Authors & Artists for Young Adults

ISSN 1040-5682

Authors & Artists for Young Adults

VOLUME 39

 **GALE GROUP**

Detroit
New York
San Francisco
London
Boston
Woodbridge, CT

Scot Peacock, *Managing Editor, Literature Product*
Mark Scott, *Publisher, Literature Product*

Alan Hedblad, *Managing Editor*
Susan Trosky, *Literature Content Coordinator*

Kristen Dorsch, Lisa Kumar, Thomas McMahon, Colleen M. Tavor, *Editors*
Shayla Hawkins, Arlene M. Johnson, Thomas Wiloch, *Associate Editors*
Alana Foster, Jennifer Kilian, Anita Sundaresan, *Assistant Editor*
Joshua Kondek, *Technical Training Specialist*

Maria Franklin, *Permissions Manager*
Edna Hedblad, *Permissions Specialist*
Shalice Shah, *Permissions Associate*

Theresa Rocklin, *Manager, Technical Support Systems*
Ryan Cartmill, *Programmer/Analyst*

Mary Beth Trimper, *Manager, Composition and Prepress*
Carolyn A. Roney, *Composition Specialist*

Dorothy Maki, *Manager, Manufacturing*
Stacy L. Melson, *Buyer*

Randy Bassett, *Image Database Supervisor*
Michael Logusz, *Graphic Artist*
Robert Duncan, *Imaging Specialist*
Pamela A. Reed, *Imaging Coordinator*
Dean Dauphinais, Robyn V. Young, *Senior Image Editors*
Kelly A. Quin, *Image Editor*

Library of Congress Catalog Card Number 89-641100
ISBN 0-7876-4672-5
ISSN 1040-5682

10 9 8 7 6 5 4 3 2 1

Printed in the United States of America

Authors and Artists for Young Adults

TEEN BOARD ADVISORS

A number of teen reading boards were consulted to help determine series' content. The teen board advisors for this volume include:

Eva M. Davis
Teen Services librarian at the Plymouth District Library in Plymouth, Michigan

Sue Holden
Head of Young Adult and Career Services at the Harborfields Public Library in Greenlawn, New York

John Manear
English teacher at Seton-Lasalle High School in Pittsburgh, Pennsylvania

Julie Roberts
Young adult librarian at the Kitchener Public Library in Kitchener, Ontario, Canada

Contents

Introduction

Authors and Artists for Young Adults is a reference series designed to serve the needs of middle school, junior high, and high school students interested in creative artists. Originally inspired by the need to bridge the gap between Gale's *Something about the Author,* created for children, and *Contemporary Authors,* intended for older students and adults, *Authors and Artists for Young Adults* has been expanded to cover not only an international scope of authors, but also a wide variety of other artists.

Although the emphasis of the series remains on the writer for young adults, we recognize that these readers have diverse interests covering a wide range of reading levels. The series therefore contains not only those creative artists who are of high interest to young adults, including cartoonists, photographers, music composers, bestselling authors of adult novels, media directors, producers, and performers, but also literary and artistic figures studied in academic curricula, such as influential novelists, playwrights, poets, and painters. The goal of *Authors and Artists for Young Adults* is to present this great diversity of creative artists in a format that is entertaining, informative, and understandable to the young adult reader.

Entry Format

Each volume of *Authors and Artists for Young Adults* will furnish in-depth coverage of twenty to twenty-five authors and artists. The typical entry consists of:

—A detailed biographical section that includes date of birth, marriage, children, education, and addresses.

—A comprehensive bibliography or filmography including publishers, producers, and years.

—Adaptations into other media forms.

—Works in progress.

—A distinctive essay featuring comments on an artist's life, career, artistic intentions, world views, and controversies.

—References for further reading.

—Extensive illustrations, photographs, movie stills, cartoons, book covers, and other relevant visual material.

A cumulative index to featured authors and artists appears in each volume.

Compilation Methods

The editors of *Authors and Artists for Young Adults* make every effort to secure information directly from the authors and artists through personal correspondence and interviews. Sketches on living authors and artists are sent to the biographee for review prior to publication. Any sketches not personally reviewed by biographees or their representatives are marked with an asterisk (*).

Highlights of Forthcoming Volumes

Among the authors and artists planned for future volumes are:

Berenice Abbott	Shelby Foote	Katherine Anne Porter
Brian Aldiss	Neil Gaiman	Philip Pullman
Amelia Atwater-Rhodes	Jack Gantos	Rick Reilly
Franny Billingsley	Edward Gorey	Jay Roach
Gary L. Blackwood	Margaret Peterson Haddix	Luis J. Rodriguez
Ken Burns	Nalo Hopkinson	Cindy Sherman
Orson Scott Card	Ji-Li Jiang	Shel Silverstein
Carolyn Coman	James Joyce	Lemony Snicket
E. E. Cummings	Susanna Kaysen	Julie Taymor
Leonardo da Vinci	A. C. LeMieux	Orson Welles
Fedor Dostoevsky	Peter Matthiessen	Gloria Whelan
W. E. B. Du Bois	Cormac McCarthy	Lois-Ann Yamanaka

Contact the Editor

We encourage our readers to examine the entire *AAYA* series. Please write and tell us if we can make *AAYA* even more helpful to you. Give your comments and suggestions to the editor:

BY MAIL: The Editor, *Authors and Artists for Young Adults,* 27500 Drake Rd., Farmington Hills, MI 48331-3535.

BY TELEPHONE: (800) 347-GALE

Acknowledgments

Grateful acknowledgment is made to the following publishers, authors, and artists for their kind permission to reproduce copyrighted material.

LAURIE HALSE ANDERSON. From a cover of *Fight for Life.* Pleasant Company, 2000. Copyright © 2000 by Laurie Halse Anderson. Reproduced by permission of Pleasant Company Publications./ From a cover of *Manatee Blues.* Pleasant Company, 2000. Cover illustration and design copyright © 2000 by Pleasant Company. Reproduced by permission./ From a jacket of *Speak.* Farrar, Straus and Giroux, 1999. Jacket art copyright © 1999 by Michael Morgenstern. Reproduced by permission of Farrar, Straus and Giroux, LLC./ Anderson, Laurie Halse, photograph by Chris Whitney/Doylestown, PA. Reproduced by permission of Laurie Halse Anderson.

LEWIS CARROLL. From a cover of *Jabberwocky.* Harry N. Abrams, 1987. Copyright © 1987 by Graeme Base. Reproduced by permission./ Carroll, Lewis, photograph. AP/Wide World Photos. Reproduced by permission./ Morris, Phyllis, in a scene from *Alice in Wonderland,* photograph. Hulton Getty/Archive Photos. Reproduced by permission.

FRANCIS FORD COPPOLA. Bridges, Jeff, in the film *Tucker,* photograph. The Kobal Collection. Reproduced by permission./ C. Thomas Howell, with Tom Cruise and Emilio Estevez, starring in the film *The Outsiders,* photograph. The Kobal Collection. Reproduced by permission./ Coppola, Francis Ford, photograph by Frank Capri. Archive Photos. Reproduced by permission./ Robert Duvall, with Albert Hall and Martin Sheen, in the movie *Apocalypse Now,* 1979, photograph. The Kobal Collection. Copyright © 1979 by United Artists Corporation. Reproduced by permission./ Gary Oldman, in the film *Bram Stoker's Dracula,* 1992, photograph. The Kobal Collection. Reproduced by permission./ Lee Strasberg, and Al Pacino, in the film *The Godfather Part II,* 1974, photograph. The Kobal Collection. Reproduced by permission./ Claire Danes and Matt Damon, in a scene from *John Grisham's The Rainmaker.* The Kobal Collection. Reproduced by permission.

CHRIS CRUTCHER. From a cover of *Running Loose.* Laurel-Leaf Books, 1983. Cover photograph by Roy Volkmann. Copyright © 1983 by Chris Crutcher. Reproduced by permission of Bantam Doubleday Dell Books for Young Readers./ From a cover of *The Crazy Horse Electric Game.* Laurel-Leaf Books, 1987. Cover photograph by Roy Volkmann. Copyright © 1987 by Chris Crutcher. Reproduced by permission of Bantam Doubleday Dell Books for Young Readers./ Crutcher, Chris, photograph by Tony Omer. Reproduced by permission of Greenwillow Books, a division of William Morrow & Company, Inc./ Charlie Talbert and Chris Owen, in a scene from *Angus,* movie still. The Kobal Collection. Reproduced by permission.

SARAH DESSEN. From a cover of *Someone Like You.* Cover illustration by Judy Pedersen. Viking, 1998. Reproduced by permission of Judy Pedersen./ Dessen, Sarah, photograph. Reproduced by permission of Sarah Dessen.

DONALD R. GALLO. From a cover of *No Easy Answers: Short Stories About Teenagers Making Tough Choices.* Edited by Donald R. Gallo. Laurel-Leaf Books, 1999. Cover illustration by Alan Mazzetti. Reproduced by permission of Random House Children's Books, a division of Random House, Inc./ From a cover of *Visions: 19 Short Stories by Outstanding Writers for Young Adults.* Edited by Donald R. Gallo. Laurel-Leaf Books, 1988. Reproduced by permission of Bantam Doubleday Dell Books for Young Readers, a division of Random House, Inc./ Gallo, Donald R., photograph by Chris Perrett. Reproduced by permission of Donald R. Gallo./ Gallo, Donald R., photograph. Reproduced by permission Donald R. Gallo./ From a cover of *Connections: Shorts Stories by Outstanding Writers for Young Adults.* Edited by Donald R. Gallo. Laurel-Leaf Books, 1989. Cover illustration by Julie E. Baker. Copyright © 1989 by Donald R. Gallo. Reproduced by permission of Random House Children's Books, a division of Random House, Inc./ From a jacket of *Time Capsule: Short Stories About Teenagers Throughout the Twentieth Century.* Delacorte Press, 1999. Jacket illustration copyright © 1999 by Ericka O'Rourke. Reproduced by permission of Ericka O'Rourke.

JAMES CROSS GIBLIN. From a cover of *Fireworks, Picnics and Flags: The Story of Fourth of July Symbols.* Clarion Books, 1983. Cover illustration copyright © 1983 by Ursula Arndt. Reproduced by permission of Houghton Mifflin Company./ Photograph from *The Century That Was: Reflections on the Last One Hundred Years.* Edited by James Cross Giblin. Atheneum Books for Young Readers, 2000. Photograph copyright © UPI/Corbis-Bettmann. Reproduced by permission./ Giblin, James Cross, drawing by William Bourne. Gale Group.

NADINE GORDIMER. From a jacket of *Living in Hope and History: Notes From Our Century.* Farrar, Straus and Giroux, 1999. Jacket design by Anne Fink. Copyright © 1999 by Nadine Gordimer. Reproduced by permission of Farrar, Straus and Giroux, LLC./ From a jacket of *Writing and Being.* Harvard University Press, 1995. Jacket painting "The Library," by Jacob Lawrence, 1969. Courtesy of the National Museum of American Art, Smithsonian Institution, Gift of S. C. Johnson and Son, Inc. Reproduced by permission./ Gordimer, Nadine, photograph. AP/Wide World Photos. Reproduced by permission.

DUANE HANSON. Hanson, Duane, photograph. AP/Wide World Photos. Reproduced by permission./ Hanson, Duane (left) standing next to a life-size sculpture, photograph. UPI/Corbis-Bettmann. Reproduced by permission.

WILL HOBBS. From a cover of *Downriver.* Dell Laurel-Leaf Books, 1996. Cover art copyright © 1992 by Robert McGinnis. Reproduced by permission of Random House Children's Books, a division of Random House, Inc./ From a cover of *River Thunder,* by Will Hobbs. Laurel-Leaf Books, 1999. Cover illustration © 1997 by Robert McGinnis. Reproduced by permission of Random House Children's Books, a division of Random House, Inc./ Hobbs, Will, photograph by Jean Hobbs. Reproduced by permission of Will Hobbs.

TIM LAHAYE AND JERRY B. JENKINS. From a cover of *Left Behind: Kids: The Underground.* Tyndale House Publishers, Inc., 1999. Cover photograph copyright © 1987 by Robert Flesher. Cover photograph copyright © 1995 by Mark Green. Reproduced by permission./ From a cover of *Left Behind: The Kids: The Vanishings.* Tyndale House Publishers, Inc., 1998. Cover photograph copyright © 1987 by Robert Flesher. Cover photograph copyright © 1995 by Mark Green. Reproduced by permission./ From a cover of *Left Behind: The Kids: Facing the Future.* Tyndale House Publishers, Inc., 1996. Cover photograph copyright © 1987 by Robert Flesher. Cover photograph copyright © 1995 by Mark Green. Reproduced by permission./ From a cover of *Left Behind: The Kids: Through the Flames.* Tyndale House Publishers, Inc., 1998. Cover photograph copyright © 1987 by Robert Flesher. Cover photograph copyright © 1995 by Mark Green. Reproduced by permission./ LaHaye, Tim (left) and Jerry B. Jenkins, photograph. Tyndale House Publishers. Reproduced by permission.

C. S. LEWIS. Anthony Hopkins, with Debra Winger, in a scene from the film *Shadowlands*, 1993, photograph. Spelling/Price/Savoy. The Kobal Collection. Reproduced by permission./ From an illustration in *The Voyage of the Dawn Treader*, by C. S. Lewis. Illustration by Pauline Baynes. Macmillan, 1964. Copyright, 1952, by The Macmillan Company. Reproduced by permission of HarperCollins Publishers Ltd. (London)./ From a cover of *Out of the Silent Planet.* Simon & Schuster, 1996. Cover illustration by Kimuko Craft. Reproduced by permission of Simon & Schuster Macmillan./ From a cover of *The Dark Tower and Other Stories.* Edited by Walter Hooper. Harcourt Brace & Company, 1977. Cover illustration by Paul Gamarello. Reproduced by permission of Paul Gamarello./ From a cover of *The Screwtape Letters.* Simon & Schuster, 1996. Cover illustration by Eunju Kang. Reproduced by permission of Simon & Schuster Macmillan./ Lewis, C. S., photograph. UPI/Corbis. Reproduced by permission.

JAN MARINO. From a cover of *Searching for Atticus,* by Jan Marino. Simon & Schuster Books for Young Readers, 1997. Cover illustration copyright © 1997 by Jenny Tylden-Wright. Reproduced by permission of Simon & Schuster Books for Young Readers, an imprint of Simon & Schuster Macmillan./ Marino, Jan, photograph. Reproduced by permission of Jan Marino.

MARK MATHABANE. From a cover of *Kaffir Boy: An Autobiography.* Touchstone, 1986. Cover photographs: (boy) © Fred House/Tony Stone Images, (landscape) © Kirsty McLaren/Tony Stone Images. Reproduced by permission of Simon & Schuster Macmillan./ From a cover of *Miriam's Song: A Memoir,* by Miriam Mathabane. Retold by Mark Mathabane. Simon & Schuster, 2000. Copyright © 2000 by Mark Mathabane. Jacket photographs (top) by Allan Penn/Nonstock, (bottom) by Gail Mathabane. Reproduced by permission of Simon & Schuster Macmillan./ Mathabane, Mark, photograph. www.mathabane.com. Reproduced by permission of Gail Mathabane.

ED MCBAIN. From a cover *Cop Hater.* Cover photograph by Ed Holub/Photonica. Pocket Books, 1999. Copyright © 1956 by Ed McBain. Copyright renewed © 1984 by Evan Hunter. Reproduced by permission of Pocket Books, a division of Simon & Schuster Macmillan./ From a cover of *Eighty Million Eyes.* Cover illustration by Danilo Ducak. Warner Books, 1966. Copyright © 1966 by Hui Corporation. Reproduced by permission of Warner Books./ From a jacket of *The Blackboard Jungle.* Illustration by Guy Fraumeni. Simon & Schuster, 1982. Copyright © 1953, 1954 by Evan Hunter. Copyright renewed © 1982 by Evan Hunter. Reproduced by permission of Simon & Schuster Macmillan./ Scene from *The Birds,* photograph. Archive Photos. Reproduced by permission./ Sidney Poitier as Gregory W. Miller and Glenn Ford as Richard Dadier in a scene from *The Blackboard Jungle.* Directed by Richard Brooks, 1955, photograph. Archive Photos. Reproduced by permission./ McBain, Ed, photograph. SAGA/FrankCapri/Archive Photos. Reproduced by permission.

GLORIA NAYLOR. From a cover of *Bailey's Cafe.* Cover illustration by Wendell Minor. Vintage Books, 1993. Copyright (c)1992 by Gloria Naylor. Reproduced by permission of Harcourt, Inc./ From a cover of *Mama Day.* Cover illustration by David Montell. Vintage Books, 1993. Copyright © 1988 by Gloria Naylor. Reproduced by permission of Vintage Books, a division of Random House, Inc./ Oprah Winfrey, starring in film *The Women of Brewster Place,* photograph. The Kobal Collection. Reproduced by permission./ Naylor, Gloria, photograph. AP/Wide World Photos. Reproduced by permission.

I. M. PEI. John F. Kennedy Library, designed by I. M. Pei. Corbis Corporation. Reproduced by permission./ Skylight diffusing light into a gallery of the Louvre Museum, designed by I. M. Pei. Corbis Corporation. Reproduced by permission./ Glass pyramid of the Louvre Museum, designed by I. M. Pei, photograph. Reuters/Corbis-Bettmann. Reproduced by permission./ Pei, I. M., photograph. Reuters/Corbis-Bettmann. Reproduced by permission.

MARY PIPHER. From a cover of *Reviving Ophelia: Saving the Selves of Adolescent Girls.* Ballantine Books, 1995. Cover photograph copyright © by Edgeworth Productions/The Stock Market. Reproduced by permission of Ballantine Books, a division of Random House, Inc./ From a cover of *The Shelter of Each Other: Rebuilding Our Families.* Ballantine Books, 1997. Cover photograph copyright © by Tom Campbell/FPG International. Reproduced by permission of Ballantine Books, a division of Random House, Inc./ Pipher, Mary, photograph. AP/Wide World Photos. Reproduced by permission.

MARSHA QUALEY. From a cover of *Close to a Killer.* Dell Laurel, 1999. Cover illustration copyright © 1999 by Cynthia Torp. Reproduced by permission of Dell Publishers, Inc./ From a cover of *Thin Ice.* Cover illustration by Joanie Schwartz. Laurel-Leaf Books, 1997. Copyright © 1997 by Marsha Qualey. Reproduced by permission of Dell Publishers, Inc./ From a jacket of *Revolutions of the Heart.* Houghton Mifflin, 1993. Jacket art copyright © 1993 Jennifer Hewitson. Reproduced by permission of the Houghton Mifflin Company./ Qualey, Marsha, photograph. Reproduced by permission of Marsha Qualey.

CHARLES M. SCHULZ. From illustrations in *PEANUTS: A Golden Celebration: The Art and the Story of the World's Best-Loved Comic Strip.* Edited and designed by David Larkin. HarperCollins Publishers, 1999. Copyright © 1999 by United Feature Syndicate, Inc. Reproduced by permission./ Schulz, Charles M., photograph. AP/Wide World Photos. Reproduced by permission.

WILLIAM SLEATOR. Sleator, William, photograph by Andrew Biggs. Reproduced by permission of William Sleator.

CAROL LYNCH WILLIAMS. From a jacket of *Carolina Autumn.* Delacorte Press, 2000. Jacket illustration copyright © 2000 by Matt Manley. Reproduced by permission of Random House Children's Books, a division of Random House, Inc./ From a cover of *If I Forget, You Remember.* Cover illustration by Robert Hunt. Yearling Books, 1999. Reproduced by permission of Random House Children's Books, a division of Random House, Inc./ From photographs from a cover of her *The True Colors of Caitlynne Jackson.* Bantam Books, 1997. Cover photographs by Michael Kornafel/FPG (top) and Rob Cage/FPG. Text copyright © 1997 by Carol Lynch Williams. Reproduced by permission of Dell Publishing, a division of Random House, Inc./ Williams, Carol Lynch, photograph. © Drew Williams. Reproduced by permission of Carol Lynch Williams.

JUNE RAE WOOD. Wood, June Rae, photograph by Vicki Grove. Reproduced by permission of June Rae Wood.

Laurie Halse Anderson

▪ Personal

"Halse" rhymes with "waltz"; born October 23, 1961, in Potsdam, NY; daughter of Frank A., Jr. (a Methodist minister) and Joyce (in management) Halse; married Gregory H. Anderson (chief executive officer of Anderson Financial Systems), June 19, 1983; children: Stephanie, Meredith. *Education:* Onondaga County Community College, A.A., 1981; Georgetown University, B.S.L.L., 1984. *Politics:* Independent. *Religion:* Quaker. *Hobbies and other interests:* Reading, running, skiing, hiking, basketball, history, travel, genealogy.

▪ Addresses

Office—P.O. Box 3407, Maple Glen, PA 19002–8407.

▪ Career

Author.

▪ Member

Society of Children's Book Writers and Illustrators, Author's Guild, PEN American Center.

▪ Awards, Honors

"Pick of the Lists," American Booksellers Association, 1996, for *Ndito Runs; Turkey Pox* was on recommended reading lists of Kansas State Librarians, Nevada Department of Education, Top of Texas Literature Review Center; National Book Award finalist in Young People's Literature, 1999, Edgar Allan Poe Award, Printz Honor Medal Book Award, *Los Angeles Times* Book Prize, and the Golden Kite award from the Society of Children's Book Writers and Illustrators, all for *Speak; Speak* was named a Best Book of 1999 by *School Library Journal,* and appeared on the American Library Association's (ALA) Honor List for excellence in literature for young adults in 2000, *Booklist*'s Top 10 First Novels of 1999, and *Horn Book*'s Fanfare Honor List; ALA Best Books for Young Adults selection, Junior Library Guild selection, Children's Book-of-the-Month selection, Parent's Guide to Children's Media Award, "Pick of the Lists," American Booksellers Association, and 100 Best Books of Fall selection, New York Public Library, all 2000, all for *Fever 1793.*

▪ Writings

NOVELS

Speak, Farrar, Straus, and Giroux, 1999.
Fever 1793, Simon and Schuster, 2000.

"WILD AT HEART" SERIES

Fight for Life: Maggie, Pleasant Company/American Girl, 2000.

Homeless: Sunita, Pleasant Company/American Girl, 2000.

Manatee Blues, Pleasant Company/American Girl, 2000.

The Trickster, Pleasant Company/American Girl, 2000.

"A TICKET TO" SERIES

Saudi Arabia, Carolrhoda Books, 2001.

PICTURE BOOKS

Ndito Runs, illustrated by Anita Van der Merwe, Henry Holt, 1996.

Turkey Pox, illustrated by Dorothy Donohue, Albert Whitman, 1996.

No Time for Mother's Day, Albert Whitman, 1999.

■ Sidelights

Laurie Halse Anderson became a finalist for the prestigious National Book Award with her first work of fiction for young adults, *Speak.* That 1999 novel won an array of honors for Anderson, the author of three earlier picture books for younger readers, for its searing portrayal of a fourteen–year–old girl who becomes mute after a sexual assault. Nancy Matson, writing for *CNN.com,* hailed Anderson as "a gifted new writer whose novel shows that she understands (and remembers) the raw emotion and tumult that marks the lives of teenagers."

Anderson was born October 23, 1961, in the northern New York town of Potsdam. Her father was a Methodist minister who wrote poetry on the side, and as a girl Anderson loved to play with his typewriter. She once commented, "I decided to become a writer in second grade. My teacher, Mrs. Sheedy–Shea, taught us how to write haiku. The giant light bulb clicked on over my head: 'Oh, my goodness! I can do this!' I hope every second grader learns how to write haiku. After Mrs. Sheedy–Shea got me writing poetry, I spent hours and hours and hours reading every book in my school library." Anderson added: "The books took me everywhere—ripping through time barriers, across cultures, experiencing all the magic an elementary school library can hold."

One book in particular that Anderson loved as a girl was *Heidi,* Johanna Spyri's classic tale about a little Swiss girl who is taken from her grandfather's

In Anderson's first novel, a National Book Award finalist, ninth–grader Melinda Sordino deals with the consequences of a sexual assault by a popular high school senior.

mountain home and sent to live in the city as companion to a wealthy, disabled girl. In later years, Anderson was strongly influenced by James Joyce's classic 1939 novel *Finnegan's Wake.* "I read this as I was struggling to find my own writing voice. It cracked open the sky above my head. I won't pretend to understand all of it, but I return to it over and over, hungry for Joyce's words," she noted in a submission to the "The Book That Changed My Life" page of the *Publishers Weekly* Web site.

In *Speak,* the narrator finds herself viciously ostracized by her peers, and Anderson recalled enduring her own traumatic experiences with high school cliques in Syracuse, New York. "I started ninth grade as a 'dirt bag,'" Anderson said in an interview for *The Book Bag* that is posted on the *bookreport.*

com Web site. "We moved to a new school district, and the dirt bags/wastecases were the people willing to forgive my unfashionable clothes and relative poverty." But Anderson joined the swim team and ran track, and her high–school experience eventually became more enjoyable. For her senior year, she took part in an exchange program with Denmark, where she lived on a pig farm and learned to speak Danish. After attending Onondaga County Community College in 1981, Anderson began studies at Georgetown University in Washington, D.C., earning a degree in languages and linguistics in 1984. By this point in her life, she had married Gregory H. Anderson, and would spend the rest of the decade as a wife and mother to two young daughters. While raising her family, Anderson also worked as reporter for the *Philadelphia Inquirer,* and as a freelance magazine writer and editor.

Anderson's first picture book was *Ndito Runs.* Illustrated by Anita Van der Merwe, it was published in 1996. The story depicts a typical morning's journey for Ndito, a Kenyan girl whose path to school traverses some of her country's characteristically stunning landscape. Ndito imagines herself as the various animals she encounters, such as the crane and the dik–dik. Anderson also wrote a second picture book that appeared in 1996. *Turkey Pox* is illustrated by Dorothy Donohue. The story follows Charity, a youngster girl who looks forward to spending the Thanksgiving holiday with her beloved grandmother. But in their haste to depart Charity's harried family does not take notice of her face. It is only when they are in the car that they realize she has awoken that day with a case of chicken pox. The discovery forces them to return home, and a snowstorm further complicates matters. The disconsolate Charity is cheered when her intrepid Nana arrives, having hitched a ride with snowplowers and bringing along her roasted turkey. The family then decorates the bird with cherries to resemble poor Charity's face.

Anderson has also written another story about Charity and her busy family. *No Time for Mother's Day,* published in 1999, finds the girl confounded by the holiday and what she might give her mother as a present. After following her parent around on a very busy Saturday, Charity realizes what her mom really needs is a day of peace and quiet. "[T]he message about modern life and how to make it just a bit simpler should hit close to home," wrote Ilene Cooper in *Booklist.*

Speak Inspired by a Dream

Speak, Anderson's first book aimed at teenage readers, was also published in 1999. Its inspiration came from a bad dream that woke the author one night in the summer of 1996. She had been plagued by nightmares all of her life, Anderson explained in an article for the *ALAN Review.* "Since I can't afford extensive psychotherapy, I write down my nightmares. . . . After an hour of scribbling in my journal or pounding the keyboard, the most horrific night–vision is reduced to a pile of sentences. And I can go back to sleep." On that night in 1996, Anderson was roused by the sound of a girl crying. Upon checking on her daughters and finding them undisturbed, she realized it had all been a dream. Wide–awake by then, she went to her desk to write, but could still hear the girl's sobbing in her head. "Once the word processor blinked awake, she stopped," Anderson wrote in the *ALAN Review.* "She made a tapping noise and blew into a microphone. 'Is this thing on?' she asked. 'I have a story to tell you.' That is how I met Melinda Sordino, the protagonist of *Speak.*"

Melinda recounts her tale in short chapters, and *Speak* is divided into the four marking periods of a school year. As it opens, Melinda's first day of high school is off to a disastrous start. No one will sit next to her on the bus, and the other students make derisive remarks about her when they are not shunning her completely. As the story unfolds, Melinda reveals the reason behind the ostracism: at an end–of–summer drinking party hosted by a group of older students, she drank too much and was sexually assaulted by a popular senior. A call made to 911 from the house brought the police, and the party was broken up. Some kids were arrested, and Melinda's "odd" behavior that night reveals to others that she was the caller.

As the weeks of her freshman year wear on, Melinda has no friends. When she sees her rapist in the halls, the young man continues to taunt her by winking at her; Melinda can only refer to him as "IT." She has told no one about the crime, and finds it increasingly difficult to communicate. She bites her lip incessantly, and her busy parents do not seem to notice the scabs or even that anything wrong. At times, Melinda's narrative recounts dialogue, which takes the form of an exchange between someone else, and Melinda's "Me," which is rarely followed by any lines. She feels stifled. "All that crap you hear on TV about communication and expressing feelings is a lie," Melinda scoffs. "Nobody really wants to hear what you have to say."

"While Melinda's smart and savvy interior narrative slowly reveals the searing pain of that 911 night. It also nails the high–school experience cold," a *Horn Book Magazine* reviewer noted. Melinda's friends from middle school have dispersed into different cliques, and her former best friend changes her name from Rachel to Rachelle and hangs out only with the foreign exchange students. Everyone else is hostile to her. "I stand in the center aisle of the auditorium, a wounded zebra in a *National Geographic* special," she describes a moment at a pep rally where she can't find a seat. Despite the trauma, Melinda emerges as a wry observer of high school life. As narrator she analyzes the various school cliques, which she tags by various names: Eurotrash, Country Clubbers, Jocks, Future Fascists of American, Suffering Artists, Thespians, Goths, and Marthas, among others. As *Speak* progresses, Melinda makes one friend, Heather, who recently moved to town, and thus knows nothing about the party or the 911 call. But Melinda is only nominally interested in being friends with the girl, who wants to be a Martha, one of the "the do–gooder bunch who collect food cans for the less fortunate and decorates the teachers' lounge," as Nancy Matson explained in *CNN.com.* The Marthas, however "are not a whit less brutal than any of the other high school cliques," Matson observed.

Melinda finds some solace in her art class, where her sympathetic teacher seems to be the only one who realizes that something is amiss in her life. As Melinda's grades decline over the marking periods, she grows increasingly withdrawn and even begins to find refuge by hiding in a closet at school. Her voice manages to assert itself in other ways besides her internal narrative: through her tree project for art class, for instance, or a piece of graffiti she begins on the wall of a bathroom stall, "Ten Guys to Stay Away From." When her ex–best friend begins dating "IT," Melinda finally begins to realize what the real cost of her silence may be. In a nightmarish denouement, she finds herself in danger again, and at last finds the voice to scream.

Reviewers of *Speak* were generous in their praise. "In a stunning first novel, Anderson uses keen observations and vivid imagery to pull readers into the head of an isolated teenager," a *Publishers Weekly* reviewer wrote. Paula Rohrlick of *Kliatt* noted that "Melinda's voice is bitter, sardonic and always believable," and predicted that the heroine's "bleak, scathingly honest depiction of the world of high school will ring true for many." A reviewer writing in the *Bulletin of the Center for Children's Books* observed that "Anderson doesn't overburden Melinda with insight or with artistic metaphors," and concluded by calling the novel "a gripping account of personal wounding and recovery." Writing for *School Library Journal*, Dina Sherman stated that *Speak* "is a compelling book, with sharp, crisp writing that draws readers in, engulfing them in the story." *Horn Book* predicted that the novel "will hold readers from first word to last." A *Kirkus Reviews* assessment commended Anderson for her engaging story

This volume in the "Wild at Heart" series shows how young Maggie tries to keep her grades from slipping while tracking down an abusive puppy breeder.

and strong characters, but pointed out that "it is its raw and unvarnished look at the dynamics" among the teenagers portrayed in *Speak* "that makes this a novel that will be hard for readers to forget."

Numerous Accolades

In addition to becoming a finalist for a National Book Award in the Young People's Literature category, *Speak* earned high marks from several other sources. It was cited as one of the best books for teens published in 1999 by the Society of Children's Book Writers and Illustrators, *School Library Journal*, the American Library Association, *Booklist, Horn Book Magazine*, and the *Los Angeles Times*. The novel's themes of ostracism and personal conviction resonated with readers of all ages. Anderson has said that in writing *Speak,* she was compelled to address issues that are universal. Melinda's act of calling the police, for instance, and the reason why no one else ever bothered to find out why she did it, seems characteristic of teen behavior. Her peers assume that she simply wanted to get everyone else in trouble. "People grab the fast, easy answer," Anderson told *The Book Bag.* "Especially in a situation like this, where Melinda's actions got everyone in trouble, her friends aren't going to explore her motives. Then there is that added twist—by being angry at Melinda (the scapegoat), they don't have to take responsibility for their own actions."

At the time that she had the nightmare that brought Melinda alive, Anderson had been reading *Reviving Ophelia,* a best–selling study from Nebraska psychologist Mary Pipher about preteen girls and the difficulties they face. "I had been processing all this information about adolescence and girls, and remembered all too vividly what it was like," Anderson told Jennifer M. Brown in a *Publishers Weekly* interview. "*Speak* is the least deliberately written book I've ever done." As the author wrote in the *ALAN Review,* she grew very attached to her heroine, whom she refers to as "Mellie," over the course of writing her story. "The ending of the book was the hardest. In fact, I had to do it three times to get it right. My patient, very smart editor, Elizabeth Mikesell, gently pushed me to do it over until I found the right ending. I was not happy about it at the time, but she was right. I was too protective of Mellie. I didn't want her to get hurt again. I couldn't stand the thought of leaving her unprotected." In fact, as Anderson told *The Book Bag,* she felt so close to her character that it was sometimes hard to remember that she existed only on paper. "When my editor called me to say she wanted to publish the book, I was really bummed because I wanted to call Melinda and tell her, she was so real to me!"

Anderson rises each day at 4:30 a.m. to write, and she keeps at it until noon—after the house empties of her daughters and husband. She researches in the afternoons. "I have two kids who do a great job of keeping me grounded, and a cat who gnaws my ankles if I don't feed her," the author told Brown in the *Publishers Weekly* interview. Anderson has also written a historical novel for teens, *Fever 1793,* which appeared in 2000. The work is set in post–revolutionary times during a yellow fever outbreak. Matilda Cook is fourteen that summer, and her family owns a coffeehouse in Philadelphia, which was also the capital of the United States at the time. When Matilda is separated from her mother and her grandfather succumbs to the epidemic, she is saved by the freed slave who works at the coffeehouse. Through her, the teen becomes involved in the Free African Society, and by the end

Brenna, a vet volunteer, becomes involved in the effort to save the Florida manatee in this work from Anderson's "Wild at Heart" series.

of the novel Matilda has emerged as the almost–adult proprietor of the coffeehouse. "Readers will be drawn in by the characters and will emerge with a sharp and graphic picture of another world," opined *School Library Journal* reviewer Kathleen Isaacs.

Despite the popularity of her other books, it has been *Speak*'s Melinda who has proved to be Anderson's most enduring, likable heroine. Anderson is a popular author on the school–and–library lecture circuit, and students often ask her if she will write another book featuring Melinda. Anderson admits that she is tempted, but will have to let any follow–up happen by itself. "Writing [*Speak*] was a bizarre experience," the author told *The Book Bag.* "I feel like Melinda dictated it to me. I would love to write another book with her so I could have her hanging out in my head again. But it's up to her. If

If you enjoy the works of Laurie Halse Anderson, you might want to check out the following books:

Brock Cole, *The Facts Speak for Themselves*, 1997.
Stephen Chbosky, *The Perks of Being a Wallflower*, 1999.
Sarah Dessen, *Someone Like You*, 1998.
Patricia Reilly Giff, *Nory Ryan's Song*, 2000.
E. L. Konigsburg, *Silent to the Bone*, 2000.

I try to resurrect her just to hammer out a sequel, it will be awful. You have to respect your characters as much as you do your friends."

■ Biographical and Critical Sources

PERIODICALS

ALAN Review, spring–summer, 2000, "Speaking Out," pp. 25–26.
Booklist, March 15, 1996, Hazel Rochman, review of *Ndito Runs*, p. 1268; September 1, 1996, Carolyn Phelan, review of *Turkey Pox*, p. 35; February 15, 1999, Ilene Cooper, review of *No Time for Mother's Day*, p. 1073; September 15, 1999, Debbie Carton, review of *Speak*; November 15, 1999, Stephanie Zvirin, review of *Speak*, p. 618; May 1, 2000, Lauren Peterson, review of *Fight for Life*, p. 1665.
Bulletin of the Center for Children's Books, November, 1996, Janice Del Negro, review of *Turkey Pox*, pp. 89–90; April, 1999, review of *No Time for Mother's Day*, pp. 271–272; October, 1999, review of *Speak*, p. 45.
Children's Book Review Service, April, 1996, p. 97.

Horn Book, fall, 1996, p. 246; September, 1999, review of *Speak*, p. 605.
Kirkus Reviews, September 19, 1999, review of *Speak*, p. 1496.
Kliatt, September, 1999, Paula Rohrlick, review of *Speak*, p. 4.
New York Times Book Review, November 19, 2000, Constance Decker Thompson, review of *Fever 1793*, pp. 45–46.
Publishers Weekly, review of *Ndito Runs*, March 18, 1996, pp. 68–69; September 20, 1996, review of *Turkey Pox*, p. 87; September 13, 1999, review of *Speak*, p. 85; December 20, 1999, Jennifer M. Brown, "In Dreams Begin Possibilities," p. 24; July 31, 2000, review of *Fever 1793*, p. 96.
School Library Journal, May, 1996, Tom S. Hurlburt, review of *Ndito Runs*, p. 84; October, 1996, Lisa Marie Gangemi, review of *Turkey Pox*, p. 84; April, 1999, Roxanne Burg, review of *No Time for Mother's Day*, p. 85; October, 1999, Dina Sherman, review of *Speak*, p. 144; July, 2000, Janie Schomberg, review of *Fight for Life*, p. 100; August, 2000, Kathleen Isaacs, review of *Fever 1793*, p. 177; December, 2000, Ronni Krasnow, review of *Homeless: Sunita*, p. 138.
Voice of Youth Advocates, December, 2000, Christine M. Hill, "Laurie Halse Anderson Speaks: An Interview," pp. 325–327; December, 2000, Dr. Stefani Koorey, review of *Fever 1793*, p. 344.

ONLINE

authors4teens.com, located at http://www.authors4teens.com/anderson/interview_full.htm.
CNN.com, located at http://www.cnn.com (May 24, 2000).
The Book Bag Web site, located at http://www.bookreport.com (May 24, 2000).
Laurie's Bookshelf, located at http://www.writerlady.com.
Publishers Weekly Web site, located at http://www.publishersweekly.com.

—*Sketch by Carol Brennan*

Lewis Carroll

those children's books considered worthy to sit on a shelf with *Alice in Wonderland*.

■ Personal

Surname is pronounced "*Dod*–son"; born Charles Lutwidge Dodgson, January 27, 1832, in Daresbury, Cheshire, England; died January 14, 1898, in Guildford, Surrey, England; buried in the old cemetery in Guildford; son (eldest of eleven children) of the Reverend Charles (rector of Daresbury) and Frances Jane (Lutwidge) Dodgson. *Education:* Richmond School, Christ Church College, Oxford University, B.A., 1854, M.A., 1857. *Hobbies and other interests:* Photography, mathematical puzzles and games.

■ Career

After completing his studies, remained at Christ Church, Oxford, for the rest of his life as a member of the teaching faculty in mathematics; ordained a deacon in the Church of England, 1861; author of books for children and of mathematical treatises; inventor of many games of mathematics and logic; amateur artist and illustrator; portrait photographer, particularly of children.

■ Awards, Honors

The Lewis Carroll Shelf Award was given annually from 1958–1979 by the University of Wisconsin to

■ Writings

FOR CHILDREN; UNDER PSEUDONYM LEWIS CARROLL

Alice's Adventures in Wonderland, illustrated by John Tenniel, Macmillan, 1865, 2nd edition, 1866, published as *Original Illustrated Alice in Wonderland*, Castle Books, 1978, published as *Alice's Adventures Underground*, Genesis, 1979, published as *Anderson's Alice*, illustrated by Walter Anderson, University of Mississippi, 1983, adaptation for young readers by the author published as *The Nursery "Alice,"* Macmillan, 1890, reprinted (with a new introduction by Martin Gardner), McGraw–Hill, 1966, Mayflower Books, 1979.

Phantasmagoria, and Other Poems, Macmillan, 1869, later edition illustrated by A. B. Frost, 1911.

Through the Looking–Glass and What Alice Found There, illustrated by Tenniel, Macmillan, 1872.

The Hunting of the Snark: An Agony in Eight Fits (nonsense verse), illustrated by Henry Holiday, Macmillan, 1876, reprinted, Potter, 1975.

Alice's Adventures in Wonderland [and] *Through the Looking–Glass,* illustrated by Tenniel, Macmillan, 1881, published as *Journeys in Wonderland,* Derrydale Books, 1979.

Rhyme? and Reason? (verses and puzzles), illustrated by Henry Holiday and A. B. Frost, Macmillan, 1883, Garland, 1976.

A Tangled Tale, illustrated by Frost, Macmillan, 1885, reprinted, Third Press, 1975.

Alice's Adventures Underground (facsimile of the original manuscript completed in 1863; illustrated by the author), Macmillan, 1886, reprinted (with a new introduction by Martin Gardner), McGraw–Hill, 1966.

Sylvie and Bruno (also see below), illustrated by Harry Furniss, Macmillan, 1889, reprinted, University Microfilms, 1967.

Sylvie and Bruno Concluded (also see below), illustrated by Furniss, Macmillan, 1893.

Three Sunsets and Other Poems (bound with *Twelve Fairy Fancies* by E. Gertrude Thompson), Macmillan, 1898.

Novelty and Romancement: A Story, Brimmer, 1925, reprinted, Folcroft, 1973.

For the Train: Five Poems and a Tale (contributions to periodical *The Train,* 1856–57), illustrated by C. H. Bennett and W. McConnell, Archer, 1932, reprinted, Folcroft, 1973.

The Rectory Umbrella [and] *Mischmasch* (contributions to early family magazines), Cassell, 1932, reprinted, Dover, 1971.

Useful and Instructive Poetry (contributions to another family magazine), introduction by Derek Hudson, Macmillan, 1954, reprinted, Folcroft, 1974.

The Jabberwocky, and More Nonsense, illustrated by Simms Taback, Dell, 1964, published as *The Jabberwocky and Other Frabjous Nonsense,* Crown, 1967, published as *Jabberwocky,* illustrated by Jane Zalben, Warne, 1977.

The Walrus and the Carpenter, illustrated by K. Rohlicek, Brunswick Press, 1965.

The Mad Gardener's Song, illustrated by Sean Morrison, Bobbs–Merrill, 1967.

The Pig–Tale, illustrated by Leonard B. Lubin, Little, Brown, 1975, Hanover Fitz, 1983.

Lewis Carroll, The Wasp in a Wig: The "Suppressed" Episode of Through the Looking Glass, Lewis Carroll Society, 1977, Macmillan, 1977.

Lewis Carroll's Jabberwocky, with annotations by Humpty Dumpty, illustrated by Jane B. Zalben, Warne, 1977.

The Lobster Quadrille, illustrated by Tony Cattaneo, Warne, 1977.

Story of Sylvie and Bruno (contains *Sylvie and Bruno* and *Sylvie and Bruno Concluded*), illustrated by Furniss, Mayflower Books, 1980.

The Complete Sylvie and Bruno, edited by Thomas Christensen, illustrated by Renee Flower, Mercury House, 1991.

COLLECTIONS

The Lewis Carroll Picture Book: A Selection from the Unpublished Writings and Drawing of Lewis Carroll, edited by nephew, Stuart Dodgson Collingwood, Unwin, 1899, reprinted, Gale, 1971, revised edition published as *Diversions and Digressions of Lewis Carroll,* Dover, 1961, published as *The Unknown Lewis Carroll: Eight Major Works and Many Minor,* Dover, 1961.

The Lewis Carroll Birthday Book, edited by Christine Terhune Herrick, Wessels, 1905.

Further Nonsense Verse and Prose, edited by Langford Reed, illustrated by Henry Mayo Bateman, Appleton, 1926.

The Collected Verse of Lewis Carroll, Dutton, 1929, reprinted as *The Humorous Verse of Lewis Carroll, the Reverend Charles L. Dodgson,* Dover, 1960.

The Lewis Carroll Book, edited by Richard Herrick, illustrated by Tenniel and Holiday, Dial Press, 1931.

A Selection From the Letters of Lewis Carroll to His Child–Friends, edited and with an introduction by Evelyn M. Hatch, Macmillan, 1933, reprinted Folcroft, 1973, R. West, 1977.

Logical Nonsense: The Works of Lewis Carroll, edited by Philip C. Blackburn and Lionel White, Putnam, 1934.

The Complete Works of Lewis Carroll, edited and with an introduction by Alexander Woollcott, illustrated by Tenniel, Modern Library, 1936, reprinted, 1966.

The Diaries of Lewis Carroll, edited by R. L. Green, two volumes, Oxford University Press, 1954, reprinted, Greenwood Press, 1971.

The Mathematical Recreations of Lewis Carroll, Volume 1: *Symbolic Logic* [and] *The Game of Logic,* Volume 2: *Pillow Problems* [and] *A Tangled Tale,* Dover, 1958.

The Works of Lewis Carroll, edited by R. L. Green, Hamlyn, 1965.

The Poems of Lewis Carroll, edited by Myra Cohn Livingston, Crowell, 1973.

The Rectory Magazine, University of Texas Press, 1976.

Lewis Carroll Observed: A Collection of Unpublished Photographs, Drawings, Poetry and New Essays, edited by Edward Guiliano, Potter, 1976.

Useful and Instructive Poetry, with an introduction by Derek Hudson, West, 1977.

The Illustrated Lewis Carroll, edited by Roy Gasson, Jupiter Books, 1978

Some Oxford Scandals: Seven "Letters to the Editor", Lewis Carroll Society, 1978.

Illustrated Lewis Carroll, Jupiter Books, 1978.

Lewis Carroll's Bedside Book, edited by Edgar Cuthwellis, Houghton, Mifflin, 1979.

The Letters of Lewis Carroll, edited by M. M. Cohen, Oxford University Press, 1979.

Lewis Carroll and the Kitchens (contains twenty–five letters not previously published and nineteen photographs), edited with an introduction and notes by M. M. Cohen, Lewis Carroll Society, 1980.

Eight or Nine Wise Words about Letter Writing, Penmeil Press, 1981.

Selected Letters of Lewis Carroll, Pantheon, 1982.

Complete Illustrated Works of Lewis Carroll, Chancellor, 1982.

The Best of Lewis Carroll, Castle, 1983.

ADULT NONFICTION; UNDER NAME CHARLES L. DODGSON

A Syllabus of Plane Algebraical Geometry [Oxford], 1860.

The Formulae of Plane Trigonometry, [Oxford], 1861.

A Guide to the Mathematical Student in Reading, Reviewing, and Writing Examples, [Oxford], 1864.

An Elementary Treatise on Determinants, Macmillan, 1867.

The Fifth Book of Euclid Treated Algebraically, [Oxford], 1868.

Euclid, Book V, Proved Algebraically, [Oxford], 1874.

Euclid and His Modern Rivals, Macmillan, 1879, reprinted, Dover, 1973.

Doublets: A Word Puzzle, Macmillan, 1879.

(Editor) *Euclid, Books I and II,* Macmillan, 1882.

The Principles of Parliamentary Representation, Harrison & Sons, 1884.

The Game of Logic, Macmillan, 1887.

Curiosa Mathematica, Macmillan, Part 1: *A New Theory of Parallels,* 1888, Part 2: *Pillow Problems Thought During Wakeful Hours,* 1893.

Symbolic Logic, Part 1: *Elementary,* Macmillan, 1895.

Feeding the Mind, Chatto & Windus, 1907, reprinted, Folcroft, 1973, West, 1977.

A Russian Journal and Other Selections from the Works of Lewis Carroll, Dutton, 1935, Dover, 1977.

Symbolic Logic: Part I and II, Clarkson Potter, 1976, reprinted and edited by W. W. Bartley III, Clarkson Potter, 1986.

Contributor, under name Charles L. Dodgson, of scientific articles to periodicals; also contributor, under pseudonym Lewis Carroll, of poems and stories to various periodicals, including *The Train, Whitby Gazette, Aunt Judy's Magazine,* and *Comic Times.*

■ Adaptations

FILMSTRIPS

The works of Lewis Carroll (especially *Alice in Wonderland*) have been featured in many filmstrips, including "Alice's Adventures in Wonderland," by Miller–Brody Productions; "Highlights from Alice's Adventures in Wonderland," by Encyclopaedia Britannica; and "You Are Old, Father William," by Doubleday Multimedia.

TELEVISION

Jonathan Miller adapted "Alice in Wonderland" for BBC–Television, and *Alice at the Palace,* an American version starring Meryl Streep, aired on American television in 1982.

STAGE

Alice, an 1886 operetta by Savile Clarke, included a song written by Carroll. Later dramatizations based on the combined works, under the title *Alice in Wonderland,* include adaptations by Eva Le Gallienne and F. Friebus, Samuel French, 1932; by Madge Miller, Children's Theatre Press, 1953; and by Anne Coulter Martens, Dramatic Publishing, 1965. "But Never Jam Today," an Afro–American adaptation for the stage, was written in 1969. Other dramatic adaptations include "Alice and Through the Looking Glass," by Stephen Moore, 1980; "Alice," by Michael Lancy, 1983; "Alice, A Wonderland Book," by R. Surrette, 1983; and "Alice" (a ballet) by Glen Tetley, 1986. "Alice in Concert" was produced in 1987 by E. Swados.

MOVIES

The first movie featuring Alice was *Alice in Wonderland* by Maienthau, 1914, starring Alice Savoy; another was produced the following year by Nonpareil. Other versions were released by Pathe Studios, 1927; Paramount, 1933; Walt Disney (animated color), 1951; "Alice of Wonderland in Paris," Childhood, 1968; Macmillan Audio Brandon Films (animated); "Alice's Adventures in Wonderland," American National, 1972; and Hanna Barbera (animated), 1965.

RECORDINGS

Recordings featuring Alice include "Adventures D'Alice au pays desmerveilles" (French), Spoken Arts; "Alice in Wonderland," read by Joan Greenwood and Stanley Holloway, Caedmon; "Alice in Wonderland," Walt Disney; "Alice in Wonderland," read by Marvin Miller and Jane Webb, Miller–Brody Productions, 1972; and "Alice in Wonderland; Through the Looking Glass," read and sung by Christopher Casson, Spoken Arts. *Through the Looking Glass* has been recorded by numerous artists for

Carroll made his own illustrations for the manuscript version of Alice Liddel's fanciful adventures, entitled "Alice's Adventures Underground."

Caedmon, Miller–Brody, and George Rose. Other Carroll works on cassette include "The Hunting of the Snark," read by Boris Karloff, Caedmon; "Nonsense Verse," read by Beatrice Lillie, Cyril Ritchard, and Stanley Holloway, Caedmon; and "Treasury of Lewis Carroll," read, sung, and arranged by Christopher Casson, Spoken Arts.

■ Sidelights

Charles Lutwidge Dodgson was an author, mathematician, teacher, and photographer who is described by Roger Lancelyn Green in *Twentieth–Century Children's Writers* as "probably the most quoted author in the English language after the Bible and Shakespeare." However, it is under the pen name Lewis Carroll that he is recognized around the world. Writing as Carroll, Dodgson is best known as the creator of *Alice's Adventures in Wonderland* and *Through the Looking–Glass,* works which are usually considered the greatest and most influential children's books to have been written in English. Lauded as a genius who fused his eccentric personal characteristics and opinions about Victorian life with a genuine love of children and childhood, Dodgson is credited with liberating juvenile literature from its history of didacticism and overt moralizing. With the "Alice" books, he ushered in the Golden Age of children's literature, a period characterized by its imaginative and purely entertaining works for the young. The stories about Alice are often praised as the first children's books that could be read with equal pleasure by both children and adults; in fact, appeal to the latter group is so strong that the tales have transcended their status as books for children to become classics of the English language.

Dodgson was born in Daresbury, a small English village where his father was rector of the church. He was the oldest of eleven children, mostly girls, and entertained the young ones with sleight–of–hand tricks and homemade marionettes which he built, and whose strings he moved himself. At the age of twelve he was sent to a boys' school in Richmond, where he composed Latin verses and wrote stories for the school magazine. However, he was tormented by the other students, an experience which may help explain his lifelong preference for the society of little girls.

"**Cheshire Puss!**" said Alice (Wasn't that a pretty name for a cat?) "Would you tell me which way I ought to go from here?"

And so the Cheshire - Cat told her which way she ought to go to visit the Hatter, and which way to go, to visit the March Hare. "They're both mad!" said the Cat.

And then the Cat vanished away, just like the flame of a candle when it goes out!

Artist John Tenniel captured the timeless spirit of Alice's encounter with the wonders of her dream world in his depiction of grotesques, such as the famous Cheshire Cat.

Tenniel's illustration of the Mad Hatter's tea party dates from 1896.

Dodgson attended Rugby in 1846 and did well in his studies there; in 1850 he entered Christ Church College, Oxford. He planned to follow in his father's footsteps as a clergyman, but he was handicapped by a stutter. Instead, he spent his life teaching, and preached an occasional sermon which his nephew, Stuart Dodgson Collingwood, describes in *The Life and Letters of Lewis Carroll* as "always delightful to listen to." In 1855 he wrote the first lines of *Jabberwocky* as an attempt to parody Anglo–Saxon poetry. He became an excellent photographer and a lecturer in mathematics in the college, and he lived for the rest of his life in rooms there. He also contributed to a small paper, *The Comic Times.* When this paper changed hands the whole staff left and began a new venture, *The Train,* for which Dodgson wrote stories and poems.

In December 1854 Dodgson was awarded the degree of bachelor of arts, and he was made a "master of the house" the next year. His duties included lecturing in mathematics and teaching private pupils. Around this time the budding author adopted the pen name Lewis Carroll (suggested by the Latin forms of his Christian name, Charles Lutwidge). Under this name he was to become known worldwide. He earned a master's degree in 1857 and continued to teach, but although he had many friends, he complained of the monotony of the college routine.

The "Alice" Books

On July 4, 1862, Dodgson took a riverboat ride with the three young daughters of the college dean, Lorina, Alice, and Edith Liddel. He told them a story about "Alice's Adventures Underground." When little Alice coaxed him to write out the story for her, he did so, calling it "Alice's Hour in Elfland." In 1864 it became *Alice's Adventures in Wonderland,* and artist John Tenniel was asked to illustrate it. Collingwood writes of his uncle: "His memory was so good that I believe that the story as he wrote it down was almost word for word the same that he had told in the boat." In time Dodgson added a sequel, *Through the Looking Glass,* which was equally popular.

These two works, which are usually treated as a whole and are loosely structured around a pack of cards and a game of chess, describe how a curious seven–year–old girl enters two dream worlds: one she enters by falling down a rabbit hole, the other by passing through a mirror. Through her experiences, which are frustrating as well as wonderful, Alice meets a host of fascinating and unusual characters, both human and anthropomorphic. As Alice meets these creatures, she is drawn into unfamiliar societies that challenge her knowledge and beliefs. She becomes involved in a series of amusing yet often disagreeable events that test her perceptions of time, space, form, and sense. Surprising and terrifying, yet with their own inherent logic, the worlds in which Alice finds herself are revealed through her reactions to them. Each book concludes with Alice ending her dream after becoming disgusted with the insanity, selfishness, and cruelty she has encountered. Critics have noted Dodgson's playful exploration of the paradoxes of thought and language; poet W. H. Auden commented: "[in the "Alice" books], one of the most important and powerful characters is not a person but the English language. Alice, who had hitherto supposed that words were passive objects, discovers that they have a life and will of their own. When she tries to remember poems she has learned, new lines come into her head unbidden and, when she thinks she knows what a word means, it turns out to mean something else."

Eventually Dodgson adapted the combined books for small children, calling it *The Nursery Alice,* with a larger type size and colored pictures. Rather than condensing the original story, he rewrote it in children's language. He also wrote a scholarly mathematical book on determinants, to the confusion of the public, which had begun to consider him a children's author. At this time, too, he took a vacation tour of Europe, keeping a diary of his travels.

Beyond Alice

Dodgson had for a long time been interested in photography, especially photographing children, and set up a studio in his Christ Church rooms. His pictures, while less known than his books, have received praise, and some have been published in *Lewis Carroll Observed* and *Lewis Carroll, Victorian Photographer.* In 1872 the author took up the study of anatomy and physiology and bought a little manual called "What to Do in Emergencies," eventually accumulating an excellent library of medical books.

In 1876, *The Hunting of the Snark* was published. Collingwood remembers that "Carroll always protested that the poem had no meaning at all," but the public loved it. That year also saw the first dramatic presentation of *Alice in Wonderland* in the form of a series of tableaux, with readings and songs. From his early days Dodgson had loved the theatre and was charmed by child performers. He offered free copies of *Alice* and *Through the Looking Glass* to sick children in hospitals. His nephew says that the author "took great pleasure in the success of his books, but the greatest pleasure of all to him was to know that they had pleased others."

In 1879 Dodgson produced *Euclid and his Modern Rivals,* the most elaborate of his mathematical books, written with a sense of humor. He gave up his lectorship at the college to devote more time to writing. In 1885 a book of mathematical problems was published. These had originally appeared in a magazine, *The Monthly Packet,* with solutions and comments (right or wrong) that had been sent in by readers. His nephew remembers him at this time as "an old bachelor . . . precise in his habits following a prescribed routine . . . and living a life of calm contentment," taking long walks in the country, telling his companions stories, or explaining some logical problem. If alone, he would "think out his books." Dodgson lived simply and distributed his income where he thought it was most needed, helping children who wished to go on the stage or friends in need.

In 1897 Dodgson published *The Game of Logic,* solving logical problems with diagrams. Early the next year he became ill with influenza, and he died on the fourteenth of January. On the white cross which marks his grave in Old Guildford Cemetery are the

Lewis Carroll

JABBERWOCKY

from *Through the Looking Glass*

Illustrated by Graeme Base

In this ballad (first published as part of *Through the Looking–Glass* in 1872) Carroll takes the reader on a romp through the English language, creating new words or reviving old ones to fit the mood of the poem.

words "Thy Will Be Done." At the suggestion of a young friend, donations from children were used to endow a cot in Children's Hospital in his memory.

If you enjoy the works of Lewis Carroll, you might want to check out the following books:

J. M. Barrie, *Peter Pan,* 1911.
Robert Louis Stevenson, *Treasure Island: A Story of the Spanish Main,* 1898.
Mark Twain, *Tom Sawyer,* 1876.
Margaret Weis, editor, *Fantastic Alice,* 1995.

After his death, critics began to analyze the "Alice" stories in a variety of interpretations which often evaluated the tales as products of Dodgson's neuro-

ses and as reactions to Victorian culture. Because of the nightmarish qualities of Alice's adventures and their violent, even sadistic, elements, the "Alice" books are sometimes considered inappropriate for children. However, Dodgson is consistently applauded as the world's best writer of nonsense, an author who successfully combined the logical with the illogical in two timeless novels which capture the essence of the child mind and are unequalled in their originality.

■ Biographical and Critical Sources

BOOKS

Aspects of Alice: Lewis Carroll's Dreamchild as Seen through the Critics, edited by Robert Phillips, Vanguard Press, 1971.

The "Alice" books have been adapted many times for film, television, and (as shown here) the stage.

Children's Books and Their Creators, edited by Anita Silvey, Houghton, 1995.

Cohen, Morton, *Lewis Carroll: A Biography,* Knopf, 1995.

Concise Dictionary of British Literary Biography, Volume 4: *Victorian Writers, 1832–1890,* Gale, 1991, pp. 111–28.

Collingwood, Stuart Dodgson, *The Life and Letters of Lewis Carroll,* Century Co., 1899.

de la Mare, Walter, *Lewis Carroll,* Faber and Faber Ltd., 1932.

Dictionary of Literary Biography, Volume 163: British Children's Writers, 1800–1880, edited by Meena Khorana, Gale, 1996.

Frey, Charles, and John Griffith, *The Literary Heritage of Childhood: An Appraisal of Children's Classics in the Western Tradition,* Greenwood Press, 1987.

Hudson, Derek, *Lewis Carroll, an Illustrated Biography,* New American Library, 1977.

Nineteenth–Century Literature Criticism, Volume 53, Gale, 1996.

Twentieth–Century Children's Writers, 3rd edition, St. James Press, 1989.

Writers for Children, Charles Scribner's Sons, 1988.

PERIODICALS

American Theatre, December, 1999, Celia Wren, "Curioser and Curioser," p. 18.

Booklist, December 15, 1993, Carolyn Phelan, review *Owls and Pussy-Cats,* p. 757; April 1, 1999, GraceAnne DeCandido, review of *Alice's Adventures in Wonderland,* p. 1412; November 1, 1999, Michael Cart, review of *Alice in Wonderland,* p. 528.

Books for Keeps, September, 1998, Helen Levens, review of *Alice's Adventures in Wonderland,* p. 28.

Children's Literature in Education, March, 1994, Virginia Lowe, "Who Dreamed It? Two Children, Philosophy and Alice, pp. 55–62.

Contemporary Review, August, 1993, Walter Strachan, "Lewis Carroll and the Hatch Sisters," p. 93; January, 1994, review of *The Hunting of the Snark,* p. 56.

Horn Book Magazine, November–December 1993, Ann A. Flowers, review of *Through the Looking Glass,* p. 759; January, 2000, review of *Alice's Adventures in Wonderland,* p. 72.

Insight on the News, December 25, 1995, Rex Roberts, "Would not, could not: Carroll in Wonderland," p. 30; January 10, 2000, R. Roberts, "Explicating Alice," p. 32.

Library Journal, March 1, 1999, Michael Rogers, review of *Alice's Adventures Underground,* p. 116.

New York Review of Books, February 15, 1996, John Bayley, "Alice, or The Art of Survival," pp. 10–13.

Notes and Queries, December, 1993, Gillian Avery, review of *Alice in Wonderland,* p. 562.

Publishers Weekly, January 5, 1990, review of *Through the Looking Glass,* p. 70; September 13, 1991, review *The Complete Bruno and Sylvie,* p. 61; August 31, 1992, review of *Jabberwocky,* p. 77; November 1, 1999, review of *Alice in Wonderland,* p. 84; November 1, 1999, review of *Alice's Adventures in Wonderland,* p. 84; December 20, 1999, "Reflections on a Looking Glass," p. 18.

UNESCO Courier, May–June 1986, Anthony Burgess, "All about Alice," p. 44.*

Francis Ford Coppola

■ Personal

Surname is pronounced *Cope*–o–la; born April 7, 1939, in Detroit, MI; son of Carmine (a musician and composer) and Italia (Pennino) Coppola; married Eleanor Neil (an artist); children: Sofia, Gian–Carlo (died, 1986), Roman. *Education:* Hofstra University, B.A. (theater arts), 1959; University of California, Los Angeles, M.F.A. (film), 1967.

■ Addresses

Agent—c/o ICM, 8942 Wilshire Blvd., Beverly Hills, CA 90211.

■ Career

Director, producer, and screenwriter, 1962—. Founder, Zoetrope Studios (film production company), 1969, and American Zoetrope, 1979—. Publisher of *City* magazine, 1975–76, and founder of *Zoetrope: All–Story*, a journal of short fiction, 1997—. Director of films, including *Tonight for Sure*, 1961;

The Playgirls and the Bellboy, 1962; *The Terror* (uncredited), 1963; *Dementia 13*, Filmgroup Inc., 1963; *You're a Big Boy Now*, Seven Arts, 1967; *Finian's Rainbow*, Warner Brothers/Seven Arts, 1968; *The Rain People*, Warner Brothers, 1969; *The Godfather*, Paramount, 1972; *The Conversation*, Paramount, 1974; *The Godfather Part II*, Paramount, 1974; *Apocalypse Now*, United Artists (UA), 1979; *One from the Heart*, Columbia, 1982; *The Outsiders*, Warner Brothers, 1983; *Rumble Fish*, Universal, 1983; *The Cotton Club*, Orion, 1984; *Peggy Sue Got Married*, Tri–Star, 1986; *Captain Eo*, 1986; *Gardens of Stone*, Tri–Star, 1987; *Tucker: The Man and His Dream*, Paramount, 1988; *New York Stories* (several short films; directed "Life without Zoe"), Touchstone, 1989; *The Godfather Part III*, Paramount, 1990; *Bram Stoker's Dracula*, Columbia, 1992; *Jack*, 1996; *John Grisham's The Rainmaker*, 1997. Producer or executive producer of films, including *THX 1138*, Warner Brothers, 1971; *American Graffiti*, Universal, 1973; *The Black Stallion*, UA, 1979; *Kagemusha*, Twentieth Century–Fox, 1980; *Hammett*, Warner Brothers, 1982; *The Black Stallion Returns*, UA, 1983; *The Escape Artist*, Warner Brothers, 1983; *Koyaanisqatsi*, 1983; *Mishima: A Life in Four Chapters*, Filmlink International/Lucasfilm, 1985; *Tough Guys Don't Dance*, Cannon Films, 1987; *Lionheart*, 1987; *Wind*, Tri–Star, 1992; *The Secret Garden*, 1993; *The Junky's Christmas*, 1993; *Mary Shelley's Frankenstein*, 1994; *My Family/Mi Familia*, 1995; *Haunted*, 1995; *Don Juan DeMarco*, 1995; *Buddy*, 1997; *Lanai–Loa*, 1998; *The Virgin Suicides*, 1999; *The Third Miracle*, 1999; *Goosed*, 1999; *Florentine*, 1999; and *Grapefruit Moon*, 2000.

Executive producer for television series and movies, including *White Dwarf*, 1995; *Tecumseh: The Last Warrior*, 1995; *Kidnapped*, 1995; *Dark Angel*, 1996; *The Odyssey*, 1997; *Outrage*, 1997; *Moby Dick*, 1998; and *First Wave*, 1998. Also owner of Niebaum-Coppola, a winery in California's Napa Valley and of Blancaneaux Lodge, a mountain resort in Belize.

■ Member

Directors' Guild of America, Academy of Motion Picture Arts and Sciences.

■ Awards, Honors

Samuel Goldwyn Award, 1962; San Sebastian International Cinema Festival award, 1970, for *The Rain People*; Academy Award for best screenplay (co–recipient), Academy of Motion Picture Arts and Sciences, 1970, for *Patton*; Academy Award nomination for best director, Academy Awards for best picture and for best screenplay based on material from another medium (co–recipient), all 1972, all for *The Godfather*; Directors' Guild of America best director citation, 1972; Golden Palm Award, Cannes Film Festival, and Academy Award nominations for best screenplay and best picture, all 1974, all for *The Conversation*; Academy Award for best picture, best director, and best screenplay based on material from another medium (co–recipient), all 1974, all for *The Godfather Part II*; named best director by Directors' Guild of America, 1974; honorary degree, Hofstra University, 1977; Golden Palm Award and FIPRESCI Prize, Cannes Film Festival, 1979, Academy Award nominations for best picture, best director, and best screenplay, and British Academy Award nomination for best picture, all 1980, all for *Apocalypse Now*; Academy Award nominations for best picture, best director, and best screenplay, all 1991, all for *The Godfather Part III*; Board of Governors Award, American Society of Cinematographers, 1998; D. W. Griffith Award, Directors Guild of America, 1998.

■ Writings

SCREENPLAYS

(And director) *Dementia 13*, American International, 1963.

(With Gore Vidal, Jean Aurenche, Pierre Bost, and Claude Brule) *Is Paris Burning?*, Paramount, 1965.

(With Fred Coe and Edith Sommer) *This Property Is Condemned*, Paramount, 1965.

(And director) *You're a Big Boy Now*, Seven Arts, 1966.

(And director) *The Rain People*, Warner Brothers, 1969.

(With Edmund H. North) *Patton*, Twentieth Century–Fox, 1970.

(With Mario Puzo; and director) *The Godfather*, Paramount, 1972.

(And director) *The Conversation*, Paramount, 1974.

(With Mario Puzo; and director) *The Godfather Part II*, Paramount, 1974.

The Great Gatsby, Paramount, 1974.

(With John Milius; and director) *Apocalypse Now*, United Artists, 1979.

(With Armyan Bernstein; and director) *One from the Heart*, Columbia, 1982.

(With S. E. Hinton; and director) *Rumble Fish*, Universal, 1983.

(With William Kennedy; and director) *The Cotton Club*, Orion, 1984.

(With Sofia Coppola; and director) "Life without Zoe" (second unit in *New York Stories*), Touchstone, 1989.

(With Mario Puzo; and director) *The Godfather Part III*, Paramount, 1990.

(And director) *John Grisham's The Rainmaker*, Paramount, 1997.

OTHER

Also publisher of *Zoetrope,* a short story magazine.

■ Adaptations

Hearts of Darkness: A Filmmaker's Apocalypse, a documentary about the filming of *Apocalypse Now,* was produced for the Showtime cable television network in 1991.

■ Work in Progress

A screenplay tentatively titled "Megalopolis".

■ Sidelights

Francis Ford Coppola rests in an elite company of American film directors who often write their own screenplays and at times produce their own movies.

In this scene from the Academy Award–winning 1974 film *The Godfather Part II*, Al Pacino and Lee Strasberg contemplate the future of the Corleone crime empire.

He has won five Academy Awards and was the first director ever to win the Golden Palm Award at the Cannes Film Festival twice. Best known for his *Godfather* trilogy of films about organized crime and his Vietnam War epic *Apocalypse Now,* Coppola has forged a career from his fascination with the themes of family love, violence, the seductions of power, and the moral bankruptcy of modern life. *Village Voice* correspondent Andrew Sarris called Coppola "a major American director, whose work is mandatory viewing for every serious cineaste."

"Few film directors have left a greater mark than Coppola on the American motion picture industry" since 1970, wrote Robert Lindsey in *New York Times Magazine.* "The first in a generation of celebrity directors whose talents were nurtured not on Hollywood's sound stages but in film schools, he co–authored 'Patton,' which in 1970 brought him the first

of his five Oscars. Also in the early 1970's, he directed two of the most honored and profitable movies of all time, 'The Godfather' and 'The Godfather Part II.' . . . Coppola's early blockbusters made him a force to be reckoned with in the motion picture business, and he used them to assert his independence from the seven Hollywood studios that finance and distribute most movies." Lindsey added that Coppola's influence "swept through the movie business at a critical time. . . . Coppola helped make American movie–making a director's medium. . . . Often swimming upstream against convention and established power, Coppola seemed to be reinventing the rules."

Almost from the start, Coppola was viewed as a maverick, an artist who believed in experimentation, who put daily worries secondary to the process of creation and the evolution of his medium.

"If Francis Ford Coppola had not existed, Hollywood would never have bothered to invent him," noted Joseph Morgenstern in *Newsweek.* "He would have gotten in the way. . . . He comes from a long, honorable line of rule breakers and system buckers—the family name is Artist." *Rolling Stone* contributor David Ehrenstein maintained that the path Coppola has blazed across the decades with his films has met "with a mixture of awe, sympathy and distrust" from critics and audiences alike.

Representing the distrustful element among American critics is *Film Comment* essayist Richard T. Jameson, who called Coppola "a totem of pseudo–style who plunders the inspiration of better artists, and confuses art with state–of–the–art." Others, such as *Partisan Review* correspondent David Denby, cited Coppola for his realistic depictions of bizarre American contradictions and moral ambiguity. "Coppola appears to be a uniquely central and powerful American talent," Denby contended. "His feeling for American surfaces—the glancing intimations of social status in gesture, tone of voice, decor, clothes—is as precise as any director's in American film history." The critic concluded, "Coppola's unusual curiosity about such things as fatherhood, marriage, power, spiritual anguish, etc., sets him apart from the run of Hollywood directors as a central interpreter of American experience, a man taking the big risks, working outside the limits of traditional genres."

Family Influences

Coppola was born in Detroit, Michigan, in 1939, the second of three children of professional flutist and composer Carmine Coppola and his wife, Italia. The

Robert Duvall, Albert Hall, and Martin Sheen share an uncharacteristically quiet moment amid the madness of the Vietnam War in 1979's *Apocalypse Now.*

director's middle name honors the famous automobile maker Henry Ford, who sponsored a radio show for the Detroit Symphony, and thereby helped to feed the Coppola family. When Coppola was still a baby, his family moved to New York City, where his father took the position of first flutist in Arturo Toscanini's NBC Symphony Orchestra. The Coppola parents were artists who were dedicated to the pursuit of excellence. Although Coppola has calculated that his family moved thirty times and he attended twenty–four schools before college, he learned an appreciation of the arts from his parents and siblings. "I think that a lot of what I'm like is from the fact that I was the audience of the most remarkable family," Coppola told *Film Comment*. "And I took it all as magic—I believed everything."

Older brother August was a particularly strong influence on young Coppola. The brothers attended movies together, shared books, and served as critics of one another's work. Coppola told *Film Comment* of his brother: "He was a very advanced kid. He was a great older brother to me and always looked out for me, but in addition, he did very well in school and received many awards for writing and other things, and he was like the star of the family and I did most of what I did to imitate him." The director admitted that his brother's proficiency as a writer stimulated him to follow that profession. "I took his short stories and handed them in under my name when I went to the writing class in high school myself," Coppola said. "My whole beginning in writing started in copying him, thinking that if I did those things, then I could be like he was. . . . At any rate, this relationship with him during those years was a powerful part of my life."

The three siblings were especially close—Coppola's sister is actress Talia Shire—because illness isolated Coppola for part of his childhood. At ten he contracted polio and was partially paralyzed and bedridden for nearly a year. During that time he was not allowed to see other children except his brother and sister, who helped to entertain him and who served as the audience for the projects he created from his bed.

The forced inactivity was made easier by Coppola's interest in gadgets such as radios, record players, and tape recorders. He used the technology at hand to create elaborate puppet shows that he staged for his family. Coppola told *New York Times Magazine*, "When you had polio then, nobody brought their friends around; I was kept in a room by myself, and I used to read and occupy myself with puppets and mechanical things. . . . I became interested in the concept of remote control, I think because I had polio. I'm good with gadgets, and I became a

tinkerer." The process of learning to tinker was one step toward a career in the film industry. Daydreaming about movies and entertaining people was another. Coppola told the *New Yorker* that during his illness he "was always hungry to be with other children." He added, "When I put on my shows alone in my room, I dreamed about the day when I would put on shows with others and people would come to see them. I was dreaming, I'm sure, about having a place like my [Zoetrope] studio, where we could learn, and teach what we learned to others."

From Music Education to Film School

As a teen Coppola earned a music scholarship for tuba to the New York Military Academy on the Hudson River. He was intensely unhappy there, however, and far from certain that he wanted to pursue music seriously. After spending a summer with his brother in Los Angeles, he returned to New York City and finished high school at Great Neck High School in Queens. Coppola began writing plays and doing theatre work at sixteen, and he carried the interest with him to Hofstra University, where he majored in theater arts.

Coppola's years at Hofstra, from 1956 to 1960, were significant for two reasons: first, he balked at the restrictive environment of the theater department and tried to organize his own student–led drama company; and second, he bought a 16mm movie camera and switched his chief focus from theater to film. He was particularly drawn to the innovative cinema work of Russian filmmaker Sergei Eisenstein. After earning his bachelor's degree in 1960, Coppola was accepted in the film school at the University of California, Los Angeles.

Right away, Coppola augmented his studies with work on commercial films. He took a job as production assistant with the well–known B–movie director Roger Corman and was soon learning the intricacies of filmmaking by performing all sorts of tasks for Corman. Early in 1962, he submitted a screenplay called *Pilma, Pilma* and won the Samuel Goldwyn Award for young writers. Coppola admitted in *Rolling Stone* that he was uncertain about his ability as a writer and was over–impressed by contemporaries who seemed to be having more success. "The issue of talent was an important thing," he said, "but then I realized that you don't have to have talent, you just have to have a lot of enthusiasm." That enthusiasm was not lost on Corman, who allowed Coppola to direct the film *Dementia 13* in 1963. A horror movie about a series of axe murders shot on location in Ireland, *Dementia 13* is not particularly remarkable. *Dictionary of Literary Biography* contributor Randall Clark noted, however, that as a twenty–three–year–old's first commercial movie, the work "did demonstrate that Coppola had passed his apprenticeship."

Soon after finishing *Dementia 13*, Coppola signed a writing contract with Seven Arts. Between 1963 and 1967 he wrote or collaborated on more than a dozen screenplays, including big–budget productions such as *This Property Is Condemned*, starring Natalie Wood, and *Is Paris Burning?* Once again his enthusiasm helped him to advance. In 1966, Seven Arts allowed him to direct a film he had written called *You're a Big Boy Now*. The work is a character study of a sensitive young man coming of age in New York City. *Saturday Review* essayist Hollis Alpert observed that the film "has not at all the look of a standard Hollywood product, as it skips along, pausing to examine some of the odder and colorfully seamy aspects of New York. It has an improvisatory air, and touches of modish mockery, particularly popular with the very young and certain film critics." In *Newsweek*, Morgenstern contended that *You're a Big Boy Now* "will wow the Presley crowd at rural drive–ins, charm the eyes off those snakes on foreign film–festival juries, pack them in at cosmopolitan art houses, make it acceptable and even fashionable for stars to play small character roles, open the way for other young directors to break into the commercial film world. . . . For kids it will be a national anthem." Such praise helped Coppola secure backing for another feature film, *The Rain People*, a small–budget art movie about a disenchanted housewife and her aimless wanderings across the country.

Opens Film Studio Zoetrope

While shooting *The Rain People* in 1969, Coppola decided to open his own independent film studio. With a four hundred thousand dollar advance from Warner Brothers, he rented a warehouse in San Francisco and founded American Zoetrope (later known as Zoetrope) Studios. At the age of thirty, Coppola had become disenchanted with Hollywood's corporate atmosphere. He wanted to put films back into the hands of their creators, and he attracted a staff of would–be movie–makers that included director/screenwriter George Lucas, Carroll Ballard, and Walter Murch, among others. In order to finance his independence, Coppola continued to take work from the standard Hollywood hierarchy. In 1970 he scored a major career coup with *Patton*.

Several other writers had already tried to craft a screenplay about controversial World War II general George Patton when Coppola was hired by Twenti-

eth Century–Fox. His script was finally filmed as *Patton* in 1970. The movie, starring George C. Scott, was one of the year's most successful, both commercially and with the critics. It won Coppola his first Academy Award, helped him to bankroll his fledgling studio, and put him on the short list for other big–budget screenplay work.

The Godfather

In 1971, faced with his studio's first financial setback, Coppola contracted with Paramount to co–write and direct a movie adaptation of Mario Puzo's best–seller *The Godfather*. His fee for the job was seventy–five thousand dollars and a six percent profit share. A London *Times* reporter noted, "Coppola perceived in *The Godfather* a journeyman assignment that might yet transcend the conventions of the gangster genre. With hindsight, *The Godfather* can be seen as the tide in Coppola's affairs which, taken at the flood, led on to fortune."

As director of *The Godfather*, Coppola insisted on including several actors—including James Caan, Al Pacino, and Marlon Brando—in the cast. His sister, Talia Shire, also received a role. Since its release in 1972, *The Godfather* has reaped near record–setting earnings. Its theme of an Italian family forging a fortune from organized crime managed to convey Mafia activities without ethnic stereotype or glamorization. In the *Journal of Popular Film*, Jonathan P. Latimer contended that watching the film "is like watching the Viet Nam War from the Pentagon; it is all a simple bookkeeping operation. . . . What we recognize, what appeals, is the fact that the film creates a kind of metaphor for life in the United States today. And, what sets it apart from other films is the fact that it not only depicts, but it also offers explanations for what have seemed to be such irrational acts in the last few years. It provides a backdrop of necessity for almost any act of mayhem, so long as you are true to your own."

The Godfather won Academy Awards for best picture of the year, best actor (Marlon Brando), and best screenplay. Coppola shared the screenplay honor with co–writer Mario Puzo. *Chicago Tribune* reviewer Dave Kehr maintained that the movie "remains one of the most solid and enduring pieces of American popular culture, an exceedingly well–told film that celebrated the protective insularity of the family against the hostility of a vast and impersonal outside world." *New Yorker* critic Pauline Kael called the work "the greatest gangster picture ever made," citing Coppola for his "wide, startlingly vivid view

C. Thomas Howell, Tom Cruise, and Emilio Estevez appear in *The Outsiders* (1983), based on the classic young adult novel by S. E. Hinton.

of a Mafia dynasty." In *American Film Now: The People, the Power, the Money, the Movies,* James Monaco wrote, "If Francis Coppola never made another film save *The Godfather,* his place in the history of American film would be assured."

Receipts from *The Godfather* helped Coppola to keep Zoetrope Studio afloat, and the company produced its own blockbusters in *The Black Stallion* and *American Graffiti.* Coppola's reputation as a screenwriter and director were enhanced by his 1974 film, *The Conversation,* a timely work about electronic surveillance. *The Conversation* won Coppola a Golden Palm award at the Cannes Film Festival and was nominated for Academy Awards for best picture and best original screenplay.

The concept of a sequel to a popular movie had not gained prominence in Hollywood by 1974, when Coppola teamed with Puzo to create *The Godfather*

Part II. The screenwriters decided to craft a film that showed, through flashback, the rise of the Corleone dynasty, interspersed with the continuing story of the family's changing relationships in the second generation. Once again a major cast, including Robert De Niro and Al Pacino, was assembled, and once again the picture was a success, winning six Academy Awards, including best screenplay and best director for Coppola.

In the *Journal of Popular Film,* John Yates claimed that, taken together, *The Godfather* and *The Godfather Part II* "are at their deepest level a brilliant revelation of the family, how it worked through the generations, and how it now falls apart." *New York Times* correspondent Larry Rohter suggested that the works "are still regarded as two of the finest films in the history of American cinema and the undisputed pinnacle of Mr. Coppola's turbulent career."

Jeff Bridges is Preston Tucker, an automotive designer driven to create the "Car of Tomorrow" in Coppola's 1988 film *Tucker: The Man and His Dream.*

Apocalypse Now and Sinking Fortunes

"Turbulent" is an apt word to describe the years following the success of *The Godfather Part II*. Coppola himself told *New York Times Magazine* that all the notoriety and awards "went to my head like a rush of perfume. I thought I couldn't do anything wrong." The director set to work on an epic Vietnam War movie from a script by John Milius. Elaborate sets were constructed in the Philippines for a sixteen–week location shoot. Unfortunately, the film that would become *Apocalypse Now* was beset by problems, from typhoons to casting changes to script rewrites. Leading actor Martin Sheen suffered a heart attack, and Coppola nearly collapsed as the filming dragged on for over a year and the costs of the project skyrocketed from $12 million to $32 million.

Apocalypse Now opened to mixed reviews in 1979, but it eventually earned several Academy Award nominations and made a large profit at the box office. Coppola, who had invested sixteen million dollars of his own money in the project, recouped

his investment as the movie went on to gross over 140 million dollars. *Apocalypse Now* is a modern interpretation of Joseph Conrad's novel *Heart of Darkness*. In the film, a military hit–man named Willard (played by Martin Sheen) is dispatched into Cambodia to "terminate" a rogue soldier (played by Marlon Brando). Although *New York Times* reviewer Vincent Canby called the finished work a "profoundly anticlimactic intellectual muddle," most critics praised the film for its graphic depiction of the insanities of war. *Washington Post* correspondent Rita Kempley concluded, for instance, that ever since *Apocalypse Now* made its debut "the chop of helicopter blades has symbolized the hell of Vietnam."

Soon after the completion of *Apocalypse Now*, Coppola engineered the purchase of the former Hollywood General Studios in Los Angeles. He invested his own money and borrowed from others in order to buy state–of–the–art equipment and renovations for the dilapidated property. Re–named Zoetrope Studios, the studio was intended to be "a paradise for creative film makers independent of the Hollywood establishment," according to Lindsey. Coppola described American Zoetrope as an experiment in fusing the latest in cinematic technology with the old–fashioned concept of contract players and directors.

Financial disaster hit soon after the release of Coppola's first film from American Zoetrope, *One from the Heart.* A musical set in Las Vegas but filmed entirely on elaborate sets, *One from the Heart* ran eleven million dollars over budget and "was greeted vitriolically by most critics," according to Aljean Harmetz in the *New York Times.* The movie cost twenty–seven million dollars to make and earned less than two million dollars at the box office. Coppola, who had sunk most of his personal fortune into the studio, was faced with payments on a debt approaching fifty million dollars. The studio was put up for auction on February 14, 1983, having released only three motion pictures. In 1987, Coppola told the *Washington Post,* "I was just so enthusiastic about movies and having an old–fashioned studio and a wacky project . . . I just wasn't careful and didn't watch exactly what was happening around me. Now, I've sort of been punished. . . . I never had my mind on money. Just the fun of it and the good company of other people . . . a group of people connected in friendship. . . . Today we don't have that anymore. It's corporate America."

His image tarnished by the management of *Apocalypse Now* and *One from the Heart,* Coppola returned to work immediately on smaller, more intimate projects that he hoped would keep his creditors at bay. He became, to quote Lindsey, "a cinematic hired gun, directing, at the rate of one a year, other people's movies for about $2.5 million apiece, plus ten percent of the profits." Two such films were *The Outsiders* and *Rumble Fish,* both based on novels by S. E. Hinton. Coppola filmed *The Outsiders* from a screenplay written by others, calling the movie "a way for me to soothe my heartache over the terrible rejection" of *One from the Heart.* After completing that work, he moved to *Rumble Fish,* directing from a script he co–wrote. *Rumble Fish,* the story of two disenchanted brothers and their alcoholic father, met a skeptical reception when it was released in 1983. As Kempley noted, however, the movie "has recently attracted cult audiences."

Digging Out of Financial Debt

In 1984, Coppola was called in to rewrite the screenplay and direct *The Cotton Club,* yet another major picture that ran over budget and took months and months to shoot. This time Coppola did not sustain

A centuries–old Count Dracula, played by Gary Oldman, seeks to reclaim his long–lost bride in *Bram Stoker's Dracula,* Coppola's 1992 film.

the damage to his own finances or to his reputation. The project was in trouble when he joined it, and he worked for a salary and a percentage of the profits. The director told the *Washington Post,* "I was frightened that I owed so much money that if I took any time off, I didn't know if I would always be in the position to command the kind of money that would be necessary to pay off the debt. . . . I didn't care that my position in the film industry might erode. I just wanted to . . . get that debt paid off. Because as long as that debt existed it meant that I couldn't go on to the next level . . . so I very definitely took one job after another so that I'd be free."

Coppola could still choose his projects with care, and he turned out at least one box–office hit, *Peggy Sue Got Married,* starring Kathleen Turner as a time–traveling homecoming queen. Other films more reflective of the writer–director's philosophies are *Tucker: The Man and His Dream,* which is about an overzealous automobile designer, and *Gardens of Stone*, which tells the story of the officers charged with burying dead soldiers in Arlington Cemetery. During the early shooting for *Gardens of Stone*, Coppola's oldest son and colleague, Gian–Carlo, was killed in a boating accident on the Chesapeake Bay. Personal grief was compounded by the slow box office business for projects such as *Tucker* and *Gardens of Stone*. Coppola had rejected several offers to write yet another *Godfather* sequel, but his waning reputation—and a lawsuit that threatened further debt—convinced him to undertake the project in 1990. Coppola and Puzo wrote another script and convinced most of the *Godfather* cast to return for another outing. The director told the *New York Times*, "I'm hoping a good reception for 'Godfather' will allow me to change my life. Most important, it'll give me a chance to think for a second, to stop worrying about my extinction and try to find something fun and enjoyable to me."

The Godfather and a Comeback

The Godfather Part III was not quite as successful as *Part I*, but it fared better than *Part II*, and the advent of home video gave the series a whole new life. In 1992 Coppola re–edited all three films into a new format that was boxed and sold for more than two hundred dollars. Ty Burr, of *Entertainment Weekly*, wrote that the digitally remastered videos' "crisp" image allows viewers to see more detail in the movies. A less expensive boxed set of the films as they were shot also sold well on the video market.

In the meantime, Coppola turned to another big–budget project, *Bram Stoker's Dracula*, a rendering of the popular Dracula story that attempted to be faithful to the original novel. In an *Entertainment Weekly* interview with Chris Nashawaty, Coppola said, "The context for *Dracula* was to do a classic but in a way that was never done before. In all my movies I

Claire Danes and Matt Damon star in *John Grisham's The Rainmaker*, a 1997 film based on the popular novel.

try to have one experiment. In *Dracula* it was to make a movie using no technology or optical effects that didn't exist when [F. W. Murnau's 1922 *Nosferatu*] was made. . . . We wanted to come up with all turn–of–the–century imagery as if it were all an absinthe dream without using anything but what Murnau had." He succeeded—reviewers praised his cinematic technique and the results of his experiment. *Washington Post* reviewer Hal Hinston wrote that *Dracula* was "Coppola's most lavish and, certainly, his most flamboyant film; never before has he allowed himself this kind of mad experimentation. And never before has he executed these feats of prestidigitation with such control, or such childlike pleasure in playing with his cinematic toys."

Reviewers were not as enthusiastic about *Jack,* Coppola's 1996 film, despite a successful box office run. The film starred Robin Williams as a child with a terrible disease that causes him to age at four times the normal rate. Owen Gleiberman of Entertainment Weekly called it "a synthetic, rather drab movie." Reviews were mixed, with one critic from *National Review* even questioning Coppola's directorial skills, saying that he "seem[ed] to have lost whatever knack he once had." However, a reviewer in *People* wrote that Coppola made the movie "quiet and sweet," by "extracting simple truths about the swift passage of life."

The next year, Coppola moved on to direct a movie based on best–selling author John Grisham's *The Rainmaker.* He wanted to take on the challenge of creating the best movie based on a Grisham novel, and according to many of the nation's reviewers, he triumphed. Stuart Klawans of the *Nation* declared that the film was "certainly the liveliest adaptation of a Grisham novel." The film follows a young lawyer, played by Matt Damon, as he takes on a powerful insurance company for refusing to pay medical bills that could save a man's life. Coppola, who also adapted the novel for film, told Nashawaty that, "At the end, it's really about when Matt asks John Voight: 'Do you even remember when you sold out?' In other words, do you really want to be a lawyer if you're not going to help people? Do you really want to be a director if you're not going to make the films that are in your heart?"

Lindsey wrote, "Mr. Coppola remains among a handful of directors—Woody Allen, Steven Spielberg, George Lucas, perhaps a few others—whose track records and names alone are likely to induce a studio to finance a new movie." His flamboyant personality and open disdain for Hollywood's corporate structures notwithstanding, Coppola has been able to command seven–figure salaries and hefty profit shares on the films to which he has lent his name. According to Gene Siskel in the *Chicago Tribune,* Coppola's fans perceive that he "simply has bigger dreams than most other filmmakers, that he wants to do more than make movies, that his goal is nothing less than revolutionizing the film business, artistically and financially."

In 1990, Coppola told the *New York Times,* "I'm very embarrassed about my career over the last 10 years. You know, an Italian family puts a lot of stock in not losing face, not making what we call *una brutta figura,* or bad showing. When you have people writing about you in a mocking way and making fun of your ideas and calling you a crackpot, that's a real *brutta figura.* I want to be considered a vital American film maker and have the country be proud of me."

If you enjoy the works of Francis Ford Coppola, you might want to check out the following films:

Full Metal Jacket, directed by Stanley Kubrick, 1987.
Goodfellas, a mob masterpiece starring Robert De Niro, directed by Martin Scorcese, 1990.
Platoon, a scathing, soldier's–eye view of Vietnam, directed by Oliver Stone, 1986.
Scarface, starring Al Pacino and directed by Brian DePalma, 1983.

Coppola insisted that his best work lies ahead, that he will not go down in history as the creator of "the greatest gangster picture ever made." He told the *New Yorker,* "It's so silly in life not to pursue the highest possible thing you can imagine, even if you run the risk of losing it all, because if you don't pursue it you've lost it anyway. You can't be an artist and be safe." He concluded, "I don't know why some of the reaction to what I do is so cynical. I know that I'm for intelligence, creativity, and friendliness, as opposed to greed, power, and hostility. Whether you're the director or the producer or the owner of a movie, as soon as you form an organization to make a picture you're a businessman. The problem is to be all that and still to be free."

■ Biographical and Critical Sources

BOOKS

Contemporary Literary Criticism, Volume 16, Gale (Detroit, MI), 1981.

Cowie, Peter, *Coppola: A Biography*, Scribner (New York City), 1990.

Dictionary of Literary Biography, Volume 44: *American Screenwriters, Second Series*, Gale (Detroit), 1986.

Goodwin, Michael, and Naomi Wise, *On the Edge: The Life and Times of Francis Coppola*, Morrow (New York City), 1989.

Johnson, Robert K., *Francis Ford Coppola*, Twayne (New York City), 1977.

Kael, Pauline, *Deeper into Movies*, Little, Brown (Boston, MA), 1973.

Lewis, Jon, *Whom God Wishes to Destroy: Francis Coppola and the New Hollywood*, Duke University Press (Durham, NC)), 1995.

Lourdeaux, Lee, *Italian and Irish Filmmakers in America: Ford, Capra, Coppola, and Scorsese*, Temple University Press (Philadelphia, PA), 1990.

Monaco, James, *American Film Now: The People, the Power, the Money, the Movies*, Oxford University Press (New York City), 1979.

Pechter, William S., *Movies Plus One*, Horizon (New York City), 1981.

PERIODICALS

American Cinematographer, August, 1991, Paula Parisi, "A Conversation with Coppola," pp. 71–73; November, 1992, George Turner, "*Bram Stoker's Dracula*: A Happening Vampire," pp. 36–46.

American Film, April, 1983.

Atlantic, August, 1976.

Chicago Sun–Times, November 11, 1992, Roger Ebert, review of *Dracula*.

Chicago Tribune, January 18, 1982; February 11, 1982; October 5, 1986; March 3, 1989; December 15, 1990.

Commentary, July, 1972; July, 1974.

Entertainment Weekly, August 6, 1996, Owen Gleiberman, review of *Jack*, p. 48; August 9, 1996, Owen Gleiberman, review of *Jack*, pp. 39–40; February 7, 1997, Ty Burr, review of *Jack*, pp. 76–77; May 2, 1997, Ty Burr, review of *The Godfather*, review of *The Godfather, Part II*, pp. 66–67; November 21, 1997, Chris Nashawaty, "A Coppola Things," pp. 56–63; November 21, 1997, Lisa Schwartzbaum, review of *The Rainmaker*, p. 100; November 1,

1999, Chris Nashawaty, "The 100 Greatest Entertainers," p. 107; December 17, 1999, "The Godfather: Part IV," p. 40.

Esquire, March, 2000, Tom Carson, "The Next Francis Ford Coppola Is . . .," p. 102.

Film Comment, October, 1983; April, 1985.

Film Quarterly, spring, 1986.

Films in Review, March–April, 1993, Edmond Grant, review of *Dracula*, pp. 131–132.

Journal of Popular Film, Volume 2, number 2, 1973; Volume 4, number 2, 1975.

Journal of Popular Film and Television, summer, 1999, Carol Corbin and Robert A. Campbell, "Postmodern Iconography and Perspective in Coppola's *Bram Stoker's Dracula*," pp. 40–48; summer, 1999, Leah M. Wyman, with others, "Primal Urges and Civilized Sensibilities: The Rhetoric of Gendered Archetypes, Seduction, and Resistance in *Bram Stoker's Dracula*," pp. 32–39.

Los Angeles Times, December 19, 1988; January 26, 1990; December 30, 1990.

Nation, April 3, 1972; December 22, 1997, Stuart Klawans, review of *The Rainmaker*, pp. 35–36.

National Review, September 16, 1996, review of *Jack*, pp. 68–69.

Newsday, December 22, 1974.

New Statesman and Society, August 2, 1996, Boyd Tonkin, "A Cinematic Offer You Can't Refuse: or How *The Godfather* Prefigured Apocalypse," p. 38.

Newsweek, February 20, 1967; November 25, 1974; December 23, 1974; June 13, 1977; January 31, 1983; October 14, 1991; November 24, 1997, David Ansen, review of *The Rainmaker*, p. 73.

New Republic, December 15, 1997, Stanley Kauffmann, review of *The Rainmaker*, p. 29.

New Yorker, March 18, 1972; April 15, 1974; December 23, 1974; November 8, 1982.

New York Times, August 12, 1979; August 15, 1979; March 18, 1980; March 21, 1980; November 23, 1980; February 11, 1982; April 16, 1982; May 3, 1987; March 1, 1989; March 12, 1989; December 23, 1990; December 25, 1990.

New York Times Magazine, August 5, 1979; July 24, 1988.

Partisan Review, Volume 43, number 1, 1976.

People, August 12, 1996, Tom Gliatto, review of *Jack*, p. 19; December 1, 1997, Leah Rozen, review of *The Rainmaker*, p. 32.

Playboy, July, 1975.

Rolling Stone, March 19, 1981; March 18, 1982.

Saturday Review, February 4, 1967; May 4, 1974.

Sight and Sound, autumn, 1972; summer, 1974; June, 1992, Lynne Tillman, "Kiss of Death," p. 33; January, 1993, Richard Dyer, "Dracula and Desire," pp. 8–12; February, 1993, Pam Cook, review of

Dracula, pp. 42–43; October, 1996, Philip Kemp, review of *Jack,* pp. 42–43; April, 1998, Philip Kemp, review of *The Rainmaker,* pp. 50–51.

Time, December 16, 1974; January 18, 1982; December 17, 1984; August 12, 1996, Richard Schickel, review of *Jack,* p. 64; December 1, 1997, Richard Schickel, review of *The Rainmaker,* p. 80.

Times (London), January 21, 1988; November 14, 1988; February 11, 1989.

Vanity Fair, June, 1990.

Variety, March 24, 1997, Peter Bart, "It's Business, not Personal," pp. 4–5; November 17, 1997, Todd McCarthy, review of *The Rainmaker,* p. 63; January 12, 1998, Richard Setlowe, "A Writer First: Coppola, with 3 Script Oscars, Gained Biz Foothold as a Crack Rewrite Talent, pp. 152–153; March 20, 2000, Peter Bart, "Renaissance Technophile," p. 2; December 18, 2000, Tim Swanson, "The Don Goes Digital," p. 3.

Village Voice, May 28, 1979; August 27, 1979; April 21, 1980; April 5, 1983.

Washington Post, February 4, 1970; December 16, 1984; May 8, 1987; August 7, 1988; March 3, 1989; December 25, 1990; November 13, 1992, Desson Howe, review of *Dracula;* November 13, 1992, Hal Hinson, review of *Dracula.**

Chris Crutcher

■ Personal

Born July 17, 1946, in Dayton, OH; son of John William (a county clerk) and Jewell (Morris) Crutcher. *Education:* Eastern Washington State College (now University), B.A., 1968. *Hobbies and other interests:* Running, basketball, swimming, biking, competing in triathlons.

■ Addresses

Home—Spokane, WA. *Agent*—Liz Darhansoff, 1220 Park Ave., New York, NY 10128.

■ Career

Writer, therapist, teacher, and child advocacy worker. Received teaching certificate, 1970; teacher, Kennewick Dropout School, Kennewick, WA, 1970–73; Lakeside School, Oakland, CA, teacher, 1973–76, director, 1976–80; Community Mental Health Center, Spokane, WA, child protection team specialist, 1980–82, child and family mental health professional, 1982–95; full–time writer, 1995—.

■ Awards, Honors

Best Book for Young Adults citations, American Library Association, for *Running Loose, Stotan!, The Crazy Horse Electric Game, Chinese Handcuffs,* and *Athletic Shorts;* Best Books, *School Library Journal,* for *The Crazy Horse Electric Game;* ALAN Award for significant contributions to young adult literature; Margaret A. Edwards Award, American Library Association, for lifetime achievement in writing books for teens, 2000.

■ Writings

FICTION; FOR YOUNG ADULTS

Running Loose, Greenwillow, 1983.
Stotan!, Greenwillow, 1986.
The Crazy Horse Electric Game, Greenwillow, 1987.
Chinese Handcuffs, Greenwillow, 1989.
Athletic Shorts (short stories), Greenwillow, 1991.
Staying Fat for Sarah Byrnes, Greenwillow, 1993.
Ironman: A Novel, Greenwillow, 1995.

OTHER

Deep End: A Novel of Suspense (psychological fiction), Morrow, 1992.

Contributor of short stories to anthologies and of articles to periodicals, including *Spokane.*

■ Work in Progress

Whale Talk, for Greenwillow, expected 2001.

■ Adaptations

Angus, a 1995 film by New Line Cinema, was based on "A Brief Moment in the Life of Angus Bethune," a short story from the collection *Athletic Shorts;* Crutcher created screenplays from his novels *Running Loose* and *The Crazy Horse Electric Game; The Deep End* has been optioned by Interscope Pictures; *Staying Fat for Sarah Burns* hs been optioned by Columbia Pictures.

■ Sidelights

Considered among the most respected American authors of young adult literature, Chris Crutcher is regarded as a dynamic and insightful writer whose works are both exciting sports stories and authentic reflections of the inner lives of his protagonists. Praised for the tough yet thoughtful nature and evocative quality of his novels and short stories as well as for the believability of both his characters and the sports background he favors, Crutcher, who has worked as a mental health professional in child and family services as well as for child advocacy, is consistently celebrated for the honesty and appeal of his books as well as for his understanding of teenagers. In 2000, the author received the coveted Margaret A. Edwards Award for his lifetime achievement in writing for teens.

Crutcher profiles young male high school students who are involved in such sports as baseball, basketball, football, swimming, wrestling, and track. While preparing for and participating in their games or meets, these characters—sensitive young people noted for being far removed from the "jock" stereotype—are faced with problems, moral dilemmas, and tough choices with which they struggle. Crutcher uses high school athletics as the proving ground for personal achievement; by testing their own limits, the boys in his books emerge from their crises as stronger and more mature individuals.

Louie Banks learns to accept that life is sometimes unfair after he is thrown off his high school football team for refusing to injure a rival player.

Throughout his works, Crutcher addresses challenging topics; his protagonists encounter sickness and death, divorce, rape and sexual abuse, disability, discrimination, AIDS, abortion, and other issues as well as pimps, prostitutes, and motorcycle and youth gangs; in addition, his characters must cope with the attitudes and actions of their parents, coaches, teammates, and friends.

Despite the seriousness of his themes, Crutcher underscores his books with positive messages that stress integrity, dignity, honor, courage, tenacity, survival, and hope. In addition, he stresses the joys of competitive sports and often includes positive friendships—between boys and between both sexes—and romantic relationships in his works. The author also invests his books with humor, which ranges from subtle wit to raw, locker room–style banter. Due to their subject matter and use of rough language, some of Crutcher's books have been censored; the author is also criticized for the complexity of his storylines and for his concentration on male protagonists, though he is also credited with creating well–realized female characters in supporting roles.

As a stylist, Crutcher writes spirited, fast–paced works that incorporate both first– and third–person narrations; he often uses the formats of the diary or personal letter to structure his books. Writing in *Twentieth–Century Children's Writers,* Bonnie O. Ericson said, "Many authors have used sports as a metaphor for the ups and downs of life, but very few with the combined humor and poignancy of Chris Crutcher. . . . [In the goal of] writing books that will hook young male readers, Crutcher is entirely successful. At the same time, he's created rich and complex works for all readers." In her essay in *Horn Book,* Christine McDonnell claimed that Crutcher "gives readers the inside story on young men, sports, and growing up," while Anita Silvey, writing in the same periodical, commented that whether Crutcher is writing "about the baseball field or the basketball court, he makes sports and the young boys who play them come alive and in the process presents the issues and problems of adolescence." *Booklist* reviewer Stephanie Zvirin called Crutcher "one of the most successful novelists writing for young adults today. . . . Chris Crutcher knows the right moves on and off the court."

Childhood Influences

Crutcher has devoted his career to helping troubled young people deal with their situations. "I'm forever being astonished at the heroism of kids who've made it," he once said in an interview with *Authors and Artists for Young Adults (AAYA).* "You look at their lives, and you look at what happened, and you don't understand why they're still standing—but they are, and they have enough strength to keep powering them on." Crutcher's experiences with young people have helped to inspire his books, and he often interweaves his own background into his novels and stories. Born in Dayton, Ohio, Crutcher grew up in Cascade, a remote logging town in central Idaho: "My dad was in the Air Force, and my parents were just passing through," he told Dave Jenkinson of *Emergency Librarian,* adding that his parents "were in Cascade before I got dry." Crutcher told *AAYA,* "It was eighty miles from the nearest

movie—and I don't mean eighty miles over freeway, I mean over two–lane highway. One street in the whole town was paved." For entertainment the town turned to high school sports, especially football, which was followed with a fierce devotion. "On a Friday afternoon you couldn't buy a tank of gas until the game was over," Crutcher recalled. The people of Cascade were typically the rugged, active kind—loggers, ranchers, and hunters. Crutcher came away with mixed feelings about these latter–day frontiersmen: he didn't always like their politics, and he didn't like hunting, either, but he admired their willingness to take care of one another. In Cascade, he observed, "there are no street people, there are no homeless people, because you can always find a place to put somebody. It's real hard to let people freeze to death if you know who they are."

Crutcher got along so well with his parents, John and Jewell Crutcher, that he dedicated his first book, *Running Loose,* to them and included them as characters. "They've been a real influence on me," he told the *Idaho Statesman.* "They let me go. It's real important to have been allowed not to carry around your parents' garbage. I knew I could take off and go hitchhiking around the country and I wouldn't lose my mom and dad." As he explained to *AAYA,* "My mother gave me a sense of passion, of doing things that weren't necessarily rational, of going with my feelings. And my dad was the balance point to that. He was a tremendously rational man, the problem solver. He gave me an ability to make things simple . . . and get to what the problem really is." As an adult counseling people about their issues, Crutcher said, "I draw far more on my dad's voice for making simple sense of things than I do for any class I ever took."

Crutcher found school "a good place to be a stand–up comic." As he told *AAYA,* "My brother was the valedictorian of his class, and it seemed like an awful lot of pressure to put on yourself, so I coasted through school." His goal was to be a "perfect C student," he explained. "If I could have done it exactly right I would never have gotten any other grade than a C, but I would screw up and get a D and then I'd need a B to counterbalance." In any case, "there were always ways to get through without doing any work"—his brother's old book reports, for instance, were a goldmine. "I was rebellious, really, and I didn't want to do anything anybody told me to do. Also, I could charm my way out of trouble." Crutcher's introduction to writing came through punishment themes: as he told Dave Jenkinson, "Teachers used to like to give me 500–word themes, and I gave them lots of reasons to do it. I would get real creative doing these because there was no school structure to them." When he was in junior high, Crutcher's journalism teacher, impressed by one of his themes, invited him to write for the school paper. Until his senior year, Crutcher recalled, "I had this column where I took pot shots at everybody." He told *AAYA,* "It was kind of a smartass thing—I would take shots at people—and I really liked it. I liked being able to say things and not have anybody have the chance to get even with me." Crutcher claimed that the only book that he read all the way through as a high school student was Harper Lee's *To Kill a Mockingbird,* which he began in preparation for a test. He recalls scanning the jacket copy to see if he could actually get out of reading the book, but once he read the first page, he was, as he told Heather Vogel Frederick of *Publishers Weekly,* "swept away"; Crutcher finished the book, he noted, "about three weeks after the test."

A Real–Life Education

Instead of academics, Crutcher was drawn to sports. "I really liked the sense of belonging," he told *AAYA.* In Cascade, he told Frederick of *Publishers Weekly,* "It didn't matter if you were a good athlete or not. You tried out for the football team with a stethoscope—if you could breathe you could play. And if you didn't show up, they'd come get you." Crutcher told *AAYA,* "My characters are always much better athletes than I was. I really didn't become proficient in basketball until after the twelfth grade—I was a bench sitter of gross proportion. In track I was somewhere in the middle. Football was probably my best sport, just because it required less athleticism." The camaraderie that Crutcher found in athletics allowed him to apply himself to team play. "Finding out how far you can push yourself if you have the support of your friends—that's very important to me about sports."

By the mid–1960s Crutcher was out of high school and studying at Eastern Washington State College. "I knew I was going to college but I didn't have any idea why," he told *AAYA.* "I was rebellious as hell—I mean rebellious with ideas—and really enjoyed it." He remained involved with sports, joining the swim team and reaching the small–college nationals, but he was not a conventional athlete. "I couldn't have been happier than when Tommie Smith and John Carlos raised their black fists at the 1968 Olympics," Crutcher noted, referring to the famous gesture of black pride made by these runners when they received their Olympic medals. "I was one of three or four lettermen at Eastern Washington who stood up for that stuff and got a lot of hate mail," Crutcher recalled. Meanwhile, he finally found something to like about school. "I took my first sociology class," he said, "and I realized that

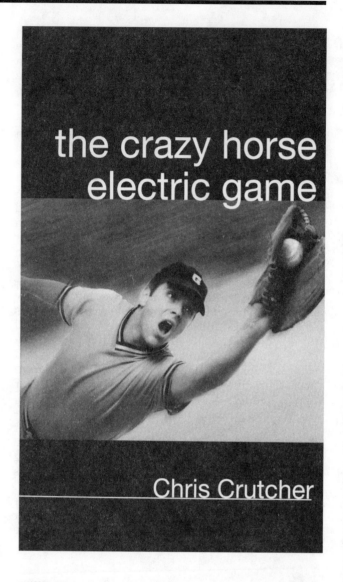

Willie Weaver turns to sports to recover his self–respect after a water–skiing accident leaves him brain–damaged in this 1987 novel.

institutions were in the world for some purpose other than what I had been told they were there for—religion as a social control or education as somebody else's idea of a social control. Things weren't exactly how I'd been told. My rebellion had a purpose."

At the beginning of his senior year, Crutcher got a phone call from the administration—he still hadn't declared a major. "I got my transcript and tried to find out what I had the most credits in," he said, "and it was psychology and sociology so I chose that, with no idea what to do with it." Next, Crutcher said, "I spent a year running around playing *Route 66* with a friend of mine"—the guys hopped in a car and flipped coins at major intersections, ending up in places like Texas and Hawaii—"and then I went back to school for a teaching credential, mostly because people said that was a saleable skill."

Alternative Teaching and Therapy

When a new, experimental school in Washington State—Kennewick Dropout School—finally made Crutcher an offer, he took it. "I got the job because I had the psych background and I wouldn't cost them much money because I didn't have any experience," he admitted. "They had a building, they put me in it, and in two years I never saw another adult in the place. It was like, 'Do what you do,' and I learned by fire." The goal was to convince the kids, usually juniors and seniors, to stay with the program long enough to get a high school diploma. "I learned a lot about what turned kids off," Crutcher said. "I did a lot of 'free–school' things. I tried a tremendous amount that *didn't work*. And the key was that I recognized that early and would just say 'This isn't working—let's stop it, it's driving me nuts.'"

When Crutcher switched to teaching in a regular high school after the money for the experimental school ran out, he felt that his situation was boring by comparison, so he headed for California. Crutcher got a job with an alternative school in Oakland, a poor city with a high crime rate. The school, Lakeside, taught students from kindergarten through twelfth grade, often on a contract from the Oakland public schools. Many were kids who'd been expelled—and "if you get thrown out of the Oakland public schools," Crutcher observed, "you've gone a ways." At first he taught the younger students, but the older ones made themselves impossible to ignore. "It was that time in the early Seventies when the learn–when–you–want–to attitude was prevalent," he recalled, "so the high school would hold classes that nobody came to. The older kids were basically out throwing water balloons at the elementary kids and terrorizing them and smoking dope and getting drunk." After about three years, he took his concerns to Lakeside's executive director. "I said, 'You know, in a lot of schools people *go*.' And he asked me if I wanted to be the director and I asked him if that paid more and he said 'no,' so I took it." Crutcher recalled, "Those were twelve–and fifteen–hour days, and I just ate it up."

Crutcher has observed that the most remarkable thing about his Lakeside experience was the "incredible togetherness" that helped to sustain the school. For his part, Crutcher said, "It was always a great challenge to make sure people knew I was fair and that the school stood for everybody." Crutcher had many chances to practice his fairness because, as director, he was also the school disciplinarian. "A lot of the high school kids would come in and just *try* to get themselves thrown out," he told *AAYA*. So he developed a novel strategy. "I said, 'You just can't *get* thrown out of here. This is it. If you're hurting people I'll send you home, but you can't get thrown out.' That really screwed people up," he admitted. "We were on equal ground then and we had to learn together." And the kids had plenty to teach Crutcher. One time he tried discussing the rules of Lakeside with a group of kids, and they pointed out, relentlessly, that he didn't really do what he had written down. Take the rule, the students said, about sending people home for bad behavior, including drug use. "That's not the rule at all," kids told him—"the rule is that if you think we're going to get hurt if we go home you won't send us there, you'll do something else." "And every one of my rules was like that," Crutcher admitted. "I started looking at what reality was, and that was tremendous for me. From then on, that was how I dealt with kids. I had a bunch of keys hanging from my belt—you could hear me coming—and I'd walk into a room and they'd say 'Crutcher is narking on us, he's looking for somebody doing drugs.' They'd expect me to say 'No I'm not,' but I'd say 'You're damn right I'm looking for drugs. Because I'm the cop and you guys are the robbers, and it's my job. I'm here to bust your butt—and I'm also here to try and find some way for you to get interested in *something*.'"

More often than not, the program worked. "I think we did some really good things," Crutcher said. "Teachers worked really hard at individualizing things for kids. We had small classrooms and kids could go as fast as they could go—you could be a good math student and a horrible English student and still stay in the same grade." The teachers at Lakeside, he declared, included some authentic heroes. "They were getting zero—I mean nothing—for money, and we all knew that they probably weren't going to stay very long. I had a teacher say to me one time, 'There's a lot of crazy things about this school, but if you can teach here you can teach anyplace. You'll never be intimidated. Ever.'"

Crutcher left Lakeside in 1980. "It was just a ripping away to leave that place," he told *AAYA*, but "I really don't like crowds and I think that growing up in the mountains really got to me. I could feel myself becoming physically agitated as it got more crowded." He went back to the Northwest, to Spokane, Washington, where he became a therapist at the Spokane Community Mental Health Center, which specialized in dealing with both family violence and the problems of young people; in addition, Crutcher became the head of Spokane's Child Protection team. Many of Crutcher's clients were referred to him from the school system, sent because they were struggling with problems beyond the scope of a guidance counselor. "As an adolescent," Crutcher recalled, "what I remember most is that I was *told* things. I was told how they worked and how I was supposed to feel and what my values were. To me therapy is allowing kids to come in, close the door, and talk about what life's really like for them. Let them know that I understand that things aren't working right. Sometimes it's just a place to come bitch—to talk about what doesn't feel good, fears that they may not be able to talk about anyplace else. It's a place for all those crazy questions about drugs, about sex, about love, and what's the difference between lust and love and need and want and all those things—because kids find themselves doing things that scare them, and they can't tell anybody they're scared. Therapy can provide a place to talk about that and not have somebody tell you what you're supposed to feel." Crutcher concluded, "Therapy is a place to come and be safe, to talk about what you don't understand and not feel silly, and know that there's somebody here who went through this, too. I didn't know the answers then either, and there are a lot of answers I don't know now, but we might—if we put our heads together—we might be able to find one."

At about the same time that Crutcher became a therapist, he also became a writer. "I recognized the need for a creative outlet in my life," he said in *Horn Book.* "In my work, the daily crisis of people's lives is so immediate. Time moves so fast. But books are so permanent. They have their own life in time." As Crutcher told *AAYA*, he wasn't the usual budding author. "As a teenager I was a famous non-reader," he said, "so I didn't engage in books, particularly fiction, until I was out of college. But I did like stories. I was told stories as a little kid a lot and I was read to a lot. Television came to Cascade when I was in the fifth grade, and I remember being really curious about why one show was funny and another wasn't when both were meant to be. I used to take stories apart; I paid close attention to how things worked among my friends—I was a real student of behavior."

Running Loose

In 1970, Crutcher went to stay with Terry Davis, a college friend and aspiring novelist who was a Stegner Fellow at Stanford. Davis was at work on his first novel, *Vision Quest*, which describes the coming

of age of a high school athlete in Spokane. The book became a best–seller when it was published in 1979 and was eventually turned into a movie; in 1997, Davis published a biography of his friend, *Presenting Chris Crutcher.* "We had a lot of the same background," Crutcher recalled, "so I got to read some of the chapters for believability. We would talk about his story and what he was trying to get across. I got to watch the raw material turn into something that's really smooth and does the job. Terry's a wonderful writer, and there was magic in that process." But it was a magic, Crutcher realized, that mere mortals could attain. "Here's a guy that I could beat one–on–one in basketball. He wasn't from outer space—he was a guy who rolled up his sleeves and did his storytelling, and I realized that writing was a human thing to do." Finally, after Crutcher left Lakeside School in 1980, he had four months free before his new job started; he had an idea, and he couldn't get *To Kill a Mockingbird* out of his head, so he dared himself to write a book. "I just sat down and wrote *Running Loose*—long–hand!" Crutcher told *AAYA.* He sent a typed copy to Davis, who recommended it to his own agent, Liz Darhansoff, in New York. Within a week Darhansoff agreed to represent Crutcher. By the time that the book was published, Crutcher remembered, "I was addicted. I just never wanted to stop." When he was writing *Running Loose,* Crutcher did not realize that he was creating a YA novel. He told Dave Jenkinson of *Emergency Librarian,* "I didn't know there was such a thing. I'd just spent ten years in the toughest school in Oakland, and so I just wrote it in that language."

In his works for teenagers, Crutcher surveys the struggle of young people to grow up and take charge of their own lives. "People always want us to *be* adults rather than *become* adults," he told *AAYA.* "Everybody wants the finished product, and nobody wants to look at how it's made." Louie Banks, the hero of *Running Loose,* knows better. "The thing I hate about life, so far, is that nothing's ever clear," he declares. "Every time you get things all figured out, somebody throws in another kink." Inspired by a conversation Crutcher overheard in a locker room fifteen years before in which a racist coach directed his players to eliminate an African American player, the novel is set in Trout, Idaho—a small town much like Crutcher's hometown of Cascade. As his senior year begins, Louie thinks his life is set. He's at peace with his parents, a good–natured, insightful couple modeled on Crutcher's own mother and father; he's a starter on the school's eight–man football team, where he's surrounded by his buddies; and he has Becky, a wonderful girlfriend. But his perfect life soon begins to unravel. The trouble begins after a game with a rival school with a challenging team anchored by

Washington, a talented black quarterback. In a bigoted harangue, Louie's coach orders the Trout team to sideline Washington with crippling tackles, and one of Louie's teammates complies. Louie denounces the play and storms off the field, ending his football career. His football buddies won't join the walkout, even if they agree with him. The coach lies his way out of the situation, and the townspeople are left to assume that Louie just lost control. Washington turns out not to be hurt very badly. Even though Louie is sure he did the right thing, he doesn't have the chance to feel very heroic. Becky dies in a pointless traffic accident, trying to drive around some rowdy kids on the only bridge in town. At the funeral, Louie hears Becky fondly eulogized by an out–of–town minister who never met her, and he rages again. However, a young track coach, who recognizes Louie's potential and respects the stand he took on the football play, recruits him for the team, and he wins the two–mile event. When the principal dedicates a memorial plaque to Becky—emblazoned with his own signature—Louie stays calm and takes care of it: he sneaks onto the school grounds and smashes up the memorial with a sledgehammer.

The solution to pain such as Louie's, Crutcher believes, lies in "letting go"—letting go of the search for a satisfying answer that doesn't exist; letting yourself admit that you're just a human being in pain. "If I keep asking why and keep not coming up with an answer," Crutcher observed, "I'm either going to get so frustrated I want to scream, or I'm just going to say 'There's no answer—hooray!' You know—'Hooray that there's no answer because I don't *have* one.'" As for sorrow, he declared, "you're not really hurt—injured—by your sadness or your grief, you're hurt by resisting it." "There's a case to be made for life being a series of losses, from the time that you lose your mother's womb, and all the times that you have to change schools, or your friends go away, or people die. If you live from zero to sixty you're going to have suffered a lot of losses. And what you can do for yourself is learn to hold yourself and grieve and allow that grief to be the focus. Just say, 'I don't need to fight this, I don't need to do anything but just feel bad. Why? Because I *do* feel bad.'" So Louie lets go: "The tears came. And man, they came. I must have lost five pounds."

Writing in *Voice of Youth Advocates*, Mary K. Chelton noted of *Running Loose*, "Best of all, . . . you love [Louie] and grieve with him when Becky dies because she is presented as a really neat person." Chelton also wrote that *Running Loose* is a "good stepping stone up from Hinton and toward titles like *Vision Quest* and *Stop Time*. Good 'bridge books' are rare and first novelists this good even rarer." *Kirkus*

Reviews claimed that Louie tells his story with "strong feeling and no crap, as he might say," and added that as a "dramatic, head–first confrontation with mendacity, fate's punches, and learning to cope, it's a zinger." Zena Sutherland of *Bulletin of the Center for Children's Books* called *Running Loose* an "unusually fine first novel," while Trev Jones in *School Library Journal* said that Louie tells his story with "sensitivity, humor, and outrage" and that the book "raises important issues for adolescents to consider."

Stotan!

For his second novel, *Stotan!*, Crutcher returned to the arena of high school sports. "One of the things I like about sports is that the rules are clear," he told *AAYA*. "I use sports in young adult fiction to talk about rules, usually back–to–back with information about the rules of life. Sports provides an arena for an athlete, or a character, to test himself or herself and learn about tenacity or about putting things in perspective." In *Stotan!*, the focus is on self–discipline. The story begins when four high–school swimmers—Walker, the team captain; Lion; Nortie; and Jeff—volunteer for "Stotan Week," an endurance test given by their coach, a Korean–American named Max II Song. When the boys sign up, they learn that a "Stotan" is a cross between a Stoic and a Spartan, and Max makes them live up to the billing with harsh exercises, exhausting laps in the pool, and a "Torture Lane" for swimmers who try to slack off. "I took Stotan Week out of real life," Crutcher confessed. "Actually I calmed it down to put in the book. My college coach was a madman, an absolute madman." Feats of physical courage, like falling off the diving board backward, were mandatory on Crutcher's team. "If you didn't do it you were doing push–ups until you couldn't walk. And then you'd have to run outside over the snowbank, wet, and bear–walk [hands and feet only]—we did all that. The Torture Lane was there, it was all there. It was *bizarre*."

Amazingly, Walker and his teammates start to like Stotan Week. Sharing the challenge brings them closer together. They discover that they can endure a lot more than they thought. They realize that the less they struggle against the pain, and the more they accept and push beyond it, the easier things get. They feel energetic and confident. When the week is over, Max tosses aside his authoritarian props—bullhorn, firehose, Airborne cap—and shares some human insights, inspired by his study of Asian philosophy. "There are lessons in this week that can serve you for the rest of your lives," he says. "Remember the times when you gave up the fight [against Max and his discipline] and just went with Stotan Week—saw which way the river was flowing and went that way too. Most times the depth of your well isn't measured in how hard you fight—how tough you are—but in your ability to see what is and go with that." The team expects their toughest challenge to be the statewide swimming meet, but they must face a far greater challenge when Jeff develops a withering case of leukemia; their Stotan wisdom helps the friends through their crisis. At Jeff's urging the team goes on to the state meet without him, where they excel—for his sake—and swim an illegal three–man relay at the finals. At the end of the book, as Walker looks back over his experiences, it's clear that he hasn't soured on life; instead, he's come to an understanding of how precious it is. "I think my job in this life is to be an observer," he writes in his diary, and concludes, "I'll be a *Stotan* observer: look for the ways to get from one to the other of those glorious moments when all the emotional stops are pulled, when you're just so . . . glad to be breathing air." *Voice of Youth Advocates* reviewer Mary K. Chelton noted that *Stotan!* depicts "beautifully the joy, pain, and emotional strength of a male adolescent friendship" and called it a "lovely story and a model of the realistic adolescent novel." Writing in *School Library Journal*, Jerry Flack called *Stotan!* "a fine coming–of–age novel," while Anita Silvey of *Horn Book* compared it to the books of John R. Tunis and Bruce Brooks's *The Moves Make the Man*, works "that use a sports setting and competition to discuss the greater issues of being young and alive."

A New Perspective on Sports

The Crazy Horse Electric Game takes a much different look at sports: it concerns a high school student who knows the thrill of having athletic talent, then loses it all and has to rebuild his life. As the novel begins, Willie Weaver is a sixteen–year–old amateur baseball player in small–town Coho, Montana, pitching for a team sponsored by the Samson Floral Shop. In the greatest moment of his career, Willie throws a winning game against a championship team sponsored by Crazy Horse Electric. By the standards of Coho, he's a living legend. Then a water–skiing accident leaves Willie brain–damaged; he's crippled and must struggle even to talk. His father, who was a winning college athlete, can scarcely stand the sight of him; friends feel awkward around him; and, most important of all, Willie hates his own life. Finally, he runs away from home and, in reality, from human contact. Willie never expected life to be so flawed—he expected it to be as perfect as the Crazy Horse Electric game. "There's a lot to hate yourself for if you listen to those expectations," Crutcher told *AAYA*, "because no one ever meets them."

Crutcher learned a different—and healthier—way of looking at life from Dr. Gil Milner, a supervising therapist in Spokane, Washington. Milner is steeped in the East Asian philosophy that appears from time to time in Crutcher's books. "He is one of the most amazing men I've ever been around," Crutcher recalled. "He's a Buddhist monk, he's been all over the world, he's an internationally renowned child psychologist, a smart and insightful guy and an absolutely *allowing* man. He does not judge people. I remember hearing him say: 'Root out self–hate.' It was one of those situations where you hear this little thing and it just spreads inside you." It made Crutcher want "to help someone else understand that—understand that what looks bad in you is just self–hate, and that you need to care for yourself more. If you care for yourself then you can care for others—that's the core to being healthy."

In the second half of *The Crazy Horse Electric Game*, Willie makes the long journey back from self–hatred to self–respect. After traveling as far as he can by bus, he finds himself in Oakland, California, at a fictionalized version of Lakeside called the One More Last Chance High School. The OMLC instructors encourage him to use physical therapy, and even basketball, to reclaim control of his body; with his pride restored, Willie becomes a valuable part of the school's community and earns his diploma. He then has the strength to return to Coho and face his family and friends, even though the reunion is a difficult one. A reviewer in *Publishers Weekly* said that *The Crazy Horse Electric Game* "resound[s] with compassion for people tripped up by their own weaknesses" and praised its "poetic sensibility and gritty realism." *Kirkus Reviews* predicted that "readers will find themselves cheered by the courageous way Willie battles back, and by the way nearly everyone gets what they deserve or work for." Writing in *Voice of Youth Advocates*, Pam Spencer noted that, as in his previous novels, Crutcher writes about a young man being forced "to dig deep for the stabilization offered in reaching one's inner strength"; the critic concluded, "Crutcher writes powerfully and movingly of Willie's attempts to 'become whole' again. . . . It's authors like Chris Crutcher who make our job of 'selling books' that much easier." *Horn Book* reviewer Anita Silvey claimed that *The Crazy Horse Electric Game* "magnificently portrays the thoughts and feelings of a crippled athlete and is a testimony to the indomitability of the human spirit."

Handcuffs of Pain

Perhaps the grittiest of Crutcher's YA novels is his fourth, *Chinese Handcuffs*, which describes the friendship between two emotionally traumatized

Charlie Talbert (center) and Chris Owen star in *Angus*, a film based on Crutcher's short story "A Brief Moment in the Life of Angus Bethune."

young people. Dillon Hemmingway grew up watching his older brother Preston destroy himself, first through drugs and then through suicide; Preston, in fact, made a point of killing himself in Dillon's presence. Dillon is close friends with Jennifer Lawless, who has been sexually abused most of her life, by her father when she was a small child, and by her stepfather in the years since. Dillon thinks he is in love with Jennifer, but she has been too deeply wounded to fully reciprocate; her emotional lifeline is sports, because the basketball court is the only place where she feels she can control her own fate. The title of the book refers to the efforts of Dillon and Jennifer to confront their pain. "Chinese handcuffs" are a classic basket–weaver's toy: they only loosen their grip when you stop pulling against them.

Dillon is so preoccupied with his brother's death that he writes long letters to him, letters that make up much of the narrative. Jennifer has similarly

strong memories of her abuse. In particular, readers see a vivid portrait of her stepfather, T. B. Himself brutalized as a child, T. B. survived through cold cunning, and now he uses it to intimidate both Jennifer and her mother. Finally Jennifer tries to kill herself, but Dillon stops her. Moved to desperate action, he gathers videotaped evidence against T. B. and uses it to drive him out of Jennifer's life; Jennifer turns T. B. in to the police. Having confronted the painful truths of his world, Dillon finds that he is no longer haunted by his brother. "I've got better things to do with my life than spend it with a pen in my hand, writing to a man who never reads his mail," he says in his last letter. "My struggle with you is finished. I'm going to let you go, push my finger in and release us from these crazy Chinese handcuffs. I wish you'd stayed, though. God, how I wish you'd stayed."

Chinese Handcuffs received some favorable response from critics. Writing in *Horn Book*, Margaret A. Bush claimed that Crutcher "constructs his painful web with intelligent insight, creating a painful, powerful story. . . . In the end the story is a compelling, well–paced, and even humorous one of human failing, survival, and hope." Writing in *Voice of Youth Advocates*, Randy Brough called *Chinese Handcuffs* a "rewarding novel, tough, topical, compelling, and well written." The strong subject matter, however, was also a cause for controversy. A notable example was the reaction of the American Library Association: its own *Booklist* magazine refused to review the book and offered a column questioning its merit. Conceding that Crutcher was "a strong writer" capable of making a "powerful moral point," *Booklist*'s Stephanie Zvirin went on to suggest that parts of the work, including Preston's suicide, were unduly graphic. She concluded that *Chinese Handcuffs* is "an unsuccessful book—and a disappointment—because the overloaded plot strains the novel's structure and diminishes the vital message Crutcher is trying to convey." In addition, *Kirkus Reviews* commented that his teenage characters "have been knocked around in Crutcher's other stories, but not to this extent. . . . Crutcher probes so many tender areas here that readers may end by feeling exhausted and emotionally bruised." However, Crutcher thinks that the amount of fan mail the book generated may have worked in the book's favor; although *Chinese Handcuffs* was almost not named an ALA Best Book for Young Adults, it did eventually receive that honor.

In response Crutcher points to the reality of his experience—and the experiences of kids. "I think there's a case to be made for being careful with language, but I want a kid to read it and believe it," he said. "I don't want some kid to say, 'God, kids don't talk like this,' because that negates everything else there. It would be nice to be able to blame things on language, because that would sure be simple—we could change the language and things would be better. Language ain't the problem. I had just come out of seven years in Oakland, for cryin' out loud, when I wrote *Running Loose*." He has a similar reaction to critics of *Chinese Handcuffs*: "My line is, Look, I *got* that stuff from kids. I *toned that down*." Crutcher knows that many of his readers are people in pain, and he suggests that he may have helped some of them through some difficult times. "Hard times are magnetic to hard times," he observed. "If I'm a kid who has had awful things happen to me, I'm going to look for other kids that have had that same experience because I want to be validated in the world. You get three or four of us together and we've got some pretty hard stories to tell. I'm not going to be running around with the quarterback on the football team or the head cheerleader." Not long after the controversy over *Chinese Handcuffs*, Crutcher was in Houston speaking to a group of students.

"A girl came up after everyone was gone and said, 'I read that book and I thought you knew me.'" At such a moment, the complaints of a few critics didn't seem to matter. "I thought, To hell with that—this is what it's really about."

In 1991, Crutcher published his first collection of short stories, *Athletic Shorts*; the volume, which includes six stories, features some of the characters from the author's novels as well as some new characters. The first story, which outlines how a fat, clumsy boy raised by two sets of homosexual parents finds dignity when he is chosen as a joke to be the king of the senior ball, and the final entry, in which Louie Banks, the title character of *Running Loose*, accepts a boy dying from AIDS as a friend even though his decision threatens his relationship with a fellow athlete, have been singled out as especially effective. Writing in *School Library Journal*, Todd Morning said, "These *Athletic Shorts* will appeal to YAs, touch them deeply, and introduce them to characters they'll want to know better." *Horn Book* reviewer Nancy Vasilakis noted, "One need not to have read Crutcher's novels to appreciate the young men within these pages. They stand proudly on their own," while *Voice of Youth Advocates* contributor Sue Krumbein concluded that all six stories "live up to the high expectations we've come to expect of Crutcher." In 1992, the author published his first book for adults, the suspense novel *The Deep End*. Called an "outstanding, yet wrenching, look into child abuse" by *School Library Journal* contributor Mike Printz, the novel was directed to adults but is considered appropriate for teenage readers. The story outlines how child therapist Wilson Corder investigates the disappearance—and eventual murder—of a young girl as well as the possible abuse of a three–year–old boy by his father, an expert in domestic violence. Printz concludes that "Crutcher's superb, sensitive style coupled with the prudent use of his unique humor makes this a first–rate, 'can't–put–it–down' novel" while *Kirkus Reviews* observed that the author's "needle–sharp focus on hurting kids makes this memorably harrowing from the starting gun."

Books on Abuse

In his next novel for young adults, *Staying Fat for Sarah Byrnes*, Crutcher features Eric Calhoune, a senior nicknamed "Moby" for his swimming ability and size; his best friend, Sarah Byrnes, suffered terrible facial burns as a small girl and has recently retreated into silence. After Sarah escapes from the psychiatric unit of a local hospital, her psychotic father Virgil—whom readers discover was the cause of his daughter's disfigurement and who refused to let her have reconstructive surgery—stabs Eric and hijacks his car when he refuses to reveal Sarah's hiding place. Eric brings in his sympathetic coach as his ally; at the end of the novel, Eric gets a new stepfather, Sarah a new set of parents, and Virgil a beating and a jail sentence. "This is a book that punches you in the stomach and never gives you a moment to breathe," wrote Susan R. Farber in *Voice of Youth Advocates,* who concluded that the novel is Crutcher's "darkest and most riveting work to date." Writing in *Horn Book,* Nancy Vasilakis called Sarah Byrnes "one of [Crutcher's] strongest female characters to date." *Kirkus Reviews* praised the novel as "pulse–pounding, on both visceral and emotional levels—a wild, brutal ride," and Janice Del Negro of *Booklist* considered it "strong on relationships, long on plot" and with "enough humor and suspense to make it an easy booktalk with appeal across gender lines."

With *Ironman,* Crutcher chronicles the senior year of Bo Brewster, who has been assigned to an anger management group after quitting the football team and calling the coach a rude name. The group's instructor, Mr. Nak, a Japanese American from Texas, gives Bo the tools to come to realizations about himself and his relationship with his vicious father; at the same time, Bo trains rigorously for an upcoming triathlon event, a race added to in intensity by the fact that Bo's father is trying to fix the event by bribing his son's main competitor. At the end of the novel, Bo competes in the triathlon with the support of the anger management group and discovers his personal strength and self–respect. Crutcher presents the story as both a third–person narrative and in the form of letters from Bo to talk–show host Larry King, the only adult the boy feels will listen to him. Writing in *School Library Journal,* Tom S. Hurlburt said, "Crutcher has consistently penned exceptional reads for YAs, and *Ironman* is one of his strongest works yet." Roger Sutton of *Bulletin of the Center for Children's Books* claimed, "If you like Crutcher, this is vintage stuff . . . [If] you haven't succumbed before, you aren't likely to now, but fans will welcome the winning formula." Writing in the *New York Times Book Review,* James Gorman noted, "The heart of the story is small and painful, and rings thoroughly true," while *Horn Book* reviewer Peter D. Sieruta concluded that *Ironman* is a novel that "doesn't strive for easy answers, but does ask many intriguing questions of both its characters and its readers."

In 1995, Crutcher became a full–time writer, although he continued to work on the Child Protection Team in Spokane, Washington. He told Heather Vogel Frederick of *Publishers Weekly,* "When it came down to it, I could not give up writing. . . . What's

known can't be unknown. As a writer and a human being . . . I have to keep myself in a position where I can scream and yell and be just obnoxious about getting something done." Crutcher once stated, "It is a joy to write a tale that is believable, that is real. Writing is also a way to express humor and to present human perspectives. I like to explore the different ways in which people make sense of what goes on around them." In an interview with Christine McDonnell in *Horn Book,* Crutcher remarked, "I want to be remembered as a storyteller, and I want to tell stories that seem real so that people will recognize something in their own lives and see the connections. We are all connected. That's what I like to explore and put into stories." Quoted in *Twentieth–Century Children's Writers,* Crutcher concluded, "My mission is to write truths as I see them, reflect the world as it appears to me, rather than as others would have it. I would like to tell stories so 'right on' that they punch a hole in the wall between young adult and adult literature." In his collection *Athletic Shorts,* Crutcher wrote, "There are a significant amount of people who . . . think kids should not be exposed in print to what they are exposed to in their lives. But I believe what I believe, and so I write my stories."

If you enjoy the works of Chris Crutcher, you might want to check out the following books:

Gillian Chan, *Glory Days and Other Stories,* 1997.
Carl Dueker, *Painting the Black,* 1997.
Adele Griffin, *Sons of Liberty,* 1997.
Tres Seymour, *The Revelation of Saint Bruce,* 1998.

Crutcher has found that some of the most gratifying comments he gets about his works come in the mail. "I get a lot of responses from kids who don't read very much," he told *AAYA,* "and that's great because I didn't read—it's like me writing to me." He described a recent batch of letters: "One said, 'My mom's dying of cancer and this book helped me come out of my shell. I've just been saying that what's happening isn't true, but it is true. And the things that Louie Banks went through tell me a way that I can let it be true, and then go on. Things *will* go on.' There were letters from kids who had just lost people, whether it was a death or not, and they learned that there is another way to look at a loss. I was astonished at these letters—that's the feedback I like."

■ Biographical and Critical Sources

BOOKS

Children's Literature Review, Gale (Detroit, MI), Volume 28, 1992, pp. 98–108.

Crutcher, Chris, *Athletic Shorts: Six Short Stories,* Greenwillow (New York City), 1991.

Crutcher, Chris, *Chinese Handcuffs,* Dell (New York City), 1991.

Crutcher, Chris, *Running Loose,* Greenwillow (New York City), 1983.

Crutcher, Chris, *Stotan!,* Dell (New York City), 1988.

Davis, Terry, *Presenting Chris Crutcher,* Twayne/Prentice–Hall (New York City), 1997.

Gallo, Donald R., editor, *Speaking for Ourselves: Autobiographical Sketches by Notable Authors of Books for Young Adults,* National Council of Teachers of English (Urbana, IL), 1990, p. 59.

Silvey, Anita, editor, *Children's Books and Their Creators,* Houghton Mifflin (New York City), 1995, pp. 181–82.

PERIODICALS

Booklist, August, 1989, Stephanie Zvirin, "The YA Connection: *Chinese Handcuffs,*" p. 1966; March 15, 1993, Janice Del Negro, review of *Staying Fat for Sarah Byrnes,* p. 1313.

Bulletin of the Center for Children's Books, May, 1983, Zena Sutherland, review of *Running Loose,* p. 165; April, 1995, Roger Sutton, review of *Ironman;* p. 269.

Emergency Librarian, January–February, 1991, Dave Jenkinson, "Portraits: Chris Crutcher," pp. 67–71.

Horn Book, September–October, 1986, Anita Silvey, review of *Stotan!,* p. 596; November–December, 1987, Anita Silvey, review of *The Crazy Horse Electric Game,* p. 741; May, 1988, Christine McDonnell, "New Voices, New Visions: Chris Crutcher,"

p. 332; July–August, 1989, Margaret A. Bush, review of *Chinese Handcuffs,* p. 487; September–October, 1991, Nancy Vasilakis, review of *Athletic Shorts,* pp. 602–3; May–June, 1993, Nancy Vasilakis, review of *Staying Fat for Sarah Byrnes,* p. 337; October, 1995, Peter D. Sieruta, review of *Ironman,* p. 606.

Idaho Statesman (Boise, ID), July 28, 1983, Lori Montgomery, "Idaho Novelist: First Book Wins Raves."

Journal of Youth Services in Libraries, summer, 2000, Chris Crutcher, "The 2000 Margaret A. Edwards Award Acceptance Speech," pp. 17–19.

Kirkus Reviews, April 15, 1983, review of *Running Loose,* p. 461; February 15, 1989, review of *Chinese Handcuffs,* p. 290; November 15, 1991, review of *The Deep End,* p. 1436; March 15, 1993, review of *Staying Fat for Sarah Byrnes,* p. 369.

New York Times Book Review, July 2, 1995, James Gorman, review of *Ironman,* p. 13.

Publishers Weekly, May 29, 1987, review of *The Crazy Horse Electric Game,* p. 79; February 20, 1995, Heather Vogel Frederick, "Chris Crutcher: 'What's Known Can't Be Unknown'," pp. 183–84.

School Library Journal, May, 1983, Trev Jones, review of *Running Loose,* p. 80; May, 1986, Jerry Fleck, review of *Stotan!,* p. 100; September, 1991, Todd Morning, review of *Athletic Shorts,* p. 278; September, 1992, Mike Printz, review of *The Deep End: A Novel of Suspense,* p. 189; March, 1995, Tom S. Hurlburt, review of *Ironman,* p. 222; June, 2000, Betty Carter, "Eyes Wide Open," pp. 42–45.

Voice of Youth Advocates, April, 1983, Mary K. Chelton, review of *Running Loose,* p. 36; April, 1986, Mary K. Chelton, review of *Stotan!,* p. 29; June, 1987, Pam Spencer, review of *The Crazy Horse Electric Game,* p. 76; June, 1989, Randy Brough, review of *Chinese Handcuffs,* p. 98; April, 1992, Sue Krumbein, review of *Athletic Shorts,* p. 26; August, 1993, Susan R. Farber, review of *Staying Fat for Sarah Byrnes,* p. 150.

OTHER

Crutcher, Chris, telephone interview with Thomas Kozikowski for *Authors and Artists for Young Adults,* March 11, 1992.*

—Sketch by Gerard J. Senick

Sarah Dessen

■ Personal

Born June 6, 1970, in Evanston, IL; married. *Education:* University of North Carolina at Chapel Hill, B.A. (with highest honors) in creative writing, 1993.

■ Addresses

Home—Chapel Hill, NC. *Office*—Department of English, University of North Carolina at Chapel Hill, Chapel Hill, NC 27599. *E–mail*—dessen@email.unc.edu.

■ Career

Writer; lecturer at University of North Carolina at Chapel Hill, 1997—. Worked as a waitress during the early 1990s.

■ Awards, Honors

Best Books for Young Adults selection, American Library Association, 1997, for *That Summer*; Best Books for Young Adults selection and Quick Pick selec-tion, both American Library Association, both for *Someone Like You;* Best Books for Young Adults se-lection and Quick Pick selection, both American Li-brary Association, and Best Book of the Year selec-tion, *School Library Journal*, all for *Keeping the Moon.*

■ Writings

That Summer, Orchard Books (New York City), 1996.
Someone Like You, Viking (New York City), 1998.
Keeping the Moon, Viking (New York City), 1999.
Dreamland, Viking (New York City), 2000.

■ Sidelights

"I always think that I get the best parts of myself from what my friends have taught me about strength and loyalty and spirit," Sarah Dessen re-flected in *Dream/Girl Online Digest*. Childhood and classmate friendships play an important role in Des-sen's popular young adult novels. She is known for her coming–of–age stories featuring strong charac-terizations of true–to–life protagonists who face pre-dicaments with which teen readers can relate. Des-sen has quickly gained a loyal following in only a few years since her first published novel, *That Sum-mer*, came out in 1996. "Why do we love Sarah Des-sen?" asked a *Dream/Girl* writer. "Because she remembers what it's like to be a teenager." Her stories, which also include *Someone Like You, Keeping the Moon,* and *Dreamland,* recognize that, as Nancy Tilly put it in *NewsBank* online, "although teens often want to be part of the 'in' crowd, adolescence, for most, is about being an outsider. It's a period of dizzying change and newness. Dessen suggests that if adults can accept the extremes of feeling and action typical of the age, they may encourage youngsters to chart paths to self–discovery and stability rather than losing themselves in the wild urge to rebel."

Dessen can recall vividly what it was like to be an awkward child and teenager. When she was young, she was a very shy girl at school, "but as I got older I tended to gravitate towards friendships with girls who were more outgoing than myself," she said in *Dream/Girl.* Never thinking of herself as being as pretty or as popular as her friends, she did not have the best self–esteem, but in her reading she was attracted to strong heroines. As a young girl, two of her favorite books were *Coming Attractions* by Fannie Flagg and *Gone with the Wind* by Margaret Mitchell. Both books feature assertive, lively female protagonists. Her mother challenged her reading abilities by giving her books that were slightly above her reading level; they were often written by Southern writers and had strong female characters in them. Dessen not only liked to read, but she liked to write stories, too. As a child, she turned her dolls into the characters in her tales, and when she was a fifth grader her teacher turned her on to history, which led her to write a series of stories about the Revolutionary War.

The Waitress–Writer

Because of her love for writing, it wasn't a surprise when Dessen decided to study creative writing at the University of North Carolina at Chapel Hill. Her father was a professor there in the English department, and Dessen recalled in *NewsBank* how that was a somewhat awkward situation for her: "I struggled mightily not to be associated with my parents, even as I majored in my father's department. It is hard to be taken seriously when your professor jubilantly remembers how you were beaned in the head with a volleyball at a department picnic at the age of six." But she was an excellent student, graduating with top honors in 1993. The only problem was that, after finishing a degree that took her five–and–a–half years to earn, she wasn't sure what to do for a career. Her parents were a little concerned when she announced that, instead of sending out resumes and searching for a position in corporate America, she wanted to con-

tinue the job she had as a waitress and work on her writing. Luckily for her, her parents were as supportive as ever of her wish to try to make it as a writer. It was, they reasoned, better than the hairstylist career she had been considering, and less surprising than her brother's choice of spending three years as a Zen Buddhist in California after attending an expensive music school.

It turned out to be the right choice for Dessen, who, despite the low prestige of the job, greatly enjoyed her work. Being a waitress had two advantages for her: it gave her time to write in the afternoons before she went to the restaurant at night, and it gave her the chance to study a wide range of personalities who came there to eat. "On a typical night," she commented in a 1996 *NewsBank* article, "I overhear snippets of dialogue, bits and pieces of people's lives coming right to me as I pass. . . . As a server, you can be almost invisible, absorbing the color and characters around you. And as a writer, I benefit daily from what people do not even know they are giving me. My rudest customer ever, who slapped my hand when I tried to remove her empty salad plate, instantly earned a place in my third novel as a bitter nasty woman, dressed in the same green pant suit and with the same features, of course. I've learned that writing well can be the best revenge." The people with whom she worked also provided material. Many of the waiters and waitresses were fascinating people: some held graduate degrees, some were artists or nursing students, or had other interesting backgrounds. Dessen also drew on the stories her best friends would tell her. "I think all good fiction starts with some truth," she told a *Dream/Girl* interviewer. "The trick is to begin with what really happened, and then change it to what you wish had happened, or what you wished you'd said."

With time to write and her parents' encouragement, Dessen found success relatively quickly. Only three years after graduating from college, her first book, *That Summer,* was published by Orchard Books. It is the story of Haven, an awkward fifteen–year–old girl who feels uncomfortable with being five feet, eleven inches tall. A lot of changes are going on in her life: her older sister, Ashley, is getting married to a guy Haven thinks is a big nerd, and is driving everyone crazy as she prepares for the wedding; Haven's father and mother are divorced, and her father is now married to annoyingly perky television weather girl, Lorna Queen; while her mother has joined a group of free–and–loose singles and has become friends with a woman Haven can't stand. Haven wishes things could be like they were four years ago, when her parents were still married and she didn't always fight with her sister. But then Ashley's former boyfriend, Sumner Lee, arrives in town, and the presence of this charming young man that Haven likes so much reminds her of the past. Sumner seems to understand what she's going through better than anyone, and Haven really likes him. But, as a *Horn Book* reviewer explained, "Haven's idealized little–girl view of him gradually changes, [and] she lets go of the past and begins to take a more active part in the present." By the end of the story, Haven has done a lot of growing up, and her feelings of awkwardness have virtually disappeared.

Many critics were impressed with Dessen's debut novel, enjoying this tale of teenage angst and growth spiced with humor and wry observations. "Dessen adds a fresh twist to a traditional sister–of–the–bride story," commented one *Publishers Weekly* contributor, "with her keenly observant narrative full of witty ironies." And Fran Lantz called Haven's maturation a "believable transformation" in a *Kliatt* article. But while many reviewers praised the book, others found some fault. *School Library Journal* critic Lucinda Lockwood, for example, found the situations clich&eacite;d and the characters "forgettable"; and Hazel Rochman of *Booklist* thought that Haven's ability to accept her body and herself by the end of the book was a little too pat a resolution. However, Rochman felt this was a minor flaw that did not seriously detract from the book. "This first novel," stated the critic, "is written with such easy grace that you want to quote sentence after sentence." *Horn Book* contributor Nancy Vasilakis similarly complimented the "fresh, unselfconscious style" of the book." Vasilakis concluded, "This is a wise book about growing up that won't give teenage readers the feeling that they are being preached to."

Friendship as a Central Theme

While the friendship between Haven and Sumner is an important part of *That Summer,* the theme of friendship takes an even more central role in *Someone Like You.* The two friends here are high–school pals Halley and Scarlett. Dessen starts the novel off quickly with a phone call to Scarlett, who learns that her boyfriend has just been killed in a motorcycle accident. Up until that point, Scarlett had always been the stronger personality in their relationship, but this tragedy and the news that Scarlett is pregnant, quickly changes their roles. Halley now has to be strong and supportive of Scarlett, who wants to have the baby even though her mother says she needs to have it aborted. But this isn't Halley's only concern. She is also falling in love with a boy named Macon Faulkner, who puts pressure on her to have sex. As these events progress in her life,

Halley keeps them a secret from her mother. This is ironic because her mother is a psychologist and author who brags that she and her daughter have a perfect relationship, even as that relationship starts to fracture. Thus the book's themes center on how two young girls struggle towards womanhood as they deal with the issues of sex and the inevitable separation of daughters from their mothers, as well as how the sisterly friendship between Halley and Scarlett pulls them through these changes.

Critics, of course, compared *Someone Like You* with Dessen's first novel, and they did so favorably for the most part. Elizabeth Devereaux, writing in the *New York Times Book Review,* felt that Dessen tries to juggle too many plotlines: "She doesn't need to bustle so much; the best thing she has going is her own steady voice." Many other reviewers agreed that it is the author's writing that really makes the book. "Dessen has a unique talent for distilling character in a few biting words," asserted Nancy Vasilakis in *Horn Book,* "and she uses her sharp sense of humor to make her points without mawkishness." Hazel Rochman of *Booklist* further observed that Dessen's portrayal of the teens friendship is perfect: "The exciting center of the story is Halley's relationship with Scarlett: here Dessen gets it exactly right." And other critics also said that Dessen's portrait of life in suburbia for middle–class kids was well done. "Dessen deals accurately, sensitively, and smoothly with growing up in suburbia," wrote Gail Richmond in *School Library Journal,* adding that the author successfully gets her message across "without preaching."

With *Keeping the Moon,* Dessen set out to approach the theme of friendship from a different angle. Her main character, Nicole "Colie" Sparks, starts off as a loner and social reject but later finds strength in new friends. Colie, who was overweight until her mother, a fitness expert, managed to get her to lose forty–five pounds, is still rejected by her peers because of the way she dyes her hair a dark black and wears a lip ring. Colie is also deeply hurt by a classmate, who spreads rumors about her being a "slut," even though Colie hasn't slept with anyone yet. When her mother goes off to Europe on a tour to promote her fitness message, Colie is sent to spend time with her nutty Aunt Mira, who lives in the seaside town of Colby, North Carolina. Mira, who illustrates greeting cards for a living, is a wrestling fan and quite the oddball. She is a social reject like Colie, with one big difference: Mira doesn't care what other people think of her.

Drawing from her own experiences as a waitress, Dessen has Colie get a job at the Last Chance Cafe, where she meets two women in their twenties, Isa-

Best friends Halley and Scarlett come to rely on each other's strength as they both learn to cope with trauma in Dessen's second novel for young adults.

bel and Morgan, who also work there. Even though they are several years senior to the fifteen–year–old Colie, the three waitresses become friends. An odd young man named Norman, who rents a room from Mira, also enters the scene. Norman is an artist who uses found objects, such as ash trays and bicycle parts, to create imaginative sculptures. Isabel and Morgan give Colie a makeover and help bolster her self–confidence, while Colie's growing affection for Norman also has a powerful effect on her. By the end of the novel, Colie is ready to face her schoolmates again and even gets revenge on the nasty girl who gave her a bad reputation.

"Dessen has set herself quite a challenge in this third book," remarked Tilly: "how to make credible the salvation of a girl teetering on the brink of damaging isolation." According to many critics, the author succeeds in doing just that. As a *Bulletin of the Center for Children's Books* critic pointed out, the author helps make Colie's transformation realistic by balancing it with her interactions with other characters. Dessen points out, through Mira, that not everyone needs to feel accepted by the crowd. The book is also "honest in its assessment of the downside of transformation," according to the reviewer, who noted that "Colie almost leaves Norman behind in the dust" toward the story's end because she thinks she's too good for him. What is appealing about *Keeping the Moon,* according to some reviewers, are Dessen's characters, especially Isabel and Morgan. *School Library Journal* contributor Cindy Darling called the two friends "great characters and the workings of their friendship is smooth, insightful, and just fun to read." Lynn Evarts concluded in *Voice of Youth Advocates* that this story of the importance of friendship "will strike a chord with young adults who need a boost developing their own self–esteem."

Addresses a More Dangerous Subject

Although Dessen's characters face a number of personal crises in her first three books, none of the roadblocks they break through are as dangerous as what Caitlin O'Koren must survive in *Dreamland.* Here, the author tackles the serious subject of physical abuse. The novel starts out somewhat like a typical Dessen story. Caitlin is jealous of her older, more popular sister, Cass, who gets good grades and has no problem snagging boyfriends. When Cass abruptly decides to follow her boyfriend to New York City, Caitlin has to deal with her parents' negative reactions. Caitlin tries to make the best of Cass's absence by being accepted into the cheerleading squad. When her parents are apathetic about this achievement, she searches for another way to obtain a sense of self–worth and finds Rogerson. Rogerson is a charismatic young man from a wealthy family. He drives a BMW, deals in marijuana, and has rebellious friends. Caitlin thinks that being with Rogerson brings out a new side of her that she likes, and she falls in love with him. Rogerson, however, has emotional problems that begin to emerge in wild mood swings that soon lead him to start hitting her. Confused and desperate, Caitlin doesn't know how to break off the relationship until Rogerson beats her right in front of other people. At this point, she is finally able to get help. Diane Masla, reviewing *Dreamland* in *Voice of Youth Advocates,* stated, "In examining the question of how much must be sacrificed to maintain a romantic relationship, Dessen has created a compassionate novel that examines how wrong love can go."

If you enjoy the works of Sarah Dessen, you might want to check out the following books:

Laurie Halse Anderson, *Speak, 1999.*
Eli Gottlieb, *The Boy Who Went Away, 1997.*
Phyllis Shalant, *The Great Eye, 1996.*

Dessen herself recalls a time in her life when she was attracted to a rebellious lifestyle, what her father called "my 'Dark Years,'" as the author recalled in *NewsBank.* It was a time "when I was not writing but instead hanging out on Franklin Street smoking cigarettes and behaving tormented." She later said, "I . . . remember so well what it was like, being that age. When everything was more intense, and I was focused only on what was going to happen that afternoon, that week, that moment." Dessen's ability to empathize so well with teenagers' lives, both the good and the bad sides, is what has made her writing so successful with young adults, and even parents, whose teens sometimes give them Dessen's books to read. Dessen, who grew up and still lives in Chapel Hill, North Carolina, feels that staying in the same town where she constantly runs into people from her past has also kept her in touch with her teenage years. "[My friends] make me laugh, still," she said in *Dream/Girl,* "and remind me where I've come from even as I'm so focused on where I'm going."

■ Biographical and Critical Sources

PERIODICALS

Booklist, October 15, 1996, Hazel Rochman, review of *That Summer,* p. 422; May 15, 1998, Hazel Rochman, review of *Someone Like You,* p. 1622; June 1, 1998, Hazel Rochman, review of *Someone Like You,* p. 1745; September 1, 1999, Michael Cart, review of *Keeping the Moon,* p. 123.

Bulletin of the Center for Children's Books, October, 1999, review of *Keeping the Moon,* pp. 49–50.

Horn Book, November–December, 1996, Nancy Vasilakis, review of *That Summer,* p. 742; July–August, 1998, Nancy Vasilakis, review of *Someone Like You,* p. 486.

Kirkus Reviews, August 15, 1999, review of *Keeping the Moon,* pp. 1309–1310.

Kliatt, November, 1998, Fran Lantz, review of *That Summer,* pp. 10, 12.

New York Times Book Review, September 20, 1998, Elizabeth Devereaux, review of *Someone Like You,* p. 33.

Publishers Weekly, September 2, 1996, review of *That Summer,* p. 132; May 18, 1998, review of *Someone Like You,* p. 80; September 20, 1999, review of *Keeping the Moon,* p. 89; September 4, 2000, review of *Dreamland,* p. 109.

School Librarian, winter, 1998, Ann G. Hay, review of *That Summer,* p. 215.

School Library Journal, October, 1996, Lucinda Lockwood, review of *That Summer,* p. 144; June, 1998, Gail Richmond, review of *Someone Like You,* p. 143; September, 1999, Cindy Darling, review of *Keeping the Moon,* p. 221; September, 2000, Gail Richmond, review of *Dreamland.*

Voice of Youth Advocates, August, 1998, Marcia Mann, review of *Someone Like You,* p. 200; December, 1999, Lynn Evarts, review of *Keeping the Moon,* p. 331; October, 2000, Diane Masla, review of *Dreamland,* p. 262.

ONLINE

Dream/Girl Online Digest, located at http://www.dgarts.com/ (May 22, 2000).

NewsBank Web site, located at http://archives.newsbank.com/ (May 22, 2000).

—*Sketch by Kevin Hile*

Donald R. Gallo

■ Personal

Born June 1, 1938, in Paterson, NJ; son of Sergio and Thelma Mae (maiden name, Lowe) Gallo; married Christie Jo Bott (an English teacher), February 14, 1997; children: Brian, Chris Perrett (stepdaughter). *Education:* Hope College, B.A., 1960; Oberlin College, M.A.T., 1961; Syracuse University, Ph.D., 1968. *Hobbies and other interests:* Travel, gardening, photography.

■ Addresses

Home—34540 Sherbrook Park Drive, Solon, OH 44139. *E-mail*—GalloDon@aol.com.

■ Career

Educator, writer, and editor. English teacher, Bedford Junior High School, Westport, CT, 1961–65; research associate, Syracuse University, 1965–67; assistant and associate professor of education, University of Colorado, 1968–72; reading specialist, Golden Junior High School, Colorado, 1972–73; professor of English, Central Connecticut State University, 1973–97; visiting faculty member, Wesleyan University, 1983; adjunct instructor, Cleveland State University, 1997–98. Has also served on the executive board or committee of numerous educational organizations, including National Council of Teachers of English (NCTE) and ALAN (president, 1986–87).

■ Member

Authors Guild, Society of Children's Book Writers and Illustrators, National Council of Teachers of English, Assembly on Literature for Adolescents of the National Council of Teachers of English, International Reading Association, Conference on English Education, Ohio Council of Teachers of English Language Arts.

■ Awards, Honors

Best Books for Young Adults 1966–1986 and Best Books for Young Adults, 1985, American Library Association (ALA), Best Books, *School Library Journal*, 1985, and nominee, Colorado Blue Spruce Award, 1988, all for *Sixteen: Short Stories by Outstanding Writers for Young Adults*; Best Books for Young Adults, ALA, Pick of the Lists, American Booksellers, and Books for the Teen Age, New York

Public Library, all 1988, all for *Visions: Short Stories by Outstanding Writers for Young Adults*; Books for the Teen Age, New York Public Library, 1990, for *Connections: Short Stories by Outstanding Writers for Young Adults*; Best Books for Young Adults, ALA, 1991, for *Speaking for Ourselves: Autobiographical Sketches of Notable Authors of Books for Young Adults*; Books for the Teen Age, New York Public Library, 1991, for *Center Stage: One–Act Plays for Teenage Readers and Actors*; Junior Literary Guild selection, Pick of the Lists, American Booksellers, and Books for the Teen Age, New York Public Library, both 1993, YALSA Humor Book list, selection for the Year's Best Fantasy and Horror, and Texas Lone Star Reading List selection, 1994–95, all for *Short Circuits: Thirteen Shocking Stories by Outstanding Writers for Young Adults*; Best Anthology/Collection, *Voice of Youth Advocates*, 1993, Books for the Teen Age, New York Public Library, and Pick of the Lists, American Booksellers, all for *Join In: Multiethnic Short Stories by Outstanding Writers for Young Adults*; Best Books for Young Adults and Quick Pick, ALA, 1998, for *No Easy Answers: Short Stories about Teenagers Making Tough Choices*.

Awarded life membership in the Connecticut Council of Teachers of English for "Exceptional Contributions to the Council," 1983; recipient of the Distinguished Service Award from the Connecticut Council of Teachers of English, 1989; recipient of the ALAN Award from the Assembly on Literature for Adolescents of the National Council of Teachers of English for "outstanding contributions to the field of adolescent literature," 1992; recipient of Certificate of Merit from the Catholic Library Association, 1995.

■ Writings

EDITOR; FOR YOUNG ADULTS

Sixteen: Short Stories by Outstanding Writers for Young Adults, Delacorte, 1984.

Books for You: A Booklist for Senior High Students, National Council for Teachers of English, 1985.

Visions: Short Stories by Outstanding Writers for Young Adults, Delacorte, 1987.

Connections: Short Stories by Outstanding Writers for Young Adults, Delacorte, 1989.

Speaking for Ourselves: Autobiographical Sketches of Notable Authors of Books for Young Adults, National Council of Teachers of English, 1990.

Center Stage: One–Act Plays for Teenage Readers and Actors, HarperCollins, 1990.

Short Circuits: Thirteen Shocking Stories by Outstanding Writers for Young Adults, Delacorte, 1992.

Speaking for Ourselves, Too–More Autobiographical Sketches of Notable Authors of Books for Young Adults, National Council of Teachers of English, 1993.

Within Reach: Ten Stories, HarperCollins, 1993.

Join In: Multiethnic Short Stories by Outstanding Writers for Young Adults, Delacorte, 1993.

Ultimate Sports: Short Stories by Outstanding Writers for Young Adults, Delacorte, 1995.

No Easy Answers: Short Stories about Teenagers Making Tough Choices, Delacorte, 1997.

Time Capsule: Short Stories about Teenagers throughout the Twentieth Century, Delacorte, 1999.

On the Fringe, Dial, 2001.

NONFICTION; FOR ADULTS

Reading Rate and Comprehension: 1970–1971 Assessment, National Assessment of Education Progress, 1972.

Recipes, Wrappers, Reasoning and Rate: A Digest of the First Reading Assessment, National Assessment of Educational Progress, 1974.

Presenting Richard Peck, Twayne, 1989.

Authors' Insights: Turning Teenagers into Readers and Writers, Boynton/Cook–Heinemann, 1992.

(With Sarah K. Herz) *From Hinton to Hamlet: Building Bridges between Young Adult Literature and the Classics*, Greenwood, 1996.

Also served as editor for the *Connecticut English Journal*, and as author and consultant for anthologies and textbooks, including *Heath Middle Level Literature Program* and *Bookmark Reading Program*. His works have been translated into French and Italian.

■ Adaptations

Sixteen and *Visions* have been adapted for audiocassette by Listening Library; *No Easy Answers* has been adapted for audiocassette by Recorded Books.

■ Work in Progress

Editing a collection of short stories about conformity, popularity, and acceptance; writing two picture books and several informational books for younger readers, including one about walls and another about the history of popular foods and snacks.

■ Sidelights

Dubbed the "Godfather of YA short stories" by Chris Crowe in the *English Journal*, Don Gallo has edited numerous award–winning anthologies dealing with themes from the moral development of teenagers to athletics and multiculturalism. His groundbreaking *Sixteen* inaugurated Gallo's interest in YA short story collections as well as the popular use of that format for younger readers. The book gathered the writings of well–known authors such as Robert Cormier and Richard Peck and ultimately found a place on the American Library Association's (ALA) Best of the Best Books for Young Adults published between 1966 and 1986. In books such as *Visions, Connections, Short Circuits, Join In, Ultimate Sports*, and *No Easy Answers*, Gallo has continued this winning formula of collecting the shorter writings of popular YA novelists and writers to present engaging anthologies.

Born in Paterson, New Jersey, in 1938, Gallo was one of those reluctant readers at whom his anthologies would later in part be targeted. He found more enjoyment in outdoor activities than in reading; sports and scouting were his main interests. As Gallo once remembered, "I did not read anything that was not required of me in school. . . . I almost never sat down to read for what we call 'pleasure.' Reading was too boring for me." Gallo became an Eagle Scout and was named Outstanding Scout in his council while in high school. He also played football and ran track. "For parents and teachers who agonize over their inability to get their otherwise bright and successful teenagers to read, I provide hope," Gallo quipped. In spite of terrible spelling skills and a limited vocabulary in high school, he went on to college and it was there he finally discovered the joys of reading.

Ernest Hemingway's *The Old Man and the Sea*, a tedious exercise in high school, suddenly came to life for him in college. "I fell in love with Hemingway's writing and his macho image. I was in that skiff with Santiago; I struggled beside him to land that magnificent fish; I raged at the sharks that attacked the marlin lashed to the boat; and I fell into bed exhausted with the old man in the end, knowing that even though we may have been beaten, we would never be defeated. Literature had finally come alive for me." He read John Steinbeck, Albert Camus, Emile Zola, Fedor Dostoyevsky, and other standard–bearers of Western literature, and as he did so his writing also improved. When an essay on e. e. cummings earned him an A and also won $25 for a school essay contest, Gallo was converted. "Al-

Gallo's second collection of short stories by famous YA authors was declared among the best books of 1988 by the American Library Association, American Booksellers, and the New York Public Library.

though my spelling was still quite poor, my writing career began at that point," Gallo once said.

Involved in religious issues and training from his teenage years, Gallo intended to attend a seminary after graduating from college; instead he went to Oberlin College where he earned a masters and a teaching certificate. Thereafter he took a teaching position in Westport, Connecticut, "one of the nation's best school systems back in the 1960s." In a sense, he received on–the–job training not only in teaching, but also in writing, for he edited a newsletter for the local education association, served as advisor to the school's literary magazine, and also kept one step ahead of his precocious students, daughters and sons of famous writers, editors, broadcast journalists, and company executives.

Develops Interest in Young Adult Literature

Married for the first time, Gallo and his wife returned to graduate school, where he earned his doctorate. Thereafter the couple found jobs in Colorado, but Gallo's interest in literature never waned. During his doctoral studies, a quiet revolution in publishing was taking place with the arrival of a

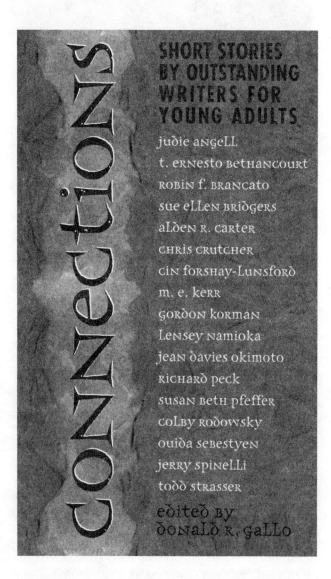

The focus is on teenage conflicts and their resolutions in Gallo's third collection of short stories, published in 1989.

new and gritty literature aimed at the YA audience and led by such writers as S. E. Hinton and Robert Lipsyte. "Although I focused a great deal of my scholarly activities on the teaching of developmental reading skills and writing skills in secondary schools at that time, I slowly began to shift my attention to books for teenagers," Gallo once commented. "I continued to read YA books voraciously and to survey students about their reading interests and habits." Moving on to a position at Central Connecticut State University, Gallo observed teenage students, tracking their reading habits and how they reacted to various books. Serving on various reading and education committees and editing professional journals, Gallo met many of the shining lights of YA literature.

Slowly Gallo began to discover a black hole in reading for young people. As he once recalled, "while most schools required students to read short stories, there were only a handful of books of short stories written by young adult novelists. Those collections had each been written by a single author." Anthologies at that time were constructed largely of stories reprinted from adult magazines. "Why weren't there any collections of good short stories about teenagers that were written by people whose novels were being read by teenagers?" Gallo asked himself. He set about to provide not so much an answer as a solution. Parlaying his wealth of knowledge about YA subjects with his acquaintanceship with a wide variety of YA novelists, Gallo solicited manuscripts for a story collection. He brought people like Robert Cormier on board, whose story, "In the Heat," had never before been published. After two years of cajoling and editing, Gallo had a book in hand, *Sixteen: Short Stories by Outstanding Writers for Young Adults*. "That collections is now viewed as a milestone in young adult literature," Gallo once stated.

Sixteen proved such a success that Gallo decided to continue with the idea of story collections. *Visions* came next, followed by *Connections* in 1989. "The procedures were the same for these volumes as for the first one: I sent letters to as many as forty–five authors, starting with the most famous people in the field, inviting them to write a story for my next book." Some, such as Judy Blume and Paula Danziger, did not feel comfortable in the short story format; others did not have the time. But for each collection he would end up with about twenty–five manuscripts from which he would cull anywhere from a dozen to sixteen of the best for the collection. Gallo brought together authors such as Richard Peck, Norma Fox Mazer, and Walter Dean Meyers for his second collection. Reviewing *Visions*, Lola H. Teubert noted in *Voice of Youth Advocates* that "these stories capture your attention continually, as each plot is timely and exciting. Whether you prefer sci-

Gallo at work in his study in 1996.

ence fiction, fantasy, living in the fast lane or current teen social problems you can take your pick from this lovely reading." A reviewer for *Kliatt* concluded that "Reluctant readers will be good candidates for this collection, because the stories are brief, and an interest in the authors may result in further reading." Gallo enlisted Colby Rodowsky, Alden R. Carter, M. E. Kerr, and Ouida Sebestyen among others for *Connections,* a collection "[i]nfused with warmth and discerning respect for young adults and their concerns," and containing "both elegant and humorous treats," according to *Kirkus Reviews.*

While these first collections were non–thematic, Gallo decided to narrow the focus with his fourth collection, *Short Circuits.* With this and following volumes, he has established books built around specific subject matter. The stories in *Short Circuits* deal with horror and the supernatural. *Kirkus Reviews* described the collection succinctly: "From both sides of the Atlantic, thirteen horror stories featuring teenagers giving good accounts of themselves in scary situations." The reviewer went on to note that Gallo prefaced each story with "a practiced teaser and ap-

pends intriguing comments about the author's life and writing." Christy Tyson noted in *Voice of Youth Advocates* that, like other Gallo collections, *Short Circuits* "is a fine collection indeed. . . . Gallo . . . has managed to pull together some truly terrifying stories that will satisfy even the most demanding horror fan." Joan Lowery Nixon, Joan Aiken, Robert Westall, Ellen Conford, and Jane McFann are among the YA writers included in this volume. *Booklist*'s Chris Sherman concluded that *Short Circuits* was "sure to be as popular as Gallo's other story collections."

Something of a departure for Gallo was the collection targeted at middle grade readers, *Within Reach,* ten tales focusing on kids who take risks. *Publishers Weekly* felt that "reluctant readers are especially likely to appreciate the accessibility of the stories' themes, conflicts and down–to–earth language." Additionally, Gallo has edited two editions of *Speaking for Ourselves,* collections of autobiographical essays from notable YA authors, as well as a volume for Twayne publishers on the YA author Richard Peck.

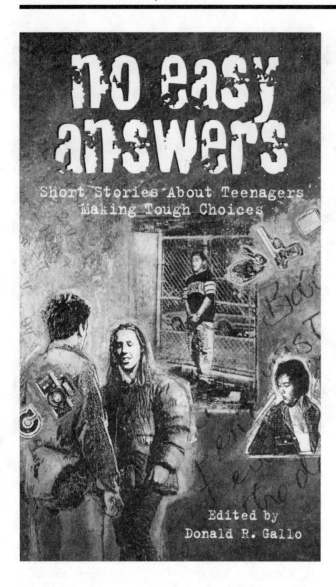

Teenagers making difficult choices and learning to live with them is the theme of this 1997 collection.

Returning to story anthologies, Gallo delivered his editorial treatment to sports with *Ultimate Sports,* including stories from such notables as Robert Lipsyte and Chris Crutcher, while multiculturalism formed the heart of *Join In,* an exploration of multiethnic experiences. Gallo included writers of color as well as white authors for these stories about teenagers of various ethnic backgrounds. *Kirkus Reviews* noted that "Gallo opens with an essay on whether authors can or should write about cultures other than their own and appends a thumbnail biography to each story." The same reviewer concluded that the collection was "[d]iverse, thought–provoking, and consistently well–written."

A Stickler for Detail

Gallo takes his editing responsibilities seriously. "My first reading of any story is for appreciation," he once said. "The next couple of readings are to confirm the general structure of the story and to note any places that don't make perfect sense. Along the way I fix mechanical errors I notice: misspellings, improper use of punctuation, subject–verb agreement, etc. . . . Because I have experienced what it feels like to have editors change pieces of my writing without my permission . . . I never change anything in anyone's writing (except for mechanical errors) without the writer's approval. . . . One of the most rewarding parts of my job is having the opportunity to read a brand new story that no one besides the author has ever seen. . . . And when my attention is grabbed on the first page, I know this is going to be a great story."

These stories demonstrate the teenage experience across the decades of the twentieth century.

If you enjoy the works of Donald R. Gallo, you might want to check out the following books:

Thomas J. Dygard, *Running Wild, 1996.*
David Gifaldi, *Rearranging and Other Stories,* 1998.
Chaim Potok, *Zebra and Other Stories,* 1998.
Michael Sterns, editor, *A Nightmare's Dozen: Stories from the Dark,* 1996.

A further theme–driven collection, *No Easy Answers,* focuses on teenagers facing moral dilemmas and dealing with the consequences of their decisions. Gallo gathered a diverse group of authors for the task, including Ron Koertge, Rita Williams–Garcia, Monica Hughes, and Graham Salisbury, to write "thought–provoking stories about such topics as peer pressure, computer blackmail, academic cheating, drug use, gang violence, and unwanted pregnancy," as Gallo once described the volume. Roxy Ekstrom praised the collection in *Voice of Youth Advocates,* noting that "Gallo knows well his YA audience." Ekstrom went on to laud Gallo's editorial abilities in all his collections. "From *Sixteen* to *Short Circuits* with stops between and beyond, he has shown his mastery at soliciting attention–grabbing short stories from the cream of the crop among YA authors." For Gallo, the self–confessed reluctant reader, this is sweet praise.

■ Biographical and Critical Sources

PERIODICALS

Booklist, November 1, 1989, p. 534; December 15, 1989, p. 826; June 1, 1990, p. 1888; December 1, 1990, p. 730; December 1, 1992, Chris Sherman, review of *Short Circuits: Thirteen Shocking Stories by Outstanding Writers for Young Adults,* p. 659; January 15, 1994, p. 918; April 1, 1996, p. 1386; March 15, 1998, p. 1218; September 15, 1999.

Bulletin of the Center for Children's Books, December, 1989, p. 83; September, 1990, p. 8; November, 1993, pp. 79–80; January, 1998, p. 159.

English Journal, March, 1997, Donald R. Gallo interview with Chris Crowe.

Horn Book, May–June, 1990, pp. 352–53.

Kirkus Reviews, December 1, 1989, review of *Connections: Short Stories by Outstanding Writers for Young Adults,* p. 1747; November 15, 1992, review of *Short Circuits: Thirteen Shocking Stories by Outstanding Writers for Young Adults,* p. 1442; December 1, 1993, review of *Join In: Multiethnic Short Stories by Outstanding Writers for Young Adults,* p. 1522.

Kliatt, January, 1989, review of *Visions: Short Stories by Outstanding Writers for Young Adults,* p. 31.

New York Times Book Review, November 15, 1987, p. 37.

Publishers Weekly, June 28, 1993, review of *Within Reach: Ten Stories,* p. 78.

School Library Journal, December, 1989, p. 124; May, 1990, p. 50; August, 1993, p. 163; October, 1995, p. 152; December, 1997, p. 124.

Voice of Youth Advocates, February, 1988, Lola H. Teubert, review of *Visions: Short Stories by Outstanding Writers for Young Adults,* p. 284; October, 1992, Christy Tyson, review of *Short Circuits: Thirteen Shocking Stories by Outstanding Writers for Young Adults,* p. 243; October, 1997, Roxy Ekstrom, review of *No Easy Answers: Short Stories about Teenagers Making Tough Choices,* p. 246.

—Sketch by J. Sydney Jones

James Cross Giblin

■ Personal

Surname is pronounced with a hard "g"; born July 8, 1933, in Cleveland, OH; son of Edward Kelley (a lawyer) and Anna (a teacher; maiden name, Cross) Giblin. *Education:* Attended Northwestern University, 1951; Western Reserve University (now Case Western Reserve University), B.A., 1954; Columbia University, M.F.A., 1955.

■ Addresses

Home—200 East 24th St., Apt. 1606, New York, NY 10010. *Office*—Clarion Books, 215 Park Ave. S., New York, NY 10003.

■ Career

Freelance writer, 1955—. Worked as a temporary typist and at the British Book Centre, 1955–59; Criterion Books, Inc., New York City, assistant editor, 1959–62; Lothrop, Lee & Shepard Co., New York City, associate editor, 1962–65, editor, 1965–67; Seabury Press, Inc., New York City, editor–in–chief of Clarion Books (for children), 1967–79, vice president, 1975–79; Houghton Mifflin Company, New York City, editor and publisher of Clarion Books, 1979–89, contributing editor, 1989—. Adjunct professor at Graduate Center of the City University of New York, 1979–83.

■ Member

Society of Children's Book Writers and Illustrators (member of board of directors), Authors Guild, Children's Book Council (president, 1976).

■ Awards, Honors

Golden Kite Award for nonfiction, Society of Children's Book Writers and Illustrators, 1982, and American Book Award for children's nonfiction, 1983, both for *Chimney Sweeps: Yesterday and Today;* Golden Kite Award for nonfiction, 1984, for *Walls: Defenses throughout History;* Boston Globe–Horn Book Nonfiction Honor Book, 1986, for *The Truth about Santa Claus;* Golden Kite Award for nonfiction, 1989, for *Let There Be Light: A Book about Windows;* American Library Association notable children's book citations, 1980, for *The Scarecrow Book,* 1981, for *The Skyscraper Book,* 1982, for *Chimney Sweeps: Yesterday and Today,* 1985, for *The Truth about Santa Claus,* 1986, for *Milk: The Fight for Purity*, 1987, for *From Hand to Mouth*, 1988, for *Let There Be Light: A Book about Windows*, 1990, for *The Riddle of the Rosetta Stone: Key to Ancient Egypt*, 1991, for *The Truth about Unicorns*, 1993, for *Be Seated: A Book about Chairs*, 1995, for *When Plague Strikes: The Black Death, Smallpx, AIDS*, 1997, for *Charles A. Lindbergh: A Human Hero*, and 2000, for *The Amazing Life of Benjamin Franklin*; Honor Book, NCTE Orbis Pictus Award for Nonfiction, 1998, for *Charles A. Lindbergh: A Human Hero*; several of Giblin's books have been Junior Literary Guild selections. In 1996 he received the *Washington Post*– Children's Book Guild Award for Nonfiction for his body of work.

■ Writings

NONFICTION; FOR CHILDREN

(With Dale Ferguson) *The Scarecrow Book*, Crown, 1980.

The Skyscraper Book, illustrated by Anthony Kramer, photographs by David Anderson, Crowell, 1981.

Chimney Sweeps: Yesterday and Today, illustrated by Margot Tomes, Crowell, 1981.

Fireworks, Picnics, and Flags: The Story of the Fourth of July Symbols, illustrated by Ursula Arndt, Clarion Books, 1983.

Walls: Defenses throughout History, Little, Brown, 1984.

The Truth about Santa Claus, Crowell, 1985.

Milk: The Fight for Purity, Crowell, 1986.

From Hand to Mouth; or, How We Invented Knives, Forks, Spoons, and Chopsticks and the Table Manners to Go with Them, Crowell, 1987.

Let There Be Light: A Book about Windows, Crowell, 1988.

The Riddle of the Rosetta Stone: Key to Ancient Egypt, Crowell, 1990.

The Truth about Unicorns, illustrated by Michael McDermott, Harper, 1991.

Edith Wilson: The Woman Who Ran the United States, illustrated by Michele Laporte, Viking, 1992.

George Washington: A Picture Book Biography, illustrated by Michael Dooling, Scholastic, 1992.

Be Seated: A Book about Chairs, HarperCollins, 1993.

Thomas Jefferson: A Picture Book Biography, illustrated by Michael Dooling, 1994.

When Plague Strikes: The Black Death, Smallpox, AIDS, illustrated by David Frampton, HarperCollins, 1995.

Charles A. Lindbergh: A Human Hero, Clarion, 1997.

The Mystery of the Mammoth Bones: And How It Was Solved, HarperCollins, 1999.

The Amazing Life of Benjamin Franklin, illustrated by Michael Dooling, Scholastic, 2000.

(Editor and author of introduction) *The Century That Was: Reflections on the Last One Hundred Years*, Atheneum, 2000.

Adolf Hitler: An Extraordinary Villain, Clarion, 2002.

FICTION; FOR CHILDREN

(Reteller) *The Dwarf, the Giant, and the Unicorn: A Tale of King Arthur*, illustrated by Claire Ewart, Clarion, 1996.

OTHER

My Bus Is Always Late (one–act play; first produced in Cleveland, OH, at Western Reserve University, 1953), Dramatic Publishing, 1954.

Writing Books for Young People (adult nonfiction), The Writer, Inc., 1990.

Also author of a play based on William Styron's novel *Lie Down in Darkness*. Contributor of original short stories to anthologies: "Three Mondays in July" in *Am I Blue? Coming out of the Silence*, edited by Marion Dane Bauer, HarperCollins, 1994; "Night of the Plague" in *Tomorrowland: Stories about the Future*, edited by Michael Cart, Scolastic Press, 1999.

Contributor of articles and stories for children to *Cobblestone*, *Cricket* and *Highlights for Children*, and of articles for adults to *Children's Literature in Education*, *Horn Book*, *Publishers Weekly*, *School Library Journal*, *Washington Post*, *The Writer*, and *Writer's Digest*.

■ Sidelights

James Cross Giblin has been a major figure in the field of children's book publishing since the 1970s. Not only has he edited the work of many important authors during his years at Clarion Books, but Giblin himself has written many nonfiction books for young readers. He has won awards and critical acclaim for his children's books, including *Chimney Sweeps: Yesterday and Today*, *The Truth about Santa Claus*, *Let There Be Light: A Book about Windows*, and *Charles A. Lindbergh: A Human Hero*. As Giblin once explained, "Nonfiction books for children aged eight to twelve [give] me the opportunity to pursue my research interests, meet interesting and stimulating experts in various fields, and share my enthusiasms with a young audience. I try to write books that I would have enjoyed reading when I was the age of my readers."

Giblin was born July 8, 1933, in Cleveland, Ohio. A shy, bookish child, he grew up in nearby Painesville. As a boy, he enjoyed the comic strip "Blondie," and, with his mother's help, he began drawing his own strips. Giblin once recalled, "I filled sketchbook after sketchbook with action–filled pictures drawn in boxes like those of the comics. Mother helped me to print the words I wanted to put in the balloons, and later I learned how to print them myself." Giblin also enjoyed going to the movies as a youngster; he once noted "My favorites weren't films made for children but spy movies set in Germany and Nazi–occupied areas such as *Casablanca.* I also liked melodramas starring emotional actresses like Bette Davis and Greer Garson, especially if they took place in exotic settings . . . or had to do with World War II."

In junior high, Giblin worked on the school paper, which helped him overcome some of his shyness. He reminisced in his autobiographical essay in *Sixth Book of Junior Authors,* "Robert K. Payne, my ninth–grade English teacher, did more than anyone to draw me out of my isolation. Mr. Payne encouraged his classes to try new things, including a mimeographed class newspaper. And he was determined that I should not only contribute pieces to the paper but also edit it." Giblin continued, "I backed away from the responsibility at first, as I backed away from so many things then. But Mr. Payne was persistent, and at last I allowed myself to become involved. Once I did, I discovered that I loved working with my classmates on the paper and thinking up ideas for each new issue."

Giblin discovered a new interest when he got to high school. He answered a notice in the local paper about auditions for a community theater production of the play *Outward Bound,* and, as he once recalled, "My parents drove me to the barn theatre on the outskirts of town, and I nervously entered the rustic auditorium. When I arrived home three hours later—one of the actors had given me a ride—I couldn't restrain my excitement. 'I got a part! I got a part!' I shouted as I raced through the darkened house to the back porch, where my parents were sitting. The director had cast me as the idealistic young Reverend Duke in the play, which tells the story of a group of English people traveling on an ocean liner who gradually realize that they have died and are on their way to Heaven . . . or to Hell." Giblin added, "As a shy youth of sixteen I might be reluctant to reveal my feelings, but I found I had no trouble expressing them through the character of the Reverend Duke. When the play was

Giblin's 1983 study looks at the ways in which symbols like the bald eagle, the American flag, the Liberty Bell, and Uncle Sam became part of Fourth of July celebrations.

over and I walked to the center of the stage to take my bow, the applause seemed like an endorsement not just of my acting but of me personally. I felt a surge of confidence that I had never known before. . . . After *Outward Bound* I was hooked on the theatre. I tried out for and got parts in all of the Le Masque Club productions . . . at Harvey High School, and the following summer I was cast in the small but funny role of the Lost Private in a professional production of the comedy *At War with the Army* at Rabbit Run Theatre in nearby North Madison."

Acting Developed into Interest in Writing

After graduating from high school, Giblin studied drama at Northwestern University. However, he was unhappy there, and after one semester he transferred to Western Reserve University (now Case Western Reserve University) near his parents' home. He did well; in addition to starring in many stage productions at Western Reserve, he won a contest to co–star in a radio drama in New York City with actress Nina Foch. As Giblin gained experience on the stage, his ambitions changed. He once noted, "The actor has very little control over his situation, and I now knew that I wanted control. So I turned my attention to directing and playwriting." An experience with an old woman on a bus inspired him to write his first play, *My Bus Is Always Late,* which was produced locally and published by the Dramatic Publishing Company in 1954.

Soon after, Giblin began studying for a Master of Fine Arts degree in playwriting at Columbia University in New York. Upon earning it, he remained in New York City to write, supporting himself by working as a temporary office employee. He became involved in efforts to adapt William Styron's novel *Lie Down in Darkness* for the stage, but the project fell through for various reasons. This failure deeply affected Giblin. He once explained, "I'd put almost a year of hard work and anticipation into *Lie Down in Darkness.* I'd drawn on my deepest feelings in order to write it, and in the process it had become my personal statement as much as Styron's. I tried to start a new play in that late spring of 1957, but I discovered, painfully, that I'd already expressed most of what I had to say in *Lie Down in Darkness.*"

After a recuperative visit home to Painesville, Giblin returned to New York in hopes of finding a more dependable career. He started out as a special–order clerk at the British Book Centre, then joined the staff of Criterion Books in 1959, first as a publicity director, and later as an editor. He enjoyed the work, especially when given the opportunity to edit books for young readers. Deciding to concentrate solely on works for children, he moved on to Lothrop, Lee and Shepard in 1962.

While working at Lothrop, Giblin started to think about writing his own books. He once recalled, "In 1964, after editing J. J. McCoy's career book, *The World of the Veterinarian,* I decided to try writing a similar book about publishing, and drafted an outline for it and several sample chapters." Though a publisher expressed initial interest in the book, in the end, it was rejected since the potential market was felt to be too small. Giblin had ambivalent feelings, as he noted in his autobiographical essay in *Sixth Book of Junior Authors:* "I really wasn't sorry. While part of me wanted to resume my writing career, another part—remembering the *Lie Down in Darkness* experience—hung back from making the necessary commitment to it."

Publishing Career Leads to Writing for Children

In the late 1960s, Giblin went to work for Seabury Press, where he was instrumental in developing the company's children's division, Clarion Books. In the 1970s, a trip to China inspired him to try another book project of his own—"an anthology of Chinese writings about the doings of Chinese young people in the years since the Communist Revolution of 1949," as he once described it. But this time the project did not go through because it was considered "too political." However, by this time Giblin was writing again, contributing articles about children's books to periodicals and lecturing at conferences of children's book writers and librarians.

In 1980, Giblin collaborated with Dale Ferguson on his first children's book, *The Scarecrow Book.* Since then, he has written several more children's nonfiction titles on a wide range of subjects, among them *The Skyscraper Book* (1981) *Walls: Defenses throughout History* (1984), and *Let There Be Light: A Book about Windows* (1988). In 1989, Giblin decided he was tired of juggling his role as editor–in–chief of Clarion Books with his expanding career as a writer, so he retired to contributing editor status.

The author's children's books have continued to range far afield. Giblin has explored such topics as milk pasteurization, Fourth of July celebrations, eating utensils, chairs, plagues, and mammoth bones, among many others. Many reviewers have praised Giblin's ability to tell complex stories in a way that is simple, understandable, and entertaining. Elizabeth S. Watson, writing in a *Horn Book Magazine* review of *The Riddle of the Rosetta Stone: Key to Ancient Egypt,* stated that "the author has done a masterful job of distilling information, citing the highlights, and fitting it all together." *New York Times Book Review* contributor Philip M. Isaacson lauded Giblin's writing skills in *Let There Be Light,* noting that the author "has condensed a daunting body of material to provide young readers with a great deal of information about the evolution and technology of windows."

Some critics have also pointed out that Giblin's accounts, while easy to understand, are loaded with valuable detail. "[His] relaxed, affable manner belies the amount of information he offers," wrote Amy L. Cohn in a *School Library Journal* review of *Chimney Sweeps: Yesterday and Today.* Other critics have observed that this wealth of information is derived from the author's painstaking research. "Giblin has such a flair for historic detail and research that he translates hordes of tales into a singular creation of Santa Claus," proclaimed a *School Library Journal* reviewer about *The Truth about Santa Claus.*

Cooper of *Booklist* wrote, "[His] writing is lively, and he wisely uses the story of Franklin's estrangement from his only living son, a Royalist, to heighten dramatic tension." Giblin's initial foray into fiction, *The Dwarf, the Giant, and the Unicorn*, met with mixed reviews. Carolyn Phelan of *Booklist* praised it as a "good read–aloud," while a *Publishers Weekly* reviewer stated that Giblin's efforts were "without memorable results."

Giblin's more recent book, *The Century That Was: Reflections on the Last One Hundred Years* is something of a departure for him, although it is a natural extension of his former work as an editor. He compiled and edited a collection of thematic essays by eleven noted children's writers, each one looking at a different aspect of life in America in the twentieth century. Hazel Rochman of *Booklist* pointed out that while editor Giblin made no effort to produce a "comprehensive" history, "The individual approaches, both personal and historical, will stimulate young people to look back and also forward to where we're going next." A *Horn Book* reviewer voiced a similar opinion, stating, "One of the older formulas of outstanding nonfiction . . . is the essay. It's back, and in fine fettle for a new generation of readers."

Women's campaigns to get the right to vote following World War I is one of many themes covered in Giblin's *The Century That Was: Reflections on the Last One Hundred Years*, a collection of historical essays published in 2000.

An evaluation of the same book in *Bulletin of the Center for Children's Books* lauded Giblin's command of his subject, stating that the author had done "his usual good job of research and well–organized presentation." Reviewing Giblin's 1999 book, *The Mystery of the Mammoth Bones*, a *Publishers Weekly* critic praised the author for having "the pacing of an ace detective [as he] unveils the painstaking steps in artist and naturalist Charles Willson Peale's 1801 discovery of mammoth bones."

In addition to his books about interesting subjects and events, Giblin has written biographies of such historical figures as founding fathers George Washington, Thomas Jefferson, Benjamin Franklin, and aviator Charles Lindbergh, and he has even started to write fiction. Like his earlier works, Giblin's non-fiction books continue to find favor with reviewers and young readers alike. For example, assessing Giblin's 2000 book about Benjamin Franklin, Ilene

---

If you enjoy the works of James Cross Giblin, you might want to check out the following books:

Carol Donoughue, *The Mystery of the Hieroglyphs: The Story of the Rosetta Stone and the Race to Decipher Egyptian Hieroglyphs*, 1999.
Richard Preston, *The Hot Zone*, 1995.
M. Jerry Weiss and Helen S. Weiss, editors, *Lost and Found: Award–winning Authors Sharing Real–Life Experiences through Fiction*, 2000.

Giblin has commented on the enjoyment that he derives from investigating the factual details of his subjects and how important this task is to his work. "I love research," the author told *Publishers Weekly* interviewer Wendy Smith. "I love going down to Washington on a vacation week and using the Library of Congress. I enjoy making things clear for readers—maybe 'clear' is a unifying word in my work as an author and editor."

PERIODICALS

Booklist, December 1, 1996, Carolyn Phelan, review of *The Dwarf, The Giant, and the Unicorn: A Tale of King Arthur*, pp. 666–667; February 15, 2000, Ilene Cooper, review of *The Amazing Life of Benjamin Franklin*, p. 1105; March 1, 2000, Hazel Rochman, review of *The Century That Was: Reflections on the Last One Hundred Years*, p. 1235.

Bulletin of the Center for Children's Books, October, 1983; February, 1985; September, 1985, review of *The Truth about Santa Claus*; November, 1986; December, 1987.

Horn Book, February, 1983, pp. 62–63; January–February, 1989, pp. 33–34; November–December, 1990, Elizabeth S. Watson, review of *The Riddle of the Rosetta Stone: Key to Ancient Egypt*, p. 758; March, 2000, review of *The Century That Was: Reflections on the Last One Hundred Years*, p. 211.

New York Times Book Review, November 21, 1982, p. 43; March 12, 1989, Philip M. Isaacson, review of *Let There Be Light: A Book about Windows*; January 16, 1994, p. 20; March 15, 1998, p. 24.

Publishers Weekly, July 26, 1985, Wendy Smith, "PW Interviews James Giblin," p. 169; November 15, 1985, p. 56; November 11, 1996, review of *The Dwarf, the Giant, and the Unicorn: A Tale of King Arthur*, p. 75; January 25, 1999, review of *The Mystery of the Mammoth Bones*, p. 97; February 28, 2000, p. 81; May 8, 2000, p. 222.

School Library Journal, January, 1983, Amy L. Cohn, review of *Chimney Sweeps: Yesterday and Today*, p. 75; October, 1985, review of *The Truth about Santa Claus*, p. 192; March, 1987, pp. 113–115; October, 1988, pp. 27–31.

Tribune Books (Chicago), April 11, 1982.

Voice of Youth Advocates, October, 2000, Leah J. Sparks, review of *The Century That Was*, p. 285.

Washington Post Book World, November 10, 1991.

Nadine Gordimer

residence, American Academy in Rome, 1984; has also lectured and taught writing at Harvard, Princeton, Northwestern, Columbia, and Tulane universities; presenter on *Frontiers* television series.

■ Personal

Born November 20, 1923, in Springs, Transvaal, South Africa; daughter of Isidore (a jeweler) and Nan (Myers) Gordimer; married Gerald Gavronsky, March 6, 1949 (divorced, 1952); married Reinhold H. Cassirer (an art gallery owner and director), January 29, 1954; children: (first marriage) Oriane Taramasco; (second marriage) Hugo, one stepdaughter. *Education:* Attended University of the Witwatersrand.

■ Addresses

Agent—Russell & Volkening, Inc., 50 West 29th St., New York, NY 10001.

■ Career

Writer. Ford Foundation visiting professor, under auspices of Institute of Contemporary Arts, Washington, DC, 1961; Hopwood Awards lecturer, University of Michigan, Ann Arbor, 1970; writer–in–

■ Member

International PEN (vice president), Congress of South African Writers, Royal Society of Literature, American Academy of Arts and Sciences (honorary member), American Academy of Literature and Arts (honorary member), Modern Language Association (honorary fellow).

■ Awards, Honors

W. H. Smith & Son Literary Award, 1961, for short story collection *Friday's Footprint and Other Stories;* Thomas Pringle Award, English Academy of South Africa, 1969; James Tait Black Memorial Prize, 1972, for *A Guest of Honour;* Booker Prize for Fiction, National Book League, 1974, for *The Conservationist;* CNA awards, 1974, 1979, 1981, and 1991; Grand Aigle d'Or (France), 1975; Neil Gunn fellowship, Scottish Arts Council, 1981; Commonwealth Award for Distinguished Service in Literature, 1981; Modern Language Association of America award, 1981; Nelly Sachs Prize (Germany), 1985; Premio Malaparte (Italy), 1986; Bennett Award, *Hudson Review,*

1986; Benson Medal, Royal Society of Literature, 1990; Commander de l'Ordre des Arts et des Lettres (France), 1991; Nobel Prize for literature, Nobel Foundation, 1991. D.Litt., University of Leuven, 1980, Smith College, City College of the City University of New York, and Mount Holyoke College, all 1985; honorary degrees from Harvard University and Yale University, both 1987, and New School for Social Research, 1988.

■ Writings

NOVELS

The Lying Days, Simon & Schuster (New York City), 1953, published with new introduction by Paul Bailey, Virago (New York City), 1983.

A World of Strangers, Simon & Schuster, 1958.

Occasion for Loving, Viking (New York City), 1963, published with new introduction by Paul Bailey, Virago, 1983.

The Late Bourgeois World, Viking, 1966.

A Guest of Honour, Viking, 1970.

The Conservationist, J. Cape (London), 1974, Viking, 1975.

Burger's Daughter, Viking, 1979.

July's People, Viking, 1981.

A Sport of Nature, Knopf (New York City), 1987.

My Son's Story, Farrar, Straus (New York City), 1990.

None to Accompany Me, Farrar, Straus, 1994.

Harald, Claudia, and Their Son Duncan, Bloomsbury, 1996.

The House Gun, Farrar, Straus, 1998.

SHORT STORIES

Face to Face (also see below), Silver Leaf Books (Johannesburg), 1949.

The Soft Voice of the Serpent and Other Stories (contains stories previously published in *Face to Face*), Simon & Schuster, 1952.

Six Feet of the Country (also see below), Simon & Schuster, 1956.

Friday's Footprint and Other Stories, Viking, 1960.

Not for Publication and Other Stories, Viking, 1965.

Livingstone's Companions, Viking, 1971.

Selected Stories (contains stories from previously published collections), Viking, 1975, also published in England as *No Place Like: Selected Stories,* Penguin, 1978.

Some Monday for Sure, Heinemann Educational (London), 1976.

A Soldier's Embrace, Viking, 1980.

Town and Country Lovers, Sylvester & Orphanos (Los Angeles, CA), 1980.

Six Feet of the Country (contains stories from previously published collections selected for television series of same title), Penguin, 1982.

Something Out There, Viking, 1984.

Reflections of South Africa: Short Stories, Systime, 1986.

Crimes of Conscience: Selected Short Stories, Heinemann, 1991.

Jump and Other Stories, Farrar, Straus, 1991.

Why Haven't You Written?: Selected Stories, 1950–1972, Viking, 1993.

OTHER

(Compiler, and editor with Lionel Abrahams) *South African Writing Today,* Penguin, 1967.

African Literature: The Lectures Given on This Theme at the University of Cape Town's Public Summer School, February, 1972, Board of Extra Mural Studies, University of Cape Town, 1972.

The Black Interpreters: Notes on African Writing, Spro–Cas/Ravan (Johannesburg), 1973.

On the Mines, photographs by David Goldblatt, C. Struik (Cape Town), 1973.

(Author of appreciation) *Kurt Jobst: Goldsmith and Silversmith; Art Metal Worker,* G. Bakker (Johannesburg), 1979.

(With others) *What Happened to Burger's Daughter; or, How South African Censorship Works,* Taurus (Johannesburg), 1980.

Lifetimes under Apartheid, photographs by David Goldblatt, Knopf, 1986.

The Essential Gesture: Writing, Politics and Places, edited and introduced by Stephen Clingman, Knopf, 1988.

Three in a Bed: Fiction, Morals, and Politics, Bennington College, 1991.

(With Ruth Weiss) *Zimbabwe and the New Elite,* Tauris & Co., 1993.

Writing and Being: The Charles Eliot Norton Lectures, Harvard University Press (Cambridge, MA), 1995.

Living in Hope and History: Notes from Our Century, Farrar, Straus, 1999.

Also author of *Our Century,* 1996; author of television plays and documentaries, including *A Terrible Chemistry,* 1981, (and director) *Choosing for Justice: Allan Boesak,* with Hugo Cassirer, 1985, *Country Lovers, A Chip of Glass Ruby, Praise,* and *Oral History,* all part of *The Gordimer Stories* series adapted from stories of the same title, 1985. Contributor to *The Heinemann Book of Contemporary African Short Stories,* Heinemann Educational (London, England), 1992; contributor to short story anthologies, including

Best Short Stories of 1993. Contributor to periodicals, including *Atlantic, Encounter, Granta, Harper's, Holiday, Kenyon Review, Mother Jones, New Yorker, Paris Review,* and *Playboy.* Gordimer's novels, short stories, and essays have been translated into twenty–five languages.

■ Adaptations

City Lovers, based on Gordimer's short story of the same title, was filmed by TeleCulture Inc./TelePool in South Africa in 1982.

■ Work in Progress

A documentary film, with son Hugo Cassirer, comparing post–apartheid Johannesburg and Berlin after the wall was brought down.

■ Sidelights

"Nadine Gordimer has become, in the whole solid body of her work, the literary voice and conscience of her society," declared Maxwell Geismar in *Saturday Review.* In numerous novels, short stories, and essays, she has written of her South African homeland and its apartheid government—under which its blacks, coloreds, and whites suffered for nearly half a century. "This writer . . . has made palpable the pernicious, pervasive character of that country's race laws, which not only deny basic rights to most people but poison many relationships," maintained Miriam Berkley in *Publishers Weekly.* Gordimer's insight, integrity, and compassion inspire critical admiration. "She has mapped out the social, political and emotional geography of that troubled land with extraordinary passion and precision," says Michiko Kakutani in the *New York Times,* observing in a later essay that "taken chronologically, her work not only reflects her own evolving political consciousness and maturation as an artist—an early lyricism has given way to an increased preoccupation with ideas and social issues—but it also charts changes in South Africa's social climate." She was honored with the Nobel Prize in literature for her novels in 1991, a sign of the esteem in which the literary world holds her work.

When she began, Gordimer was only one of a number of novelists working in South Africa after World War II. "Some of the writers, like [Alan] Paton, turned to nonfiction or political work; even more, most notably [Peter] Abrahams and Dan Jacobson, expatriated," explained John Cooke in *The Novels of Nadine Gordimer: Private Lives/Public Landscapes.* "By the early sixties Gordimer was almost the only member of the postwar group to continue producing fiction from within the country. That she should be the survivor was not altogether surprising, for she was in essential ways more a product of South Africa than her contemporaries. She attended university at home, not in England as colonial writers so regularly have; she did not travel abroad until she was thirty."

"Gordimer seemed particularly unsuited to prosper as a writer in her arid land," Cooke continued, "because of the disjunction between her temperament and the situation she confronted. More than any of her contemporaries, Gordimer was initially drawn to private themes." Her novels and short stories are, at bottom, about complicated individuals caught in awkward or impossibly complex situations. "Her writing [is] so subtle that it forces readers to find their way back from her works into her mind," said Firdaus Kanga in the *Times Literary Supplement;* "her characters are powerful precisely because you cannot sum them up in a line or even a page."

South Africa's Whites Confronted

Much of Gordimer's fiction focuses upon white middle–class characters. It frequently depicts what Geismar described as "a terrified white consciousness in the midst of a mysterious and ominous sea of black humanity." But the "enduring subject" of her writing has been "the consequences of apartheid on the daily lives of men and women, the distortions it produces in relationships among both blacks and whites," said Kakutani. Her first novel, *The Lying Days,* is drawn from her own personal experience and tells about a young woman who comes into contact with the effects of apartheid when she has an affair with a social worker. *A World of Strangers* is about the efforts of a British writer to bring together his white intellectual friends with his black African intellectual friends. In *Burger's Daughter,* considered by some to be her best novel, Gordimer examines white ambivalence about apartheid in the person of Rosa, who can no longer sustain the anti–apartheid cause of her imprisoned Afrikaner father after his death. This work, like several others before it, was banned in South Africa, but the ban was quickly removed because of the critical attention the novel had attracted in the West. The story of the banning and acceptance of *Burger's Daughter* is related in *What Happened to Burger's Daughter: or, How South African Censorship Works,* published in 1980.

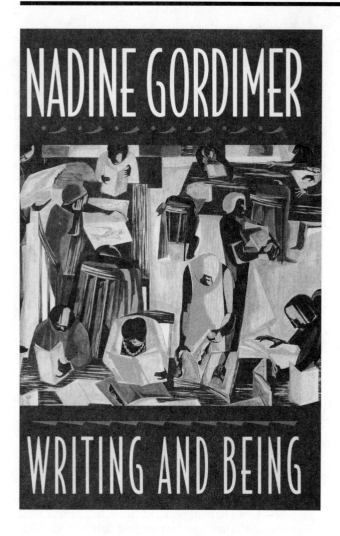

Gordimer considers the relationship between writers' experiences of "real life" and the fiction they produce in this 1995 volume.

Both *The Lying Days* and *A World of Strangers* end with a note of hope for a better future for South Africans. Gordimer's later novels, however, take a more pessimistic tone. *A Guest of Honour,* which won the James Tait Black Memorial Prize in 1973, tells of the return of Colonel James Bray to his African homeland. Bray had been exiled by the previous government for his espousal of black revolutionary ideology. Upon his return, however, Bray discovers that the new revolutionary government is just as corrupt and self–interested as the previous government was. When he speaks out publicly against the new government, it targets him for assassination. *The Conservationist,* awarded the Booker Prize (England's highest literary honor) the following year, tells about the uneasy relationship between a white landowner and the black squatters who have settled on his estate. "Beginning with *A Guest of Honour,*" Cooke concluded, "Gordimer's novels are informed by a tension between . . . two impulses: she at once observes her world from without and envisions it from within. Through this double process, the fruit of her long apprenticeship, Gordimer creates masterful forms and shapes despite the 'low cultural rainfall' of her world."

These forms and shapes also appear in Gordimer's short fiction. *Jump and Other Stories*—published shortly before the author received the Nobel Prize—contains stories that approach her favorite themes in a variety of ways. She tells about a white man out for a jog, who is caught up in a black gang killing and is saved by a black woman who shelters him. "A single truth is witnessed," wrote John Edgar Wideman in the *New York Times Book Review,* "a truth somehow missing in most fiction by white Americans that purports to examine our national life. No matter how removed one feels oneself from the fray, race and race relations lie at the heart of the intimate, perplexing questions we need to ask of ourselves: Where have I been? Where am I going? Who am I?" "Ms. Gordimer can be a merciless judge and jury," Wideman concluded. "Her portraits obtain a Vermeer–like precision, accurate and remorseless, with no room for hope, for self–delusion, no room even for the small vanities of ego and self–regard that allow us to proceed sometimes as if at least our intentions are honorable."

The Nobel Prize, Concern for Apartheid

The Swedish Academy had considered Gordimer as a Nobel Prize nominee for years before she finally received the award in 1991. Several commentators, while congratulating her on her accomplishment, noted that the struggle against apartheid remained unfinished. "On the day of the announcement that Nadine Gordimer would receive the 1991 Nobel Prize for literature, a tribute to the complex and intimate stories she has written about racism's toll on people's lives in her native South Africa," wrote Esther B. Fein in the *New York Times,* "Nelson Mandela still did not have the right to vote." Mandela, who later became president of South Africa, had been released from his political prison, but the basic tenets of apartheid prevented him from exercising the rights of citizenship. When South African president F. W. De Klerk announced that the policy of separation would end, reviewers wondered where the Nobel laureate would turn her attention. "With apartheid finally ended," Diana Jean Schemo declared in the *New York Times,* "the novelist waxes exultant over a sense of renewal in her homeland; the urgency is gone, but the turn of mind remains."

"For the whole of her literary career, Gordimer has grappled with the intricacies and distortions of life under a certain political system, a specific regime of oppression," noted Diane Simon in the *Nation*. With the ending of apartheid and the enfranchisement of South African blacks, critics scanned Gordimer's fiction for evidence of how this supremely political writer's focus would change. Her novel, *None to Accompany Me,* looks at the fortunes of two families—one black, one white—as they move into the new, post–apartheid, era. "The repressions, the . . . laws and persecutions, the campaigns of resistance, the exiles, the detentions, the bannings and brutalities–all these horrors of the past are finished," observed Sonya Rudikoff in *African Writers.* She continued, "What remains is the damage done to society and to personal relations." "*None to Accompany Me* is a sustaining achievement, proving Gordimer once again a lucid witness to her country's transformation and a formidable interpreter of the inner self," Anne Whitehouse averred in *Chicago Tribune Books.* While some viewed this as a step away from the public themes of her earlier novels and short stories, Simon observed that all of Gordimer's main characters are actively involved in the political life of the new South Africa.

By contrast, Gordimer's second post–apartheid novel, *The House Gun,* while it also explores the relationships between blacks and whites in the newly transformed South Africa, is arguably more concerned with the politicization of her characters' personal lives. The Lindegards are an affluent white couple who learn that their only son, Duncan, has committed a murder using a gun intended to protect the house from thieves. They hire a black lawyer to represent him and begin the painful process of emerging out of the sheltered lives they have created. Through these events, Gordimer explores the question, "Does a violent society provoke violence in nonviolent individuals?" "The story deftly brings homes a tricky truth," remarked Walter Kirn in *Time:* "Peace can be as perilous as war, and even more confusing to negotiate." The novel's other underlying question, which asks if the level of violence in South Africa is higher than in Europe because of its large black population, is "the racial question that haunts Gordimer's novel," according to Jack Miles in the *New York Times Book Review.* Miles went on to describe *House Gun* as an "elegantly conceived, flawlessly executed novel." While Michiko Kakutani in the *New York Times* dubbed the novel "little more than a courtroom thriller, dressed up with some clumsy allusions to apartheid's legacy of violence and the uses and misuses of freedom," *Library Journal* reviewer Edward B. St. John contended that *House Gun* is "much more ambitious" than the courtroom dramas of Scott Turow or John Grisham, adding that "Gordimer's

In this memoir, published in 1999, Gordimer explains what it was like to be a political dissident in apartheid South Africa.

trademark prose style . . . seems especially well suited to capturing the moral ambiguities of South African life." "Gordimer's great fiction has always personalized the political," observed Hazel Rochman in *Booklist,* but in this novel, the author "moves in the opposite direction, taking the personal intimacy of family, friend, and lover into the glare of the public sphere."

Gordimer's turn of mind reaches out in two directions: politically, she follows the fortunes of other first–class "third world" writers such as Egyptian Naguib Mahfouz, Nigerian Chinua Achebe, and Israeli Amos Oz. "Her attention is turned on writers whose work seems most engaged in the questions that have absorbed her for much of her life," Schemo wrote: "how justice, wealth, power and

If you enjoy the works of Nadine Gordimer, you might want to check out the following books and films:

David Goodman, *Fault Lines: Journeys into the New South Africa*, 1999.

Rian Malan, *My Traitor's Heart: A South African Exile Returns to Face His Country, His Tribe and His Conscience*, 1991.

V. S. Naipaul, *In a Free State*, 1984.

A Dry White Season, a film starring Donald Sutherland and Marlon Brando.

---

freedom are parceled out in a society, and the repercussions for its people." In the essays collected in *Living in Hope and History: Notes from Our Century*, the author addresses politics and morals, writers and culture, and, first of all, life as a white liberal in South Africa. Here especially, Gordimer "speaks with the authority of the insider," according to Hazel Rochman in *Booklist*, "bearing witness to what it has been like, as a white citizen and writer, to live in Johannesburg" during the years of apartheid and through the upheavals that accompanied the transition to a post–apartheid regime. Critics noted that Gordimer herself has frequently called her fiction more truthful than her nonfiction, and agreed that, as a reviewer for *Publishers Weekly* claimed, the pieces found in *Living in Hope and History* "shouldn't be expected to attain the nuance and depth of Gordimer's best fiction, but some of them are devastating." Gordimer herself once told interviewer Beth Austin in the *Chicago Tribune*: "I began to write, I think, out of the real source of all art, and that is out of a sense of wonderment about life, and a sense of trying to make sense out of the mystery of life. That hasn't changed in all the years that I've been writing. That is the starting point of everything that I write."

■ **Biographical and Critical Sources**

BOOKS

Bazin, Nancy Topping, and Marilyn Dallman Seymour, editors, *Conversations with Nadine Gordimer*, University Press of Mississippi (Jackson), 1990.

Brodsky, Joseph, *New Censors: Nadine Gordimer and Others on Publishing Now*, Cassell Academic, 1996.

Chapman, Michael, editor, *The Drum Decade: Stories from the 1950s*, University of Natal Press (Pietermaritzburg, South Africa), 1989.

Clingman, Stephen, *The Novels of Nadine Gordimer: History from the Inside*, University of Massachusetts Press, 1992.

Cooke, John, *The Novels of Nadine Gordimer: Private Lives/Public Landscapes*, Louisiana State University (Baton Rouge), 1985.

Cox, C. Brian, editor, *African Writers*, Scribner's, 1997, pp. 277–290.

Driver, Dorothy, Ann Dry, Craig MacKenzie, and John Read, *Nadine Gordimer: A Bibliography of Primary and Secondary Sources, 1937–1992*, Hans Zell, 1994.

Dubbeld, Catherine Elizabeth, *Reflecting Apartheid: South African Short Stories in English with Socio–Political Themes, 1960–1987: A Select and Annotated Bibliography*, South African Institute of International Affairs, 1990.

Ettin, Andrew Vogel, *Betrayals of the Body Politic: The Literary Commitments of Nadine Gordimer*, University Press of Virginia, 1993.

Head, Dominic, *Nadine Gordimer*, Cambridge University Press, 1995.

Kamm, Antony, *Biographical Companion to Literature in English*, Scarecrow, 1997, pp. 215–216.

King, Bruce, editor, *The Later Fiction of Nadine Gordimer*, St. Martin's Press, 1993.

Nell, Racillia Jillian, *Nadine Gordimer: Novelist and Short Story Writer: A Bibliography of Her Works and Selected Criticism*, University of the Witwatersrand, 1964.

Newman, Judie, *Nadine Gordimer*, Routledge, 1990.

Smith, Rowland, editor, *Critical Essays on Nadine Gordimer*, G. K. Hall, 1990.

Wagner, Kathrin, *Rereading Nadine Gordimer*, Indiana University Press, 1994.

Yelin, Louise, *From the Margins of Empire: Christina Stead, Doris Lessing, Nadine Gordimer*, Cornell University Press, 1998.

PERIODICALS

America, October 31, 1981, p. 264; December 15, 1984, p. 410; November 18, 1989, p. 361; June 6, 1992, Jerome Donnelly, review of *Jump and Other Stories*, p. 518; December 12, 1998, Augusta Rohrbach, review of *The House Gun*, p. 15.

Antioch Review, fall 1998, Rosemary Hartigan, review of *The House Gun*, p. 496.

Artforum, March 1998, interview with Nadine Gordimer, p. S21.

Atlantic Monthly, January, 1960; October, 1994, Phoebe–Lou Adams, review of *None to Accompany Me*, p. 131; February, 1998.

Atlas, January, 1980, p. 30.

Booklist, October 1, 1958; January 10, 1960; August, 1992, p. 2022; June 1, 1994, p. 1862; August 1994, Stuart Whitewell, review of *None to Accompany Me,* p. 1989; September 15, 1995, Hazel Rochman, review of *Writing and Being,* p. 129; October 15 1997, H. Rochman, review of *The House Gun,* p. 362; August, 1999, review of *Jump and Other Stories,* p. 2025; September 1, 1999, H. Rochman, review of *Living in Hope and History,* p. 57.

Bulletin of Bibliography, Volume 36, 1979; Volume 42, number 1, 1985.

Business Week, September 8, 1980, p. 17.

Canadian Forum, February, 1984, p. 17; April, 1989, p. 27.

Canadian Literature, summer, 1992, W. H. New, review of *Jump and Other Stories,* p. 194.

Chicago Sunday Tribune, September 21, 1958.

Chicago Tribune, May 18, 1980; December 7, 1986; November 12, 1987; October 4, 1991.

Christian Century, May 26, 1982, p. 642.

Christian Science Monitor, January 10, 1963; November 4, 1971; May 19, 1975; September 10, 1979.

Commentary, February, 1992, Jillian Becker, "Nadine Gordimer's Politics," p. 51.

Commonweal, October 23, 1953; July 9, 1965; November 4, 1966; December 5, 1980, p. 702; November 30, 1984, pp. 662, 667–668; March 10, 1989, p. 150.

Contemporary Literature, winter, 1995, Nancy Topping Bazin, interview with Nadine Gordimer, p. 571.

Cosmopolitan, August, 1981, p. 24.

Detroit News, September 2, 1979; June 7, 1981; May 31, 1989.

Encounter, August, 1971; February, 1975.

English Journal, March, 1990, p. 70.

Entertainment Weekly, January 24, 1992, review of *My Son's Story,* p. 52; November 4, 1994, Vanessa V. Friedman, review of *None to Accompany Me,* p. 69.

Explicator, winter, 1993, Rosalie Otero, "Nadine Gordimer's *The Conservationist,*" p. 116.

Extrapolation, spring, 1992, pp. 73–87.

Glamour, November, 1990, p. 174.

Globe and Mail (Toronto), July 28, 1984; June 6, 1987; January 5, 1991; October 5, 1991.

Harper's, February, 1963; April, 1976; November, 1990, p. 27.

Hudson Review, spring, 1980; spring, 1992, Gary Krist, review of *Jump and Other Stories,* p. 146; summer, 1995, Alan Davis, review of *None to Accompany Me,* p. 325.

Insight on the News, January 9, 1995, Jeffrey Staggs, review of *None to Accompany Me,* p. 27.

Interview, December, 1988, p. 140.

Library Journal, September 1, 1958; September 1, 1980, p. 1751; March 15, 1981, p. 680; December, 1985, p. 99; March 1, 1987, p. 70; April 15, 1987, p. 98; January, 1988, p. 41; July, 1988, p. 70; October 15, 1988, p. 91; May 15, 1990, p. 120; November 1, 1990, p. 124; August, 1991, p. 149; March 1, 1993, p. 122; April 1, 1993, Sister M. Anna Falbo, review of *July's People,* p. 148; August, 1994, Edward B. St. John, review of *None to Accompany Me,* p. 1989; September 15, 1994, Michael Rogers, reviews of *The Lying Days* and *Occasion for Loving,* p. 95; February 1, 1995, p. 114; September 1, 1995, Carol A. McAllister, review of *Writing and Being,* p. 176; November 1, 1997, E. B. St. John, review of *The House Gun,* p. 115.

London Magazine, April–May, 1975.

Los Angeles Times, July 31, 1984; December 7, 1986.

Los Angeles Times Book Review, August 10, 1980; April 19, 1987; April 3, 1988; April 2, 1989; October 28, 1990.

Maclean's, August 3, 1981, p. 43; November 2, 1981, p. 21; August 13, 1984, p. 52, June 1, 1987, p. 50; November 14, 1994, John Bemrose, review of *None to Accompany Me,* p. 104.

Modern Fiction Studies, summer, 1987.

Mother Jones, June, 1984, p. 56; December, 1988, p. 50.

Ms., July, 1975; June, 1981, pp. 41, 90; July, 1984, p. 33; September, 1987, p. 28.

Nation, June 18, 1971; August 18, 1976; January 3, 1981, p. 22; June 6, 1981, p. 226; June 25, 1983, p. 809; May 2, 1987, p. 578; May 30, 1987, p. 731; December 26, 1988, p. 726; December 17, 1990, p. 777; October 16, 1995, Maureen Howard, review of *Writing and Being,* p. 431; March 2, 1998, Diane Simon, review of *The House Gun,* p. 25; December 13, 1999, Susie Linfield, "Why, the Beloved Country," p. 26.

National Review, December 25, 1981, p. 1561.

New Leader, June 29, 1981, p. 17; June 25, 1984, p. 18; April 20, 1087, p. 18.

New Orleans, December, 1984, p. 87; November, 1985, p. 31.

New Republic, May 18, 1987, p. 33; November 28, 1988, p. 28; October 24, 1994, Caryl Phillips, review of *None to Accompany Me,* p. 34.

New Statesman, May 16, 1980, p. 751; September 11, 1981, p. 18; March 23, 1984, p. 27; April 10, 1987, p. 27; December 4, 1987, p. 30.

New Statesman and Nation, August 18, 1956.

New Statesman & Society, September 23, 1988, p. 35; December 15, 1989, p. 39; September 21, 1990, p. 40; September 16, 1994, Julie Wheelwright, review of *None to Accompany Me,* p. 38.

Newsweek, May 10, 1965; July 4, 1966; March 10, 1975; April 19, 1976; September 22, 1980; June 22, 1981, p. 78; July 9, 1984, p. 71; August 4, 1986, p.

29; May 4, 1987, p. 78; October 1, 1990, p. 40; October 14, 1991, p. 40.

New York, August 25, 1980, p. 54; June 22, 1981, p. 64; February 3, 1986, p. 40; October 22, 1990, p. 119.

New Yorker, June 7, 1952; November 21, 1953; November 29, 1958; May 12, 1975; June 22, 1981, p. 114; June 29, 1987, p. 87.

New York Herald Tribune Book Review, May 25, 1952; October 4, 1953; October 21, 1956; September 21, 1958; January 10, 1960; April 7, 1963.

New York Review of Books, June 26, 1975; July 15, 1976; October 23, 1980, p. 46; August 13, 1981, p. 14; July 16, 1987, p. 8; March 30, 1989, p. 12; November 21, 1991, p. 27; December 5, 1991, p. 16; December 1, 1994, Michael Wood, review of *None to Accompany Me,* p. 12.

New York Times, June 15, 1952; October 4, 1953; October 7, 1956; September 21, 1958; May 23, 1965; October 30, 1970; September 19, 1979; August 20, 1980; May 27, 1981; December 28, 1981; July 9, 1984; January 14, 1986; April 22, 1987; December 28, 1987; October 5, 1990; January 1, 1991; October 4, 1991, pp. A1, C28; October 10, 1991, p. C25; December 8, 1991, p. 22; September 16, 1994, p. C31; November 28, 1994, pp. C11, C15.

New York Times Book Review, January 10, 1960; September 11, 1966; October 31, 1971; April 13, 1975; April 18, 1976; August 19, 1979; August 24, 1980, pp. 7, 31; December 7, 1980, p. 51; June 7, 1981, pp. 26, 226; February 7, 1982, p. 38; August 8, 1982, p. 23; December 5, 1982, p. 75; June 24, 1984, p. 40; July 29, 1984, p. 7; August 16, 1984, p. 3; February 16, 1986, p. 29; August 31, 1986, p. 20; May 3, 1987, pp. 1, 22; July 19, 1987, p. 1; November 27, 1988, p. 8; October 21, 1990, pp. 1, 21; December 2, 1990, p. 81; June 2, 1991, p. 21; September 29, 1991, p. 7; September 25, 1994, p. 7; December 24, 1995, p. 11; October 6, 1996, p. 102; January 16, 1998; February 1, 1998, p. 10.

Paris Review, summer, 1983.

Partisan Review, spring, 1998, Millicent Bell, review of *The House Gun,* p. 259.

People Weekly, March 26, 1984, p. 104; August 20, 1984, p. 15; January 5, 1987, p. 18; May 4, 1987, p. 22; October 18, 1991, p. 14; October 21, 1991, p. 52; January 19, 1998, "After the Revolution," p. 37.

Playboy, January, 1992, Claudia Dreifus, "Checking In," p. 32.

Progressive, January, 1982, p. 53; January, 1992, Claudia Dreifus, "Nadine Gordimer: 'I've Never Left Africa,'" p. 30.

Publishers Weekly, June 27, 1980, p. 79; April 20, 1984, p. 82; May 23, 1986, p. 99; March 6, 1987; April 10, 1987, p. 80; November 6, 1987, p. 40; September 30, 1988, p. 54; August 17, 1990, p. 53; August

30, 1991, p. 69; October 18, 1991, p. 14; July 11, 1994, review of *None to Accompany Me,* p. 61; August 14, 1995, review of *Writing and Being,* p. 63; November 11, 1996, p. 66; October 20, 1997, p. 52; March 16, 1998, Paul Nathan, "Nobelist's Film Deal," p. 21; August 16, 1999, review of *Living in Hope and History,* p. 66.

Research in African Literatures, summer, 1997, Susan Greenstein, review of *Writing and Being,* p. 145; spring, 2000, "Where the Banalities Are Enacted," p. 95.

San Francisco Chronicle, May 26, 1952; November 9, 1953; January 24, 1960.

Salmagundi, winter, 1992, Robert Boyers, review of *My Son's Story,* p. 188; winter, 1997, Karen Lazar, "'A Feeling of Realistic Optimism': An Interview with Nadine Gordimer," p. 149.

Saturday Review, May 24, 1952; October 3, 1953; September 13, 1958; January 16, 1960; May 8, 1965; August 20, 1966; December 4, 1971; March 8, 1975; September 29, 1979; May, 1981, p. 67.

Sewanee Review, spring, 1977.

Spectator, February 12, 1960; September 17, 1994, Caroline Moore, review of *None to Accompany Me,* p. 39; November 18, 1995, Barbara Trapido, review of *Writing and Being,* p. 55; February 7, 1998, B. Trapido, review of *The House Gun,* p. 29.

Tikkun, January–February, 1990, p. 67; May–June, 1995, Todd Pitock, "Unloved Back Home," p. 76 and Melanie Kaye–Kantrowitz, review of *None to Accompany Me,* p. 79.

Time, October 15, 1956; September 22, 1958; January 11, 1960; November 16, 1970; July 7, 1975; August 11, 1980, p. 70; June 8, 1981, p. 79; July 23, 1984, p. 95; April 6, 1987, p. 76; October 29, 1990, p. CT12; October 14, 1991, p. 91; January 19, 1998, Walter Kirn, "The Stockholm Syndrome: Is the Nobel a Curse?," p. 66.

Times (London), December 16, 1982; March 22, 1984; April 2, 1987; September 6, 1990.

Times Literary Supplement, October 30, 1953; July 13, 1956; June 27, 1958; February 12, 1960; March 1, 1963; July 22, 1965; July 7, 1966; May 14, 1971; May 26, 1972; January 9, 1976; July 9, 1976; April 25, 1980; September 4, 1981; March 30, 1984; April 17, 1987; September 23–29, 1988; October 4, 1990; October 11, 1991, p. 14; April 1, 1994, pp. 10–11; September 9, 1994, Rosemary Dinnage, review of *None to Accompany Me,* p. 20; December 1, 1995, Edward W. Said, review of *Writing and Being,* p. 7.

Tribune Books (Chicago), September 9, 1979; June 7, 1981; July 29, 1984; April 26, 1987; December 11, 1988, pp. 8–9; October 14, 1990; September 25, 1994, pp. 1, 9.

U.S. News & World Report, January 27, 1986, p. 65; May 25, 1987, p. 74.

Village Voice, September 17, 1980.

Voice Literary Supplement, September, 1984.

Washington Post, December 4, 1979.

Washington Post Book World, November 28, 1971; April 6, 1975; August 26, 1979; September 7, 1980; May 31, 1981; July 15, 1984; May 3, 1987; November 20, 1988; October 2, 1994.

Wilson Library Journal, February, 1994, p. 94.

Wilson Quarterly, autumn, 1995, review of *Writing and Being,* p. 89.

Women's Review of Books, December 1994, Vivian Gornick, review of *None to Accompany Me,* p. 5; April 1998, June Unjoo Yang, review of *The House Gun,* p. 221.

World Literature Today, autumn, 1984; spring, 1992, Michael Thorpe, review of *Crimes of Conscience,* pp. 390–391; winter, 1996, Carol Ludtke Prigan, review of *Writing and Being,* p. 227.

World Press Review, October, 1987, p. 61.

Yale Review, winter, 1982, p. 254; winter, 1988, p. 243.*

Duane Hanson

■ Personal

Born Duane Elwood Hanson, January 17, 1925, in Alexandria, MN; died of non–Hodgkin's lymphoma January 6, 1996, in Boca Raton, FL; son of Dewey O. (a dairy farmer) and Agnes (Nelson) Hanson; married Janice Roche, 1950 (divorced), married Welsa Host, 1968; children: (first marriage) Craig, Paul, Karen; (second marriage) Maja, Duane Jr. *Education:* Studied at a college in Iowa and at the University of Washington; Macalester College, B.A., 1946, Cranbrook Academy of Art, M.F.A., 1951.

■ Career

Art instructor, Twin Falls, ID, 1946–47; traveling salesman, Webb Publishing Company, St. Paul, MN, 1949; art instructor at Decorah High School, Iowa, 1949–50, Edgewood School, Greenwich, CT, 1951–52, Wilton Junior High School, Wilton, CT, 1952–53, United States Army High School, Munich, Germany, 1953–57, United States Army High School, Bremerhaven, Germany, 1957–60, United States Army High School, Atlanta, GA, and Oglethorpe University, Atlanta, 1962–65; assistant professor, Miami–Dade Junior College, Miami, FL, 1965–69; artist, 1969–96, lived and worked in Davie, FL, 1974–96. *Exhibitions:* "Human Concern/Personal Treatment," group show at Whitney Museum of American Art, New York City, 1969; solo shows at O. K. Harris Gallery, New York City, 1970, 1972, 1974, 1976, 1980, 1984, and at the Museum of Contemporary Art, 1974; Württembergischer Kunstverein, Stuttgart, 1974; Louisiana Museum, Humlebaek, Denmark, 1975; Portland Art Museum, OR, 1977; Corcoran Gallery, Washington, DC, 1977; Whitney Museum, 1978, Cranbrook Academy of Art, Bloomfield Hills, MI, 1985; Carl Milles Gärden, Lindingö, Sweden, 1986; Fort Worth Art Museum, TX, 1994; retrospective at Whitney Museum, 1999.

■ Awards, Honors

Grant for sculpture, Ella Lyman Cabot Trust, 1963; sculpture award, Florida State Fair Arts Exhibition, 1968; Blair Award, Art Institute of Chicago, 1974; D.A.A.D. grant to work in Berlin, Germany, 1974; named Florida Ambassador of the Arts, 1983; Moetti Award, 1984; Florida Prize, for outstanding achievements in sculpture, 1985; inducted into Florida Artists Hall of Fame, 1992; Artistic Achievement Award, Broward County Cultural Affairs, 1995; DHL, 1979, and LHD, 1985, both from Nova University.

■ Sidelights

Art historians have deemed Duane Hanson to be one of the most important American sculptors of the twentieth century. His lifelike forms, with their realistically translucent skin and authentically unstylish clothes, have stirred viewers to recognize themselves or their own class prejudices. As an artist, Hanson eschewed aesthetic conventions and concentrated on a largely invisible segment of society. Coming into contact with Hanson's figures, noted an *American Artist* review of Martin H. Bush's *Sculptures by Duane Hanson*, "was like bumping into real people with life stories as rich in detail as the sculptures." The artist enjoyed a successful three-decade career before his January 1996 death at age seventy-one from non-Hodgkin's lymphoma.

Hanson was born on January 17, 1925, in the rural hamlet of Alexandria, Minnesota, where his Swedish-heritage parents were dairy farmers. In 1930, the family moved to Parkers Prairie, an isolated farming community of seven hundred residents. Hanson, a sickly child, suffered from various allergies. Though the Great Depression dominated much of his childhood, he later said that his parents' self-sufficiency meant their household remained relatively unaffected by the economic crisis. His father built their house and barn, for instance, and his mother tended to a flourishing garden that provided food for the table. The Hansons rarely purchased anything from a store.

"The subject matter that I like best deals with the familiar lower and middle class American types of today. To me, the resignation, emptiness and loneliness of their existence captures the true reality of life for these people."

—Duane Hanson

Hanson's father passed his mechanical dexterity on to his son. As Duane Hanson entered his teens, he grew to be a skilled carver with his mother's butcher knife, whittling on any type of wood he could find and turning logs and even broomsticks into imaginative forms. Not even the human form daunted him: at age thirteen Hanson carved his own "Blue Boy," inspired by the Thomas Gainsborough painting of the same name. He had seen this painting—which depicts a fanciful eighteenth-century youth in blue satin breeches—inside the sole art history tome in the Parkers Prairie public library. Hanson knew that it was possible to pursue art as a career, but he had no contact at all with anyone who might serve as a role model or inspiration. He was sixteen when he first visited an art museum on a 1941 trip to Minneapolis.

Macalester College's First-ever Art Major

After graduating from high school in 1943, in the midst of World War II, Hanson was declared ineligible for military service because of his medical history of allergies. He enrolled in Iowa's Luther College, but was disappointed by the few art classes the school offered. Making a bold decision, he headed west to Seattle, where professors in the University of Washington art department were encouraged of his sculpting talents. Hanson returned to Minnesota for his senior year, enrolling in Macalester College. When he graduated in 1946, it was as the school's first-ever art major.

After college, Hanson drifted for several years. He was an art instructor in Idaho and Iowa, then for a time did graduate studies in art at the University of Minnesota; he even worked as a traveling salesman. Hanson married in 1950, and the following year earned his M.F.A. from the respected Cranbrook Academy of Art in Michigan. There, Hanson studied under two well-known sculptors of the era: Carl Milles and stone carver Bill McVey. Of Swedish extraction like Hanson, Milles was known for creating graceful abstract figures in monumental public sculptures. Milles even invited his protégé to return to Sweden with him to work as his assistant, but Hanson declined. At the time, Hanson was making abstract sculptures that followed the predominant artistic movement of the postwar era in America. "I did a little clay modeling, carved wood, cast in bronze and did a little welding in steel," he recalled in an interview with *ARTnews* writer Ellen Edwards in 1978. "I got to the point where I said to myself, so what? They were pretty statements that didn't amount to much. . . . There was no attempt to communicate any deep feeling or to say anything about how I felt."

Space-Age Plastics Spurred New Work

In 1953, Hanson made a significant change in his life when he moved to what was then known as West Germany to teach art in high schools run by the U.S. Army for the children of its personnel. He lived in Munich and Bremerhaven for seven years. A burgeoning friendship with artist George Grygo, whom he had met there, brought about a crucial change in the direction of Hanson's art. Grygo, a sculptor as well, showed Hanson how to work with polyester resins and fiberglass, two relatively new materials. When Hanson returned to the United States in 1960, he discovered the work of George Segal, who was carving lifelike forms in white plaster. Segal was part of the emergent Pop Art movement, a reaction to the staidness of the American art scene and to the abstract art that had dulled Hanson's creativity. Pop Art sought to elevate the commonplace to the status of "art;" it drew inspiration and mimicked the styles of the everyday world, from lurid comic–book illustration to boldly colored advertising art.

By 1965, Hanson was teaching at an Army high school in Atlanta, as well as nearby Oglethorpe College. At the same time, he became increasingly interested in domestic political life. The U.S. government was stepping up its military involvement in Vietnam, and Hanson's high school graduates faced a year–long combat stint and the possibility of returning home in body bags. Furthermore, civil–rights issues were making headlines on a daily basis, from the murders of voter–registration workers in the Deep South to urban riots in Los Angeles. Hanson and others witnessed a pervasive sense of dissatisfaction and distrust that seemed to be taking hold on a generation of young people.

The first art to emerge from Hanson's studio that dealt with themes from this new era was a two–foot–tall, mixed–media work titled "Abortion." In 1966, the abortion procedure was illegal in many states, so doctors and even non–medical professionals performed the technique in secret. The conditions were often unsanitary, and there was little follow–up care. As a result, women who had abortions sometimes bled to death. Hanson's sculpture depicted a dead young woman, visibly pregnant, lying on table and covered with a sheet. The work had been inspired by a spate of recent newspaper stories in south Florida, where he had recently moved, about women who died in this way. When the sculpture was included in a "Sculptors of Florida" show, it caused a sensation. Hanson was praised for bringing the issue to the forefront in such a disturbing manner, but he was also condemned by more conservative critics. Hanson decided to recreate "Abortion" in a life–sized version that he hoped would magnify its impact. However, when he did so he was unhappy with the result and eventually destroyed the larger work.

Shockingly Realistic Commentaries

The success of that first new work finally spurred Hanson's creativity, and he began making extremely realistic sculptures inspired by other news stories. These included a young woman, who had been sexually assaulted and nailed to a tree, and another work that depicted a suicide by hanging. Hanson soon grew dissatisfied with these works as well, finding them too sensationalist even for his own taste, and he destroyed them. He was more satisfied with "War," a gory work from 1967 that marked Hanson's first use of fiberglass, polyester resin, and direct casting from live models. It depicted five Vietnam servicemen—four dead soldiers and the fifth in his own final moments. Hanson also sculpted "Race Riot," "Gangland Victim"—a disfigured corpse that has washed ashore—and "Accident," the last one depicting a young man pinned underneath his motorcycle wreckage. These works, all from the late 1960s, established Hanson's reputation as a serious artist by forcing viewers "to face challenging issues without the psychic distancing inherent to television and newspaper reports," commented a critic for *USA Today*.

The sculptures also created outrage, and two were even banned by a Miami museum, whose director told the media that visitors came to art museums to see "pretty things." Under fire from conservative critics in Florida, Hanson decided that his work might find a more receptive audience elsewhere. He sent some slides to a famous Pop Art dealer in New York, Ivan Karp, who liked Hanson's life–sized, graphic style very much and arranged for "Riot," "Accident," and "Pieta" to be included in a 1969 group show at the Whitney Museum of American Art. The show, titled "Human Concern/Personal Treatment," assembled images from the less savory aspects of humanity as portrayed by artists through the ages. Hanson's work created a sensation and secured his reputation in the larger art community. When Karp urged Hanson to relocate to New York City, the artist did just that. As a result, for a few years in the early 1970s, he worked in a studio on Bleecker Street, at the time located in one of the city's more run–down neighborhoods. The first piece Hanson completed in New York depicted a trio of winos—the neighborhood's predominant citizenry in the 1970s—in "Bowery Derelicts."

After a solo show at the O.K. Harris Gallery in 1970, Hanson began working on a series of sculptures that depicted American stereotypes. These included "Cowboy," "Football Players," and "Baton Twirler," among others. However, Hanson was unhappy with their overall sense of stiffness. That same year, however, he also created "Supermarket Shopper," the first of his works to satirize contemporary American lifestyles. It depicts an overweight woman, clad in too–tight clothes and her hair in curlers, behind a shopping cart loaded with convenience foods. As an essay by Barbara Cavaliere in *Contemporary Artists* explained, Hanson wanted to show "the horror and waste within our contemporary society" with such works, and "Supermarket Shopper" ushered in a new era for him as an artist. In subsequent sculptures like "Tourists" and "Shoppers," he lampooned the complacency of the American lifestyle, and created tableaux in which everyday figures appear grossly satiated by the ease of their lives. As Cavaliere's essay noted, "waste is seen on another plane, that of the ordinary classes of Americans, who, steeped in overabundance, become careless in habits and appearances, lumpy, sloppy and filling themselves with junk to excess."

Hanson would maintain his interest in the average American for the rest of his career. Eventually, he came to consider these portrayals of tourists, manual laborers, and the ordinary citizen as his interpretation of a style that he called "expressionist realism." Such works struck a chord with the public, who quickly recognized the stereotypes that Hanson was depicting. An *American Artist* article described one work, "Shoppers": "The man, already bored, carried a package; the woman's eyes gleamed with the prospect of a bargain." Hanson cast such works from real models, using friends and even people he approached on the street. He began by taking several photographs to uncover their personality, and the casting process started when sections of the subject's body were coated with petroleum jelly. They were then covered in liquid silicone rubber, which sets quickly, and then plaster or fiberglass was added, which helped the mold retain its shape. This rather uncomfortable process included the head and face; when the silicone dried, it was sliced off and then a liquid like polyester resin or polyvinyl was injected into the mold. After that hardened, Hanson then soldered the body parts together, and polychromed the skin in oil. Initially he used wigs for his subjects, but when he began to use vinyl over plastic in the late 1970s, the softer material allowed him to sew real hair onto the scalps. Lifelike eyeballs, teeth, and realistic clothing and accessories added to the overall effect; sometimes Hanson even cajoled his models into donating their own items for the piece.

Created Diverse Body of Work

The involved process meant that just one lifelike figure took Hanson several months to create, and groupings more than a year. Works from the decade included "Tourists" (1970), an older couple burdened by the accessories of travel; the "Executive" (1971) in his overcoat and fedora, slumped over in exhaustion; the very realistic "Businessman," also from 1971, was once placed in the lobby of Wall Street office building, but had to be removed when it became a public nuisance. Reactions to these less humorous pieces spurred Hanson to create works that emitted that same sense of quiet desperation. After some time in West Germany in 1972, the artist showed his first cleaning woman ("Putzfrau," 1972), followed by other works in a similar vein, such as "Old Man Playing Solitaire" (1973), "Woman with Laundry Basket" (1974), "Rita: The Waitress" (1975), and "House Painter" (1977).

Hanson moved back to Florida in 1973, making his home in a suburb of Fort Lauderdale. By now, his household included three children from his first marriage and two by his second wife, Welsa Host. In 1978, the first national exhibition of Hanson's work set attendance records at the Whitney Museum and toured the United States for two years; art–lovers and the curious flocked to see Hanson's lifelike forms. One work, "Photographer," depicted a man kneeling amidst his lenses and equipment in front of another of Hanson's sculptures; gallery viewers always walked around him rather than in front of him.

Vilified as Entertainer, Not Artist

By the 1980s, Hanson had abandoned much of the satire in his work, adopting a more empathetic approach that attempted to show the disappointment and desperation that shadowed people from the bottom rungs of the economic ladder through much of their lives. As Hanson told *Contemporary Artists* in the early 1990s, "The subject matter that I like best deals with the familiar lower and middle class American types of today. To me, the resignation, emptiness and loneliness of their existence captures the true reality of life for these people." A 1993 show at Helander Gallery, Hanson's first in New York since 1984, showed only five male figures, from all walks of life. They included an executive, a security guard, and a cowboy. Reviewer Jerry Saltz, writing in *Art in America*, typified the criticism that some in the art establishment leveled at Hanson's work: "This work is about voyeurism," Saltz chided. "You feel a distinct sense of transgression in looking at it. You gaze fixedly at these solitary men who can't look back at you. This is what feels somehow perverse, and the work bears an odd relationship to pornography in this way."

At other times, Hanson's work was compared to wax–museum entertainment. But others appreciated the special niche that Hanson had created as an art-

Which one is real? Hanson (left) stands next to one of his life–size sculptures.

ist with works that struck a chord with the general public as well. As *National Review* journalist James Gardner wrote in a review of a 1999 retrospective at Whitney Museum of American Art in New York City, "Hanson's world consists of people whom we see everywhere, but who are largely invisible, as if they existed at the very peripheries of our vision," Gardner remarked. He added, "It is Hanson's gift, by bracketing [these people] within the context of art, to reveal them for the first time. Hanson has Tom Wolfe's unerring eye for the details that betray class and status."

If you enjoy the works of Duane Hanson, you might want to check out the following:

The sculptures of Carl Milles, with whom Hanson studied in the 1940s and 1950s.
The works of George Grygo, a German–born artist who introduced Hanson to industrial materials like polyester resin and fiberglass.
The works of sculptor George Segal, an early figure in the Pop Art movement.
The multimedia works of American Pop artist Jeff Koons.

Duane Hanson died of non–Hodgkin's lymphoma in January of 1996. His works have become part of the canon of contemporary American art of the twentieth century. "Hanson took sculpture off its pedestal and removed the boundaries that separated art from life," declared *USA Today* three years after his death. "His intention was to represent a cross–section of American society by focusing on the singularities of individuals." However, the *U.S.A. Today* writer added, "Perhaps the ultimate paradox of Hanson's realism is that his lifelike figures seem incapable of escaping their situations. In the end, the courage with which they seem to endure this fate expresses the dignity and nobility that Hanson found in the common American."

■ Biographical and Critical Sources

BOOKS

Artists: From Michelangelo to Maya Lin, UXL (Detroit), 1995, pp. 174–180.
Bush, Martin H., *Sculptures by Duane Hanson*, Wichita State University, 1986.
Contemporary Artists, fourth edition, edited by Joann Cerrito, St. James Press, 1996, p. 479–481.
Varnedoe, Kirk, *Duane Hanson*, Abrams, 1985.

PERIODICALS

American Artist, January, 1986, review of *Sculptures by Duane Hanson*, pp. 104–105.
Art in America, September–October, 1970, "Presenting Duane Hanson"; January, 1993, Jerry Saltz, "Duane Hanson at Helander," p. 104; October, 1999, Robert Taplin, "Duane Hanson at the Whitney," p. 164.
Art International, "Martin Bush Interviews Duane Hanson," September, 1977.
ARTnews, April, 1978, Ellen Edwards, interview with Duane Hanson, p. 56.
Interview, "Duane Hanson Confounded by Ivan Karp," March, 1978.
National Review, February 8, 1999, James Gardner, "Art: Still Lives," p. 60.
USA Today (Magazine), May, 1999, "Duane Hanson: Artful Master of Super–Realism," p. 36.

■ Obituaries

PERIODICALS

New York Times, January 10, 1996, p. 18.
Time, January 22, 1996, p. 15.*

—*Sketch by Carol Brennan*

Will Hobbs

■ Personal

Born August 22, 1947, in Pittsburgh, PA; son of Gregory J. and Mary (Rhodes) Hobbs; married Jean Loftus (a former teacher and realtor; currently Hobbs's literary agent), December 20, 1972. *Education:* Stanford University, B.A., 1969, M.A., 1971. *Hobbies and other interests:* Hiking in the mountains and canyons, white water rafting, archeology, and natural history.

■ Addresses

Office—5 Sunridge Circle, Durango, CO 81301.

■ Career

Pagosa Springs, CO, and Durango, CO, public schools, taught junior high and senior high reading and English, 1973–89; writer, 1990—.

■ Member

Authors Guild, Society of Children's Book Writers and Illustrators, Phi Beta Kappa.

■ Awards, Honors

Notable Trade Book in the Field of Social Studies, National Council for the Social Studies–Children's Book Council (NCSS–CBC), 1988, and Colorado Blue Spruce Young Adult Book Award, 1992, both for *Changes in Latitudes;* Notable Trade Book in the Field of Social Studies, NCSS–CBC, 1989, Best Books for Young Adults, American Library Association (ALA), 1989, Teachers' Choice citation, International Reading Association, 1990, Regional Book Award, Mountains and Plains Booksellers Association, 1990, all for *Bearstone;* Pick of the Lists, American Booksellers Association (ABA), 1991, Best Books for Young Adults and Best Books for Reluctant Young Adult Readers citations, ALA, 1992, 100 Best Young Adult Books of the Past 25 Years, ALA, 1994, California Young Readers Medal, 1995, and 100 Best Young Adult Books of the Twentieth Century, ALA, 2000, all for *Downriver;* Best Books for Young Adults, ALA, 1993, for *The Big Wander;* Pick of the Lists, ABA, 1993, Best Books for Young Adults, ALA, 1993, Spur Award, Western Writers of America, and Colorado Book Award, all for *Beardance;* Notable Trade Book in the Field of Social Studies, NCSS–CBC, 1995, for *Kokopelli's Flute;* Top 10 Best Books for Young Adults and Quick Picks for Reluctant Young Adult Readers citations, ALA, 1996, Notable Trade Book in the Field of Social Studies, NCSS–CBC, 1996, Spur Award, Western Writers of America, Colorado Book Award, and 100 Best Young Adult Books of the Twentieth Century, ALA, 2000, all for *Far North;* Pick of the Lists, ABA, 1997, and Edgar Allan Poe Award, Mystery Writers of America, 1998, both for *Ghost Canoe;* Pick of the Lists, ABA, 1997, and Colorado Center for the Book Award, 1998, both for *Beardream*; Young Adult Choice selection, International Reading Association, 1998, for *River Thunder*; Best Books for Young Adults and Quick Picks for Reluctant Young Adult Readers, ALA, Pick of the Lists, ABA, and Teachers' Choice, International Reading Association, all 1998, all for *The Maze*; Best Books for Young Adults, ALA, Pick of the Lists, ABA, Quick Picks for Reluctant Readers, ALA, and Notable Children's Trade Book in the Field of Social Studies, NCCS–CBC, all 1999, all for *Jason's Gold*. All of Hobbs's titles have been nominated for various state readers' choice awards.

■ Writings

Changes in Latitudes, Atheneum, 1988.
Bearstone, Atheneum, 1989.
Downriver, Atheneum, 1991.
The Big Wander, Atheneum, 1992.
Beardance, Atheneum, 1993.
Kokopelli's Flute, Simon & Schuster, 1995.
Far North, Morrow, 1996.
Beardream, illustrated by Jill Kastner, Simon & Schuster, 1997.
Ghost Canoe, Morrow, 1997.
River Thunder, Delacorte, 1997.
Howling Hill, illustrated by Jill Kastner, Morrow, 1998.
The Maze, Morrow, 1998.
Jason's Gold, Morrow, 1999.
Down the Yukon, HarperCollins, 2001.

Contributor of articles to periodicals, including *Horn Book, ALAN Review, Journal of Youth Services in Libraries, Journal of Adolescent and Adult Literacy, Book Links, Signal, Voices from the Middle, Voice of Youth Advocates*, and numerous state journals.

■ Adaptations

Hobbs's novels are available in unabridged audiocassette recordings from Recorded Books, Inc., Bantam Doubleday Dell Audio, and Listening Library. *Bearstone* was adapted as a play by Karen Glenn, published in *Scholastic Scope*, January 14, 1994.

■ Sidelights

Author Will Hobbs has a unique way of beginning each day. He winds up a toy pterodactyl and watches it cross his desk. By the time it gets to the other side, he must start writing. That's the deal. For about six hours a day he commits himself to the task of putting something on paper, and, he once explained in an interview for *Authors and Artists for Young Adults (AAYA)*, "I owe at least three books, especially *Beardance*, to that little guy. I might have given up if it hadn't been for my deal with the pterodactyl." Hobbs's wilderness–based novels, which include *Bearstone, Kokopelli's Flute,* and *Far North*, have been well received by both his young adult audience and reviewers alike. He knows this audience very well because he taught reading and English for seventeen years, mostly in Durango, Colorado.

Hobbs's father was an engineer in the Air Force, so the family moved often. Born in Pittsburgh, Pennsylvania, the author was only six months old when the family moved to the Panama Canal Zone. After that, his moves included Virginia, Alaska, California, and Texas. Being close to his three brothers and one sister made the moves easier. They were all involved in scouting, and Hobbs developed a love for nature and the outdoors at an early age. Hobbs explained in his interview that his mother "contributed the gusto to my makeup. She feels that life is best lived as an adventure. At the age of seventy-three she rafted the Grand Canyon." His father introduced him to rivers in Alaska. Hobbs recounted, "Years later he joined me for three trips up the Pine River, where *Bearstone* takes place. It's my idea of heaven on earth, and I'll always be able to find him up there."

Although Hobbs has hiked and backpacked in many regions, it was the Southwest that captured his imagination. He spent two summers during high school and two during college in New Mexico as a guide and camp director at Philmont Scout Ranch. In 1973, with his wife, Jean, he moved to southwestern Colorado. There he enjoys the beauty of the San Juan Mountains and the nearby Weminuche Wilderness, the largest wilderness area in Colorado. Hobbs lives at the edge of Durango, in a wooded area adjoining thousands of acres of public land. From his writing desk in his upstairs office, he looks out at snow–capped mountain peaks. Nieces and nephews come for backpacking trips, river trips, and other explorations of the Southwest. Hobbs and his wife have no pets at present, but from their home they have seen black bears, coyotes, badgers, and bald and golden eagles, and "in late winter, a herd of elk comes out of the forest in the late afternoons and browses in the meadow, digging up the grass under the snow."

Hobbs's 1991 novel tells the story of an reckless, unplanned rafting expedition through the Grand Canyon.

Ventures into Publishing

Hobbs was thirty–three before he started writing novels. It was the summer of 1980. The story was *Bearstone,* and it took six different manuscripts and eight years before it was published. In the *California Reader,* Hobbs noted that the writing of *Bearstone* "fulfilled my dream of setting a story for others to enjoy in the upper Pine River country of the Weminuche Wilderness, one of three favorite places in the geography of my heart." It is in wilderness settings such as this that many of his characters are tested—to push themselves and to learn their limits. Their journeys are often difficult.

School Library Journal contributor George Gleason described *Bearstone* as "far above other coming–of–age stories." *Bearstone* tells the story of a Ute Indian boy from Utah, Cloyd Atcitty, who has been sent by his tribe to a group home in Colorado. When that doesn't work out, he is sent to spend the summer with an old rancher. Angry and hostile, Cloyd distrusts the old man's affection. While exploring the mountains nearby, Cloyd discovers an Indian burial site and a small bearstone. Thus he begins his self–discovery as he renames himself "Lone Bear" and learns how to "live in a good way," as his grandmother has taught him.

Cloyd and the old man, Walter Landis, have dreams. Walter wants to reopen his old gold mine, and Cloyd wants to explore the mountains his ancestors knew. Together they ride up to the high country and grow closer. A bear hunter who is an old friend of Walter's visits their camp, and Cloyd tells the man about a large bear he saw near the Continental Divide. It turns out that the bear is a grizzly, and it is illegal to kill them. However, the hunter does kill the bear as Cloyd tries in vain to shout a warning. Later the hunter lies to the game warden about the circumstances. Cloyd faces the dilemma of whether to tell and get revenge, or keep silent.

Cloyd's story continues in *Beardance,* which Hobbs published in 1993. Cloyd and his old friend, Walter, are riding into the mountains together in search of a lost gold mine when they hear about the sighting of a mother grizzly with three cubs. Because the male grizzly bear killed in *Bearstone* was believed to be the last grizzly in Colorado, Cloyd is overjoyed and wants to find these bears. He meets a wildlife biologist named Ursa, who is also in the mountains searching for the bears, and ultimately risks his life by staying on alone, with winter approaching, in a heroic attempt to save two orphaned grizzly cubs. His people, the Utes, have a tradition of closeness with bears, which helps Cloyd find the strength for this act of bravery by entering the spirit world in which people and bears are relatives. Praising Hobbs's "satisfying conclusion," Merlyn Miller observed in a review for *Voice of Youth Advocates* that *Beardance* "weaves Native American legends with real adventure. Not only is Cloyd connected with his ancestry, but he's focused with courage, determination, and strength."

While, as a first novel, *Bearstone* would be a struggle for its author, its sequel was another story. According to Hobbs, *Beardance* started with the image of the boy denning with bears, but "I began too early in the action. It was only when I threw away my first eight chapters and began with the boy and the old man riding into the mountains, that the story began to click. After that I had to hang onto my hat—the story took off at a gallop."

The character of Cloyd, the protagonist of both *Bearstone* and *Beardance,* is based on a student from a Durango group home whom Jean Hobbs had taught. The old rancher who teaches Cloyd so much about life and forgiveness is also based on someone Hobbs knows. The author had helped this rancher bring in hay, gaining a feel for the ranching life and listening to his stories about the mine that he was going to reopen someday. After *Bearstone* came out, Hobbs was invited to visit Native American students from the home in Durango, who identified with Cloyd. Hobbs wrote in the *California Reader* that it was "a big honor, especially to see how attached they were to [the story]."

In *Beardream* (1997), Hobbs's first picture book, he revisits the relationship between native people and bears. Illustrated by Jill Kastner, this is a companion book to his novels *Bearstone* and *Beardance*. Written for younger readers, *Beardream* describes how a boy called Short Tail awakens an oversleeping grizzly bear from hibernation, and how, in ancient times, the Ute people learned the beardance from the bears. In an author's note at the end of *Beardream*, Hobbs stated: "It is my belief that future generations of the human family will have greater and greater need for the inspiration of native wisdom, which sees humankind not apart from nature, but as a part of nature."

Although *Bearstone* was the first novel Hobbs wrote, it was not his first published novel. *Changes in Latitudes,* written second, was the first to be published, in 1988. The author stated that this story came much more easily for him, after the many revisions of *Bearstone*. Hobbs starts his stories, as he said in his *AAYA* interview, "usually with a single image that I have a strong feeling about." The image in this case came from a photo in *National Geographic* of a sea turtle swimming underwater. Letting his imagination take over, the author wondered what it would be like to swim with the turtles, and he began to find a story in which he could encourage his readers to care about endangered species. What he ended up with is a novel about two kinds of endangered species: the turtles and a family that is on the verge of breaking up. The novel's title is drawn from Jimmy Buffett's song, "Changes in Latitudes, Changes in Attitudes."

"The character I knew right from the first line, better than any I've created before or since, was Travis, the narrator in *Changes in Latitudes,*" Hobbs noted. Travis, the oldest of three kids, is cynical and self–absorbed. At sixteen he attempts to hide himself from his problems by withdrawing into his own "cool" world. On vacation in Mexico with his mother, who has taken the trip without their father,

Travis is only close to his little brother, Teddy. It is through Teddy that Travis becomes interested in the plight of the sea turtles. Nancy Vasilakis, writing in *Horn Book*, applauded Hobbs's talents as he "neatly balances the perilous situation of these ancient lumbering sea creatures against the breakdown of his family." She also commended the author for his "sensitive ear for the language of the young." When Teddy dies trying to rescue some of the turtles, Travis discovers that he can't run away from problems and relationships, and that hurt will, indeed, make you stronger.

Thrilling Adventures

"'October in the mountains,' Al said with a grin. 'You live a whole lot closer to the edge.'" The leader of a group of young people participating in an outdoor program, Al offers his prophetic wisdom at the beginning of Hobbs's third novel, *Downriver*. The idea for this story—which is set in another of the author's favorite places, the Grand Canyon—came from Hobbs's desire to have readers experience one of the great American adventures. Having rowed his raft through the rapids of the Grand Canyon ten times himself, Hobbs knows intimately the dangers and the beauty of the journey. Narrated by Jessie, a fifteen–year–old girl who's been sent away from home, this adventure story takes seven teens down the Grand Canyon where they are tested over and over again. Jessie begins the journey feeling that she has no future: "I could see nothing but the frightening dark tunnel that was my future. I saw no images there, no hopes, only blackness." She and the rest of the group, known as "The Hoods in the Woods," leave their leader behind and take off on their own. Now they're making their own decisions, some good and some bad, and living with the consequences. It is the journey down the river that helps Jessie to find a new life and her way back home as well.

Although *Downriver* takes place in a setting that Hobbs knows well, it was not an easy book to write. It took three drafts, using different narrators each time, before he settled on Jessie. "The first two didn't end up in the story," he commented. "I guess I was auditioning them as narrators, and when their voices didn't prove to be the one to tell the story, I didn't have other roles for them to play." Although his characters are often based on someone he knows, Hobbs describes them as "coming into their own in their interactions with events and other characters in ways I could never have predicted. Sometimes I'm amazed by the depth they insist on." For example, he had created a two–dimensional character sketch of Star, the homeless girl in *Downriver*, before he started writing. When he placed her as Jessie's cabin–mate in the story, he found out more about her, and "she kept fascinating and surprising me throughout the story."

Jessie and her companions are back together in *River Thunder*, published in 1997. In this story Jessie gets a chance to row the entire Colorado River through the Grand Canyon herself. Troy, the powerful personality who emerged as the group's leader in *Downriver*, tries to convince Jessie and the others that he's changed for the better. Unexpectedly high water on the river forces them all to confront their fears and to face the raging rapids of the Colorado together if they are to survive.

Hobbs was fourteen years old in 1962, the same age as Clay Lancaster in *The Big Wander*. "I recognize a kindred spirit in Clay Lancaster. We both have an adventuring outlook, we're both romantics, and goofy things tend to happen to both of us," Hobbs explained. He placed Clay in Glen Canyon in the summer of 1962, the last summer before it was flooded by Lake Powell. To write the story, Hobbs kept an image in his mind of a boy, a burro, and a dog adventuring in a "blank spot on the map," the magnificent canyon country of Utah. Clay and his brother head for the Southwest to look for a missing uncle, but the brother returns home. On his own, with no one to tell him what to do, Clay takes off on a big wander—a journey that leads him to a Navajo family, through remote canyons, and eventually to his uncle. In the process he has adventures escaping the dangers of quicksand, flash floods, and bad guys, and finds time for a little romance. Reviewer Kathleen Beck was quick to praise *The Big Wander*, calling it "a rousing adventure with an appealing hero" in *Voice of Youth Advocates*. *Booklist* critic Chris Sherman similarly hailed the work in a starred review, describing it as "an adventure that most teens would love to experience themselves."

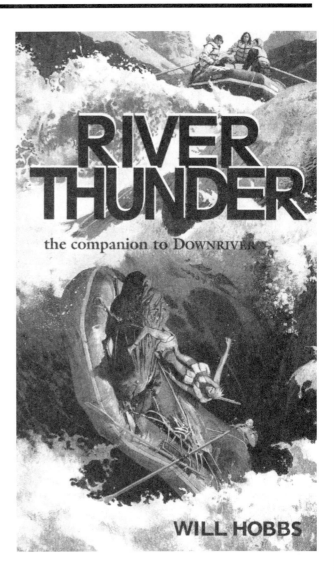

Jessie, the narrator and protagonist of *Downriver*, reunites with her friends and travels the length of the Colorado River.

An Avid Researcher

When Hobbs writes a story, first he reads and reads. He does research about the settings, backgrounds, and historical events that will provide the foundation for his stories. For *The Big Wander* he hiked into his settings, then studied maps, photos, and writings about the canyons and the places "no one knew." In addition to reading, he watched old westerns in the evenings. He knew that he wanted the uncle to be a former rodeo star, which would qualify him as a hero akin to Clay's big–screen heroes from the westerns. However, it was an anti–western, *The Misfits*, that gave him the idea of including the wild horses that Clay's uncle was trying to save.

While Hobbs was doing research for *The Big Wander* he developed ten plot outlines. He knew his character, but he wasn't sure about the problem he wanted him to solve. Each of Hobbs's protagonists has to learn to survive alone, but ultimately is able to achieve personal goals by establishing a strong relationship with someone else. When Hobbs decided that Clay's missing uncle would be involved in saving the wild horses, the author had found the problem he needed. When he added Sarah, who had grown up on a ranch, Hobbs had the necessary members of a team.

According to Hobbs, the novel turned out very differently than he had anticipated. He called it "a song of innocence, with such a whimsical tone and so many comic incidents." Humor is a key ingredient, and the lighthearted tone is set from the first page when Clay and his brother are riding in the noisy old pickup. Hobbs had two former students in mind as an audience as he created the novel. Both were reluctant readers, but Hobbs knew they liked stories that had adventure and humor. Describing his second draft, the author said, "I'd be dreaming about the story as I slept, and wake up reaching for a scratch–pad. I'd find myself writing intuitively, racing, just trying to keep up with my fingers. . . . When I wrote that last chapter, I was Clay Lancaster, and I was galloping down the Escalante on that spotted pony."

In 1995's *Kokopelli's Flute*, the world of dreamlike fantasy enters into Hobbs's Western settings. Thirteen–year–old Tepary Jones and his dog, Dusty, journey to the ruins of an ancient Anasazi cliff house overlooking the austere canyons near his home on a seed farm in New Mexico. Hoping to be able to see a total eclipse of the full moon from this remote location, Tep soon realizes that he is not as alone as he first believed; he surprises looters searching for Anasazi artifacts and chases them away. Picking up an old flute made of eagle bone, which the looters dropped in their hurry to get away, the teen finds himself in the grip of an ancient magic, which transforms him each night into a bushy–tailed woodrat. With the help of Dusty, his loyal golden retriever, Tep is able to track down the pothunters, and also to obtain medicinal herbs from the ancient cliff dwelling which save his mother from the deadly hantavirus. Hobbs "blends fantasy with fact so smoothly that the resulting mix can be consumed without question," wrote Darcy Schild in a review in *School Library Journal*, while in *Voice of Youth Advocates* Nancy Zachary called *Kokopelli's Flute* "an engaging and delightful tale."

Far North (1996) takes readers into the rugged wilderness of Canada's Northwest Territories. Gabe Rogers, almost sixteen and fresh from Texas, has enrolled in a boarding school in Yellowknife in order to be closer to his father, who works on nearby diamond exploration rigs. His roommate, Raymond Providence, a native boy from a remote Dene village, decides to quit school after only a few months, and on a flight home in a small bush plane, both Raymond and Gabe end up stranded on the banks of the Nahanni River. This winter survival story is described by *Horn Book* contributor Mary M. Burns as "a thrill–a–minute account of their struggle, against seemingly impossible odds." The critic added that "this is not just another page–turner; there are deeper issues addressed," such as the differences between the two boys' cultures.

In an author's note at the end of *Far North*, Hobbs describes spending several weeks rafting down the Nahanni River himself, with his wife Jean and one other friend, in the summer of 1993. As they were portaging their raft and canoe around the Nahanni's huge waterfall, twice as high as Niagara, Hobbs began to think about a novel taking place in this setting. He did extensive reading and research after returning home, learning about the history and the people of the Northwest Territories. He also read personal accounts such as R. M. Patterson's book *Dangerous River*, which provided Hobbs with a first-hand account of survival under winter conditions. This research shows in the finished novel; as Diane Tuccillo stated in *Voice of Youth Advocates*, "This classic Hobbs adventure takes readers to a rugged, amazing wilderness few know. Characters are well–drawn, and excitement and energy penetrate their entire trek." The American Library Association named *Far North* one of the Top Ten Young Adult Books of 1996.

Still in the outdoor adventures vein, 1997's *Ghost Canoe* is Hobbs's first mystery novel, and the 1998 winner of the Edgar Allan Poe Award for Best Young Adult Mystery. Set in 1874 along the storm–tossed coast of Washington's Olympic Peninsula, this story follows fourteen–year–old Nathan MacAllister, the son of a lighthouse keeper. When a mysterious shipwreck leaves behind a set of unexplained footprints on the shore, Nathan suspects something is amiss. The ship's captain washes ashore with a stab wound to the heart, and Nathan spies a plume of smoke from a sea cave along the shore, leading Nathan to believe that a mysterious and dangerous stranger is hiding nearby. Writing in *School Library Journal*, Gerry Larson called *Ghost Canoe* "a winning tale that artfully combines history, nature, and suspense."

The novel features rich descriptions of the lifestyle and customs of the Makah, the native people living in this setting. While Nathan attempts to solve the mystery, he forges a close friendship with Lighthouse George, a local fisherman who delivers the mail to Nathan's father at the lighthouse in his handmade canoe, carved from a single cedar log. With George at his side, Nathan learns about everything from canoe building to fishing and whaling, as he participates in the life of the local Makah village. The novel "was inspired by the canoes themselves," Hobbs explained in his author's note. "The great canoes are once again being carved from Western red cedar trees by native people . . . and paddled on the waters of the Pacific. They are a sight to see." The result of this inspiration is an exciting historical mystery–adventure. "What a read!" exclaimed *Booklist* contributor Chris Sherman, adding that "Hobbs really knows how to please his readers." The author attributes this skill to his many years in the classroom, working with students the same age as his young readers.

Although Hobbs has experienced first–hand many of the adventures he writes about, his descriptions of hang gliding in *The Maze* are based on time spent with friends who fly, watching them jump off cliffs and soar. Recalling flying dreams from his childhood, Hobbs knew he wanted his young character to actually fly. "The idea for *The Maze*," he explains in his Author's Note, "came as I trained a spotting scope on a juvenile condor soaring above the majestic Vermilion Cliffs near the Grand Canyon. My wife, Jean, and I were huddled there with three hardy bird biologists on a bitterly cold, windy day in late December 1996. . . . I started thinking about putting fledgling condors together with a 'fledgling boy' in a story." Like Icarus, young Rick Walker would attempt to fly out of his own personal labyrinth, a life of foster homes and dead ends. Hobbs set the story in the Maze, a remote region of Canyonlands National Park in Utah, "for thematic purposes and for its stunning beauty." Todd Morning, in his review in *School Library Journal*, asserted: "What sets this book apart is the inclusion of fascinating details about the condors and hang gliding, especially the action–packed description of Rick's first solo flight above the canyons. . . . Many young readers will find this an adventure story they can't put down." The dedication page reads, "To Derek James, whose luminous cover paintings invite readers into my stories." James is the artist who has done the cover art for eight of Hobbs's novels.

Howling Hill, Hobbs's second picture book, is set in the same rugged country as his novel, *Far North*. Illustrated by Jill Kastner, the story follows a young wolf pup named Hanni who becomes separated from her family. "Hobbs, master of the YA survival story, turns his attention to picture books with this riveting fictionalized account of a lost wolf cub," maintained Julie Corsaro in her review in *Booklist*. "This should have an enormous appeal to Hanni's human counterparts as they venture into larger worlds of school and neighborhood."

Set amid the actual events of the Klondike gold rush of 1897–98, *Jason's Gold* follows young Jason Hawthorn as he races to catch up to his brothers who have taken off for the gold fields in Canada's Yukon. Along the way he meets the not–yet–famous Jack London, but mostly he travels alone, with King, a husky he rescues from a madman. "*Jason's Gold* goes back to my childhood in Alaska in the 1950s—my memories of the winter darkness and the northern lights and rusting gold dredges," Hobbs explains in his Author's Note. As he did in *Far North*, Hobbs creates an action–packed adventure story filled with vivid descriptions of bone–chilling cold, personal courage and friendship.

After he finished writing Jason's Gold, Hobbs couldn't resist heading back up to the Northland to find out what came next for Jason. The result was Down the Yukon. "At the end of the first book," Hobbs explains in the Author's Note to Down the Yukon, "Jamie had promised she'd come back, and there was so much left to explore—not only Jason and Jamie's relationship but the Yukon River itself. Together, the two of them might float clear across Alaska. The historical context, I realized, would be the 1899 rush to Cape Nome, where gold had been discovered in the beaches of the Bering Sea." Jason and Jamie find themselves paddling together in a canoe in a Great Race across Alaska, hoping to win a $20,000 prize so they can buy back the family sawmill. With them is a small black dog named Burnt Paw. Down the Yukon is a compelling tale of adventure, danger, greed, and love—a story so vivid it brings readers straight into the heart of the Gold Rush.

If you enjoy the works of Will Hobbs, you might want to check out the following books:

Robert Barlow Fox, *To Be a Warrior,* 1997.
Meredy Maynard, *Blue True Dream of the Sky,* 1997.
P. J. Petersen, *White Water,* 1997.
Sherry Shahan, *Frozen Stiff,* 1998.

Hobbs advises young writers, "Put the readers in your characters' shoes. Let them smell, hear, see, taste, and touch through your characters' senses." Thus, the fortunate reader who has "seen" the rugged wilderness, "touched" the fur of the cubs, "tasted" the snow as it tumbled down during the avalanche, "heard" the rushing waters in the Grand Canyon, and "smelled" the campfires of Walter and Cloyd, have lived in these worlds. In his article "Teaching a Will Hobbs Novel?" for the *Colorado Reading Council Journal*, Hobbs stated, "I believe that if kids come to care about and identify with the characters in stories, they will also learn more about and ultimately care more about preserving the treasures of our natural world."

■ Biographical and Critical Sources

BOOKS

Gallo, Donald R., editor, *Speaking for Ourselves Too*, National Council of Teachers of English, 1993.

Seventh Book of Junior Authors and Illustrators, Wilson, 1996, pp. 133–35.

Writers for Young Adults, edited by Ted Hipple, Charles Scribner's Sons, 1997, pp. 121–29.

PERIODICALS

ALAN Review, fall, 1994.

Booklist, October 15, 1992, Chris Sherman, review of *The Big Wander*, p. 424; May 1, 1997, Chris Sherman, review of *Ghost Canoe*; September 1, 1997, p. 106; September 1, 1998, Julie Corsaro, review of *Howling Hill*, p. 126.

California Reader, winter, 1992, Will Hobbs, "Living and Writing *Bearstone*," pp. 15–16.

Colorado Reading Council Journal, spring, 1993, Will Hobbs, "Teaching a Will Hobbs Novel?," pp. 7–9.

Horn Book, May–June, 1988, Nancy Vasilakis, review of *Changes in Latitudes*, p. 358; January–February, 1993, p. 91; March–April, 1996; November–December, 1996, Mary M. Burns, review of *Far North*, p. 745.

Journal of Youth Services in Libraries, spring, 1995.

Kirkus Reviews, March 15, 1997, p. 462.

Kliatt, September, 1999, p. 8.

Publishers Weekly, February 12, 1988, p. 88; February 1, 1991, pp. 80–81; November 2, 1992, p. 72.

School Library Journal, March, 1988, pp. 212, 214; September, 1989, George Gleason, review of *Bearstone*, p. 272; March, 1991, p. 212; November, 1992, p. 92; December, 1993, p. 134; October, 1995, Darcy Schild, review of *Kokopelli's Flute*, p. 134; April, 1997, Gerry Larson, review of *Ghost Canoe*; September, 1997, p. 217; October, 1998, Todd Morning, review of *The Maze*, p. 136.

Voice of Youth Advocates, December, 1992, Kathleen Beck, review of *The Big Wander*, p. 279; December, 1993, Merlyn Miller, review of *Beardance*, p. 292; February, 1996, Nancy Zachary, review of *Kokopelli's Flute*, p. 372; February, 1997, Diane Tuccillo, review of *Far North*, p. 328.

ONLINE

Will Hobbs Web site, located at http://www.willhobbsauthor.com.

OTHER

Hobbs, Will, interview with Caroline S. McKinney for *Authors and Artists for Young Adults*, 1995.

Tim LaHaye and Jerry B. Jenkins

Jerry B. Jenkins: *Home*—P.O. Box 88288, Black Forest, CO 80908. *Office*—820 North LaSalle Dr., Chicago, IL 60610.

■ Personal

Tim LaHaye: Born April 27, 1926, in Detroit, MI; son of Francis T. (an electrician) and Margaret (a fellowship director; maiden name, Palmer) LaHaye; married Beverly Jean Ratcliffe (a writer and lecturer), July 5, 1947; children: Linda (Mrs. Gerald Murphy), Larry, Lee, Lori. *Education:* Bob Jones University, B.A., 1950, Western Conservative Baptist Seminary, D.Min., 1977. *Religion:* Baptist. *Hobbies and other interests:* Flying his own twin–engine plane, skiing, football.

Jerry B. Jenkins: Full name Jerry Bruce Jenkins; born September 23, 1949, in Kalamazoo, MI; son of Harry Phillip (a police chief) and Bonita Grace (Thompson) Jenkins; married Dianna Louise Whiteford, January 23, 1971. *Education:* Attended Moody Bible Institute, 1967–68, Loop College, 1968, and William Rainey Harper College, 1968–70. *Politics:* Independent. *Religion:* Jesus Christ. *Hobbies and other interests:* Photography, tournament table tennis, Scrabble club.

■ Addresses

Tim LaHaye: *Home*—2447 Camino Monte Sombra, El Cajon, CA 92021.

■ Career

Tim LaHaye: Pastor of Baptist churches in Pickens, SC, 1948–50, and in Minneapolis, MN, 1950–56; Scott Memorial Baptist church, El Cajon, CA, senior pastor, 1956–81. Host, with wife, of weekly thirty-minute television program *LaHayes on Family Life,* 1982—. President of Christian Heritage College, 1970–76; lecturer for Family Life Seminars, 1972—. *Military service:* U.S. Army Air Forces, 1944–46; became sergeant.

Jerry B. Jenkins: WMBI–FM–AM–Radio, Chicago, IL, night news editor, 1967–68; Day Publications, Mount Prospect, IL, assistant sports editor, 1968–69; Des Plaines Publishing Co., Des Plaines, IL, sports editor, 1969–71; *Tri–City Herald,* Kennewick, WA, sportswriter, 1971; Scripture Press Publications, Wheaton, IL, associate editor, 1971–72, managing editor, 1972–73; Inspirational Radio–Television Guide, Chicago, executive editor, 1973–74; *Moody Monthly* (magazine), Chicago, managing editor, 1974–75, editor, 1975–81, director, 1978–81; Moody Press, Chicago, director, 1981–83; Moody Bible Institute, Chicago, manager of Publishing Division, 1983–85, vice–president of Publishing Branch, 1985—. Visiting lecturer in advanced journalism, Wheaton Graduate School, 1975—.

■ Awards, Honors

Tim LaHaye: D.D. from Bob Jones University, 1962.

Jerry B. Jenkins: Novel of the Year nomination, *Campus Life* magazine, for *Margo;* Biography of the Year Award, *Campus Life* magazine, 1980, for *Home Where I Belong;* Religion in Media Angel Award for *Meaghan* and *Margo's Reunion;* Evangelical Christian Publishers Association Gold Medallion nomination for *The Night the Giant Rolled Over* and *Rekindled: How to Keep the Warmth in Marriage.*

■ Writings

"LEFT BEHIND" SERIES

Left Behind, Tyndale House, 1995.
Tribulation Force, Tyndale House, 1996.
Nicolae, Tyndale House, 1997.
Soul Harvest, Tyndale House, 1998.
Assassins: Assignment—Jerusalem, Target—Antichrist, Tyndale House, 1998.
Apollyon, Tyndale House, 1999.
The Indwelling: The Beast Takes Possession, Tyndale House, 2000.
The Mark: The Beast Rules the World, Tyndale House, 2000.

"LEFT BEHIND: THE KIDS" SERIES

The Vanishings, Tyndale House, 1998.
Second Chance, Tyndale House, 1998.
Through the Flames, Tyndale House, 1998.
Facing the Future, Tyndale House, 1998.
Nicolae High, Tyndale House, 1999.
The Underground, Tyndale House, 1999.
Busted, Tyndale House, 2000.
Death Strike, Tyndale House, 2000.
The Search, Tyndale House, 2000.
On the Run, Tyndale House, 2000.
Into the Storm, Tyndale House, 2000.
Earthquake, Tyndale House, 2000.

NONFICTION FOR ADULTS

Are We Living in the End Times?, Tyndale House, 1999.
Have You Been Left Behind?, Tyndale House, 1999.
Revelation Unveiled, Zondervan, 1999.

BY TIM LAHAYE

Spirit–Controlled Temperaments, Tyndale House, 1966.
How to Be Happy Though Married, Tyndale House, 1968.
Transformed Temperaments, Tyndale House, 1971.
The Beginning of the End, Tyndale House, 1972.
How to Win Over Depression, Zondervan, 1973.
Revelation Illustrated and Made Plain, Zondervan, 1973.
Spirit Controlled Temperament, Tyndale House, 1973.
(With wife, Beverly LaHaye) *The Act of Marriage: The Beauty of Sexual Love,* Zondervan, 1976.
The Bible's Influence on American History, Master Book, 1976.
How to Study the Bible for Yourself, Harvest House, 1976.
The Bible's Influence on American History, Creation–Life, 1976.
Understanding the Male Temperament, Fleming H. Revell, 1977.
Your Temperament Can Be Changed, Tyndale House, 1978.
Six Keys to a Happy Marriage, Tyndale House, 1978.
The Unhappy Gays, Tyndale House, 1978.
(With John D. Morris) *The Ark on Ararat,* Lakeland, 1979.
(With Barbara Trump) *Forgiven Love,* Jeremy Books, 1979.
The Battle for the Mind, Fleming H. Revell, 1980.
The Battle for the Family, Fleming H. Revell, 1981.
(With Bob Phillips) *Anger Is a Choice,* Zondervan, 1982.
The Battle for the Public Schools, Fleming H. Revell, 1982.
The Battle for the Mind Study Guide, Fleming H. Revell, 1983.
How to Manage Pressure, Zondervan, 1983.
(With Beverly LaHaye) *Spirit–Controlled Family Living,* Fleming H. Revell, 1983.
The Hidden Censors, Fleming H. Revell, 1984.
The Coming Peace in the Middle East, Zondervan, 1984.
(With Beverly LaHaye) *Practical Answers to Common Questions about Sex in Marriage,* Zondervan, 1984.
(With Beverly LaHaye) *What Lovemaking Means to a Woman,* Zondervan, 1984.
(With Beverly LaHaye) *What Lovemaking Means to a Man,* Zondervan, 1984.
How to Win Over Depression, Zondervan, 1985.
Sex Education Is for the Family, Zondervan, 1985.
Increase Your Personality Power, Tyndale House, 1986.
(With Beverly LaHaye) *Our Favorite Verse,* Accent Books, 1986.

The Race for the Twenty–First Century, Thomas Nelson, 1986.

Spirit–Controlled Temperament, Walker & Company, 1986.

Faith of Our Founding Fathers, Wolgemunt & Hyatt, 1987.

Life in the Afterlife, Tyndale House, 1987.

Why You Act the Way You Do, Tyndale House, 1988.

Finding the Will of God in a Crazy, Mixed–up World, Zondervan, 1989.

Four Steps to an Intimate Marriage, Tyndale House, 1989.

How to Study Bible Prophecy for Yourself, Harvest House, 1990.

If Ministers Fall, Can They Be Restored?, Zondervan, 1990.

The Beginning of the End, Tyndale House, 1991.

I Love You, But Why Are We So Different?, Harvest House, 1991.

Transforming Your Temperament, Arrowood Press, 1991.

Transformed Temperaments, Tyndale House, 1993.

(With Beverly LaHaye) *A Nation without a Conscience*, Tyndale House, 1994.

No Fear of the Storm, Multnomah, 1994.

(With Beverly LaHaye) *The Spirit–Filled Family*, Harvest House, 1995.

How to Win Over Depression, Zondervan, 1996.

Jesus, Who Is He?, Multnomah, 1997.

(With Beverly LaHaye) *Alike in Love*, New Leaf Press, 1998.

(With Beverly LaHaye) *Family*, New Leaf Press, 1998.

Gathering Lilies from among the Thorns, New Leaf Press, 1998.

(With Beverly LaHaye) *Home and Hearth*, New Leaf Press, 1998.

Opposites Attract, Harvest House, 1998.

Rapture under Attack, Multnomah, 1998.

Transforming Your Temperament, Inspirational Press, 1998.

Understanding the Last Days, Harvest House, 1998.

(With Thomas Ice) *Charting the Future*, Harvest House, 1999.

(With Beverly LaHaye and Mike Yorkey) *The Act of Marriage after 40: Making Love for Life*, Zondervan, 2000.

BY JERRY B. JENKINS

You CAN Get thru to Teens, Victor Books, 1973.

Sammy Tippit: God's Love in Action, Broadman, 1973.

VBS Unlimited, Victor Books, 1974.

(With Hank Aaron and Stan Baldwin) *Bad Henry*, Chilton, 1974.

The Story of the Christian Booksellers Association, Thomas Nelson, 1974.

(With Pat Williams) *The Gingerbread Man: Pat Williams Then and Now*, Lippincott, 1974.

Stuff It: The Story of Dick Motta, Toughest Little Coach in the NBA, Chilton, 1975.

(With Sammy Tippit) *Three Behind the Curtain*, Whitaker House, 1975.

(With Paul Anderson) *The World's Strongest Man*, Victor Books, 1975.

(With Madeline Manning Jackson) *Running for Jesus*, Word, Inc., 1977.

(With Walter Payton) *Sweetness*, Contemporary Books, 1978.

(With Sammy Tippit) *You, Me, He*, Victor Books, 1978.

(With B. J. Thomas) *Home Where I Belong*, Word, Inc., 1978.

Light on the Heavy: A Simple Guide to Understanding Bible Doctrines, Victor Books, 1978.

(With Sammy Tippit) *Reproduced by Permission of the Author*, Victor Books, 1979.

The Luis Palau Story, Fleming H. Revell, 1980.

The Night the Giant Rolled Over, Word, Inc., 1981.

(With Pat Williams) *The Power within You*, Westminster, 1983.

(With Robert Flood) *Teaching the Word, Reaching the World*, Moody, 1985.

(With Pat Williams) *Rekindled: How to Keep the Warmth in Marriage*, Fleming H. Revell, 1985.

A Generous Impulse/The Story of George Sweeting, Moody Press, 1987.

(With Meadowlark Lemon) *Meadowlark*, Thomas Nelson, 1987.

(With Pat and Jill Williams) *Kindling*, Thomas Nelson, 1987.

(With Christine Wyrtzen) *Carry Me*, Moody Press, 1988.

(With Deanna McClary) *Commitment to Love*, Thomas Nelson, 1989.

Hymns for Personal Devotion, Moody Press, 1989.

Twelve Things I Want My Kids to Remember Forever, Moody Press, 1991.

Winning at Losing, Moody Press, 1993.

(With Sammy Tippit) *No Matter What the Cost*, Thomas Nelson, 1993.

Life Flies When You're Having Fun, Victor Books, 1993.

(With Gary and Carol Almy) *Addicted to Recovery*, Harvest House, 1994.

Still the One: Tender Thoughts from a Loving Spouse, Focus on the Family, 1995.

And Then Came You: The Hopes and Dreams of Loving Parents, Focus on the Family, 1996.

(With Brett Butler) *Field of Hope: An Inspiring Autobiography of a Lifetime of Overcoming the Odds*, Thomas Nelson, 1997.

(With Bill Gaither) *Homecoming: The Story of Southern Gospel Music through the Eyes of Its Best–Loved Performers*, Zondervan, 1997.

(With Rev. Bill Graham) *Just As I Am*, HarperCollins/Zondervan, 1997.

FICTION FOR ADULTS; BY JERRY B. JENKINS

The Operative, Harper & Row, 1987.

The Deacon's Woman (short stories), Moody Press, 1992.

'Twas the Night Before, Viking, 1998.

Though None Go with Me, Zondervan, 2000.

FICTION FOR CHILDREN; BY JERRY B. JENKINS

Rookie, Multnomah Books, 1997.

"GLOBAL AIR TROUBLESHOOTERS" SERIES; BY JERRY B. JENKINS

Crash at Cannibal Valley, Multnomah Books, 1996.

Terror in Branco Grande, Multnomah Books, 1996.

Disaster in the Yukon, Multnomah Books, 1996.

"MARGO MYSTERY" SERIES; BY JERRY B. JENKINS

Margo, Jeremy Books, 1979.

Karlyn, Moody Press, 1980.

Hilary, Moody Press, 1980.

Paige, Moody Press, 1981.

Allyson, Moody Press, 1981.

Erin, Moody Press, 1982.

Shannon, Moody Press, 1982.

Lindsey, Moody Press, 1983.

Meaghan, Moody Press, 1983.

Janell, Moody Press, 1983.

Courtney, Moody Press, 1983.

Lyssa, Moody Press, 1984.

Margo's Reunion, Moody Press, 1984.

"JENNIFER GREY MYSTERY" SERIES; BY JERRY B. JENKINS

Heartbeat, Victor Books, 1983.

Three Days in Winter, Victor Books, 1983.

Too Late to Tell, Victor Books, 1983.

Gateway, Victor Books, 1983.

The Calling, Victor Books, 1984.

Veiled Threat, Victor Books, 1984.

"THE BRADFORD FAMILY ADVENTURE" SERIES; BY JERRY B. JENKINS

Daniel's Big Surprise, Standard Publishing, 1984.

Two Runaways, Standard Publishing, 1984.

The Clubhouse Mystery, Standard Publishing, 1984.

The Kidnapping, Standard Publishing, 1984.

Marty's Secret, Standard Publishing, 1985.

Blizzard!, Standard Publishing, 1985.

Fourteen Days to Midnight, Standard Publishing, 1985.

Good Sport/Bad Sport, Standard Publishing, 1985.

In Deep Water, Standard Publishing, 1986.

Mystery at Raider Stadium, Standard Publishing, 1986.

Daniel's Big Decision, Standard Publishing, 1986.

Before the Judge, Standard Publishing, 1986.

"DALLAS O'NEIL AND THE BAKER STREET SPORTS CLUB" SERIES; BY JERRY B. JENKINS

The Secret Baseball Challenge, Moody Press, 1986.

The Scary Basketball Player, Moody Press, 1986.

The Mysterious Football Team, Moody Press, 1986.

The Weird Soccer Match, Moody Press, 1986.

The Strange Swimming Coach, Moody Press, 1986.

The Bizarre Hockey Tournament, Moody Press, 1986.

The Silent Track Star, Moody Press, 1986.

The Angry Gymnast, Moody Press, 1986.

DALLAS O'NEIL MYSTERIES; BY JERRY B. JENKINS

Mystery of the Kidnapped Kid, Moody Press, 1988.

Mystery of the Mixed–Up Teacher, Moody Press, 1988.

Mystery of the Missing Sister, Moody Press, 1988

Mystery of the Scorpion Threat, Moody Press, 1988.

Mystery on the Midway, Moody Press, 1989.

Mystery of the Golden Palamino, Moody Press, 1989.

Mystery of the Skinny Sophomore, Moody Press, 1989.

Mystery of the Phony Murder, Moody Press, 1989.

"TOBY ANDRES AND THE JUNIOR DEPUTIES" SERIES; BY JERRY B. JENKINS

The House of Tunnels, Moody Press, 1996.

The Man With the Terrible Secret, Moody Press, 1996.

The East Side Bullies, Moody Press, 1996.

The Neighborhood's Scariest Woman, Moody Press, 1996.

"TARA CHADWICK" SERIES; BY JERRY B. JENKINS

Springtime Discovery, Moody Press, 1990.
Time to Tell, Moody Press, 1990.
Operation Cemetery, Moody Press, 1990.
Scattered Flowers, Moody Press, 1990.

OTHER

Jenkins is also a contributor to periodicals, including *Reader's Digest, Parade, Moody Monthly, Power, Contact, Coronet, Saturday Evening Post,* and *Campus Life.*

■ Adaptations

Left Behind has been adapted as a film that was released as a video in 2000.

■ Sidelights

No event in recent history has sparked media hype or captured public attention the way the turn–of–the–Millennium did. In addition to the countless hours of television and radio programming devoted to the subject, all of the newspaper and magazine articles, and the mass uncertainty sparked by the dreaded Y2K "computer bug," publishers unleashed what *Publishers Weekly* described as a "tsunami" (a Japanese term for a tidal wave) of books with religious themes. Many of these books deal with the end of the world, a scenario forecast by some Christian fundamentalists who interpret the Scriptures literally. Several of these doomsday books became best sellers, none more so than the "Left Behind" novels, which have deftly turned Biblical prophecies about the Second Coming of Jesus Christ into mass market literary entertainment. Despite the fact they include none of the sexual content, nudity, or blasphemy that is a staple of so much contemporary mass–market fiction, sales of the "Left Behind" books have rivaled those of such superstar authors as Stephen King and John Grisholm.

With eight novels already in print and another four scheduled to be published in the next two years, the series' total sales have exceeded ten million copies, and the "Left Behind" Web site reportedly receives more than twenty–five thousand hits per day. "This may not be the apocalypse, but it's certainly publishing history," J. C. Furnas observed in a recent article in the journal *American Scholar.*

In the first volume of the "Left Behind: The Kids" series, Judd, Vicki, Lionel, and Ryan face the prospect of an Apocalyptic future together.

The "Left Behind" series is the brainchild of two men: the team of Jerry B. Jenkins, a successful evangelical Christian author who also does the writing for the syndicated comic strip "Gil Thorp," and Reverend Tim LaHaye, a retired Southern Baptist minister, author, and broadcaster. LaHaye first had the idea for a novel about the apocalypse back in 1981, but he is not a fiction writer. Until he met Jenkins, LaHaye had never found the right person to team with him on the project. A literary agent introduced the pair in 1992, and they immediately became friends. Soon they also agreed to become literary collaborators. California–based LaHaye creates the plots for the "Left Behind" novels based on biblical texts. He then sends his outlines to Jenkins, who lives in Colorado. Jenkins works ten hours per day until he produces a first draft of each book, which he gives to LaHaye for further work and to ensure that the plot's theological underpinnings are consistent with biblical prophecies outlined in the book of Revelations. Although LaHaye is Jenkins' senior by twenty–three years, the two men seem to be in perfect sync, and their system works to perfection. "It's like a father–son thing," Jenkins told *People Weekly* reporter Thomas Fields–Meter in a 1998 interview.

The third volume of the "Left Behind: The Kids" series continues the adventures of the four friends.

Michigan–born Authors

Tim LaHaye was born in Detroit, Michigan, in 1926. His father, who was an electrician, died of a heart attack when his son was just nine. It was the midst of the Great Depression, and times were tough. La-Haye's mother took a job in a Ford auto factory to support her three children. LaHaye worked to help put himself through school, and it was while doing a stint as a lifeguard at a Christian summer camp that he decided to become a preacher. With that in mind, LaHaye enrolled at Bob Jones University in Greensville, South Carolina. There he met and fell in love with fellow student Beverly Davenport, whom he married in 1947. Following his graduation from Bob Jones three years later with a bachelor of arts degree, LaHaye served a Baptist congregation in Minneapolis, Minnesota. He stayed for six years before moving on to Scott Memorial Church in San Diego, California. In addition to his duties as a preacher, LaHaye helped to start a small Christian college at nearby El Cajon, California, and also supported his wife, Beverly, in her work as the host of a syndicated Christian radio talk show and founder of a conservative public policy lobby group known as Concerned Women for America.

LaHaye, who has always loved words and now has more than forty books to his credit, wrote his first work in 1966. Over the course of the next ten years, he produced five more inspirational "self–help" books, which are based on aspects of his work as a preacher. In 1976, LaHaye teamed up with his wife on a self–help marriage guide called *The Act of Marriage*. LaHaye enjoyed that initial experience of working with another person on a book; in the years since, he has done so repeatedly, co–authoring fifteen nonfiction books (twelve of them with his wife), in addition to the "Left Behind" novels that he and Jenkins have done together. LaHaye left the pulpit in 1981 to devote himself full time to writing and promoting his own political beliefs.

LaHaye's "Left Behind" writing partner comes from a somewhat more secular background, but one thing that the two men have in common is the strength of their evangelical beliefs; religion has always played a pivotal role in the life of Jenkins. Born in 1949 in Kalamazoo, MI, and the son of a police chief, Jenkins attended Moody Bible Institute in Chicago, Illinois, Loop College, and William Rainey Harper College. During his student days, he worked part time as the night news editor at a Chicago radio station and as a sports reporter and editor, first in Des Plaines, Illinois, and then, after graduating, in Kennewick, Washington. In late 1971, Jenkins took a job as an editor with the religious publisher Scripture Press Publications in Wheaton, Illinois. In the years since, he has held a variety of jobs with the

In this 1998 novel, Judd, Vicki, Lionel, and Ryan learn the story of the Antichrist through the eyes of someone who has met him personally.

Chicago–based Moody Press (owned by the Moody Bible Institute), including vice–president for publishing and his current writer–at–large position.

Jenkins wrote his first book in 1973. It is a self–help guide for parents entitled *You CAN Get thru to Teens*. Once he began writing, there was no stopping him. The prolific Jenkins' literary output has been astounding. He wrote nine books in the three years 1973–75, and today the Jenkins bibliography includes more than one hundred and thirty titles. He has primarily written in four genres: biography, marriage and family self–help, children's fiction,

and adult fiction. Among Jenkins' most successful efforts have been "as–told–to" autobiographies of star baseball players Orel Hershiser and Nolan Ryan, and his collaboration with Billy Graham on the evangelist's 1997 memoirs, *Just As I Am*. All three books made the *New York Times* bestseller list. Despite this, until he and LaHaye teamed up on the "Left Behind" series, Jenkins remained relatively unknown. In an informational blurb that appears on his Web site, the self–effacing author jokingly refers to himself as the "most famous writer no one's ever heard of." While that statement may once have been true, it isn't any more, despite Jenkins' claims to the contrary. The phenomenal success of the "Left Behind" books has changed all that forever.

"This is out of our control," the marketing director for Tyndale House Publishers proclaimed in a March 1999 interview with reporter Stephen Rabey in *Christianity Today*. "We aren't engineering all of this success. It's God really using it in a mighty way." LaHaye expressed a similar notion when he explained what has motivated him and Jenkins to continue the series. "We are using fiction to teach biblical truth," he told Rabey.

Jenkins has also highlighted a couple of other key factors, which he says have contributed to the success of the first eight "Left Behind" books: their simplicity and their strong story lines. "I'm not smart enough to write a book that's hard to read," Jenkins said in a recent conversation with an interviewer for *Amazon.com*. "I have mentor/teacher–type characters in each book who explain what's going on." Jenkins went on to outline what he says are the three guiding principles of good fiction writing: "appealing characters, a sense of tension and expectancy, and a page–turning quality." Millions of readers apparently agree, for they have made the "Left Behind" books "the most successful Christian fiction series ever," as Thomas Field–Meyer reported in *People Weekly*.

Plot Straight Out of the Scriptures

In his *Amazon.com* interview, Jenkins explained that the "Left Behind" books' complex and at times fantastic story lines spring from a detailed apocalyptic chronology that LaHaye has devised. He created it by drawing upon a lifetime of experiences preaching and studying the Bible. "The prophecy [of the Second Coming] is laid out in Scripture, so astute students know roughly where we're going," Jenkins said. "But as for the fiction, I have only vague ideas and am often surprised."

The friends are involved in printing and distributing an underground newspaper in this sixth volume of the "Left Behind: The Kids" series.

It took Jenkins and LaHaye three years to plan and write the first book in what has become their signature creation. *Left Behind*, the flagship novel from which the series draws its name, was published in November 1995. That book opens the authors' epic story in memorable fashion. It's the wee hours of the morning, and Captain Rayford Steele, the handsome, middle–aged pilot of a Boeing 747 airliner flying over the Atlantic en route to London, is in the cockpit of his plane. Sitting there in the dark, he's reveling in adulterous thoughts about his "drop–dead gorgeous" senior flight attendant, Hattie Durham. Steele has grown impatient with his own beautiful wife, Irene, who has become a born–again Christian. "Rayford tried to tell himself it was his wife's devotion to a divine suitor that caused his mind to wander. But he knew the real reason was his own libido," Jenkins writes.

The pilot's amorous reveries are interrupted by a breathless Hattie, who reports that dozens of passengers have disappeared from the airplane; these people are gone, having evaporated into thin air, leaving behind on their seats piles of their clothing and articles of personal property and valuables, including eyeglasses, hearing aids, jewelry, and other items. A stunned Captain Steele promptly turns the airliner around and returns home to Chicago. There he learns that his wife and son, Raymie, a born–again Christian like his mother, have also disappeared from the family's suburban home. Steele and his nineteen–year–old daughter, Chloe, a skeptic where religion is concerned, then set out to solve the mystery of what has happened to Irene and Ramie Steele. A visit to the church where the pair worshiped provides Rayford and Chloe with the shocking answer to their question.

The pastor of the church, a man named Bruce Barnes, explains that Jesus Christ has come again, and that he has led all true believers off to Heaven. Everyone else—including the pastor himself, whose own faith in Jesus has at times wavered—has been left behind in "the Rapture." However, all is not lost, yet. Barnes tells Rayford that it's not too late to convert or to become a "true believer" who will be saved from eternal damnation in the second, and final, Rapture. Steele, his daughter, and the pastor become born–again Christians, of course, and they then set out to spread their message and take up the battle against the emerging legions of evil, who are also on the march.

The disappearance of millions of people has left the wicked world in utter chaos. As governments and other man–made institutions begin to crumble, an obscure Romanian politician named Nicolae Carpathia—proclaimed to be the "sexiest man alive" by *People* magazine—steps into the void. The charismatic Carpathia, who it turns out is really the Antichrist and is supported by a shadowy cabal of international financiers, becomes the leader of the world by preaching a seductive internationalist message that touts disarmament, a one–world currency, and an all–powerful United Nations.

As the *Left Behind* plot thickens, a crack news magazine journalist named Cameron "Buck" Williams begins to investigate the Rapture. Williams, who chanced to be a passenger on the fateful flight when those passengers began to disappear, befriends Rayford, Chloe, and Pastor Barnes. Williams also converts, but he inadvertently adds to the world's troubles when he introduces Hattie Durham to Carpathia. The flight attendant falls for the Romanian demagogue's utopian message and soon becomes his personal assistant and his lover. The *Left Behind* saga moves on from there. The subsequent novels in the series chronicle the adventures of Rayford, Buck, and their Tribulation Force, what reviewer John D. Spalding described in *Christian Century* as a "little group . . . a sort of Green Berets" of believers as they battle Carpathia. The story will culminate in the inevitable apocalyptic battle between the forces of good and evil.

Surprising Success

Following the unexpected success of *Left Behind*, seven subsequent books in the series have been published. A feature film directed by Victor Sarin was released on video in the fall of 2000, and four more novels are in the works. The "Left Behind" series has become one of the real commercial success stories of Christian publishing. The authors reportedly have earned an estimated five million dollars so far. Jenkins devotes twenty per cent of his earnings to Christian charities, while LaHaye is using his share of the money to publish in several languages a book he has written about the life of Jesus Christ.

Despite the "Left Behind" series' remarkable popularity and commercial success, it has received surprisingly little attention in the mainstream media. Those reviews that have appeared have tended to be skeptical and less than enthusiastic in their assessments. Reviewer Douglas E. Winter commented in the *Washington Post Book World*, "The novels are a competent but stodgily written blend of B–movie science fantasy and horror with the tenets of pre–millennial dispensationalism. . . . Although this is not great fiction, it is effective evangelism, using fear as its paramount means of persuasion." Reviewing *Left Behind*, Melissa Hudak wrote in *Library Journal* that the novel "is riddled with cardboard characterization and creaky dialog." In a January 2000 *Atlantic Monthly* feature article that attempted to explain the popularity of the "Left Behind" phenomenon, Michael Joseph Gross wrote, "Jenkins and LaHaye have done a masterful job of using conservative Christian media networks to purvey their message, build their image, and make their fortune." *Booklist* reviewer Ray Olsen stated that the "Left Behind" novels, like other "conservative Christian controversialist literature," are marred by what he termed "errors of factual detail," "failures of logic," and "ranting when neither data nor logic supports a position."

Not all reviewers—and certainly not the book–buying public—agreed. Reviews of the "Left Behind" series that have appeared in dispassionate scholarly journals and the conservative or religious–oriented media often have been more sympathetic. An example of the former is J. C. Furnas, who, writing in *American Scholar*, allowed, "I found *Left Behind* rattling good reading, professionally terse yet fluid, a real page turner." An example of the latter is John D. Spalding, who opined in *Christian Century*, "Though full of diatribes and unflattering portrayals of women, liberals, Jews, Californians and the media, *Left Behind* is suspenseful and surprisingly well–written. . . . [It] leaves readers waiting for a sequel." *National Review* critic Mathew Scully praised Jenkins' "gift for plot and dialogue" and noted that "if you take the story on its own terms, it's a page turner."

Even more neglected by reviewers is the success of the junior "Left Behind" series—a dozen books so far that parallels the plot of the adult version. The junior series follows the adventures of four young people as they battle the forces of the Antichrist that invade their high school.

In addition to these books, both LaHaye and Jenkins have continued to write works on their own. LaHaye has published more than a dozen new inspirational self–help books, both on his own and in collaboration with his wife and other writing partners. Meanwhile, the energetic Jenkins has somehow managed to find time and energy to continue to write the syndicated *Gil Thorpe* comic strip for Tribune Media Services, as well as other novels such as the young adults baseball story called *The Rookie*, the Christmas romantic fantasy *'Twas the Night Before*, and a planned new fictional series that begins with a book called *Though None Go with Me*.

If you enjoy the works of Tim LaHaye and Jerry B. Jenkins, you might want to check out the following books:

Jonathan R. Cash and Jonathan M. Cash, *The Age of the Antichrist*, 1999.
Bill Myers, *Blood of Heaven*, 1996.
Frank E. Peretti, *The Visitation*, 1999.

Regardless of what else Jenkins and LaHaye may write, their names have been inseparably linked as the co–authors of the "Left Behind" series, which if all goes as planned will not conclude until 2003. The large and devoted readership the series enjoys provides the authors with a forum few other writers of Christian fiction enjoy. The rewards that this brings the two men are as huge as the responsibility they now bear. "I feel the pressure . . . of writing for a waiting audience," Jenkins said in his interview with Amazon.com. "It's intimidating to know that you can write a bad book and it will sell more than a million [copies]." Speaking with Thomas Fields–Meyer in *People Weekly*, LaHaye said, "I feel humble that God has given us a vehicle to affect the minds of other people."

■ Biographical and Critical Sources

PERIODICALS

American Scholar, winter, 2000, J. C. Furnas, "Millennial Sideshow," p. 87.

Atlantic Monthly, January, 2000, Michael Joseph Gross, "The Trials of the Tribulations," p. 122.

Booklist, October 15, 1994, Ray Olsen, "Nation without a Conscience," p. 376; November 1, 1995, p. 455; October 1, 1996, p. 304; March 1, 1997, p. 1111; July, 1997, p. 1775; June 1, 1998, p. 1669; October 15, 1998, p. 374; February 1, 1999, p. 940; January 1, 2000, p. 874; February 15, 2000, p. 1128.

Christian Century, May 22, 1996, John D. Spalding, review of *Left Behind*, pp. 587–591.

Christian Science Monitor, November 25, 1996, p. 12.

Christianity Today, March 24, 1982, p. 348; May 7, 1982, pp. 60–61; February 17, 1984, p. 48; September 7, 1984, pp. 56–61; October 5, 1984, pp. 54–59; December 14, 1984, p. 57; January 13, 1985, p. 65; January 17, 1986, pp. 40–42; September 1, 1997, pp. 22–27; March 1, 1999, Stephen Rabey, "Apocalyptic Sales Out of this World," p. 19.

Electronic News, November 28, 1994, pp. 34–35.

English Journal, January, 1985, pp. 26–34.

Humanist, March–April, 1981, pp. 7, 50; July–August, 1981, pp. 13–14.

Kirkus Reviews, September 15, 1998, p. 1330.

Library Journal, June 1, 1998, p. 94; November 1, 1998, p. 127; May 15, 1999, Melissa Hudak, review of *Left Behind*, p. 147; September 1, 1999, p. 172; December, 2000, review of *The Act of Marriage after 40: Making Love for Life*, p. 164.

Magazine of Fantasy and Science Fiction, February, 1999, p. 35.

Mother Jones, January, 1986, pp. 14–19; July–August, 1986, pp. 46–57.

Nation, August 22, 1981, pp. 149–150; July 9, 1983, pp. 51–52.

National Review, December 21, 1998, Mathew Scully, "Apocalypse Soon," p. 62.

New York Review of Books, October 12, 1989, pp. 49–54.

Newsweek, July 6, 1981, pp. 48–49.

People Weekly, December 14, 1998, Thomas Fields–Meyer, "In Heaven's Name," p. 139.

Present Tense, winter, 1985, pp. 22–30.

Publishers Weekly, June 7, 1991, p. 46; September 14, 1998, p. 50; July 26, 1999, p. 82; November 15, 1999, p. 56; September 18, 2000, "'Left Behind' Is Not," p. 24.

School Library Journal, September, 1982, p. 140; May, 1983, p. 94.

Voice of Youth Advocates, April, 1994, p. 56.

Washington Post Book World, September 12, 1999, Douglas E. Winter, review of *Left Behind* and *Assassins*, p. 9.

West Coast Review of Books, May, 1985, p. 58.

ONLINE

Amazon.com, http://www.amazon.com (May 22, 2000).

Jerry Jenkins Web site, http://www.jerryjenkins.com (October 3, 2000).

"Left Behind" series Web site, http://www.leftbehind.com (October 3, 2000).

Tim LaHaye Web site, http://www.timlahaye.com (October 3, 2000).*

—*Sketch by Ken Cuthbertson*

C. S. Lewis

■ Personal

Full name Clive Staples Lewis; also wrote as Clive Hamilton and N. W. Clerk; born November 29, 1898, in Belfast, Ireland; died November 22, 1963, in Oxford, England, of heart failure after an extended illness; son of Albert James (a solicitor) and Flora Augusta (a mathematician; maiden name, Hamilton) Lewis; married Joy Davidman Gresham (a poet and novelist), 1956 (died, 1960); stepchildren: David Gresham, Douglas Gresham. *Education:* Attended Malvern College, 1913–14; University College, Oxford, A.B. (classics; first class honors), 1922, A.B. (English; first class honors), 1923. *Religion:* Anglican. *Hobbies and other interests:* Walking.

■ Career

University College, Oxford University, Oxford, England, philosophy tutor and lecturer, 1924; Magdalen College, Oxford University, fellow and tutor in English literature, 1925–54; Magdalene College, Cambridge University, Cambridge, England, professor of Medieval and Renaissance English, 1954–63. Ballard Matthews Lecturer, University of Wales, 1941; Riddell Lecturer, University of Durham, 1942; Clark Lecturer, Trinity College, Cambridge, 1944. *Military service:* British Army, Somerset Light Infantry, 1917–18; became second lieutenant. *Member:* British Academy (fellow), Royal Society of Literature (fellow), Athenaeum, Sir Walter Scott Society (president, 1956), Socratic Club (president and speaker), Inklings, British Academy (fellow), University College (fellow), Magdalen College (honorary fellow).

■ Awards, Honors

Hawthornden Prize, 1936, and Gollancz Memorial Prize for Literature, 1937, both for *The Allegory of Love*; D.D., University of St. Andrews, 1946; Docteur–es–Lettres, Laval University, 1952; Carnegie Medal Commendation, British Library Association, 1955, for *The Horse and His Boy*; Carnegie Medal, 1957, for *The Last Battle*; D.Litt., University of Manchester, 1959; Lewis Carroll Shelf Award, 1962, for *The Lion, the Witch, and the Wardrobe*; honorary doctorate, University of Dijon, 1962, and University of Lyon, 1963.

■ Writings

"CHRONICLES OF NARNIA" SERIES FOR CHILDREN; ILLUSTRATED BY PAULINE BAYNES

The Lion, the Witch, and the Wardrobe: A Story for Children, Macmillan, 1950.

Prince Caspian: The Return to Narnia, Macmillan, 1951.

The Voyage of the "Dawn Treader," Macmillan, 1952.

The Silver Chair, Macmillan, 1953.

The Horse and His Boy, Macmillan, 1954.

The Magician's Nephew, Macmillan, 1955.

The Last Battle, Macmillan, 1956.

The Complete Chronicles of Narnia, seven volumes, Penguin, 1965, published as *The Chronicles of Narnia,* Macmillan, 1983.

"SPACE" TRILOGY; SCIENCE FICTION NOVELS

Out of the Silent Planet, John Lane, 1938, Macmillan, 1943, abridged edition, Macmillan, 1973.

Perelandra, John Lane, 1943, Macmillan, 1944, new edition published as *Voyage to Venus,* Pan Books, 1960.

That Hideous Strength: A Modern Fairy–Tale for Grown-ups, John Lane, 1945, Macmillan, 1946, abridged edition published as *The Tortured Planet,* Avon, 1958.

Space Trilogy (boxed set), Macmillan, 1975.

NOVELS; FOR ADULTS

The Pilgrim's Regress: An Allegorical Apology for Christianity, Reason and Romanticism, Dent, 1933, Sheed & Ward, 1935, revised edition, Fount, 1977.

The Screwtape Letters (first published in *Guardian,* 1941), Bles, 1942, Macmillan, 1943, revised edition published as *The Screwtape Letters and Screwtape Proposes a Toast,* Bles, 1961, Macmillan, 1962.

The Great Divorce: A Dream (first published in weekly installments in *Guardian*), Bles, 1945.

Till We Have Faces: A Myth Retold, Bles, 1956, Harcourt, 1957.

RELIGIOUS WORKS

The Problem of Pain, Centenary Press, 1940, Macmillan, 1943.

The Weight of Glory, S.P.C.K., 1942, revised and expanded edition, Macmillan, 1980.

Broadcast Talks: Right and Wrong; A Clue to the Meaning of the Universe and What Christians Believe, Bles, 1942, published as *The Case for Christianity,* Macmillan, 1943.

Christian Behaviour: A Further Series of Broadcast Talks, Macmillan, 1943.

Beyond Personality: The Christian Idea of God, Bles, 1944, Macmillan, 1945.

(Editor and author of preface) *George MacDonald: An Anthology,* Centenary Press, 1945, Macmillan, 1947, published as *George MacDonald: 365 Readings,* Collier, 1986.

Miracles: A Preliminary Study, Macmillan, 1947.

The Trouble with X, The Church Union, Church Literature Association, 1948.

Reflections on the Psalms, Harcourt, 1958, Phoenix Press, 1985.

Shall We Lose God in Outer Space?, S.P.C.K., 1959.

The Four Loves, Harcourt, 1960, Collins, 1987.

The Humanitarian Theory of Punishment, Abingdon, 1972.

LITERARY CRITICISM

The Allegory of Love: A Study in Medieval Tradition, Oxford University Press, 1936.

(With Eustace M. W. Tillyard) *The Personal Heresy: A Controversy,* Oxford University Press, 1939.

Rehabilitations and Other Essays, Oxford University Press, 1939.

A Preface to "Paradise Lost": Being the Ballard Matthews Lectures, Delivered at University College, North Wales, 1941, Oxford University Press, 1942, revised edition, 1960.

Hamlet: The Prince or the Poem? (lecture), H. Milford, 1942.

(Editor and author of commentary) Charles Williams, *Arthurian Torso: Containing the Posthumous Fragment of "The Figure of Arthur,"* Oxford University Press, 1948, Eerdmans, 1974.

The Literary Impact of the Authorized Version: The Ethel M. Wood Lecture Delivered before the University of London on 20th March, 1950, Athlone Press, 1950, Fortress Press, 1963, revised edition, 1967.

Hero and Leander (lecture), Oxford University Press, 1952.

English Literature in the Sixteenth Century, Excluding Drama, Clarendon Press, 1954, published as *Poetry and Prose in the Sixteenth Century,* 1990.

De Descriptione Temporum: An Inaugural Lecture, Cambridge University Press, 1955.

Studies in Words, Cambridge University Press, 1960, second edition, 1967.

An Experiment in Criticism, Cambridge University Press, 1961.

They Asked for a Paper: Papers and Addresses, Bles, 1962.

The Discarded Image: An Introduction to Medieval and Renaissance Literature, Cambridge University Press, 1964.

Studies in Medieval and Renaissance Literature, edited by Walter Hooper, Cambridge University Press, 1967.

Spenser's Images of Life, edited by Alastair Fowler, Cambridge University Press, 1967.

Shelley, Dryden, and Mr. Eliot in Rehabilitations, Richard West, 1973.

LETTERS

Beyond the Bright Blur, Harcourt, 1963.

Letters to Malcolm: Chiefly on Prayer, Harcourt, 1964.

Letters of C. S. Lewis, edited by brother, W. H. Lewis, Harcourt, 1966.

Letters to an American Lady, edited by Clyde S. Kilby, Eerdmans, 1967.

Mark vs. Tristram: Correspondence between C. S. Lewis and Owen Barfield, edited by Walter Hooper, Lowell House Printers, 1967.

They Stand Together: The Letters of C. S. Lewis to Arthur Greeves (1914–1963), edited by Walter Hooper, Macmillan, 1979.

Letters to Children, edited by Lyle W. Dorsett and Marjorie Lamp Mead, foreword by Douglas H. Gresham, Macmillan, 1985.

Letters: C. S. Lewis and Don Giovanni Calabria, Servant (Ann Arbor, MI), 1988.

C. S. Lewis Letters: A Study in Friendship, translation from the Latin by Martin Moynihan, Servant, 1988.

The Latin Letters of C. S. Lewis, edited by Don G. Calabria, St. Augustine's Press, 1998.

POETRY

(Under pseudonym Clive Hamilton) *Spirits in Bondage: A Cycle of Lyrics,* Heinemann, 1919, published under name C. S. Lewis, Harcourt, 1984.

(Under pseudonym Clive Hamilton) *Dymer,* Macmillan, 1926.

Poems, edited by Walter Hooper, Bles, 1964, Harcourt, 1965.

Narrative Poems, edited by Walter Hooper, Bles, 1969, Harcourt, 1972.

COLLECTED AND SELECTED WORKS

Rehabilitations, 1939, published as *Rehabilitations and Other Essays,* Folcroft, 1980.

The Weight of Glory, and Other Addresses, Macmillan, 1949, revised edition, 1980.

Mere Christianity (contains revised and enlarged versions of radio talks, *The Case for Christianity, Christian Behaviour,* and *Beyond Personality*), Macmillan, 1952.

The World's Last Night, and other Essays (includes *Shall We Lose God in Outer Space?*), Harcourt, 1960.

Screwtape Proposes a Toast and Other Pieces, Collins, 1965, published as *Screwtape Proposes a Toast,* Fontana, 1970.

Of Other Worlds: Essays and Stories, edited by Walter Hooper, Bles, 1966, Harcourt, 1967.

A Mind Awake: An Anthology of C. S. Lewis, edited by Clyde S. Kilby, Bles, 1968, Harcourt, 1969.

Selected Literary Essays (includes part of *Rehabilitations and Other Essays, De Descriptione Temporum,* and part of *They Asked for a Paper: Papers and Addresses*), edited by Walter Hooper, Cambridge University Press, 1969.

C. S. Lewis: Five Best Books in One Volume, Iversen Associates, 1969.

God in the Dock: Essays on Theology and Ethics, edited by Walter Hooper, Eerdmans, 1970, published in England as *Undeceptions: Essays on Theology and Ethics,* Bles, 1971, new edition published in England as *First and Second Things,* Fount, 1985.

Fern–Seed and Elephants and Other Essays on Christianity, edited by Walter Hooper, Fontana, 1975.

The Dark Tower and Other Stories (includes two unfinished novels), edited by Walter Hooper, Harcourt, 1977.

The Joyful Christian: 127 Readings from C. S. Lewis, Macmillan, 1977.

Six by Lewis, Macmillan, 1978.

The Visionary Christian: One Hundred and Thirty–one Readings from C. S. Lewis, selected by Chad Walsh, Macmillan, 1981.

On Stories and Other Essays on Literature, edited by Walter Hooper, Harcourt, 1982.

The Business of Heaven: Daily Readings from C. S. Lewis, edited by Walter Hooper, Harcourt, 1984.

Of This and Other Worlds, edited by Walter Hooper, Fount, 1984.

Boxen Stories, Collins, 1985.

The Seeing Eye and Other Selected Essays from Christian Reflections, Ballantine, 1986.

The Inspirational Writings of C. S. Lewis, Arrowood Press, 1987.

The Essential C. S. Lewis, Macmillan, 1988.

The Quotable Lewis, Tyndale House, 1990.

Readings for Meditation and Reflection, Walker & Co., 1998.

C. S. Lewis on Faith, Thomas Nelson, 1998.

C. S. Lewis on Grief, Thomas Nelson, 1998.

C. S. Lewis on Love, Thomas Nelson, 1998.

C. S. Lewis on Joy, Thomas Nelson, 1998.

OTHER

The Abolition of Man; or, Reflections on Education with Special Reference to the Teaching of English in the Upper Forms of Schools, Oxford University Press, 1943, Macmillan, 1947.

Vivisection, New England Anti–Vivisection Society, c. 1947.

Surprised by Joy: The Shape of My Early Life (autobiography), Bles, 1955, Harcourt, 1956.

(Under pseudonym N. W. Clerk) *A Grief Observed* (autobiography), Faber, 1961, Seabury, 1963, published under name C. S. Lewis, Walker & Company, 1988.

(Author of introduction) *Selections from Layamon's "Brut,"* edited by G. L. Brook, Clarendon Press, 1963.

Essays Presented to Charles Williams, Eerdmans, 1966.

Essays on the Death Penalty, third edition, St. Thomas Press, 1978.

C. S. Lewis at the Breakfast Table, and Other Reminiscences, edited by James T. Como, Macmillan, 1979.

The Grand Miracle, Ballantine, 1983.

(With Owen Barfield) *A Cretaceous Perambulator (the Re–examination Of)* (parody), limited edition, edited by Walter Hooper, Oxford University C. S. Lewis Society, 1983.

Boxen: The Imaginary World of the Young C. S. Lewis (collection of early maps, histories, and sketches), edited by Walter Hooper, Harcourt, 1985.

Present Concerns (essays), edited by Walter Hooper, Harcourt, 1986.

Timeless at Heart, edited by Walter Hooper, Fount, 1988.

All My Road before Me: The Diary of C. S. Lewis, 1922–1927, Harcourt, 1991.

Also contributor to books, including *Essays on Malory,* edited by J. A. W. Bennett, Clarendon Press, 1963; *Christian Reflections,* edited by Walter Hooper, Eerdmans, 1967, Fount, 1981; (author of commentary) Charles W. S. Williams, *Taliessin through Logres* [and] *The Region of the Summer Stars* [and] *Arthurian Torso,* Eerdmans, 1974; (contributor of letters) *A Severe Mercy: C. S. Lewis and a Pagan Love Invaded by Christ, Told by One of the Lovers,* by Sheldon Vanauken, Harper, 1977; *Eglerio!: In Praise of Tolkien,* edited by Anne Etkin, decorations and illustrations by Lucy Matthews, Questi Communications, 1978; *Christian Childhoods: An Anthology of Personal Memories,* edited by Celia Van Oss, Crossroad, 1986; and *The Collier Christian Library* (three–volume boxed set), Macmillan, 1988.

Contributor to the proceedings of the British Academy and to *Essays and Studies by Members of the English Association.* Lewis's papers are held at the Bodleian Library at Oxford University, Oxford, England, and in the Marion Wade Collection at Wheaton College, Wheaton, Illinois.

TELEVISION

The Lion, the Witch, and the Wardrobe (animated), Lord & King Associates, CBS–TV, April 1–2, 1979.

The Chronicles of Narnia (miniseries), PBS–TV, 1989.

CASSETTES AND RECORDS

The Chronicles of Narnia: The Lion, the Witch and the Wardrobe, Caedmon, 1978.

The Chronicles of Narnia: Prince Caspian, Caedmon, 1979.

The Chronicles of Narnia: The Voyage of the "Dawn Treader," Caedmon, 1979.

The Chronicles of Narnia: The Silver Chair, Caedmon, 1980.

The Chronicles of Narnia: The Horse and His Boy, Caedmon, 1980.

The Chronicles of Narnia: The Magician's Nephew, Caedmon, 1980.

The Chronicles of Narnia: The Last Battle, Caedmon, 1981.

Other cassette recordings of Lewis's work include *Out of the Silent Planet,* Books on Tape, *Perelandra,* Books on Tape, *Philiu,* Word Books, *Storge,* Word Books, *That Hideous Strength,* Books on Tape, and *The Four Loves,* Catacomb. Other recordings have been made of *The Four Loves,* Word Books, and *Agape* (title means "Divine Love"), Word Books.

PICTURE BOOKS; ILLUSTRATED BY DEBORAH MAZE

Edmund and the White Witch, HarperCollins, 1997.
Lucy Steps through the Wardrobe, HarperCollins, 1997.
Aslan, HarperCollins, 1998.
Aslan's Triumph, HarperCollins, 1998.
The Wood between the Worlds, HarperCollins, 1999.

OTHER

William Nicholson based his biographical play *Shadowlands* on Lewis's life and memoirs. He adapted the work for British television in 1985, and also as the 1993 film *Shadowlands,* starring Anthony Hopkins as C. S. Lewis and Debra Winger as Joy Gresham.

■ Sidelights

"Writing a book is much less like creation than it is like planting a garden or begetting a child," revealed fantasist, scholar, and Christian apologist C.

S. Lewis in *Letters of C. S. Lewis;* "in all three cases we are only entering as *one* cause into a causal stream which works, so to speak, in its own way. I would not wish it to be otherwise." In beginning such classic works as *The Screwtape Letters, Out of the Silent Planet,* and the seven Chronicles of Narnia, the author explained in *Letters to Children,* "I see pictures. . . . I have no idea whether this is the usual way of writing stories, still less whether it is the best. It is the only one I know: images always come first." Such images—a faun carrying an umbrella, an English lamppost in the midst of a snowy forest, a beautiful yet awesome Lion—distinguish one of the best–loved books in all children's literature, *The Lion, the Witch, and Wardrobe.* Yet Lewis was a versatile writer whose academic studies have proven long–lasting and whose writings on religion have inspired generations of Christians. Indeed, all of Lewis's many writings are distinguished by the faith that the author adopted wholeheartedly in his early thirties, as well as by an imaginative felicity of expression and an intellectual depth that make them entertaining as well as thought–provoking.

Clive Staples Lewis was born in 1898 in Belfast, Ireland, where his father, Albert, worked as a solicitor. His mother, Flora, was a mathematician of sharp intellect and sunny disposition, and Lewis, who was known to the family as "Jack," enjoyed an early childhood filled with reading, drawing, and imaginative games with his elder brother, Warren. Unfortunately, Flora Lewis died of cancer when Jack was only nine, leaving him devastated. As he recounted in *Surprised by Joy: The Shape of My Life:* "With my mother's death all settled happiness, all that was tranquil and reliable, disappeared from my life. There was to be much fun, many pleasure, many stabs of Joy; but no more of the old security. It was sea and islands now; the great continent had sunk like Atlantis." Lewis was sent by his father to an English boarding school shortly after Flora Lewis's death, an abrupt transition that permanently soured the relationship between father and son. Lewis attended a series of schools and colleges until 1914, when he left school to be privately tutored by William Kirkpatrick, who had been headmaster of Albert Lewis's school. Kirkpatrick's instruction was challenging, but Lewis was a precocious student who was well–read, creative, and eager to learn. He was well prepared when he entered Oxford's University College in 1917, but he only spent a single term there before being called to serve in World War I. In April 1918 he was wounded at the Battle of Arras in France and spent several months recuperating from his wounds. Afterwards he returned to Oxford, which he would call home for the majority of his lifetime.

In the first volume of the "Space Trilogy," Lewis begins the story of Dr. Ransom and his abduction by aliens from the planet Malacandra.

Lewis's university training was steeped in classical learning and English literature, and he preferred the medieval and Renaissance works that would later inform much of his fiction. During his time there he met the poet William Butler Yeats and hoped for his own career as a poet. His first book was a collection of verses, published in 1919 under the pseudonym Clive Hamilton and titled *Spirits in Bondage: A Cycle of Lyrics.* The poems were not particularly successful, however, and after taking degrees in both classics and English, earning first class honors in both, Lewis became a fellow of Oxford in 1925. He began what was to become a long and esteemed career as a teacher and scholar, and he became popular for his lectures, which were distinguished by their depth of content and by Lewis's animated means of expression. His academic writings were similarly noteworthy; his first published study, 1936's *The Allegory of Love*, used examples from little–known as well as classic works to argue that the concept of "romantic love" is a relatively recent occurrence. A *Times Literary Supplement* critic hailed the study as "plainly a great book—one which is destined to outlive its particular conclusions as few works of literary scholarship contrive to do." During his early academic career, Lewis also became involved in a literary group that met weekly in Oxford to discuss literature; the Inklings, as they called themselves, also included fellow medieval scholar J. R. R. Tolkien, who would go on to author the classic "Lord of the Rings" fantasy trilogy.

In 1929, Lewis had an experience that was to change his life and the course of his literary career. Although he had been raised in a religious household, by the time he was a young adult Lewis had become an atheist, a fashionable position for a young intellectual to hold. Having passed the age of thirty, however, the scholar had a mystical experience while on a summer trip; by the time he returned to Oxford, he felt compelled by evidence to acknowledge the existence of God. He related this experience in *Surprised by Joy:* "You must picture me alone in [my] room in Magdalen [College], night after night, feeling, whenever my mind lifted even for a second from my work, the steady, unrelenting approach of Him whom I so earnestly desired not to meet. . . . I gave in, and admitted that God was God, and knelt and prayed: perhaps, that night, the most dejected and reluctant convert in all England." Within a few years, aided by conversations with the Inklings, Lewis had accepted Christianity and joined the Anglican church.

Having himself come from an atheistic background to Christianity through reasoned contemplation, Lewis found that he had much to say in support of his new–found religion. In 1933 he published *The Pilgrim's Regress: An Allegorical Apology for Christianity, Reason and Romanticism*, which *Renascence* contributor Andrew Wheat considered "one of the best guides to Lewis's thought because, in spite of its apparent shortcomings, it is a masterful illustration (not simply codification) of a conversion." The work was just the first of dozens of books, lectures, and radio broadcasts that Lewis was to give on Christian life and thought. These works brought him great renown, as everyday readers appreciated their conversational approach, creative use of allegories and analogies, and clearly articulated logic. In *First Things*, Richard John Neuhaus examined the appeal

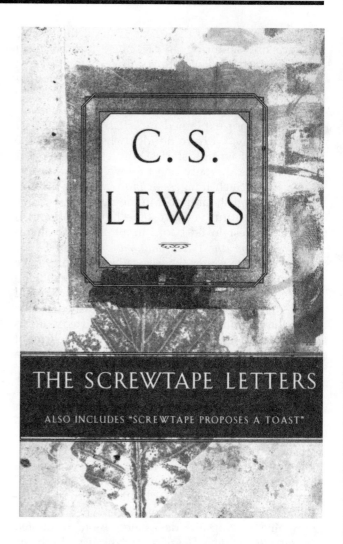

Taking the form of a series of letters from a senior demon named Screwtape to his nephew Wormwood, this 1942 book examines orthodox Christian theology.

of Lewis's religious writings: "Lewis frequently published what is personal, always in the expectation that it would engage the like experience of other persons. . . . Throughout his writings, one detects between the lines the inquiry posed to his readers, 'Is it not true? Do you not find it to be so?'" As a result, a *Times Literary Supplement* writer related, "for the last thirty years of his life no other Christian writer in [Britain] had such influence on the general reading public as C. S. Lewis. Each new book from his pen was awaited with an eagerness which showed that thousands of intelligent men and women had acquired a taste for his distinctive idiom and had come to rely on him as a source of moral and intellectual insight."

Spirits and Space

Although Lewis had experimented with narrative in his 1926 poem *Dymer,* it was not until the late 1930s that he composed his first work of mainstream fiction. Published in 1938, *Out of the Silent Planet* opens a science fiction trilogy that "is heavily laden with religious allegory," as David L. Russell described it in the *Dictionary of Literary Biography.* The hero of the series is a literary scholar named Elwin Ransom, who finds himself kidnapped by the evil Dr. Weston and taken to the planet Mars, whose inhabitants call it "Malacandra." Although Ransom is intended as a sacrifice to the supposedly "uncivilized" natives, he discovers that the mysterious leaders of the planet, known as the *eldila,* are actually beings of light reminiscent of Biblical angels. Ransom is "adopted" by the Malacandrans despite his Earth origins, Earth being looked on suspiciously as the "silent planet" because it is wrapped in a dark shroud that divides it from the rest of the universe. Together Ransom and his new friends capture Weston and his accomplice Devine, foiling their sinister scheme for the planet. While the novel is more speculative fiction than true science fiction—Lewis glosses over scientific details such as Weston's manner of space travel—it has nevertheless proved popular with a wide spectrum of readers, including the author's friend Tolkien, who did not always favor Lewis's approach to fiction.

Five years later Lewis published the next volume in the series, *Perelandra,* which is the name given to the planet Venus by its inhabitants. In order to save the innocence of the Perelandrans, Ransom is mysteriously transported to the planet in an attempt to rescue the Green Lady, who serves as an Eve figure. Set against them once again is Weston, who has forgotten his humanity and become the "Un–Man," the manifestation of evil on the planet. Ransom realizes he has an opportunity to save the Eden of this planet and struggles to help the Green Lady resist the temptation offered by Weston. The novel concludes with Ransom learning from Perelandra's "Adam" that events on Earth may soon come to a turning point and that there will be an opportunity to escape the grip of the Devil. Although there is little science in the novel—Venus is portrayed as a watery world populated with floating islands—the invention of the world is of the highest standard. Calling *Perelandra* "a truly remarkable book," Leonard Bacon remarked in *Saturday Review* that the novel "is the result of the poetic imagination in full blast and should never have been written in prose, however excellent." Discussing these first two novels in *America,* Charles A. Brady stated that their "Miltonic grandeur of conception [is] the greatest exercise of pure imagination in immediately contemporary literature."

Lewis concluded his trilogy with 1945's *That Hideous Strength: A Modern Fairy–Tale for Grownups.* Written during the turmoil of World War II, *That Hideous Strength* reflects the horrific tales coming out of Nazi Germany and contains an indictment of fascism and unchecked technology along with its spiritual lessons. The novel opens on Earth, where fallen *eldila* have influenced the government to create a soulless, semi–fascist state that is attempting to impose social engineering on its subjects through the National Institute of Coordinated Experiments (NICE). The plot follows the lives of a young academic couple, Mark and Jane Studdock, as they find themselves on opposite sides of the upcoming struggle: the ambitious Mark on the side of the devils and the seeress Jane on that of the angels. Eventually, Jane allies herself with the ancient mage Merlin and a small Christian enclave to not only rescue Mark's soul but also foil NICE's plans to "free" humanity from corporeal existence. While Russell believed that the work "is a mixture of fantasy and realism demanding more of readers than many are willing to give," *College English* contributor Charles Moorman found it "Lewis's most complex and impressive use of myth in fiction." *That Hideous Strength* "is more timely today than when the book was published in 1945," Phillip E. Johnson argued in a March 2000 *First Things* article, observing that the possibilities of genetic engineering make the events in the novels more plausible than ever. The critic contended that the novel "is a thrilling story that I enjoy more each time I reread it, but I have heard others say that the action is contrived, the characters one–dimensional, and the tone didactic. I suppose you could say the same of *Paradise Lost.*" *Extrapolation* contributor A. K. Nardo likewise hailed the epic dimension of Lewis's "Space" trilogy, concluding that "what are merely artificial constructs to delineate kinds of poetry on earth become living realities in the heroic world of Mars and the pastoral world of Venus. Through identification with Ransom, the reader tastes what, Lewis seems to believe, is almost impossible in the modern world: pure epic and pure lyric experiences."

During the same time he was penning his "Space" trilogy, Lewis produced one of his most popular and enduring works, one that, along with his wartime radio talks, was to make him famous throughout Britain. Using a lighthearted approach, *The Screwtape Letters* presents the "advice" that the experienced devil Screwtape gives to his young nephew Wormwood on how to warp the character of a Christian. Unfortunately for the hapless Wormwood's hopes, the young man in question has the Church and a "nauseating" young Christian woman to sway him away from damnation. In *First Things,* Gilbert Meilaender suggested that "part of the enduring power of *The Screwtape Letters* [is that]

Screwtape knows how much the ordinary and the everyday count for in our spiritual life," and thus many of his instructions involve normal, commonplace human activities. In addition, according to Russell, *The Screwtape Letters* "reveals Lewis as a talented satirist and humorist," while Bacon wrote in the *Saturday Review of Literature* that "whatever you may think of the theses of Mr. Lewis . . . the fact remains that [*The Screwtape Letters*] is a spectacular and satisfactory nova in the bleak sky of satire."

In 1945, the author followed up this success with another satirical novel, *The Great Divorce: A Dream,* an allegorical story that takes place on a bus trip from hell to heaven. As the souls travel towards paradise, they are guided by George MacDonald, the British fantasist whose literary fairy tales provided inspiration to Lewis's own work. *Christianity Today* contributor Philip Yancey praised the author's "wonderfully imaginative portrait" of heaven, as well as how he emphasized its "sheer moral necessity." Along with *The Screwtape Letters*, Richard Jenkyns noted in the *New Republic, The Great Divorce* is "the best" of all of Lewis's "enduring" devotional works.

In the late 1940s Lewis came to another major turning point, this time in his career as a writer. He had suffered an embarrassing defeat in a debate with Christian philosopher Elizabeth Anscombe, and he began doubting the legitimacy of his own religious works. As he reflected on what he wanted to accomplish with his writing, he considered children's fantasy as a potential instrument to teach about the great truths of life. It was not such a great leap as one might think for this bachelor scholar to begin writing for children. As he later related in *On Stories, and Other Essays in Literature:* "When I was ten, I read fairy tales in secret and would have been ashamed if I had been found doing so. Now that I am fifty I read them openly. When I became a man I put away childish things, including the fear of childishness and the desire to be very grown up." Recalling fondly the classic fantasies of such authors as George MacDonald, as well as the Northern sagas and medieval romances he studied in his work, Lewis dreamed up a world populated with talking animals, mythical creatures, and evil witches. Appearing throughout the series is Aslan, the great Lion, a Christ–like figure who encourages, redeems, and creates. As Lewis explained in one of his *Letters to Children:* "I did not say to myself 'Let us represent Jesus as He really is in our world by a Lion in Narnia'; I said 'Let us *suppose* that there were a land like Narnia and that the son of God, as He became a Man in our world, became a Lion there, and then imagine what would happen.'"

A group of children find themselves aboard a Narnian ship in *The Voyage of the "Dawn Treader,"* the third volume in the popular "Chronicles of Narnia" series.

Through the Wardrobe Door

Lewis published the first of these fantasies in 1950 with *The Lion, the Witch, and the Wardrobe,* which introduces readers to the land of Narnia and the human family the Pevensies, who help liberate it from darkness. The novel opens as four siblings—Peter, Susan, Edmund, and Lucy—are visiting the country home of a family friend during the Second World War. While playing hide–and–seek on a rainy day, Lucy Pevensie finds a remarkable wardrobe that leads her into an enchanted forest. Although she meets a friendly faun during her initial visit, she learns that Narnia is under the spell of the sinister White Witch, who makes it "always winter and never Christmas." When Lucy later brings her brothers and sister into Narnia, they discover that only they can fulfill the prophecy that will end the winter and free the creatures of Narnia. After a series of challenges and battles similar to those found in a medieval quest, the Pevensies face the White Witch with the aid of Aslan, the great lion. Because Edmund has betrayed his siblings and submitted to the power of the White Witch, however, Aslan must sacrifice himself in Edmund's place in order to defeat her evil. Although some critics were concerned that the violence in the book might not be appropriate for children, initial reviews of the book were mainly positive. A *Times Literary Supplement* reviewer, for instance, noted that "the fairy story is admirable at fairy–story level; but also at the deep, unformulated level of myth. It never loses its vitality, its fantasy, its emotional vividness; it never becomes that tiresome thing, allegory." "In the story Lewis gives life to the deepest principles of his Christian faith," Russell explained. "He presents a world corrupted with a powerful evil, full of dangerous temptation; humanity is seen as often weak and prone to erring ways, but with the capacity for devotion and even heroism if guided by the unconditional love of the godhead, who is also the redeemer."

This 1977 volume brings together all of Lewis's shorter fiction under a single cover for the first time.

Lewis and the Pevensies return to Narnia in the second book in the series, 1951's *Prince Caspian.* The four siblings are standing on a train platform when they are suddenly summoned to the magical land they once ruled. Because time runs faster in Narnia, however, they discover that hundreds of years have passed since they were last there and the land has fallen into tyrannical hands. These new rulers, the Telmarines, have silenced the talking animals, banished the dwarves and dryads, forbidden magic, and denied the existence of Aslan. Although the current heir to the Narnian throne, Prince Caspian, has true Narnian blood in him and is inclined to believe everything he has heard of Old Narnia, his throne has been usurped by his malicious uncle Miraz. Caspian is eventually forced to leave his home and, in a manner recalling traditional initiation tales, he manages to overcome obstacles and regain his throne with the aid of the Pevensies and the creatures of Narnia. Within this rousing adventure of intrigue and battles, Lewis addresses issues of faith and belief, as first one person and then another must be convinced of the truth of Old Narnia and its rulers. Lucy, however, never loses her faith, and so when the children become lost it is she who is able to guide them to safety with the help of Aslan. A *New York Herald Tribune Book Review* critic found this second installment better than the first and observed that "here we have style and imagination as seldom met in modern books."

Susan and Peter are too old to return to Narnia for a third adventure, and so Lucy and Edmund are joined by their disbelieving and unimaginative cousin Eustace Scrubb in 1952's *The Voyage of the "Dawn Treader."* Lucy and Edmund are staying with the Scrubbs while their parents are on a trip, and they are finding their cousin a boring pest who jeers at their tales of Narnia and Aslan. Even when the three children are magically transported to a Narnian sea, where they find the now–King Caspian leading a voyage to find his father's seven missing loyal lords, Eustace remains stubbornly disbelieving and gratingly annoying. His constant complaining accompanies Caspian and his crew as they have a series of adventures reminiscent of the classic voyages of the *Odyssey* and the *Aeneid.* It is only after Eustace is turned into a dragon and is rescued by the efforts of Aslan that he becomes a more sensitive, less selfish person. This theme of spiritual rebirth is an important part of the novel, as is "the importance of balance and moderation in life," as Russell described it. Hailing the "thrilling action" that occurs throughout the book, a *New York Herald Tribune Book Review* writer noted that "it is a complicated, different sort of fairy tale, exciting and beautiful."

Eustace is allowed another visit to Narnia in the next volume in the series, 1953's *The Silver Chair.* The novel opens with a strong critique of the pseudointellectual, so–called "modern" schools that Lewis loathed for their dehumanizing atmosphere and lack of spirituality. Eustace attends such a school, and it is while he is comforting a fellow student, Jill, that the two are chased by bullies and discover a door into Narnia. Aslan has called them there to perform the task of finding and saving Prince Rilian, the sole son and heir of the now–elderly King Caspian. The two are immediately separated after Jill accidentally pushes Eustace off a mountain, so only Jill hears Aslan tell of the four Signs they must follow to achieve their quest. Because she is late in catching up to Eustace, however, Jill does not tell him the first Sign in time, and the two spend the rest of their adventures trying to find Rilian without the guidance of the signs. They are aided in their quest by Puddleglum, a doleful, frog-like creature of the marshes who serves as a guide and as a source of humor. They eventually find Rilian underground in the clutches of the evil Green Witch, and they defeat her and restore Rilian to his home. Lewis used the classic pattern of an underworld descent and victorious return for Eustace and Jill's adventures; in addition, he has Puddleglum give an impassioned speech about his faith in the face of the Witch's attempts to convince him of its falseness. Roger Lancelyn Green considered this volume one of the best in the series, noting in *Henry Treece, C. S. Lewis, and Beatrix Potter* that Lewis "construct[ed] a complete and single unity with each incident growing naturally as part of the whole, and conjur[ed] up the characters, strange and ordinary, against marvelous and unexpected backgrounds, as if the circumstances and not the author had called them into being."

Lewis used a different model for the next volume in the series: he goes back in time to the era of the Pevensies' reign, places the action wholly within Narnia, and uses only Narnian characters. *The Horse and His Boy* is the story of Shasta, who has been raised by a fisherman in Calormen, the sinister, totalitarian country to the south of Narnia. By chance Shasta discovers that he is not truly a fisherman's son, but rather a foundling who is more a slave than a foster child. As his "father" is about to sell him to a Calormene lord, Shasta escapes with Bree, a talking horse who has been kidnapped from Narnia. Together the two set out for the North and freedom, gaining a pair of companions in the noble girl Aravis and her Talking Horse, Hwin, and also meeting King Edmund and Queen Susan along the way. As Shasta and Aravis escape Calormen, they overhear Calormene plans to attack neighboring Archenland, travel through the desert, help Edmund and Lucy thwart the Calormene attack, and

discover Shasta's true identity. As is customary in the Narnia books, Aslan appears in a revelation scene to one of the characters, this time explaining that his designs are not always meant to be grasped by mere mortals. While the novel explores themes of identity, it is also "one of the most consistently exciting of the Chronicles," according to Russell, "and is not without its share of good comic scenes." In *Renascence*, Mervyn Nicholson called *The Horse and His Boy* "a charming and rich text," one that follows in the best traditions of adventure writers such as H. Rider Haggard.

Beginnings and Endings

For the sixth volume in his tales of Narnia, Lewis once again eschewed chronological order so that he could tell of the origins of the land of Narnia. *The Magician's Nephew* opens in turn–of–the–century London and introduces the reader to Digory Kirke, a child who will later become the professor of *The Lion, the Witch, and the Wardrobe.* Digory lives in the city with his sick mother, his aunt, and his peculiar Uncle Andrew. When Digory and his friend Polly Plummer find one of Andrew's magical rings lying about, they are transported to the magical Wood between the Worlds; when they try to return home, they instead find themselves in the dark and lifeless land of Charn. Digory's curiosity leads to the awakening of the evil Queen Jadis, who will later become the White Witch, and she escapes Charn and takes the children to London, wreaking havoc on the city. In the ensuing turmoil, the children, Uncle Andrew, and an unsuspecting cabbie are taken to another place, where they witness the creation of Narnia through a song of Aslan. Because Queen Jadis was present as well, however, her evil has been let loose in this new land. Because it was Digory's mistake that permitted this, Aslan sends the boy on a quest to find a magical talisman to protect the land. In the process Digory fights temptation and matures both emotionally and spiritually, finally returning home with a cure for his mother. The novel has an interesting combination of poetry and humor, for, as Russell observed, it contains "one of the loveliest of creation stories" (Aslan's song), as well as "one of Lewis's finest comic scenes" (the escapades of Queen Jadis in London). G. Taylor noted in *School Librarian and School Library Review* that children will read and absorb the morals of the story because "the writing is so fresh and vivid, the characters, however fantastic, so solid, [and] the adventures so exciting."

Having published one volume in each of seven years, Lewis finally concluded his saga in the 1956 novel *The Last Battle.* Like *The Horse and His Boy,* The

Last Battle takes place entirely within Narnia; the land is once again under the shadow of evil, as a sinister ape named Shift is passing off the donkey Puzzle as Aslan. The king of Narnia, Tirian, is deceived and captured by Shift, and calls Eustace and Jill into Narnia from their places on a rushing train. Although they help free Tirian and expose Puzzle as a fraud, the land is still in trouble, for Narnians have come to doubt the true Aslan. As the children and their allies try to deal with this crisis of faith, they must also confront the invading Calormenes. In the midst of this they discover that Shift has created another false god: Tashlan, a fearsome combination of the Calormene god Tash and Aslan. People believe that he resides in a Stable, and those who enter it are struck down with fear. When Tirian and the children enter, however, they discover only lightness, for their belief in Aslan has brought them into Paradise. In what Russell called "one of the most hopeful conclusions in all children's literature," Aslan takes the children into a new creation: "Now at last they were beginning Chapter One of the Great Story, which no one on earth has read: which goes on for ever: in which every chapter is better than the one before." "*The Last Battle* is an apocalyptic vision and, properly speaking, a *tour de force*," Nicholson asserted in *Renascence*. "To present a vision of the end of the world, with its Biblical symbolism and references to the book of Revelation, in the form of a children's story, is a remarkable achievement."

In the more than forty years since Lewis concluded his saga, it has become one of the best-loved works in children's literature. According to Nicholson, this was due to how Lewis imaginatively worked within the traditions of fantasy; he "absorbed, recreated, and transmitted literary materials from other authors," including such classic storytellers as George Macdonald, E. Nesbit, and H. Rider Haggard. Nevertheless, some critics have found fault with the series, citing problems ranging from preachiness, cardboard characters, and flat dialogue to an emphasis on violence and vengeance. Other observers, however, believe that the depth and imagination displayed in the Narnia books far outweigh any such shortcomings. "Although every story in the series is a reworking in Narnian terms of some aspect of Christian theology," Diana Waggoner argued in *The Hills of Faraway*, "the seven Chronicles of Narnia are among the freshest and most enchanting of fantasies, because they are an utterly satisfying expression of Lewis's imagination." She further explained that "Narnia itself . . . comes alive despite any flaws in the stories, because Lewis makes it a real place." Similarly, *Junior Bookshelf* critic M. S. Crouch noted that what distinguishes the books is "the fact that the author has something to say." As a result, the critic wrote, "after all the inadequacies of expres-

sion and of characterisation, one comes to the last page of the last of these seven strange books with deep satisfaction mingled with regret. It has been a memorable experience and a privilege to visit the great magical world of Narnia." As Charles A. Brady concluded in *America*, the seven volumes "mark, it seems to me, the greatest addition to the imperishable deposit of children's literature since [Kipling's] the *Jungle Books*."

Even as he was working on the Narnia Chronicles, Lewis was also making progress in his academic career. In 1954 he finally achieved a professorship, although it was offered at Cambridge University instead of at Oxford, where he had studied and taught for over thirty years. That same year he also published his most noteworthy critical work: 1954's *English Literature in the Sixteenth Century, Excluding Drama*, later published as *Poetry and Prose in the Sixteenth Century*. "Most literary criticism is dated within its own generation," Russell observed, "but Lewis's remains highly readable, provocative, and, perhaps more significantly, in print more than three decades after his death—a forceful testimonial to his powers as a scholar." Analyzing the author's literary criticism in *Renascence*, Stephen Logan claimed that Lewis's extensive background in literature and the classics made him able to "enlighten us as to the conditions we must observe if we are to take the past, and the literature of the past, on their own terms." As a result, Logan stated, Lewis "is thus uniquely able, in our times, to restore to us a sense of that community with the past which it has become one of the distinctive, proud obsessions of our age to spurn."

The author's scholastic knowledge also informed his last novel, 1956's *Till We Have Faces: A Myth Retold*. It is "the most enduring of Lewis's imaginative works and yet the least understood," Ralph C. Wood claimed in the *Christian Century*. "Here all of Lewis's central themes—the problem of evil, the relation of the natural to the supernatural, the efficacy of prayer, the nature of sacrifice, the place of poetry in the life of the mind, the foreshadowing of Christian revelation in pagan religion—are interwoven in an enticing and elusive design." The novel reworks the myth of Cupid and Psyche, in which a beautiful human princess is compelled to marry a winged serpent, whom she comes to love; when she seeks out her husband's true form, however, she is cast out and left to wander the world in search of him. Lewis adapts this story of transgression and redemption by setting it in the pre–Christian world of Glome, a brutal and uncivilized land, and by focusing on the character of Psyche's unattractive and resentful older sister, Orual. Orual loves her sister dearly, but in a selfish and possessive way. When Psyche finds fulfillment in sacrificing herself to save

Anthony Hopkins portrays Lewis and Deborah Winger plays his wife, Joy Gresham, in *Shadowlands*, a 1993 film that received two Academy Award nominations.

their people, Orual cannot understand it and threatens to kill herself unless Psyche disobeys their gods. When Psyche is eventually banished, Orual is similarly unable to understand why she has lost her sister, having received no answer upon asking her native goddess. The title of the novel refers to Orual's eventual understanding of why the gods do not answer her questions: "Why should they hear the babble that we think we mean? How can they meet us face to face till we have faces?" "This is an answer that is as powerful . . . as it is troubling," Brian Murphy wrote in his study *C. S. Lewis,* and concluded that in later works such as *Till We Have Faces,* "Lewis says that life is a preparation—not, as William Butler Yeats said, a preparation for something that never happens—but a readying for seeing God."

Lewis also examined his life as he examined his faith, publishing two autobiographies during his lifetime. In the 1955 work *Surprised by Joy: The Shape of My Early Life,* the author explores his childhood and his late–blooming acceptance of Christianity. *Nation* contributor May Swenson likened the work to a "long drawn out and intricate conversation" that is "fascinating because of [Lewis's] intellect and charm, plus the story–telling dexterity of a top-notch mystery writer." The title of this memoir gained added significance the following year, when the nearly sixty–year–old bachelor married the American writer Joy Davidman Gresham. They had begun corresponding after she had converted to Christianity, inspired by reading his books; after her husband abandoned her, she moved to England. They married in a civil ceremony so that Gresham could remain in England, but the intellectual match

soon grew into love, particularly when she was diagnosed with cancer shortly after their marriage. They eventually remarried in a religious service, expecting her to die very soon. Although the couple miraculously gained additional happy years together when her disease went into remission, Joy died in July 1960, leaving Lewis heartbroken. He dealt with his feelings of loss by writing, and in 1961 used the pseudonym N. W. Clerk to publish *A Grief Observed,* which Russell stated "is still admired for its profoundly personal examination of bereavement." The story of Lewis's relationship with Joy Gresham was later told by William Nicholson in his play *Shadowlands;* the playwright adapted the work for television in 1985, and also as the 1993 film *Shadowlands,* starring Anthony Hopkins and Debra Winger as the scholar and his wife.

Lewis himself was suffering from ill health by the time his wife passed away, and in 1963 he resigned his Cambridge post because of a chronic heart and bladder condition. He retired to his Oxford home, from which he had commuted while working in Cambridge, and there his brother attended to him until his death on November 22, 1963. His death was a footnote in the papers, as that was also the day President Kennedy was assassinated, but since his death Lewis's reputation has only grown. His Christian writings have sold in the millions, and various conferences and societies have been organized around them. "To make ordinary people think about historic Christianity, and to see and feel the strength and attraction of the case for it, was Lewis's goal throughout," J. I. Packer asserted in *Christianity Today* as one of the reasons for his lasting influence. "The combination within him of insight with vitality, wisdom with wit, and imaginative power with analytical precision made Lewis a sparkling communicator of the everlasting gospel." "No venue was too modest, no reader too unlearned, no idea too unremarkable to be spared his gifts, if those gifts, however deployed, might profit the reader," James Como remarked in *Wilson Quarterly,* adding that this "humility" made Lewis "accessible and adaptive." "He gives us something better [than theology]," Gilbert Meilaender wrote in *First Things:* "the feel, the quality, of a life truly lived before God."

His fictional writings have been no less influential. Writing of the "Space" trilogy and the "Chronicles of Narnia," Waggoner noted that "what Lewis contributed to mythopoetic fantasy was specificity, which it had never had before. . . . He pointed out that a mystical vision, far from being vague and unreal, should be more vivid, more real, more memorable than ordinary life." It is this intensity and thoroughness of imagination that has made the Narnia books so enduring, and even more popular today

If you enjoy the works of C.S. Lewis, you might want to check out the following books and films:

T. A. Barron, *The Ancient One*, 1992.
Pamela Dean, *The Whim of the Dragon*, 1989.
Tanith Lee, *Black Unicorn*, 1991.
Mark E. Rogers, *The Riddled Man*, 1992.
Shadowlands, a film about Lewis's marriage to Joy Gresham, starring Anthony Hopkins and Debra Winger, 1995.

than when first published. "The Narnia books are more than simply *in* another world; they create and establish that world as the proving ground for obedience, belief, sacrifice, redemption, and so many more self–transcendent messages that we cannot record all of them," Donald Glover asserted in *C. S. Lewis: The Art of Enchantment*. As a result, the critic concluded, "all readers seem to agree, even if they agree about nothing else to do with Lewis, that here he made his most influential and lasting mark on literature and on his readers."

■ Biographical and Critical Sources

BOOKS

Children's Literature Review, Volume 27, Gale (Detroit, MI), 1992.
A Christian for All Christians: Essays in Honor of C. S. Lewis, Regnery, 1992.
Dictionary of Literary Biography, Volume 160: *British Children's Writers, 1914–1960*, Gale, 1996, pp. 134–149.
Ford, Paul F., *Companion to Narnia*, Macmillan, 1987.
Glover, Donald E., *C. S. Lewis: The Art of Enchantment*, Ohio University Press, 1981.
Green, Robert Lancelyn, Margery Fisher, and Marcus Crouch, *Henry Treece, C. S. Lewis, and Beatrix Potter*, Bodley Head, 1969, pp. 131–154.
Green, Robert Lancelyn, and Walter Hooper, *C. S. Lewis: A Biography*, Harcourt, 1974.
Hanney, Margaret Patterson, *C. S. Lewis*, Ungar, 1981.
Hein, Rolland, *Christian Mythmakers*, Cornerstone Press, 1988.
Hooper, Walter, *Past Watchful Dragons: The Narnian Chronicles of C. S. Lewis*, Collier, 1979.
Howard, Thomas, *The Achievement of C. S. Lewis*, Harold Shaw, 1980.
Lawlor, John, *C. S. Lewis: Memories and Reflections*, Spence (Dallas, TX), 1998.
Lewis, C. S., *Surprised by Joy: The Shape of My Early Life*, Bles, 1955, Harcourt, 1956.
Lewis, C. S., *The Last Battle*, Macmillan, 1956.
Lewis, C. S., *Letters of C. S. Lewis*, edited by W. H. Lewis, Harcourt, 1966.
Lewis, C. S., *On Stories, and Other Essays on Literature*, edited by Walter Hooper, Harcourt, 1982.
Lewis, C. S., *Letters to Children*, edited by Lyle W. Dorsett and Marjorie Lamp Mead, Macmillan, 1985.
Murphy, Brian, *C. S. Lewis*, Starmont House, 1983.
Sayer, George, *Jack: C. S. Lewis and His Times*, Macmillan, 1998.
Schakel, Peter J., *Reading with the Hearts: The Way into Narnia*, Eerdmans, 1979, pp. 131–135.
Waggoner, Diana, *The Hills of Faraway: A Guide to Fantasy*, Atheneum, 1978.
Wilson, A. N., *C. S. Lewis: A Biography*, Norton, 1990.

PERIODICALS

America, May 27, 1944, Charles A. Brady, review of *Perelandra*; October 27, 1956, Charles A. Brady, "Finding God in Narnia," pp. 103–105.
Children's Literature, Volume 12, 1984, Dennis B. Quinn, "The Narnia Books of C. S. Lewis: Fantastic or Wonderful?," pp. 105–121.
Christian Century, August 30, 1995, Ralph C. Wood, "The Baptized Imagination: C. S. Lewis's Fictional Apologetics," p. 812.
Christian History, February, 2000, Ted Olsen, "C. S. Lewis," p. 26.
Christianity Today, April 23, 1976, Cheryl Forbes, "Narnia: Fantasy, But . . .," pp. 6–10; October 25, 1993, Mary Michael, "Our Love Affair with C. S. Lewis," p. 34; September 7, 1998, J. I. Packer, "Still Surprised by Lewis," p. 54; October 26, 1998, Philip Yancey, "What's a Heaven For?," p. 104.
College English, May, 1957, Charles Moorman, review of *That Hideous Strength*.
Extrapolation, summer, 1979, A. K. Nardo, review of the "Space" trilogy.
First Things, August–September, 1998, Gilbert Meilaender, "The Everyday C. S. Lewis," p. 27; December, 1998, Richard John Neuhaus, "C. S. Lewis in the Public Square," p. 30; March, 2000, Phillip E. Johnson, review of *That Hideous Strength*, p. 48.
Horn Book, October, 1963, Lillian H. Smith, "News from Narnia," pp. 470–473.

Junior Bookshelf, November, 1950, Eleanor Graham, review of *The Lion, the Witch, and the Wardrobe,* p. 198; November, 1956, M. S. Crouch, "Chronicles of Narnia," pp. 245–253.

Language Arts, May, 1976, Susan Cornell Poskanzer, "Thoughts on C. S. Lewis and the Chronicles of Narnia," pp. 523–526.

Nation, June 2, 1956, May Swenson, review of *Surprised by Joy;* February 1, 1999, Michael Joseph Gross, "Narnia Born Again," p. 28.

National Review, December 2, 1991, James Como, review of *All My Road before Me,* p. 50; December 11, 1995, Russell Kirk, review of *Surprised by Joy,* pp. 126–127.

New Republic, May 28, 1990, Richard Jenkyns, review of *C. S. Lewis: A Biography,* p. 35.

New York Herald Tribune Book Review, November 11, 1951, review of *Prince Caspian,* p. 5; November 16, 1952, review of *The Voyage of the "Dawn Treader,"* p. 3.

New York Times Book Review, September 30, 1956, Chad Walsh, "War in Narnia," p. 46.

Renascence, fall, 1998 (special Lewis issue), James Como, "Rhetorica Religii," p. 3, Andrew Wheat, "The Road before Him," p. 21, Mervyn Nicholson, "C. S. Lewis and the Scholarship of Imagination in E. Nesbit and Rider Haggard," p. 41, Stephen Logan, "Old Western Man for Our Times," p. 63.

Saturday Review, April 8, 1944, Leonard Bacon, review of *Perelandra.*

Saturday Review of Literature, April 17, 1943, Leonard Bacon, review of *The Screwtape Letters.*

School Librarian and School Library Review, December, 1955, G. Taylor, review of *The Magician's Nephew,* p. 438.

Times Educational Supplement, February 6, 1981, Gerald Haigh, "Through the Wardrobe," p. 24.

Times Literary Supplement, February 28, 1942; November 17, 1950, review of *The Lion, the Witch, and the Wardrobe,* p. vi; October 7, 1955; May 11, 1956, review of *The Last Battle,* p. v; January 7, 1965; March 23, 1967; August 11, 1989.

Wilson Quarterly, spring, 1994, James Como, "Mere Lewis," p. 109.*

—Sketch by Diane Telgen

Jan Marino

workshops at Bread Loaf Writer's Conference, Bennington College, and Long Island University. Workshop leader for Society of Children's Book Writers and Illustrators, Writer's Voice at Silver Bay, Hofstra Writer's Conference, Barbara Bush Literacy Council, among many others.

■ Personal

Born 1936, in Boston, MA; daughter of Ernest D. and Helen (Brown) Rejo; married Leonard Marino (an artist and illustrator); children: Leonard E., Christopher J., Betsy E. *Education:* Graduated from Katherine Gibbs School, 1950s; graduated from Nassau Community College; attended Hofstra University and New School for Social Research.

■ Addresses

Home—P.O. Box 201771, Denver, CO 80220.

■ Career

Client coordinator at an investment counseling firm, 1972–85; author and lecturer, 1985—. Instructor in writing, Long Island University, C. W. Post College, and Southampton College. Participant in writing

■ Member

Society of Children's Book Writers and Illustrators, Author's Guild, Poets & Writers, Rocky Mountain Women's Institute.

■ Awards, Honors

"Book for the Teen Age," New York Public Library, Editor's Choice, *Booklist,* Best Book, *School Library Journal,* and Alabama Reading Incentive Award, all 1992, all for *The Day That Elvis Came to Town;* "Book for the Teen Age," New York Public Library, 1993, for *Like Some Kind of Hero.*

■ Writings

Eighty–Eight Steps to September, Little, Brown (Boston, MA), 1989.

The Day That Elvis Came to Town, Little, Brown (Boston, MA), 1991.

Like Some Kind of Hero, Little, Brown (Boston, MA), 1992.

For the Love of Pete, Little, Brown (Boston, MA), 1993.

The Mona Lisa of Salem Street, Little, Brown (Boston, MA), 1995.

Searching for Atticus, Simon & Schuster Books for Young Readers (New York), 1997.

Write Me a Happy Ending, Simon & Schuster Books for Young Readers (New York), 2001.

Contributor to the *New York Times* and *Boston Globe;* Marino's young adult–novels have been translated and published in England, France and Italy.

■ Work in Progress

The Rainbow Connection, a young adult novel to be published by Simon & Schuster; *Absolution,* a young adult novel; *Driving,* an adult novel.

■ Sidelights

Young–adult novelist Jan Marino has won accolades for her sensitive portrayals of adolescents experiencing rather tough, often family–centered crises. Peopled with adults who in some cases could be described as eccentric, Marino's novels usually end on a positive note and affirm a teen's ability to solve dilemmas and grow from them. All of Marino's novels, including *Eighty–Eight Steps to September* and *Searching for Atticus,* have garnered positive reviews and a devoted readership. Marino is a Colorado resident who also leads workshops that encourage teens to develop crisis–management skills through creative writing.

Marino was born in 1936 in Boston. As she once stated, "In the house were I grew up there was a leather–bound set of the Harvard Classics. At the age of eight or so, I decided to read all fifty volumes—always known to have one foot in fantasyland. The first five titles rather intimated me and so I went on to number six, *Poems and Songs* by Robert Burns. Since I loved to sing and imagined myself a poet, this volume appeared to be the perfect beginning. But when I asked my mother over and over to explain what the poet meant by, 'Ha! Whaur ye gaun, ye crowlin ferlie?' and 'Sal–alkali o'midge–tail clippings' my mother gently suggested I move on.

"I did. To Volume 29, Charles Darwin's *Voyage of the Beagle.* But when I learned on page one that the *Beagle* wasn't the four–legged variety, but a 'ten–gun brig in her Majesty's Navy,' and page two described 'singular encrustations, atmospheric dust with infusoria, and the causes of a discoloured sea,' my interest vanished.

"Discouraged, but not defeated, I followed my mother's not–so–gentle suggestion to move on to Volume 17: *Aesop, the Brothers Grimm, and Hans Christian Andersen's Folklore and Fable.* I loved it from the start, even though it caused me considerable concern. I worried about Hansel and Grethel, Little Red Cap and all the rest. How could a father lead his children into the forest and leave them? How could a mother let a little girl go off alone to visit her ailing grandmother? And what about Snow White? What was she thinking of when she neglected to invite the dwarves to her wedding? I was bitterly disappointed, so I wrote my own endings. Hansel and Grethel's father sent the stepmother off into the forest. Little Red Cap took a taxi to Grandma's and she and Grandma ate sweet cakes and had a happy visit. And, at her wedding Snow White danced the night away with the dwarves. I was good at making up endings that pleased me. I could do that for any story. Except one.

"When I was nine, my brother Robbie died. I remember the sadness and silence that filled the house. Nobody spoke of him. Determined never to forget him, I wrote stories and poems about him, but it wasn't until *Eighty–Eight Steps to September* that I truly came to accept the loss of him."

Puts Feelings Down in Words

It was nearly forty years later that Marino explored this painful time in her life in novel form. After graduating from the Katherine Gibbs School in Boston, she married an artist, with whom she had three children. The family lived on Long Island, and she worked for a number of years as a client coordinator at an investment counseling firm. But when her youngest child entered junior high, Marino began taking college courses, where she was encouraged by teachers to develop her writing talents further. Marino attended both Long Island's Hofstra University as well as the New School for Social Research in New York City, and won scholarship grants to the Bread Loaf Writer's Conference at Bennington College and other workshops. She eventually quit her job in 1985, wrote for Long Island newspapers, and began work on *Eighty–Eight Steps,* which was published four years later.

The novel is set in 1948 and at first, depicts the contentious sibling rivalry between eleven–year–old Amy and her brother Robbie. They fight constantly, and Amy, who recounts these memories in the novel, reveals herself as stubborn. When Robbie goes into the hospital, her obstinacy initially helps her deny the situation, believing that her brother is eventually going to come home. But one morning her father tells her that her brother has died. The family's grief–stricken days, and Amy's emergence as a less obdurate young person, carry the work to its conclusion. "Few authors, fledgling or established, can create a consistently believable first–person child narrator; with Amy Marino accomplishes this feat poignantly," declared an essay on the author in *Children's Books and Their Creators.*

"So many scenes in *Eighty–Eight Steps* are just the way they happened back then," Marino explained, "especially the scene where Amy's father tells her that Robbie is dead. 'He's gone, Amy,' he says. 'Robbie's gone. Goddamnit. He didn't make it.' My father never swore, and I never saw him cry, but he did both that morning.

"And when Amy's teacher, Miss Farrell, calls her into the cloakroom to ask about Robbie, Amy is determined not to cry, just as I was. Instead she concentrates on Miss Farrell's nose. 'I looked up and kept my eyes on her nostrils, trying to count the little hairs I saw. I bit my lip and said nothing. I prayed I wouldn't cry, because all the kids were in the classroom waiting for the three o'clock bell to ring.'"

Examines Events from the Past

Marino's family history also helped her create the characters and setting for her next young–adult story, *The Day That Elvis Came to Town.* This 1991 novel follows some hardships experienced by Wanda, whose family runs a boarding house. Her father drinks, which brings periodic crises to the household, but when a bi–racial jazz singer named Mercedes Washington becomes a boarder, Wanda is enchanted by the glamorous life Mercedes apparently leads. Soon she comes to realize that Mercedes' status in the South in 1963 is a difficult and even dangerous one. "Not a writer of mere problem novels, Marino offers Wanda no quick fixes or easy outs," observed *Children's Books and Their Creators* about this work.

As Marino remarked, "While not all of my books are autobiographical, each one of them has a little bit of my past in them. *The Day That Elvis Came to*

Fifteen–year–old Tessa has to deal with the problems surrounding her father's service in Vietnam as well as her own romantic entanglements in Marino's 1997 novel.

Town is set in a boarding house in Georgia. I never lived in the South, nor did I ever live in a boarding house, but my aunt owned a boarding house in Cambridge, Massachusetts. Since Harvard was close by, my aunt had a wonderful assortment of boarders. One was a professor at Harvard who prefaced every conversation with a quote. He also found his way into *Elvis,* as did my aunt. The setting for *Like Some Kind of Hero* is really Oyster Bay, the town where my children grew up. Ted, the 'hero,' is a composite of my two sons."

Like Some Kind of Hero was Marino's third novel published by Boston's Little, Brown, and it appeared in 1992. Its protagonist, Ted, is a talented classical guitarist, but craves acceptance for more "normal" teen traits. He decides to become a lifeguard, and finds he can indeed excel in this as well, but in the end conflicts force him to choose between artistic talent and social acceptance. Marino's next novel, *For the Love of Pete,* was published in 1993. Set in Georgia in the 1970s, it recounts the difficulties experienced by Phoebe, whose mother died in childbirth, and whose father was never told that the infant survived. Phoebe lives with her well–to–do grandmother, whose household staff includes the English butler, Bishopp, an African–American cook and his brother, and the eccentric chauffeur.

When Phoebe's grandmother becomes ill, she must enter a nursing home, and the family fortune dwindles. Fearing for her future, her grandmother decides that Phoebe must be sent to her next of kin—the father who did not know she even existed. The staff is enlisted with the task of taking Phoebe from Georgia to Maine in a vintage automobile. Bertie, the chauffeur, refuses to drive on the interstate highways, so they must take the back roads; along the way they meet interesting characters, but it is Phoebe's inner turmoil that forms the basis of the plot in *For the Love of Pete.* The servants are really the only family she has ever known, and she is devastated about having to leave them; moreover, she is apprehensive about her father, and wonders whether or not he will love her as they do. "The cast is vividly developed," opined Betsy Hearne in *Bulletin of the Center for Children's Books,* and "Phoebe's narration is consistent and believable." The novel won similar praise from other quarters as well. "There is humor when the story's strong personalities bicker and Phoebe's anguish about leaving all that is familiar is realistically conveyed," wrote Jacqueline Rose for *Voice of Youth Advocates.*

Traces of the Author's Life

"The butler in *For the Love of Pete,* Bishopp, was a butler I once knew and loved," Marino once recalled. "And Pa in *The Mona Lisa of Salem Street* is the grandfather I always wanted but never had." Published in 1995, this fifth novel from Marino also chronicles an adolescent who is without a conventional family structure. Twelve–year–old Nettie DeAngelus and her shy, quiet little brother, John Peter, are orphans who have been shunted about to the homes of various family members. As a last resort, they are handed over to their grandfather in Boston.

Nettie is initially unhappy with this situation, and considers the grandfather "Pa," a retired undertaker, decidedly eccentric. He lives above his former funeral home and talks to his deceased wife, and Nettie is determined not to form a bond with him—partially because she has been forced to live with so many different relatives. But to her surprise, John Peter likes Pa from the start, and his stutter even abates. As they settle into their new life in this Italian–American neighborhood of Boston known as North End, Nettie and John Peter make friends with the children across the street, whose mother is the "Mona Lisa" of the title. Nettie envies the children for their "normal" life, though in reality their mother suffers from a phobia that makes it impossible for her to leave the house; instead she sits by the window and watches the action on the street, as if she is framed in a painting.

Nettie also envies her older aunt, who still has delusions of a career on the stage and promises Nettie extravagances that never materialize. *The Mona Lisa of Salem Street*'s crisis occurs when the grandfather decides to take a job in order to support them better. This panics Nettie; she is fearful that they will again be forced to move on to other relatives, and resolves to help in any way so that they might stay. She fixes dinner one afternoon, but sets the kitchen afire; traumatized, she runs away, but Pa finds her, offers forgiveness, and assures her that she and her brother will never have to leave again. "The story invokes great sympathy for Nettie and her brother and for the grandfather, too, who was lost and alone until his grandchildren arrive and gave him reason to live again," remarked Merlyn Miller in *Voice of Youth Advocates.* Miller also termed it a novel "filled with sadness, yet the reader is rewarded with a happy ending." Nettie's journey from a guarded, somewhat unfriendly adolescent "to someone who is able to come to terms with her parents' death and deal realistically with her own life makes a natural and affecting narrative," asserted Nancy Vasilakis in *Horn Book.*

The Effects of Vietnam

Marino's first book for Simon & Schuster—where her longtime editor had been hired and then brought her along as an author—was the 1997 novel *Searching for Atticus.* The author described this work as "the story of sixteen–year–old Tess's yearning to have a father like Atticus Finch from Harper Lee's *To Kill a Mockingbird,* my favorite book and fictional character." Instead, Tessa's father is a Milwaukee surgeon whose life changes irrevocably when he volunteers for a tour of duty as a field surgeon in the Vietnam War. He comes back to Wisconsin a far different man, traumatized by his experiences, and unable to practice medicine at all.

Tessa accompanies her father on a road trip down South so that he might look into a job opening, but he suffers a nervous breakdown and they instead spend the summer with an aunt in Taloosa. There, Tessa makes a new friend, Selina, and they begin working together at a day camp on the grounds of a Roman Catholic convent. Tessa also develops a crush on an older boy, Caleb, a handsome senior with a promising future. Caleb tries to seduce Tessa, who discovers that he has also had a relationship with a new entrant to the women's religious community. When the postulant became pregnant, he had arranged for an abortion. Caleb believes that Tessa will blackmail him with this secret and keep him from entering West Point in the fall. When Caleb pushes her from a ladder, her father is there to save her.

"Tessa is fully believable in her emotional confusion," remarked Janice M. Del Negro in *Bulletin of the Center for Children's Books,* who termed *Searching for Atticus* "a solid work of fiction with some admirably drawn characters who grow and change in realistic and satisfying ways." An assessment from Chris Crowe in *Voice of Youth Advocates* echoed that of many other reviewers of Marino's young–adult novels: "Marino has well–developed main characters and makes good use of dialogue and action to advance the plot and provide needed exposition," Crowe wrote.

If you enjoy the works of Jan Marino, you might want to check out the following books:

Chris Lynch, *Johnny Chesthair,* 1997.
Patsy Baker O'Leary, *With Wings as Eagles,* 1997.
Marilyn Reynolds, *But What About Me?,* 1996.
G. Clifton Wisler, *Mustang Flats,* 1997.

Marino describes her next work, *Write Me a Happy Ending,* as "the story of sixteen–year–old Jake Haddam's acceptance of his gay father." The author further noted that the work "is set in the Florida Keys,

a place I know well." Marino continues to draw upon her past to create her characters, though there is one family member who "has not found her way into my work—as yet," the author once noted about her grandmother. "She found me terribly annoying as a child, always telling me how dramatic I was. How I daydreamed. How I never missed a trick. How I eavesdropped on adult conversations. How she hoped I would one day outgrow what she called 'character defects.' As yet, I haven't and hope I never will.

"I love to write. To read. I've gone through much of my father's set of the Harvard Classics, but none pleases me as much as Volume 17. I love to imagine. To create characters. Yes, there are days of frustration. Days when I stare at the lifeless computer screen. Days when my characters refuse to talk to me. But give up? Never. I cajole. I plead and beg until I hear their voices. And when my computer screen finally comes alive, I am beyond happy."

■ Biographical and Critical Sources

BOOKS

Children's Books and Their Creators, edited by Anita Silvey, Houghton Mifflin, 1995, p. 234.

PERIODICALS

Booklist, March 1, 1995, pp. 1242–1243.
Bulletin of the Center for Children's Books, July–August, 1993, Betsy Hearne, review of *For the Love of Pete,* p. 362; December, 1997, Janice M. Del Negro, review of *Searching for Atticus,* p. 134.
Horn Book, July–August, 1995, Nancy Vasilakis, review of *The Mona Lisa of Salem Street,* p. 459.
Kirkus Reviews, May 15, 1993, p. 665.
Publishers Weekly, July 28, 1997, p. 75.
Voice of Youth Advocates, June, 1993, Jacqueline Rose, review of *For the Love of Pete,* p. 91; August, 1995, Merlyn Miller, review of *The Mona Lisa of Salem Street,* pp. 161–162; December, 1997, Chris Crowe, review of *Searching for Atticus,* p. 318.

Mark Mathabane

Member

Authors Guild.

Awards, Honors

Christopher Award, 1986; Speaker of the Year, National Association for Campus Activities, 1993; White House Fellow, 1996–97.

Personal

First name originally Johannes; name changed, 1976; born 1960, in Alexandra, South Africa; son of Jackson (a laborer) and Magdelene (a washerwoman; maiden name, Mabaso) Mathabane; emigrated to the United States, became U.S. citizen; married Gail Ernsberger (a writer), in 1987; children: Stanley, Arthur, Bianca, Nathan. *Education:* Attended Limestone College, 1978, St. Louis University, 1979, and Quincy College, 1981; Dowling College, B.A., 1983; attended Columbia University, 1984. *Religion:* "Believes in God."

Writings

Kaffir Boy: The True Story of a Black Youth's Coming of Age in Apartheid South Africa, Macmillan, 1986, published as *Kaffir Boy: Growing out of Apartheid,* Bodley Head, 1987.

Kaffir Boy in America: An Encounter with Apartheid, Scribner, 1989.

(With Gail Mathabane) *Love in Black and White: The Triumph of Love over Prejudice and Taboo,* HarperCollins, 1992.

African Women: Three Generations, HarperCollins, 1994.

Miriam's Song: A Memoir, Simon and Schuster, 2000.

Addresses

Home—341 Barrington Park Lane, Kernersville, NC 27284.

Sidelights

"What television newscasts did to expose the horrors of the Vietnam War in the 1960s, books like *Kaffir Boy* may well do for the horrors of apartheid

Career

Lecturer and writer, 1985—.

in '80s," Diane Manuel predicted in a 1986 *Chicago Tribune Book World* review of *Kaffir Boy: The True Story of a Black Youth's Coming of Age in Apartheid South Africa*. In that book, author Mark Mathabane's first, he recounts his early life in the black township of Alexandra, outside Johannesburg. The eldest of his parents' seven children, the author lived in dire poverty and constant fear, until he almost miraculously received a scholarship to play tennis at an American college. *Washington Post Book World* critic Charles R. Larson hailed *Kaffir Boy* as "violent and hard–hitting," while Peter Dreyer in the *Los Angeles Times Book Review* described Mathabane's autobiography as "a book full of a young man's clumsy pride and sorrow, full of rage at the hideousness of circumstances, the unending destruction of human beings, [and] the systematic degradation of an entire society (and not only black South African society) in the name of a fantastic idea."

The Alexandra of *Kaffir Boy* was a place of overwhelming poverty and deprivation, of incessant hunger, of horrific crimes committed by the government and citizen gangs, and of fear and humiliation. It was a township where many of the black residents either spent hours searching in garbage dumps for scraps of food discarded by Johannesburg whites or prostituted themselves for meals. It was a place where "children grow up accepting violence and death as the norm," as Charles Larson reflected. One of Mark Mathabane's childhood memories is of his being startled from sleep, terrified to find police breaking into his family's shanty in search of persons who emigrated illegally—as his parents had—from the "homelands," or tribal reserves. His father, Jackson Mathabane, was imprisoned following one of these raids and was repeatedly jailed after that. Mathabane recalls in *Kaffir Boy* how his parents "lived the lives of perpetual fugitives, fleeing by day and fleeing by night, making sure that they were never caught together under the same roof as husband and wife" because they lacked the paperwork that allowed them to live with their lawful spouses. His father was also imprisoned—at one time for more than a year with no contact with his family—for being unemployed, losing jobs as a laborer because he lacked the "proper documents."

However, those blacks who lived in the urban ghettos near Johannesburg were actually better off than those who were forcibly resettled in the outlying homelands. "Nothing is more pathetic in this book than the author's description of a trip he takes with his father to the tribal reserve, ostensibly so that the boy will identify with the homelands," wrote Larson. "The son, however, sees the land for what it really is—barren, burned out, empty of any meaning for his generation." In *Kaffir Boy* Mathabane de-

picts the desolation of the Venda tribal reserve as "mountainous, rugged and bone–dry, like a wasteland. . . . Everywhere I went nothing grew except near lavatories. . . . Occasionally I sighted a handful of scrawny cattle, goats and pigs grazing on the stubbles of dry brush. The scrawny animals, it turned out, were seldom slaughtered for food because they were being held as the people's wealth. Malnutrition was rampant, especially among the children." Charles Larson noted that the visit to the homeland backfires when the "boy [becomes] determined to give up his father's tribal ways and acquire the white man's education."

Window into Another World

Although Mathabane had the opportunity to get at least a primary education, so grim was his life that by age ten he contemplated suicide. "I found the burden of living in a ghetto, poverty–stricken and without hope, too heavy to shoulder," he explained in his memoir. "I was weary of being hungry all the time, weary of being beaten all the time: at school, at home and in the streets. . . . I felt that life could never, would never, change from how it was for me." But his first encounter with apartheid sparked his determination to overcome the adversities.

Mathabane's grandmother was a gardener for an English–speaking liberal white family in an affluent Johannesburg suburb. One day she took her grandson to work, where he met Clyde Smith, the employer's eleven–year–old son. "My teachers tell us that Kaffirs [blacks] can't read, speak or write English like white people because they have smaller brains, which are already full of tribal things," Smith told Mathabane, the author recalled in *Kaffir Boy*. "My teachers say you're not people like us, because you belong to a jungle civilization. That's why you can't live or go to school with us, but can only be our servants."

Determined to prove young Smith wrong, Mathabane resolved to excel in school. He even taught himself English—although blacks were only allowed to learn tribal languages at the time—through comic books that his grandmother brought home from the Smith household. "I had to believe in myself and not allow apartheid to define my humanity," Mathabane pointed out.

Mrs. Smith also gave Mathabane an old wooden tennis racket. After teaching himself to play, he then sought coaching. As his game improved, he began to fare well at tournaments and gained recognition as a promising young athlete. In 1973 Mathabane attended a tennis tournament in South Africa where the late American tennis player Arthur Ashe publicly condemned apartheid. Ashe became Mathabane's hero, "because he was the first free black man I had ever seen," the author was later quoted as saying by the *New York Times*. After watching Ashe play against other professionals, Mathabane strove to do as well as his hero. Eventually, Mathabane became one of his country's top players, and this gave him opportunities to meet influential white tennis players who did not support apartheid; 1972 Wimbledon winner Stan Smith, another American tennis professional, befriended Mathabane and urged him to apply for tennis scholarships at American schools. When Mathabane did so, he won one; *Kaffir Boy* ends with the author boarding a plane headed for South Carolina.

Lillian Thomas in the *New York Times Book Review* asserted that "it is evident that [Mathabane] wrestled with the decision whether to fight or flee the system" in South Africa. The author was involved in the 1976 township uprisings in Soweto, where more than 600 black people were killed when police opened fire on a peaceful student protest. However, Mathabane continued to be friends with whites whom he had met at his athletic club. He also was the only black in a segregated tournament that was boycotted by the Black Tennis Association, but he participated believing that he would meet people who could help him leave South Africa. Afterward he ran for his life when attacked by a gang of blacks who resented his association with whites.

David Papineau in the *Times Literary Supplement* did not find fault with Mathabane for leaving South Africa. In a 1987 review, the critic contended that Mathabane "does make clear the limited choices facing black youths in South Africa today. One option is political activity, with the attendant risk of detention or being forced underground. . . . Alternatively you can keep your head down and hope for a steady job. With luck and qualifications you might even end up as a white–collar supervisor with a half–way respectable salary."

A Different Form of Apartheid

Mathabane continued his life story in *Kaffir Boy in America: An Encounter with Apartheid,* which chronicles his experiences in 1978 as a student at Limestone College, South Carolina. Although armed with copies of the Declaration of Independence and the U.S. Constitution, Mathabane learned that the United States was not the promised land after all.

"Like . . . Claude Brown's *Manchild in the Promised Land* . . . in every way as important and exciting."—*THE WASHINGTON POST*

In this 1986 memoir about growing up black in racist South Africa, Mathabane relates the story of his personal struggle against apartheid.

Kaffir Boy in America is an account of Mathabane's efforts to get a good education and of his early career as a journalist and writer. Along the way, Mathabane struggled to understand American popular culture and racial attitudes. Writing in the *Journal of Modern African Studies,* Mwizenge S. Tembo observed that "*Kaffir Boy in America* shows the extent of the contradictions that exist in the world's leading superpower." A *Library Journal* reviewer stated that *Kaffir Boy in America* was "generally well–written," but "like many sequels, this one lacks the power of the original." Lorna Hahn of the *New York Times Book Review* praised Mathabane's fairness in his discussion of American attitudes toward South Africa, and she described *Kaffir Boy in America* as "an inspiring account of a young man's self–realization and his commitment to the self–realization of others."

With *In Love in Black and White: The Triumph of Love over Prejudice,* which Mathabane coauthored with his American wife, Gail Ernsberger, the author responded to people who criticized his decision to marry a white woman. In chapters divided into each spouse's perspective, this 1992 book describes the hostility that interracial marriages still face from both races. The Mathabanes discuss their initial reactions to each other when they met as graduate students in New York, their rocky courtship and secret marriage, public reaction to their marriage from blacks and whites in both New York and North Carolina, and their experiences in raising biracial children. *Kirkus Reviews* called *In Love in Black and White* "a personal and candid account of what it means to break an intransigent taboo—and a heartwarming affirmation of love and commitment." Writing in the *New York Times Book Review,* Andrea Cooper described the book as "lively" and she praised both Mathabane's "obvious intelligence and quiet passion" and Gail Mathabane's "specific, informal and visual" treatment of the problems of marrying outside one's race.

Returned Home for Inspiration

In 1994, Mathabane published his fourth work of nonfiction. *African Women: Three Generations* recounts of the life stories of his mother, grandmother, and sister to tell the larger tale of what it meant to grow up female and black in South Africa under apartheid and the legacy of colonialism. Under apartheid, the family lives of black women were torn apart as their men were forced to travel far from home to look for work. Each woman's story involves violent beatings and abuse by husbands and lovers, desperate poverty and hunger, the deaths of children, and the effects of both witchcraft and Christianity on their lives.

African Women is written in two parts. The first, set in South Africa, is the story of each woman's life as told from her own first–person perspective, as though she had dictated her tale to Mathabane; the second involves the reunion of the Mathabane women with their Americanized son on the Oprah Winfrey television show. Some reviewers found it odd that Mathabane sent his American wife to South Africa to interview his own relatives. Writing in *New Statesman & Society,* Victoria Brittain noted that all the women in the book have the same voice and "it is unmistakably the voice of the son, grandson, and brother, who escaped from the townships

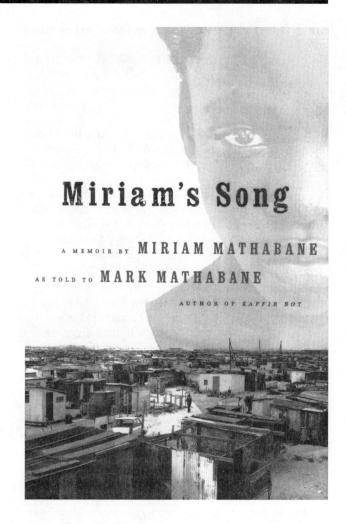

Mathabane's younger sister tells a story of institutionalized abuse and sexual assault, both under apartheid and during its aftermath, in this 2000 work.

with a tennis scholarship to America, and later graduated from the Columbia School of Journalism." Meanwhile, a *Booklist* reviewer suggested that while "the political is made personal in scenes of daily confrontation," the book would have benefited from "tighter editing." Writing in the *New York Times Book Review,* Veronica Chambers questioned Mathabane's decision to tell the women's stories in what she felt was his own voice rather than theirs. She also noted that because Mathabane failed to sketch the larger social and political context in the book, the women's problems seemed to be "boyfriends and cheating husband." Chambers added, "With *African Women: Three Generations,* it feels as though [Mathabane's literary] well is beginning to run dry."

In his introduction to *African Women,* Mathabane explained why he chose to write the book so that it reads as if the women are recounting their lives in their own words. "In telling these stories in the first person, through the eyes of each of the three characters, I have sought to avoid intruding on the ways of my grandmother, mother and sister saw, felt, thought, and acted," he wrote. "I was surprised by how differently we often saw the same thing and reacted to the same experience. For instance, my father, with his strange moods and domineering and stubborn pride, was far more of a tyrant and abuser than I had let myself remember."

Apartheid from a Child's Perspective

Mathabane's fifth book, *Miriam's Song: A Memoir*, was published in 2000. It uses the same narrative approach to focus on the sorrows that befell his younger sister, born in 1969. Like her brother, Miriam was rescued by an overseas educational opportunity. Again, the story is told in a first-person voice, and the scenes of life in Alexandra—their household's chronic poverty, a parents' combative marriage, the cruelty of Miriam's teachers at a township school—are especially vivid when told from a child's perspective. "It is evening. I'm sitting on the kitchen floor in front of a cozy fire from a red-hot *mbawula*, a brazier, watching Mama cook dinner," *Miriam's Song* recalls. "I have no toys to play with, so I often watch Mama do chores. Our house, which overlooks a donga (gully) and a dusty street called Hofmeyer, is in yard number forty-seven on Thirteenth Avenue. It has two small rooms, three small windows with several broken panes, and no running water, electricity, or indoor toilet."

Like Mathabane's other books, *Miriam's Song* provides literary snapshots of daily life under apartheid. Miriam recounts a dinner of porridge and chicken intestines in the midst of reliving a particularly horrific school day, when she had been whacked with a heavy ruler after failing a fingernail inspection. Then when the crying six-year-old girl wiped her nose on her sleeve, her enraged teacher smacked her on the head. But Miriam's mother must borrow fingernail clippers from a neighbor, and even a simple handkerchief is beyond their means. After her father disparages a school that would punish so young a child for such an infraction, Miriam explains to readers that such a school was the only education available to her, and harshness was part of the system there. "Black schools had to abide by the strict discipline rules set by the Department of Bantu Education, and corporal punishment was high on the list of those rules," she and Mathabane point out in *Miriam's Song*.

A Tale of Redemption

Interwoven into *Miriam's Song* is the gripping story of the end of apartheid in South Africa. During Miriam's teen years, opponents to the system made the black townships the focal point of protest, and places like Alexandra descended into a dangerous spiral of police violence and armed uprisings. Mathabane and his sister also recount the particular obstacle facing black South African women: in an economic situation where poverty is nearly insurmountable, and alcoholism and abusive relationships are often the rule rather than the exception. Rape and unplanned pregnancies kill many young women's dreams of finding careers or lives outside the townships. As she entered her teen years, Miriam was determined to finish high school, and she dreamed of becoming a nurse. She found solace in the religion of her mother, a devout Christian, and managed to save a small nestegg for her future. Sadly, these funds were stolen by a family member, and then when her boyfriend sexually assaulted her and she becomes pregnant. At that point, it appears that her dream is lost. But then her brother in America comes to her rescue. *Miriam's Song* ends as his *Kaffir Boy* did, with Miriam leaving South Africa for college.

New York Times Book Review writer Mary Ellen Sullivan praised the book's dramatic account of political activity in Alexandra, which Sullivan asserted "brings a critical chapter of South African history to life." The reviewer also termed the way in which Mathabane let his sister tell her own story one of *Miriam's Song*'s finest attributes: the elder brother, she wrote, "perfectly captures her guileless wisdom."

In the years since its publication, Mathabane's *Kaffir Boy* has become a part of the curriculum in high schools and colleges across the U.S. The author is a popular speaker on college campuses, and in 1996 he was named a White House fellow to the Department of Education. The eighteen fellows conducted research trips to Panama and South Africa as part of this yearlong fellowship. The year concluded with Mathabane and his colleagues submitting educational initiatives they had devised to the Department.

Mathabane, his wife, and their four children, live in North Carolina. In a 1990 interview, Mathabane told Bruce W. Nelan of *Time* that he found the American South markedly different from his college experiences in New York City. The far more segregated urban north is similar to what life was like in South Africa under apartheid—some whites in northern cities, Mathabane said, "seldom set foot in a ghetto.

They know nothing about the real life of black people. They react to what they see on television. I know because that is the way they reacted to me." In North Carolina, by contrast, Mathabane saw "that in places in the South where change has occurred, it has been genuine. Many white people go out of their way not to be seen as racists, not to give a racial connotation to any situation."

If you enjoy the works of Mark Mathabane, you might want to check out the following books:

Rudolfo A. Anaya, *Bless Me, Ultima,* 1995.
Andre Philippus Brink, *Imaginings of Sand,* 1999.
Antjie Krog, *Country of My Skull: Guilt, Sorrow, and the Limits of Forgiveness in the New South Africa,* 1999.
Margaret McCord, *The Calling of Katie Makanya: A Memoir of South Africa,* 1998.

In his lectures to high school and college students, Mathabane recounts his own story, through it stressing the need to use any opportunity available. He sees education—and even a substandard one, be it in Bantu or a problem–plagued American urban public system—as the salvation. "With education you are made to accept the universality of human beings," he told Nelan in *Time.* "You can see yourself in other people."

■ Biographical and Critical Sources

BOOKS

The Schomburg Center Guide to Black Literature, Gale, 1996.
St. James Guide to Young Adult Writers, 2nd edition, St. James Press, 1999.

PERIODICALS

Africa Today, July/September, 1996, Sheldon W. Weeks, review of *African Women—Three Generations,* p. 329.

Booklist, February 15, 1994, Hazel Rochman, review of *African Women—Three Generations,* p. 1034.
Chicago Tribune Book World, April 13, 1986, Diane Manuel, review of *Kaffir Boy.*
Christian Science Monitor, May 2, 1986; April 25, 1994; February 21, 1995.
Journal of Modern African Studies, December, 1990, Mwizenga S. Tembo, review of *Kaffir Boy in America,* p. 723.
Kirkus Reviews, November 15, 1991, review of *Love in Black and White.*
Library Journal, April 15, 1986, Elizabeth Widenmenn, review of *Kaffir Boy,* p. 76; June 1, 1989, review of *Kaffir Boy in America,* p. 116; December, 1991, A.O. Edmonds, review of *Love in Black White,* p. 158; April 1, 1994.
Los Angeles Times Book Review, March 30, 1986, Peter Dreyer, review of *Kaffir Boy.*
New Statesman & Society, March 30, 1995, Victoria Brittain, review of *African Women—Three Generations,* p. 37.
Newsweek, March 9, 1992, Laura Shapiro, review of *Love in Black White,* p. 62.
New York Times, March 2, 1987; September 24, 1987; December 14, 1997.
New York Times Book Review, April 27, 1986; August 13, 1989; February 16, 1992, Andrea Cooper, review of *Love in Black and White;* July 31, 1994, p. 25; August 13, 2000, Mary Ellen Sullivan, review of *Miriam's Song.*
People Weekly, July 7, 1986; February 17, 1992, Susan Shapiro, review of *Love in Black and White,* p. 25.
Publishers Weekly, February 28, 1986, Genevieve Stuttaford, review of *Kaffir Boy,* p. 111; April 28, 1989, review of *Kaffir Boy in America,* p. 66; December 6, 1991, review of *Love in Black and White,* p. 53; March 21, 1994, review of *African Women—Three Generations,* p. 62.
Sage, spring, 1995.
School Library Journal, February, 2001, Jane S. Drabkin, review of *Miriam's Song: A Memoir,* p. 145.
Seventeen, August 1987, Lesley Poindexter, review of *Kaffir Boy,* pp. 242+.
Time, November 12, 1990, Bruce W. Nelan, "Taking the Measure of American Racism," p. 16.
Times Literary Supplement, August 21, 1987.
Washington Post Book World, April 20, 1986, Charles R. Larson, review of *Kaffir Boy.*

ONLINE

Mark Mathabane Web site, located at http://www.mathabane.com (January, 2001).*

Ed McBain

mobile Association and selling lobsters for a whole-sale lobster firm, both New York City; worked for Scott Meredith Literary Agency, New York City, for about eighteen months. *Military service:* U.S. Navy, 1944—46. *Member:* Phi Beta Kappa.

■ Personal

Also writes under name Evan Hunter and under pseudonyms Curt Cannon, Hunt Collins, Ezra Hannon, and Richard Marsten; born Salvatore Albert Lombino, October 15, 1926, in New York, NY; son of Charles and Marie (Coppola) Lombino; name legally changed to Evan Hunter; married Anita Melnick, October 17, 1949 (divorced); married Mary Vann Finley, June, 1973 (divorced); married Drasica Dimitrijevic, September 4, 1997; children: (first marriage) Ted, Mark, Richard; (second marriage) Amanda Eve Finley (stepdaughter). *Education:* Attended Cooper Union, 1943—44; Hunter College (now Hunter College of the City University of New York), B.A., 1950. *Politics:* Democrat.

■ Addresses

Agent—c/o Gelfman Schneider, 250 West 57th St., New York, NY 10107.

■ Career

Writer. Taught at a vocational high school in New York City, 1950; held various jobs, including answering the telephone at night for American Auto-

■ Awards, Honors

Mystery Writers of America Award, 1957, for short story "The Last Spin"; Grand Master Award, Mystery Writers of America, 1986, for lifetime achievement; Cartier Diamond Dagger Award, Crime Writers Association (Britain), c. 1999, for lifetime achievement.

"87TH PRECINCT" SERIES

Cop Hater (also see below), Simon & Schuster, 1956.

The Mugger (also see below), Simon & Schuster, 1956.

The Pusher (also see below), Simon & Schuster, 1956.

The Con Man (also see below), Simon & Schuster, 1957.

Killer's Choice, Simon & Schuster, 1957.

Killer's Payoff, Simon & Schuster, 1958.

Lady Killer, Simon & Schuster, 1958.

Killer's Wedge, Simon & Schuster, 1958.

'Til Death, Simon & Schuster, 1959.

King's Ransom, Simon & Schuster, 1959.

Give the Boys a Great Big Hand, Simon & Schuster, 1960.

The Heckler, Simon & Schuster, 1960.

See Them Die, Simon & Schuster, 1960.

Lady, Lady, I Did It!, Simon & Schuster, 1961.

Like Love, Simon & Schuster, 1962.

The Empty Hours (three novellas), Simon & Schuster, 1962.

Ten Plus One, Simon & Schuster, 1963.

Ax, Simon & Schuster, 1964.

He Who Hesitates, Delacorte, 1965.

Doll, Delacorte, 1965.

Eighty Million Eyes, Delacorte, 1966.

The 87th Precinct (includes *Cop Hater, The Mugger, The Pusher,* and *The Con Man*), Boardman, 1966.

Fuzz (also see below), Doubleday, 1968.

Shotgun, Doubleday, 1969.

Jigsaw, Doubleday, 1970.

Hail, Hail, the Gang's All Here, Doubleday, 1971.

Sadie When She Died, Doubleday, 1972.

Let's Hear It for the Deaf Man, Doubleday, 1972.

87th Precinct: An Ed McBain Omnibus, Hamish Hamilton, 1973.

Hail to the Chief, Random House, 1973.

Bread, Random House, 1974.

The Second 87th Precinct Omnibus, Hamish Hamilton, 1975.

Blood Relatives, Random House, 1975.

So Long as You Both Shall Live, Random House, 1976.

Long Time No See, Random House, 1977.

Calypso, Viking, 1979.

Ghosts, Viking, 1980.

Heat, Viking, 1981.

Ice, Arbor House, 1983.

Lightning, Arbor House, 1984.

Eight Black Horses, Avon, 1985.

Poison, Morrow, 1987.

Tricks, Morrow, 1987.

McBain's Ladies: The Women of the 87th Precinct, Mysterious Press, 1988.

Lullaby, Morrow, 1989.

McBain's Ladies, Too, Mysterious Press, 1989.

Vespers, Morrow, 1990.

Widows, Morrow, 1991.

Kiss, Morrow, 1992.

Mischief, Morrow, 1993.

Romance, Warner (New York City), 1995.

Nocturne, Warner (New York City), 1997.

The Big Bad City, Simon & Schuster, 1999.

The Last Dance, Simon & Schuster, 2000.

"MATTHEW HOPE" SERIES; CRIME NOVELS

Goldilocks, Arbor House, 1978.

Rumpelstiltskin, Viking, 1981.

Beauty and the Beast, Hamish Hamilton, 1982, Holt, 1983.

Jack and the Beanstalk, Holt, 1984.

Snow White and Rose Red, Holt, 1986.

Cinderella, Holt, 1986.

Puss in Boots, Holt, 1987.

The House that Jack Built, Holt, 1988.

Three Blind Mice, Mysterious Press, 1991.

Mary, Mary, Warner (New York City), 1993.

And All through the House, Warner (New York City), 1994.

There Was a Little Girl, Warner (New York City), 1994.

Gladly, the Cross–Eyed Bear, Warner (New York City), 1996.

The Last Best Hope, Warner (New York City), 1998.

UNDER NAME EVAN HUNTER

The Evil Sleep, Falcon, 1952.

The Big Fix, Falcon, 1952, published under pseudonym Richard Marsten as *So Nude, So Dead*, Fawcett, 1956.

Find the Feathered Serpent, Winston, 1952.

Don't Crowd Me, Popular Library, 1953, published in England as *The Paradise Party*, New English Library, 1968.

The Blackboard Jungle, Simon & Schuster, 1954.

Second Ending, Simon & Schuster, 1956, published as *Quartet in H*, Pocket Books, 1957.

The Jungle Kids (short stories), Pocket Books, 1956.

Strangers When We Meet (also see below), Simon & Schuster, 1958.

A Matter of Conviction, Simon & Schuster, 1959, published as *The Young Savages*, Pocket Books, 1966.

The Remarkable Harry (juvenile), Abelard, 1960.

The Last Spin and Other Stories, Constable, 1960.

The Wonderful Button (juvenile), Abelard, 1961.

Mothers and Daughters, Simon & Schuster, 1961.

Happy New Year, Herbie, and Other Stories, Simon & Schuster, 1963.

Buddwing, Simon & Schuster, 1964.

The Paper Dragon, Delacorte, 1966.

A Horse's Head, Delacorte, 1967.

Last Summer, Doubleday, 1968.

Sons, Doubleday, 1969.

Nobody Knew They Were There, Doubleday, 1971.

The Beheading and Other Stories, Constable, 1971.

Every Little Crook and Nanny, Doubleday, 1972.

The Easter Man (a Play), and Six Stories (also see below), Doubleday, 1972.

Seven, Constable, 1972.

Come Winter, Doubleday, 1973.

Streets of Gold, Harper, 1974.

The Chisholms: A Novel of the Journey West (also see below), Harper, 1976.

Me and Mr. Stenner (juvenile), Lippincott, 1977.

Walk Proud (also see below), Bantam, 1979.

Love, Dad, Crown, 1981.

Far from the Sea, Atheneum, 1983.

Lizzie, Arbor House, 1984.

Criminal Conversation, Warner (New York City), 1995.

Privileged Conversation, Warner (New York City), 1996.

Me and Hitch (memoir), Faber & Faber (Boston), 1997.

Contributor to *Best Detective Stories of the Year 1955,* edited by David Coxe Cook, Dutton, 1955.

UNDER PSEUDONYM RICHARD MARSTEN

Rocket to Luna (juvenile), Winston, 1953.

Danger: Dinosaurs (juvenile), Winston, 1953.

Runaway Black (crime novel), Fawcett, 1954.

Murder in the Navy (crime novel), Fawcett, 1955, published under pseudonym Ed McBain as *Death of a Nurse,* Pocket Books, 1968.

The Spiked Heel (crime novel), Holt, 1956.

Vanishing Ladies (crime novel), Pocket Books, 1957.

Even the Wicked (crime novel), Permabooks, 1957, published in England under pseudonym Ed McBain, Severn House, 1979.

Big Man (crime novel), Pocket Books, 1959, published in England under pseudonym Ed McBain, Penguin, 1978.

Contributor to *Dames, Danger, and Death,* edited by Leo Marguiles, Pyramid, 1960.

PLAYS; UNDER NAME EVAN HUNTER

The Easter Man, produced in Birmingham, England, at Birmingham Repertory Theatre, 1964, produced under title *A Race of Hairy Men!* on Broadway at Henry Miller's Theater, April, 1965.

The Conjuror, produced in Ann Arbor, MI, at Lydia Mendelssohn Theatre, November 5, 1969.

Stalemate, produced in New York City, 1975.

SCREENPLAYS AND TELEVISION SCRIPTS; UNDER NAME EVAN HUNTER

Strangers When We Meet (based on his novel of the same title), Columbia Pictures, 1960.

The Birds (based on a short story by Daphne du Maurier), Universal Pictures, 1963.

Fuzz (based on his novel of the same title), United Artists, 1972.

Walk Proud (based on his novel of the same title), Universal Pictures, 1979.

The Chisholms (Columbia Broadcasting System mini-series and weekly television series), Alan Landsburg Productions, 1979-80.

Also author of *The Legend of Walks Far Woman* (television movie), 1982; *Dream West* (television mini-series), 1985; and *Columbo: Undercover* (television movie), 1994.

OTHER

(Under pseudonym Hunt Collins) *Cut Me In,* Abelard, 1954, published as *The Proposition,* Pyramid Books, 1955.

(Under pseudonym Hunt Collins) *Tomorrow's World,* Bouregy, 1956, published as *Tomorrow and Tomorrow,* Pyramid Books, 1956, published in England under pseudonym Ed McBain, Sphere, 1979.

(Under pseudonym Curt Cannon) *I'm Cannon—For Hire* (crime novel), Fawcett, 1958.

(Under pseudonym Curt Cannon) *I Like 'Em Tough* (short stories), Fawcett, 1958.

(Under pseudonym Ezra Hannon) *Doors* (crime novel), Stein Day, 1975.

Also author of "Appointment at Eleven" for *Alfred Hitchcock Presents,* 1955-61. The Mugar Memorial Library of Boston University holds Hunter's manuscripts.

■ Adaptations

MOVIES AND TELEVISION

The Blackboard Jungle, Metro-Goldwyn-Mayer, 1955.

Cop Hater, United Artists, 1958.

The Muggers (based on *The Mugger*), United Artists, 1958.

The Pusher, United Artists, 1960.

The Young Savages (based on *A Matter of Conviction*), United Artists, 1961.

High and Low (based on *King's Ransom*), Toho International, 1963.

Mr. Buddwing (based on *Buddwing*), Metro–Goldwyn–Mayer, 1967.

Last Summer, Twentieth Century–Fox, 1969.

Sans Mobile Apparent (title means "Without Apparent Motive"; based on *Ten Plus One*), President Films, 1971.

Le Cri du cormoran le soir au–dessus des jonques (title means "The Cry of the Cormorant at Night over the Junks"; based on *A Horse's Head*), Gaumont International, 1971.

Every Little Crook and Nanny, Metro–Goldwyn–Mayer, 1972.

Ed McBain's 87th Precinct: Lightning (television movie), 1995.

Ed McBain's 87th Precinct: Ice (television movie), 1996.

McBain's breakout novel, first published in 1954 under the name Evan Hunter, was based in part on his own experiences as a teacher in a vocational high school.

The film rights to the Evan Hunter novel *Criminal Conversation* have been purchased by actor Tom Cruise's company, Cruise–Wagner Productions.

■ Work in Progress

Rain after Sundown, an Evan Hunter novel; the book for the musical *The Night They Raided Minsky's.*

■ Sidelights

In 2001, veteran crime writer Ed McBain teamed up with acclaimed literary novelist and screenwriter Evan Hunter to write *Candyland: A Novel of Obsession;* the book opens with the type of in–depth character study and examination of moral issues for which Hunter is famous, and it concludes with the kind of detailed police investigation that McBain has popularized in dozens of thrillers. Dedicated fans of these authors' work will know, however, that Ed McBain and Evan Hunter are the same person. One of today's most versatile, prolific, and best–selling writers, McBain/Hunter has numerous novels, short stories, plays, and film scripts to his credit. Better known to millions throughout the world under his pseudonym Ed McBain, the originator of the "87th Precinct" detective series, the author, under his own name of Evan Hunter, has also created such thought–provoking best–sellers as *The Blackboard Jungle, Sons, Mothers and Daughters, Streets of Gold,* and *Love, Dad.* He prefers to keep these two identities strictly separate, he once explained, because "I don't like to confuse critics who are very easily confused anyway. I also do not like to confuse readers. I wouldn't like a woman, for example, who had read *Mothers and Daughters* by Evan Hunter, to pick up *The Heckler* by Ed McBain and find that it's about mayhem, bloodshed and violence. I think this would be unfair to her and unfair to me as well."

McBain was born Salvatore Albert Lombino in 1926 and grew up in the East Harlem and North Bronx neighborhoods of New York City. He discovered a talent for art, and after graduating from high school he began studying at the Cooper Union, an advanced school for the arts. He soon discovered, however, that although he had been the best artist at his high school, most of his fellow students at Cooper were more talented and dedicated to art than he was. He left school, joined the U.S. Navy,

Glenn Ford (center) and Sidney Poitier (right) appear in the 1955 film *The Blackboard Jungle,* based on McBain's novel.

and was stationed on a ship in the Pacific. The posting lent itself to developing his future career, for World War II had ended and he saw little action. "When I got into the navy I began writing and sending the stories off to various magazines," McBain once stated. "I was on a destroyer in the peacetime Pacific and there wasn't much else to do." Not very familiar with the publishing market, the young man sent most of his stories to the big glossy magazines of the day. He submitted his stories under a series of pseudonyms, figuring that the obviously ethnic name "Lombino" might hinder his chances, but he still found little success.

Undeterred, after leaving the navy McBain entered New York's Hunter College with the intent of studying to become a writer. He graduated Phi Beta Kappa in 1950 and began having some success sell-ing science fiction stories to pulp magazines. The author also managed to sell two science fiction novels in the early 1950s, but even this was not enough to support his growing family. He took other jobs to supplement his writing income: selling lobsters, playing jazz piano, teaching at a vocational school, and finally working as a literary agent. These last two jobs were to prove the turning point in his career, for as an agent he could place his work more easily, and his time as a teacher provided the inspiration for what was to become his breakthrough novel, *The Blackboard Jungle.* After his editor suggested that the pseudonym "Evan Hunter" (taken from the names of his high school and college) would help sell the book better than "Salvatore Lombino," the author legally adopted Evan Hunter as his name.

Though it appeared four years after he made his first serious attempts to write for publication, *The Blackboard Jungle* caused the twenty–eight–year–old author to be labeled an "overnight" success. A semi–autobiographical work, *The Blackboard Jungle* tells the story of an idealistic young man who confronts the often violent realities of trying to teach a group of sullen, illiterate, delinquent teenagers in a big–city vocational high school. Written in what was then politely termed the "vernacular," Hunter's dramatic indictment of both the inadequacies of teacher training colleges and of the New York City school system is "a nightmarish but authentic first novel," according to a *Time* critic. *New York Herald Tribune Book Review* contributor Barbara Klaw pointed to Hunter's "superb ear for conversation," "competence as a storyteller," and "tolerant and tough–minded sympathy for his subject" as some of the book's best features. Nathan Rothman of the *Saturday Review* felt that it is free of the "distortions and dishonesty" of many newspaper articles on the same topic. And even though *Nation* critic Stanley Cooperman believed that Hunter "makes only cursory attempts to probe the wellsprings of the action he photographs so well," he concluded that the ex–substitute teacher "succeeds in dramatizing an area heretofore neglected in fiction." The book was an immediate best–seller, and, along with the ground-breaking film adaptation starring Glenn Ford and Sidney Portier, helped awaken America to the troubles of youthful alienation and juvenile delinquency. Assessing the book nearly thirty years after its publication, *Dictionary of Literary Biography Yearbook* contributor Ralph F. Voss stated that the story of *The Blackboard Jungle* "is an absorbing one in which the idealism inherent in the American democratic concept of public education comes into full clash with the cynicism and frustration of burnt-out students and teachers."

Although Hunter's *The Blackboard Jungle* is still regarded as a classic, the pseudonym the author adopted two years later is the one by which most readers recognize him today. He once related the story of the birth of "Ed McBain" as follows: "When I was beginning to write, I wrote a great many detective stories for the pulp magazines. I wrote not only police stories, but private eye and man–on–the–run and woman–in–jeopardy, the whole gamut. After *The Blackboard Jungle* was published, Pocket Books did the reprint of it. I had an old mystery novel kicking around that I had not yet sold, and there was a pseudonym on it, but not Ed McBain. We sent it to Pocket Books as a possibility for a paperback original. The editor there at the time, a man named Herbert Alexander, was a very bright guy.

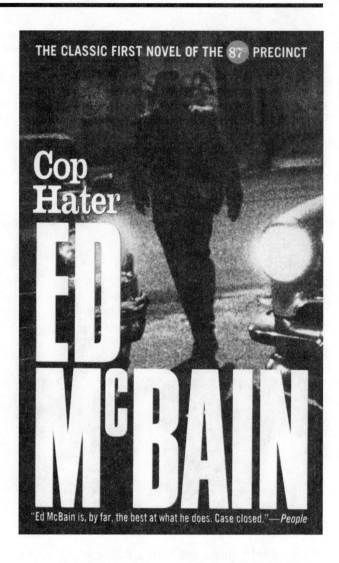

This 1956 crime novel opened McBain's "87th Precinct" series, which now numbers more than fifty volumes.

He recognized the style and called my agent and said, 'Is this our friend Hunter?' My agent said, 'Yes, it is,' and Alexander said, 'Well, I'd like to talk to him.'

"We had lunch one day," the author continued, "and the gist of the conversation was that the mainstay of Pocket Books was [the mystery writer] Erle Stanley Gardner; he had sold millions of books and they would just republish each title every three or four years with new jackets. They kept selling as if they were new books all the time. But he was getting old and they were looking for a mystery writer who could replace him, so they asked me if I had any ideas about a mystery series. I said I would think about it. I got back to them and I said that it seemed to me—after all the mysteries I'd written—that the only valid people to deal with crime were cops, and I would like to make the lead character, rather than a single *person,* a *squad* of cops instead—so it would be a conglomerate lead character. They said, 'OK, we'll give you a contract for three books and if it works we'll renew it.' I started writing the series."

Finding Solutions in the Details

Published in 1956, *Cop Hater* was the debut of McBain's "87th Precinct" series, novels that are known as "police procedurals" in the mystery trade. As the author once remarked, "I spent months in research in the precincts, in the cars, in the courts, and at the labs before I wrote the first book." This was time well spent, for as Voss commented, "from its earliest novels, the 87th Precinct series has been noted for its accuracy and authenticity in describing police procedures." The series is set in Isola, a metropolis that bears a striking resemblance to New York City, and features various policemen and detectives of the city's 87th Precinct as they work together to solve crimes. Although the squad as a whole is the focus of the series, one detective who appears frequently is Steve Carella, whose relationship with his wife, the beautiful deaf–mute Teddy, is developed throughout the novels as well. In over forty years, McBain has published fifty books in the series, giving him plenty of room to introduce and evolve numerous characters, from cops to criminals to informants, and explore various storylines, from humorous to gruesome. Throughout each novel, McBain includes "crisp believable dialogue" and meticulous detail that makes him "the most consistently skillful writer of police novels," according to Julian Symons in *Mortal Consequences.*

Other critics have likewise observed that the tales of 87th Precinct have managed to remain inventive and interesting. Reviewing the ninth of the series, *'Til Death, New York Times Book Review* writer Anthony Boucher noted that it "nobly upholds the traditions of the 87th Precinct: it is a fresh, human, humorous, exciting novel about a vivid and unusual situation." The same critic observed that the thirteenth installment, *See Them Die,* proves that "McBain, fortunately, is not concerned with writing according to the McBain formula, and can sometimes depart from it almost entirely." Commenting on *Bread,* which falls mid–way through the series, *Washington Post Book World* critic Jean M. White wrote that "McBain not only solves an exciting case but, as always, captures a feeling for the problems of everyday law enforcement on the streets." Besides memorable characters, Julian Symons stated in the *New York Times Book Review,* "the 87th Pre-

cinct stories also offer the pleasures of much crisp, credible dialogue that is never too smart for its own good or our enjoyment, and some alert observations about the contemporary scene." Even after more than thirty volumes, the critic concluded, in *Calypso* "the narrative grip and storytelling zest are still there."

While the scope of the series has allowed McBain to introduce and explore new characters, he still makes room to catch up with old favorites. In 1992's *Kiss,* for example, Carella winds his way through a series of events that lead him to being involved with his father's killer. The plot also twists around Carella investigating the attempted murder of a stockbroker's wife. The 1997 installment *Nocturne* has Carella and Hawes investigating the death of a former concert pianist. "Followers of this 40–year–old series will be satisfied, as always, and new fans will be captured by this latest example of McBain's enduring virtuosity," a *Publishers Weekly* critic observed. The 1999 volume *The Big Bad City,* concerning the murder of a nun with an unconventional past, likewise contains "a startlingly real cast of suspects and witnesses and a terrifically entertaining mix of cop dialogue, gritty city atmosphere and action," according to another *Publishers Weekly* writer. *Booklist* contributor Wes Lukowsky similarly praised the book, calling it "another solid entry in an amazing series that has always set the standard for intelligent police procedurals." The appearance in 2000 of the fiftieth volume in the series, *The Last Dance,* drew additional tributes to the author's ability to not only keep his work fresh but improve upon previous volumes. Terming this tale of murder in the worlds of theater and high society "one of the best" in the series, a *Publishers Weekly* reviewer noted that *The Last Dance* is "a cop story that's as strong and soulful as the urban heart of American [McBain] celebrates so well." In *Booklist,* Lukowsky characterized the volume as containing McBain's "typically accomplished mix of police procedure, characterization, social commentary and tight plotting that has long distinguished this landmark series."

As the "87th Precinct" series has progressed, McBain has not shied away from depicting, often graphically, the violence that police officers often encounter. "That came," the author revealed to *Crime Time Online* interviewer Barry Forshaw, "because I was riding with the cops. I'd get out of a cop's car, you'd walk over to the curb and there'd be a guy lying in the gutter with his brains all over the sidewalk. . . . As a writer, I felt you couldn't pull punches in this area. If you wanted your books to be authentic, then it was essential to tell the truth." The author likened the changes in his books to the evolution of movie violence over the past forty years. "But what they don't do in the mov-

Two detectives team up to solve the on–screen murder of a television personality in this "87th Precinct" novel.

ies—and what I try to do in the books—is to represent the fact that when you get shot it *hurts*."

As Ed McBain, the author later branched out to begin a new mystery series, and in 1978 lawyer Matthew Hope made his debut in *Goldilocks*. Set on Florida's Gulf Coast instead of in the big city, the novel begins with a man returning home to find his family murdered; he falls under suspicion, and it is up to his lawyer to discover the truth of the matter. In subsequent volumes, Hope is involved in various cases that recall other fairy tales, if in a bizarre and sometimes gruesome fashion. In addition to the clever plots, the series has become popular for its protagonist, for Hope is not the stereotypical clever and confident sleuth of standard mystery fiction.

He has a barely successful law practice, often losing cases to smarter attorneys, and has an ex–wife who treats him with scorn. These "artful dodges from the stereotypes of the genre" help make the 1984 installment, *Jack and the Beanstalk*, a "*tour de force* of the genre," according to *Best Sellers* contributor D. V. O'Brien. A *Publishers Weekly* reviewer concurred with this assessment, calling this story of a client and his pilfered wealth "racy, intricate, well–crafted suspense."

The 1994 novel *There Was a Little Girl* is also one of McBain's Matthew Hope mysteries. Hope, however, is unconscious through most of the action of the novel. His condition remains a mystery until his colleagues are able to untangle the events leading up to his coma. The trail of evidence leads them to Hope's most recent job, looking for land for a circus. Part of the problem with this novel, Richard Gid Powers claimed in the *New York Times Book Review*, is that by getting Hope out of the action "you have to identify with the supporting characters and, frankly, they are not of star caliber." The critic nevertheless concluded that "this is an amazingly accomplished, richly enjoyable three–ring circus of a book directed by a ringmaster at the top of his form." John Skow commented in *Time* that "the author's secret appears to be the steadiness of his gaze. He looks straight at whatever he is describing, concentrating utterly . . . on, say, why bears are more dangerous than tigers in animal acts."

After thirteen volumes, McBain concluded the series with 1998's *The Last Best Hope*; he revealed to Forshaw that in addition to the extra research required to write the books, "it's always been difficult for me to justify an amateur solving crimes: someone hired by somebody to defend them. He has to be there, for instance, at the showdown, which is not logical. You'd rarely find a lawyer in that position. In fact, you'd rarely find a police detective in that position." In this concluding volume, the author resolves that problem by bringing in Steve Carella of the 87th Precinct to assist Hope as he tries to locate a missing husband. The case is not as simple as it first seems, as two separate romantic triangles and a museum heist figure into the case. While the plot is "tangled," a *Publishers Weekly* critic observed, "with McBain's skilled handling, it's crystal clear and an absolute delight." *Booklist* reviewer Lukowsky similarly hailed the author's control over a "brilliantly complex" plot, and concluded that this "stellar work by one of crime fiction's very best" is "McBain's best crime novel in years."

Hunting Epic Scope and Themes

"The nice thing about the '87th Precinct' is that I can deal with any subject matter so long as it's criminally related," McBain once said. "With the Ed

McBain (as Evan Hunter) wrote the screenplay for *The Birds,* Alfred Hitchcock's classic 1963 horror film.

McBain novels, I only want to say that cops have a tough, underpaid job, and they deal with murder every day of the week, and that's the way it is, folks. With the Hunters, the theme varies and I'll usually ponder the next book for a long, long time—until it demands to be written." Most of these "Hunter" novels exhibit definite thematic concerns, occasionally inspired by biographical or autobiographical material, but often just "intellectual concepts that come to me and take a while to develop before they're put down on paper," as the author described it. As Hunter, the author has written a great deal about young people, especially the relationship between the young and their elders (usually parents). "I don't know why I've been attracted to writing about young people," he remarked to *Publishers Weekly* interviewer Robert Dahlin. "I guess from *Blackboard Jungle,* it's been a situation that's always appealed to me, the idea of adults in conflict with

the young. I think part of my fascination is with America as an adolescent nation and with our so–called adult responses that are sometimes adolescent." Often these same novels contain elements of current topical interest as well—the state of the American educational system in *The Blackboard Jungle,* the emptiness of post–World War II middle–class life in *Mothers and Daughters,* the Vietnam War in *Sons,* and the anti–Establishment "hippie" movement of the late 1960s and early 1970s in *Love, Dad.*

The 1969 novel *Sons,* for instance, follows three generations of the Tyler family through their participation in America's major conflicts of the twentieth century. Grandfather Bertram leaves the woodlands of Wisconsin to fight in World War I and defend the interests of democracy, but soon finds his ideals in conflict with the realities of warfare in the trenches.

His son Will becomes a fighter pilot during World War II, despite Bertram's doubts about the usefulness of war. Grandson Wat is born into a more troubled world, as American business expansion has made political relations with the world more ambiguous and complex. Wat's death in Vietnam is symbolic of the contrasting philosophies of his father and grandfather and within America as a whole. *Sons* "is a powerful novel that says something about the chronic problems that retard the pursuit of the American Dream," John D. Foreman remarked in *Best Sellers*. Foreman further praised how Hunter "catches the speech and character of the three generations of this century with great subtlety." While he found the characters overshadowed by the novel's themes, Voss noted that "its multigenerational view of the Tylers' painfully coming of age with America and its persistent questioning of America's myths make it Hunter's most ambitious novel after *The Blackboard Jungle*."

For the 1974 Hunter novel *Streets of Gold*, the author drew on his background once again, this time using his experiences growing up Italian American and his former job as a jazz pianist. The novel follows the transformation of Ignazio Di Palermo, a blind third–generation Italian American trained as a classical musician, into Dwight Jamison, a popular jazz pianist. The novel is both an examination and an indictment of the American dream, as Ignazio becomes successful but realizes what he has had to give up—a loving and supportive family—to attain it. While a *New Yorker* writer found the "familiarity" of Ignazio's rise and fall "depressing," the critic added that "much of the book has a definite personal stamp, and its evocations of jazz . . . are pleasant." Calling the novel "probably [Hunter's] finest to date," Voss found it "a serious examination of America's myth of unlimited opportunity for immigrants." Similarly, the 1976 Western epic *The Chisholms* "evokes some freshness from the tritest materials and focuses our concern on complex, often perverse, human beings rather than on the vacuous panoramic vista that too often dominates this genre," James R. Frakes observed in the *New York Times Book Review*.

Even as he has become better known for his McBain novels, the author has continued to produce novels as Evan Hunter that have earned positive critical attention. The 1981 novel *Love, Dad* follows the turbulent relationships within a family during the late 1960s; *Washington Post Book World* contributor Stanley Ellin found it "an exceptionally rewarding and entertaining novel." "Hunter's interest is primarily in his characters—their reflexes, preoccupations, foibles," Helen Rogan observed in a *Harper's* review of the 1983 novel *Far from the Sea*. "Instead of dumping stereotypes into a situation, he shows how the small details animate people." As a result, this story of a family facing the terminal illness of their patriarch makes for an "unsparing and personally felt novel of how we go about the business of dying in the late twentieth century," according to Richard Freedman in the *New York Times Book Review*.

Criminal Conversation, a 1995 novel, involves issues of law and order, as well as loyalty and duty. In this book, Michael Welles is an assistant district attorney whose assignment is to find incriminating evidence on mobster Andrew Faviola. During video surveillance of Faviola, Welles discovers that his wife is having an affair with the crime boss. Welles is then torn between his dedication to his job and his love for his wife. Chris Petrakos complained in *Tribune Books* that the "characters seem a little thin," but overall commended the novel's fast pace and interesting plot. *New York Times Book Review* contributor Michael Anderson felt that some of the story is derivative, but he praised the storytelling and pacing, commenting that Hunter "unfolds them like the master he is." The rights to the book were purchased by actor Tom Cruise's production company for potential adaptation as a motion picture.

As Evan Hunter, the author has also written several film and television screenplays. While some have been adapted from his own books, his most famous script is that for the classic 1963 film directed by Alfred Hitchcock, *The Birds*. Taking just the premise from a story by Daphne du Maurier—ordinary birds suddenly attacking people—Hunter crafted a fable about nature taking revenge against the species that has defiled it. The film is considered one of Hitchcock's most terrifying works, although the great director tended to de–emphasize the role of the writer in creating his films. "Which is fair enough," the author told Forshaw, "as he was undoubtedly the main reason for their greatness. But his best films *are* well written." Hunter later recounted his working relationship with Hitchcock—besides *The Birds*, he was involved in the early drafts of the director's film *Marnie*—in the 1997 memoir *Me and Hitch*, which itself was well received as an insightful portrait of a film legend.

"Whether he is writing the whodunit, the potboiler, the pulp or the serious novel, [Hunter/McBain] is a thoroughly profession writer: a 'pro,'" Al Morgan stated in the *New York Herald Tribune Lively Arts and Book Review*. "His style has drive, pace, tempo, and authenticity." As Evan Hunter, the author shows himself as "a serious and honorable writer trying to entertain us, and also trying to tell us, now and again, some useful things about our lives," according to *New York Times Book Review* contributor Ivan Gold. "Hunter's claim to be considered a serious writer rests largely on his stories of American families and their relationships to America's sustaining myths," Voss likewise suggested, adding that "in novels such as *Sons* and *Streets of Gold*, his claim is well based." As McBain, the author "invented the American police procedural as we know it," Marilyn Stasio observed in the *New York Times Book Review*. Besides establishing a certain style for the genre, the critic continued, "McBain also demystified the traditional detective hero and brought him down to earth." McBain allowed his precinct of cops to change and evolve just like a real squad would, Stasio concluded, and thus his "real achievement is how [he] has managed to sustain the continuity of the series for nearly half a century without sacrificing its freshness. Indeed, the most recent novels . . . are among the best."

If you enjoy the works of Ed McBain, you might want to check out the following books:

Rex Burns, *Body Guard*, 1991.
Frederick D. Huebner, *Methods of Execution*, 1994.
Stephen Lewis, *And Baby Makes None*, 1991.
William G. Tapply, *The Spotted Cats*, 1991.

As he so aptly demonstrated in the joint Hunter–McBain novel *Candyland*, the author has no difficulty in making his two literary identities distinguishable. As he told Selwyn Raab in a *New York Times Book Review* interview, "changing writing styles is like an actor taking on a different part." His versatility, while pleasing readers, has created some difficulties with critics and fellow authors, he recalled to Raab. "I'm not quite accepted among mystery writers because they suspect that I think I'm slumming when I'm Ed McBain. And I'm not quite accepted in the 'literary community' because I write mystery novels." The author is not complaining, however; as he remarked in his interview with Forshaw, "I'm satisfied to have made one movie at least as Evan Hunter which will be remembered. And as long as people remember the 87th Precinct books, that'll be satisfaction enough for me." It is the reader, after all, for whom the author writes. As he explained to *Publishers Weekly* interviewer Dahlin, "The whole reason I write anything is so that someone somewhere will say, 'Oh, yeah. I feel that way too. I'm not alone.'" "I guess you simply have

to write what you feel deeply," the author once remarked, "and you have to write it as well as you can and hope that it will strike a responsive chord somewhere out there."

■ Biographical and Critical Sources

BOOKS

Contemporary Authors New Revision Series (interview), Volume 5, Gale (Detroit, MI), 1982, pp. 277–281.

Contemporary Literary Criticism, Gale, Volume 11, 1979, pp. 279–280, Volume 31, 1985, pp. 217–229.

Dictionary of Literary Biography Yearbook: 1982, Gale, 1983, pp. 291–299.

Dove, George N., *The Boys from Grover Avenue: Ed McBain's 87th Precinct Novels*, Bowling Green State University Popular Press, 1985.

Newquist, Roy, *Conversations*, Rand McNally, 1967.

Symons, Julian, *Mortal Consequences: A History—From the Detective Story to the Crime Novel*, Harper, 1972, p. 205.

PERIODICALS

Armchair Detective, summer, 1992, p. 282; spring, 1995, p. 104.

Best Sellers, October 15, 1966, Anne Keehan, review of *Paper Dragon*, p. 259–260; June 15, 1968; August 15, 1969, John D. Foreman, review of *Sons*, pp. 185–186; March 15, 1971, William B. Hill, review of *Nobody Knew They Were There*, p. 536; June, 1984, D. V. O'Brien, review of *Jack and the Beanstalk*, p. 93.

Booklist, January 1, 1998, Wes Lukowsky, review of *The Last Best Hope*, p. 743; January, 1999, W. Lukowsky, review of *The Big Bad City*, p. 548; December, 1999, W. Lukowsky, review of *The Last Dance*, p. 197.

Books, June, 1970.

Books and Bookmen, January, 1969.

Catholic World, August, 1958, Riley Hughes, review of *Strangers When We Meet*, p. 391.

Chicago Sunday Tribune, January 22, 1956; June 8, 1958; May 28, 1961, Victor P. Hass, "Tormented Psyches and Quivering Ids," p. 3.

Choice, June, 1970.

Detroit News, January 16, 1983.

Globe and Mail (Toronto), October 19, 1985; June 21, 1986; February 28, 1987.

Harper's, December, 1967; June, 1968, Katherine Gauss Jackson, review of *Last Summer,* p. 94; January, 1983, Helen Rogan, review of *Far from the Sea,* p. 76.

Kirkus Reviews, February 15, 1993, p. 175; June 15, 1993, p. 745.

Los Angeles Times, May 14, 1981; February 4, 1983.

Los Angeles Times Book Review, May 8, 1994, p. 11.

Nation, December 4, 1954, Stanley Cooperman, "Violence in Harlem," pp. 493–494.

New Statesman, January 10, 1969.

Newsweek, March 8, 1971; July 11, 1983, David Lehman, "Murder Most Entertaining," pp. 70–71.

New Yorker, January 13, 1975, review of *Streets of Gold,* pp. 90, 93.

New York Herald Tribune Book Review, October 17, 1954, Barbara Klaw, "Garbage Can of the Schools," p. 4; January 15, 1956, Wilder Hobson, "Hot Music and Cold Turkey," p. 8; July 20, 1958, Robert C. Healey, "An Infidelity in Suburbia," p. 5.

New York Herald Tribune Lively Arts and Book Review, May 21, 1961, Al Morgan, "Gulf between Generations," p. 28.

New York Times, January 8, 1956; June 15, 1958; June 12, 1968; April 10, 1981; April 19, 1985; February 20, 1987; July 3, 1987.

New York Times Book Review, January 8, 1956, James Kelly, "H Stands for Hell," p. 27; June 7, 1959, Anthony Boucher, review of *A Matter of Conviction,* p. 27; October 4, 1959, A. Boucher, review of *'Til Death,* p. 26; July 31, 1960, A. Boucher, review of *The Heckler,* p. 23; December 11, 1960, A. Boucher, review of *See Them Die,* p. 40; May 28, 1961; October 20, 1968; July 16, 1969; September 28, 1969, Richard P. Brickner, "From the Woods of Wisconsin to the Jungles of Vietnam," p. 54; September 19, 1976, James R. Frakes, review of *The Chisholms,* pp. 42–43; May 6, 1979, Julian Symons, "Procedure at the 87th Precinct," p. 12; May 10, 1981, Ivan Gold, "Family Relations," p. 14; January 16, 1983, Richard Freedman, "Father and Son," p. 12; May 22, 1994, p. 35; October 2, 1994, Richard Gid Powers, review of *There Was a Little Girl,* p. 27; April 16, 1995, p. 29; February 16, 1996, p. 27; April 14, 1996, p. 21; January 10, 1999, Marilyn Stasio, review of *The Big Bad City,* p. 18; January 30, 2000, M. Stasio, "Cop Story," p. 13, and Selwyn Raab, "Writing Under an Assumed Name," pp. 13–14.

Observer (London), April 5, 1970.

People, December 19, 1977; April 3, 1995, p. 97.

Publishers Weekly, April 3, 1981, Robert Dahlin, "PW Interviews: Evan Hunter," pp. 6–7; February 3, 1984, review of *Jack and the Beanstalk,* p. 398; November 29, 1991, p. 48; March 21, 1994, p. 53; December 18, 1995, p. 39; March 24, 1997, review of *Nocturne,* p. 62; February 23, 1998, review of *The Last Best Hope,* pp. 54–55; December 7, 1998, review of *The Big Bad City,* p. 54; October 18, 1999, review of *The Last Dance,* p.74; October 23, 2000, Robert Dahlin, review of *Candyland,* p. 45.

San Francisco Chronicle, July 9, 1961.

Saturday Review, October 9, 1954, Nathan Rothman, "Cold–War Class," pp. 16–17; January 7, 1956; April 24, 1971; September 9, 1972.

Springfield Republican, July 9, 1961.

Time, October 11, 1954, review of *The Blackboard Jungle;* June 9, 1958; March 8, 1971; April 26, 1993, p. 65; October 17, 1994, John Skow, review of *There Was a Little Girl,* p. 84.

Times (London), August 20, 1981; September 11, 1982; July 11, 1985.

Times Literary Supplement, November 21, 1958; July 28, 1961; January 25, 1968; May 28, 1970; July 13, 1973, "The Slippery Slopes," p. 797.

Tribune Books (Chicago), February 2, 1992; May 15, 1994, p. 7.

Virginia Quarterly Review, summer, 1968.

Washington Post Book World, November 17, 1974, Jean M. White, "The Case of the Cornflake Crunch," p. 4; March 29, 1981, Stanley Ellin, "Daughter of the Revolution," p. 5; December 20, 1981, Jean M. White, review of *Heat,* p. 8; January 19, 1983; June 24, 1984; March 15, 1992, p. 10; April 16, 1995, p. 6.

Writer, April, 1969.

Writer's Digest, April, 1971, Fran Krajewski, "An Exclusive Re–Visit with Evan Hunter," pp. 24–26.

ONLINE

Crime Time On–Line, http://www.crimetime.co.uk/ (December 5, 2000).*

—Sketch by Diane Telgen

Gloria Naylor

■ Personal

Born January 25, 1950, New York, NY; daughter of Roosevelt (a transit worker) and Alberta (a telephone operator; maiden name, McAlpin) Naylor. *Education:* Brooklyn College of the City University of New York, B.A., 1981; Yale University, M.A., 1983.

■ Addresses

Agent—Sterling Lord Literistic, 65 Bleecker St., New York, NY 10012–2420.

■ Career

Missionary for Jehovah's Witnesses in New York, North Carolina, and Florida, 1968–75; worked for various hotels in New York, NY, including Sheraton City Squire, as telephone operator, 1975–81; writer, 1981—; One Way Productions, New York, NY, president, 1990—. Writer in residence, Cummington Community of the Arts, 1983; visiting lecturer, George Washington University, 1983–84, and Princ-

eton University, 1986–87; cultural exchange lecturer, United States Information Agency, India, 1985; scholar in residence, University of Pennsylvania, 1986; visiting professor, New York University, 1986, and Boston University, 1987; Fannie Hurst Visiting Professor, Brandeis University, 1988. Senior fellow, Society for the Humanities, Cornell University, 1988; executive board, Book of the Month Club, 1989–94; producer, One Ways Productions, 1990; visiting scholar, University of Kent, 1992; playwright, Hartford Stage Company, 1994.

■ Awards, Honors

American Book Award for best first novel, 1983, for *The Women of Brewster Place;* Distinguished Writer Award, Mid–Atlantic Writers Association, 1983; National Endowment for the Arts fellowship, 1985; Candace Award, National Coalition of 100 Black Women, 1986; Guggenheim fellowship, 1988; Lillian Smith Book Award, Southern Regional Council, 1989, for *Mama Day.*

■ Writings

FICTION

The Women of Brewster Place, Viking (New York City), 1982.

Linden Hills, Ticknor & Fields (New York City), 1985.

Mama Day, Ticknor & Fields (New York City), 1988.

Bailey's Cafe, Harcourt (New York City), 1992.

(Editor) *Children of the Night: The Best Short Stories by Black Writers, 1967 to the Present,* Little, Brown (Boston), 1995.

The Men of Brewster Place, Hyperion (New York City), 1998.

Also author of unproduced screenplay adaptation of *The Women of Brewster Place,* for American Playhouse, 1984, and of an unproduced original screenplay for Public Broadcasting System's "In Our Own Words," 1985. Contributor of essays and articles to periodicals, including *Southern Review, Essence, Ms., Life, Ontario Review,* and *People.* Contributing editor, *Callaloo,* 1984—. "Hers" columnist for *New York Times,* 1986.

Oprah Winfrey stars in *The Women of Brewster Place,* an adaptation of Naylor's debut novel.

■ Adaptations

The Women of Brewster Place was adapted as a miniseries, produced by Oprah Winfrey and Carole Isenberg, and broadcast by American Broadcasting Co. (ABC–TV) in 1989; it became a weekly ABC series in 1990, produced by Winfrey, Earl Hamner, and Donald Sipes.

■ Sidelights

"I . . . wanted to be a writer from the time I was twelve or thirteen years old. But whether that was going to be a probable goal for me didn't come up as an issue for me until my college years," novelist Gloria Naylor told interviewer Charles H. Rowell of *Callaloo* in a 1997 interview. "It was in my college years that I began to learn about [black women] writers like Toni Morrison and Zora Neale Hurston. . . . [H]aving those role models around helped me when I began to feel that I could be a writer."

Naylor's first novel, *The Women of Brewster Place,* which features a cast of seven strong–willed black women, won the American Book Award for best first fiction in 1983. Naylor has continued her exploration of the black female experience in two subsequent novels that remain focused on women, but she has also expanded her fictional realm. In *Linden Hills,* for example, Naylor uses the structure of the Italian poet Dante Alighieri's thirteenth century classic *Inferno* to create a contemporary allegory about the perils of black materialism and the ways in

which denying one's heritage can endanger the soul. Naylor's third novel, *Mama Day,* draws on another literary masterpiece—William Shakespeare's play *The Tempest*—and artfully combines the Bard's elements with black folkloric strains.

By drawing on traditional western sources, Naylor places herself firmly in the literary mainstream, broadening her base from its ethnic roots. Unhappy with what she calls the "historical tendency to look upon the output of black writers as not really American literature," Naylor told interviewer William Goldstein of *Publishers Weekly* in a 1983 interview that her work attempts to "articulate experiences that want articulating—for those readers who reflect the subject matter, black readers, and for those who don't—basically white middle class readers."

Born in 1950, Naylor grew up in the Harlem area of New York City. Her father was a public transit worker. Her mother worked as a telephone operator, a job that Naylor herself would also hold at several hotels during her time as a student at Brooklyn College. Naylor was an avid reader throughout her childhood, but she chose not to attend college after graduating from high school in 1968. Naylor felt disillusioned by the world she saw around her and was devastated by the assassination of the Rev. Martin Luther King in April of that year. Instead, Naylor spent seven years as a missionary for her mother's church, the Jehovah's Witnesses, believing that she could make a difference in people's lives on a personal level instead. In 1977, at the age of twenty–five, she entered Brooklyn College. Although Naylor wanted to be a writer, she had encountered few role models for herself in the literature that she studied in the educational system of her era; the curriculum was dominated by male writers of European heritage. However, inspired by classics from African–American literature that she discovered in the African Studies Department at Brooklyn College, she decided to tell her own story.

Publishing Contract and Yale

Naylor began writing *The Women of Brewster Place* while she was still a student, and she found a publisher before she graduated. Naylor was thirty–one when she got her diploma in 1981. Upon doing so, she was offered a full scholarship for graduate studies at Yale University. Its campus in New Haven, New Jersey, was "close to New York, and I didn't want to be too far from my family at that point," Naylor told *Callaloo* interviewer Charles D. Rowell. She also recalled that when she was a student at the Ivy League school, she sometimes took the train to New York's Grand Central Station simply to spend some hours there, "because sometimes I would just feel suffocated in that whole campus setting."

Naylor's first novel grew out of a desire to reflect the diversity of the black experience—a diversity that she feels neither the black nor the white critical establishment has recognized. Reviewing *The Women of Brewster Place* in the *Washington Post,* Deirdre Donahue wrote: "Naylor is not afraid to grapple with life's big subjects: sex, birth, love, death, grief. Her women feel deeply, and she unflinchingly transcribes their emotions. . . . Naylor's potency wells up from her language. With prose as rich as poetry, a passage will suddenly take off and sing like a spiritual. . . . Vibrating with undisguised emotion, *The Women of Brewster Place* springs from the same roots that produced the blues. Like them, her book sings of sorrows proudly borne by black women in America."

To date, Naylor has linked her novels by carrying over characters from one narrative to another. In *The Women of Brewster Place,* one of the young residents is a refugee from Linden Hills, an exclusive black suburb. Naylor's second novel spotlights that affluent community, revealing the material corruption and moral decay that would prompt an idealistic young woman to abandon her home for a derelict urban neighborhood. Though *Linden Hills,* as the book is titled, approaches the Afro–American experience from the upper end of the socioeconomic

Naylor tells the story of an island matriarch with strange healing powers in this 1988 novel.

spectrum, it is also a black microcosm. This book "forms the second panel of that picture of contemporary urban black life which Naylor started with in *Women of Brewster Place,*" noted *Times Literary Supplement* contributor Roz Kaveney. "Where that book described the faults, passions, and culture of the good poor, this shows the nullity of black lives that are led in imitation of suburban whites."

In addition to shifting her focus, Naylor also raised her literary sights in her second novel. *Linden Hills,* which some critics described as being a contemporary allegory with gothic overtones, is an ambitious undertaking structurally modeled after Dante's *Inferno.* Among its many accomplishments, Dante's Italian masterpiece describes the nine circles of hell, Satan's imprisonment in their depths, and the lost

In 1992 Naylor published this story of characters meeting and mixing in a mystical restaurant.

souls condemned to suffer with him. In Naylor's modern version, "souls are damned not because they have offended God or have violated a religious system but because they have offended themselves. In their single–minded pursuit of upward mobility, the inhabitants of Linden Hill, a black, middle–class suburb, have turned away from their past and from their deepest sense of who they are," Catherine C. Ward wrote in the journal *Contemporary Literature*.

To correspond to Dante's circles, Naylor uses a series of crescent–shaped drives that ring the suburban development. Her heroes are two young street poets—outsiders from a neighboring community who hire themselves out to do odd jobs so they can earn Christmas money. "As they move down the hill, what they encounter are people who have

'moved up' in American society . . . until eventually they will hit the center of their community and the home of my equivalent of Satan," Naylor told William Goldstein of *Publishers Weekly*. Naylor's Satan is one Luther Nedeed, a combination mortician and real estate tycoon, who preys on the residents' baser ambitions to keep them in his sway.

Mama Day "Turns The World "Upside Down"

Naylor's third novel, *Mama Day*, is named for its main character—a wise old woman with magical powers whose name is Miranda Day, but whom everyone refers to as Mama Day. This ninety–year–old conjurer made a walk–on appearance in *Linden Hills* as the illiterate, toothless aunt who hauls about cheap cardboard suitcases and leaky jars of preserves. But it is in *Mama Day* that this "caster of hoodoo spells . . . comes into her own," according to *New York Times Book Review* contributor Bharati Mukherjee. "The portrait of Mama Day is magnificent," she declared.

Mama Day lives on Willow Springs, a wondrous island off the coast of Georgia and South Carolina that has been owned by her family since before the Civil War. The fact that slaves are portrayed as property owners demonstrates one of the ways that Naylor turns the world upside down, according to Rita Mae Brown, writing in the *Los Angeles Times Book Review*. Another way, Brown continued, is "that the women possess the real power, and are acknowledged as having it." When Mama Day's grandniece Cocoa brings George, her citified new husband, to Willow Springs, he learns the importance of accepting mystery. "George is the linchpin of *Mama Day*," Brown explained. "His rational mind allows the reader to experience the island as George experiences it. Mama Day and Cocoa are of the island and therefore less immediately accessible to the reader. The turning point comes when George is asked not only to believe in Mama Day's power but also to act on it. Cocoa is desperately ill. A hurricane has washed out the bridge so that no mainland doctor can be summoned." Only Mama Day has the power to help George save her life. She gives him a task, which he bungles because he is still limited by purely rational thinking. Ultimately, George is able to save Cocoa, but only by great personal sacrifice.

The plot twists and thematic concerns of *Mama Day* have led some reviewers to compare the work to Shakespeare. "Whereas *Linden Hills* was Dantesque, *Mama Day* is Shakespearean, with allusions, however oblique and tangential, to *Hamlet*, *King Lear*, and, especially,*The Tempest*," *Chicago Tribune Books* critic John Blades wrote. "Like Shakespeare's fantasy, Naylor's book takes place on an enchanted island. . . . Naylor reinforces her Shakespearean connection by naming her heroine Miranda." Mukherjee also believes that *Mama Day* "has its roots in *The Tempest*. The theme is reconciliation, the title character is Miranda (also the name of Prospero's daughter), and Willow Springs is an isolated island where, as on Prospero's isle, magical and mysterious events come to pass."

Naylor's ambitious attempt to elevate a modern love story to Shakespearean heights "is more bewildering than bewitching," according to Blades. "Naylor has populated her magic kingdom with some appealingly offbeat characters, Mama Day foremost among them. But she's failed to give them anything very original or interesting to do." Mukherjee also acknowledges the shortcomings of Naylor's mythical love story, but asserts, "I'd rather dwell on *Mama Day*'s strengths. Gloria Naylor has written a big, strong, dense, admirable novel; spacious, sometimes a little drafty like all public monuments, designed to last and intended for many levels of use."

A Sequel About Black Men

The Women of Brewster Place became Oprah Winfrey's first venture into television producing outside of her popular talk show. Naylor's saga was the basis for a mini-series that aired on ABC in 1989, and became weekly fare on the network the next year. Though an entirely new literary generation of female-centered black fiction had emerged by the 1990s, "*The Women of Brewster Place* remained a defining achievement," *Essence* writer Tamala Edwards asserted. Naylor's 1998 novel, *The Men of Brewster Place*, returned readers to that same setting, this time to tell the stories of the men in the lives of the original characters. Naylor said this fifth novel was inspired by the Million Man March in Washington, D.C., which took place in the fall of 1995, as well as by the death of her father. Both events helped Naylor reassess certain ideas she held about men and their roles in the lives of African-American women. As she told Edwards in *Essence*, she wanted her new novel's characters to be "a microcosm of the Black man in America."

The seven men in *The Men of Brewster Place* occupy the same tenement block as the characters in the first novel, and Naylor revives one of original characters, a man who was murdered, to serve as the new novel's narrator. The men's dissimilar economic circumstances and attitudes provide the microcosmic panorama that Naylor hoped to portray:

one is a playwright, another an ambitious minister. There is also a gay character, a drug dealer, and a man who is unhappily married, but is a committed father. Comparisons with Naylor's famous debut were inevitable, and reviews were mixed.

David Bahr, reviewing *The Men of Brewster Place* for *The Advocate*, claimed that "this work aspires higher" than its namesake, "both in its pared-down prose and reigned-in emotionalism." Yet Bahr found the characters too stereotypical, and "ultimately unconvincing." *Booklist* reviewer Donna Seaman echoed that judgment in her own review: the novel's "characters remain flat," Seaman declared, "and their stories are cautionary tales, intriguing in terms of the issues they raise yet a touch too facile and melodramatic." However, a *Publishers Weekly* reviewer judged *The Men of Brewster Place* a success. "Naylor lends these archetypal situations complexity and depth," the reviewer stated, and he or she went on to praise the way in which Naylor has joined the individual stories and themes into a conclusion possessing "a grace note of optimism that is as credible as it is moving."

If you enjoy the works of Gloria Naylor, you might want to check out the following books and films:

David Bradley, *South Street*, 1975.
Paule Marshall, *Daughters*, 1991.
Al Young, *Seduction by Light*, 1988.
Beloved, a film starring Oprah Winfrey and Danny Glover, 1998.

Naylor, along with other African-American women novelists, weathers criticism that she and writers like Terry McMillan portray black men in a negative light. She has said that she only writes from experience. "I say to my audience, 'I'm telling your mother's story. Now what could be wrong with that?'" she stated in her 1998 *Essence* interview with Edwards. "There's a lot of self-censorship in our community, which is a shame. People feel they need to write role models, not just good characters."

■ Biographical and Critical Sources

BOOKS

Black Literature Criticism, Gale, 1992.
Contemporary Literary Criticism, Gale, Volume 28, 1984, Volume 52, 1989.

Encyclopedia of World Literature in the Twentieth Century, third edition, St. James Press, 1999.

Fowler, Virginia C., *Gloria Naylor: In Search of Sanctuary,* Prentice Hall, 1996.

Gloria Naylor: Strategy and Technique, Magic and Myth, edited by Shirley A. Stave, University of Delaware Press, 2000.

Gloria Naylor's Early Novels, edited and with an introduction by Margot Anne Kelly, University Press of Florida, 1999.

Hall, Chekita T., *Gloria Naylor's Feminist Blues Aesthetic,* Garland, 1998.

Harris, Trudier, *The Power of the Porch: The Storyteller's Craft in Zora Neale Hurston, Gloria Naylor, and Randall Kenan,* University of Georgia Press, 1996.

Modern Women Writers, compiled and edited by Lillian S. Robinson, Continuum, 1996, pp. 339–346.

Reference Guide to American Literature, third edition, edited by Jim Kamp, St. James Press, 1994.

Whitt, Margaret Early, *Understanding Gloria Naylor,* University of South Carolina Press, 1999.

PERIODICALS

Advocate, April 14, 1998, David Bahr, review of *The Men of Brewster Place,* p. 73.

African American Review, summer, 1994, p. 173; spring, 1995, Maxine Lavon Montgomery, "Authority, Multivocality, and the New World Order in Gloria Naylor's *Bailey's Cafe,*'" p. 27, Gary Storhoff, "'The Only Voice Is Your Own': Gloria Naylor's Revision of *The Tempest,*" p. 35.

American Visions, Dale Edwyna Smith, review of *Children of the Night,* p. 26.

Antioch Review, summer, 1996, Ed Peaco, review of *Children of the Night,* p. 365.

Black Issues in Higher Education, December 10, 1998, Jackie Thomas, review of *The Men of Brewster Place,* p. 31.

Booklist, December 1, 1995, Kathleen Hughes, review of *Children of the Night,* p. 609; January 1, 1996; March 1, 1998, Donna Seaman, review of *The Men of Brewster Place,* p. 1045; January 1, 1999, Barbara Baskin, review of *The Men of Brewster Place,* p. 900.

Callaloo, winter, 1997, Charles H. Rowell, "An Interview with Gloria Naylor," pp. 197–192.

Chicago Tribune Book World, February 23, 1983; January 31, 1988, John Blades review of *Mama Day.*

Christian Science Monitor, March 1, 1985.

Commonweal, May 3, 1985, Robert Jones, review of *Linden Hills,* p. 283.

Contemporary Literature, Volume 28, number 1, 1987.

Detroit News, March 3, 1985; February 21, 1988.

Ebony, May, 1998, review of *The Men of Brewster Place,* p. 14.

English Journal, January, 1994, p. 81; March, 1994, p. 95.

Essence, June, 1998, Tamala Edwards, "A Conversation with Gloria Naylor," p. 70.

Library Journal, June 1, 1998, p. 187.

Los Angeles Times, December 2, 1982.

Los Angeles Times Book Review, February 24, 1985; March 6, 1988, Rita Mae Brown, review of *Mama Day.*

London Review of Books, August 1, 1985.

Ms., June, 1985, Susan McHenry, review of *The Women of Brewster Place,* p. 18.

New Republic, September 6, 1982.

New York Times, February 9, 1985; May 1, 1990.

New York Times Book Review, August 22, 1982; March 3, 1985; February 21, 1988, Bharati Mukherjee, review of *Mama Day,* p. 7.

People, June 22, 1998, p. 39.

Publishers Weekly, September 9, 1983, William Goldstein and Steve Sherman, "A Talk with Gloria Naylor," p. 35; December 11, 1995, review of *Children of the Night,* p. 56; February 23, 1998, review of *The Men of Brewster Place,* p. 49.

San Francisco Review of Books, May, 1985.

Times (London), April 21, 1983.

Times Literary Supplement, May 24, 1985, Roz Kaveney, review of *Linden Hills.*

Twentieth Century Literature, spring, 1995, Jocelyn Hazelwood Donlon, "Hearing Is Believing," p. 16.

Tribune Books (Chicago), January 31, 1988.

Washington Post, October 21, 1983, May 1, 1990.

Washington Post Book World, March 24, 1985; February 28, 1988.

Women's Review of Books, August, 1985.

Writer, December, 1994, p. 21.

I. M. Pei

■ Personal

Born Ieoh Ming Pei, April 26, 1917, in Canton, China; emigrated to the United States, 1935; became a naturalized citizen, 1948; son of Tsuyee (a bank executive) and Lien Kwun (Chwong) Pei; married Eileen Loo, 1942; children: Ting, Chien, Li, Liane. *Education:* Massachusetts Institute of Technology, B. Arch., 1940; Harvard Graduate School of Design, M.Arch., 1946.

■ Addresses

Office—88 Pine St., New York, NY 10005.

■ Career

Harvard Graduate School of Design, instructor, later became assistant professor, 1945–48; Webb and Knapp, New York City, director of architecture, 1948–55; I. M. Pei & Associates (changed to Pei, Cobb, Freed & Partners in 1989), New York City, architect, 1955—. Served on National Defense Re-

search Committee, 1943–45; American Academy and Institute of Arts and Letters, Washington, DC, chancellor, 1966–70. Member of the National Council on the Humanities, Washington, DC, 1966–70, Urban Design Council of the City of New York, 1967–72; National Urban Policy Task Force, American Institute of Architects, 1970–74; Corporation of the Massachusetts Institute of Technology, Cambridge, MA, 1972–77 and 1978–83; and Task Force on the West Front of the US Capitol, American Institute of Architects, 1978–80.

■ Member

American Institute of Architects (fellow), American Academy and Institute of Arts and Letters, American Academy of Arts and Sciences, American Society of Interior Designers (honorary fellow), National Academy of Design (academician), American Philosophical Society, Royal Institute of British Architects (corporate member), Institut de France (foreign associate), New York City Partnership, Inc. (board of directors), Museum of Fine Arts, Boston (elected honorary member of board of overseers), Royal Academy of Arts, London (honorary academician), Chinese Academy of Engineering (foreign member), l'Academie d'Architecture de France.

■ Awards, Honors

Arnold Brunner Award, National Institute of Arts and Letters, 1961; Medal of Honor, American Institute of Architects, New York Chapter, 1963; Golden

Door Award, International Institute of Boston, 1970; For New York Award, City Club of New York, 1973; Thomas Jefferson Memorial Medal, University of Virginia, 1976; Elsie de Wolfe Award, American Society of Interior Designers, New York Chapter, 1978; Gold Medal for Architecture, American Academy of Arts & Letters, 1979; Gold Medal, American Institute of Architects, 1979; President's fellow, Rhode Island School of Design, 1979; Gold Medal of Honor, National Arts Club, 1981; Mayor's Award of Honor for Art and Culture, city of New York, 1981; Gold Medal, Academie d'Architecture, France, 1981; Pritzker Architecture Prize, 1983; National Medal of Art, National Endowment for the Arts, 1988; Praemium Imperiale for Lifetime Achievement in Architecture, Japan Art Association, 1989; UCLA Gold Medal, University of California at Los Angeles, 1990; First Award for Excellence, Colbert Foundation, 1991; Presidential Medal of Freedom, 1993; Officier de la L'égion d'Honneur, 1993; New York State Governor's Arts Award, 1994; Medal of Arts Ambassador for the Arts Award, National Endowment for the Arts, 1994; Gold Medal for Outstanding Achievement in Architecture, Architectural Society of China, 1994; Jerusalem Prize for Arts & Letters, Bazalel Academy of Arts & Design of Jerusalem, 1994; Jacqueline Kennedy Onassis Medal, Municipal Arts Society (New York City), 1996; Premio Internazionale Novecento La Rosa d'Oro (Italy), 1996; Independent Award, Brown University, 1997; Edward MacDowell Medal, MacDowell Arts Colony, 1998, for outstanding contributions to the arts; fellow, American Institute of Architects; BZ Kulturpreis (Germany), 1999; Cultural Laureate, Historic Landmark Preservation Center (New York City), 1999; honorary fellow, American Society of Interior Designers. Honorary doctorates from University of Pennsylvania, 1970, Chinese University of Hong Kong, 1970, Pace University, 1972, Rensselaer Polytechnic Institute, 1978, as well as from Harvard University, New York University, Carnegie–Mellon University, Northeastern University, University of Massachusetts, University of Rochester, Brown University, Dartmouth College, Columbia University, University of Colorado, University of Hong Kong, and the American University of Paris.

■ Sidelights

I. M. Pei is considered one of the most important architects of the post–World War II era. His modernist works, which alternately soar above city streets or nestle inside rugged mountain terrain, have earned Pei enthusiastic praise for their grace, craftsmanship, and unusual forms. The most famous projects associated with his name include a wing for the National Gallery of Art in Washington, D.C. and a major renovation at Paris's Musée du Louvre. He was also the surprising choice to design the Rock and Roll Hall of Fame in Cleveland, Ohio. "Pei himself says little," remarked John Winter in an essay for *Contemporary Architects.* "Unlike most great architects of the century, he does not teach, lectures rarely, writes little, does not theorize in public. It is all there in the buildings."

Pei was born Ieoh Ming Pei on April 26, 1917, in Canton, China. The second of five children, he was the son of a Bank of China executive whose family wealth descended from land holdings. Pei's mother, whom he has said influenced him deeply, was a musician and a devout Buddhist. When Pei was still in his infancy, he and his family relocated to Hong Kong, then a British colony. There, the boy began to learn English in earnest. This enabled him to enroll at St. John's Middle School when his family moved once again, this time to Shanghai. Sadly, this stage of Pei's life was disrupted by the death of his mother, which occurred when he was 13.

By the 1920s, Shanghai was arguably China's most vibrant big city. As a youngster, Pei was fascinated by its thriving financial district, where one new building rose to an unprecedented twenty–three stories. Rejecting his father's hopes that he would become a doctor, Pei decided to study architecture in the United States. He arrived in 1935, enrolling at the University of Pennsylvania. However, he found the architecture program there too conservative for his liking. Transferring to the Massachusetts Institute of Technology in Cambridge, Massachusetts, he decided to study engineering, but when an astute professor urged him to rethink the decision, Pei switched back to architecture. He had always planned to return to China, but by the time he graduated in 1940, his native country was at war with Japan; late the following year, the United States entered World War II. Recruited by the U.S. government to participate in the war effort, Pei worked for National Defense Research Committee from 1943 to 1945, using his architecture degree to research more effective methods of destroying buildings.

Settled in New York City

Pei's personal life was also busy. In 1942, he married a Chinese–American woman from Boston, Eileen Loo. He also began working toward a graduate degree in his field, and won acceptance to the rigorous program at Harvard University's Graduate School of Design. Under the leadership of Walter Gropius, founder of the famous Bauhaus school of

Pei's controversial 1983 glass pyramid design now graces the front of the Louvre museum in Paris, France.

design in Germany, the department was considered the leader in modernist architecture at the time. A refugee from the Nazis and their closure of the Bauhaus facilities, Gropius and his adherents stressed craftsmanship, clean geometric lines, a respect for materials, and most importantly, the idea that the form of something—a piece of furniture or a home—should be guided by functional principles. Also studying alongside Pei at Harvard at the time were several fellow modernists who would also enjoy careers as eminent postwar architects, including Philip Johnson and Paul Rudolph. All were profoundly influenced by another refugee from Nazi Germany, the modernist Ludwig Miës van der Rohe. This first director of architecture for the Bauhaus group was becoming extremely active in American architecture at the time, and would design memorable additions to the skylines of New York, Chicago, and other large North American cities.

Pei earned his master's degree in architecture in 1946 and for a time taught as an assistant professor at Harvard. He still hoped to return to China, but the country's emerging political situation made that possibility increasingly unlikely: the civil war that brought the Communists to power in China in 1949 was raging. Mao Tse Tung's victorious Reds deemed families like Pei's, who had been part of China's prosperous middle class, to be "enemies of the state." Thus Pei looked for a permanent position in the U.S. In 1948 he took a job with Webb and Knapp, a New York City development firm. It was an unusual move for the Harvard–trained architect, for though he was hired as the firm's director of architecture, most Harvard alumni immediately went to work for architectural firms, not commercial real–estate companies.

Pei quickly made a name for himself at Webb and Knapp. He created a roof garden for its Madison Avenue headquarters, complete with a dining room above that boasted a spectacular view of city, and he was involved in the acclaimed Hyde Park Redevelopment project in Chicago. Pei also attracted other innovative young architects to the firm. One of their biggest projects, completed the same year that Pei struck out on his own, was the Mile High Center in Denver in 1955. With its black–faced frame, visible columns and beams, and silver porcelain air–conditioning drops, the much–discussed project gave ample evidence the imaginative Pei was ready to take the Miës van der Rohe–inspired style in some bold new directions.

Pei launched his own New York City architectural firm in 1955, I. M. Pei & Associates, which would later include partners Henry Cobb and James Ingo Freed. The firm continued to take on the same kind of commissions for high–rise housing, urban renewal projects, and office complexes with which Pei had earned his reputation at Webb and Knapp. His work from this era includes the Place Ville Marie in Montreal; high–rise apartment buildings in Kips Bay, New York, and Society Hill, Philadelphia; the Town Center Plaza in Washington, D.C.; and some of the 1966–67 Bedford–Stuyvestant area renewal plan. In 1968, Pei received his first art museum commissions for structures in Des Moines, Iowa, and Syracuse, New York.

The scope of Pei's work as an architect took on an increasingly public profile, and earned him a correspondingly prestigious reputation. Just a year after her husband's 1963 assassination, Jacqueline Kennedy selected Pei to design the planned John F. Kennedy Library Complex in Boston. Pei's firm also completed an airline terminal at J. F. Kennedy Airport in New York, and a skyscraper that became an impressive addition to the Toronto skyline; the Toronto–Dominion Center, completed in 1972, rises adjacent to a skyscraper that was designed by Miës van der Rohe. "Miës is black, Pei is silver, but both are clear, clean skeletal structures and stand happily together," noted John Winter in his *Contemporary Architects* essay on Pei's work.

In Boston, Pei's firm was commissioned, with Cobb serving as design partner, by the John Hancock Insurance Company to create its new corporate headquarters on Copley Square. Pei assisted Cobb as a design partner and contributor for this project. The Hancock Tower project was plagued with problems from the start: its dominance of the site, an historic plaza, at a towering eight hundred feet of steel and glass, was the first controversial issue. During construction, work tools and materials fell from above and smashed stained–glass windows in an adjacent church. Finally, the Hancock Tower's large plate–glass windows began popping out after the first bad storm of the winter. They were quickly sealed with plywood, which earned the building the deri-

sive nickname "Ply in the Sky." Pei's firm faced a potentially disastrous lawsuit initiated by Hancock, but the matter was eventually settled to the satisfaction of all parties.

Pei's first overseas project came in Singapore in 1976 with the design of a bank building. Around this same time, he won a prestigious commission from the National Gallery of Art to create a much–needed East Building. The Washington museum, part of the Smithsonian Institution, opened in 1941 to house the collection of its main benefactor, Andrew Mellon, but the holdings had increased in subsequent decades and needed new galleries. Paul Mellon selected Pei to design the addition, which had to work itself into a trapezoidal plot of land at the base of Capitol Hill that had always been reserved for expansion. It was near Pennsylvania Avenue, the National Mall, and sat on the presidential inaugural route. Such a site presented an unusual set of difficulties: the building needed to possess a certain dignity to match its surroundings, but the trapezoidal patch of land was the first hurdle to conquer. "I sketched a diagonal line across the trapezoid and produced two triangles," Pei was quoted as saying in a 1999 interview with Heidi Hinnish of *School Arts*. "That was the beginning."

A Resounding Success

The National Gallery's East Building became two triangles for that trapezoidal space: an isosceles triangle for the exhibition hall, and a right triangle that housed offices, library, and a research center. The isosceles motif was repeated throughout the design of the public space, with the marble for the floor sliced into the same shape and the steel frame that housed the skylights also containing the form. For the material, Pei used the same pink Tennessee marble as the original building, but realizing that marble changes size with temperature, each stone was laid separately and allowed to settle. The National Gallery project made Pei one of the best–known architects in America. In 1979, his John F. Kennedy Library Complex finally opened—fifteen years after Pei had won the commission—and it earned him a gold medal from the American Institute of Architects.

Throughout the 1980s, Pei continued to win impressive commissions: after relations with China were normalized in the late 1970s, Pei was invited to design a Beijing hotel and traveled to his homeland for the first time since 1935. He and his partners also completed such projects as the Jacob K. Javits

A skylight designed by Pei diffuses light into a gallery of the Louvre.

Convention Center Plaza in New York, the new headquarters for International Business Machines, Inc. (IBM) outside of the city.

Pei completed another significant Asian project in 1989, the Bank of China Tower in Hong Kong, but this one also had a personal relevance for him: the firm's origins on the island colony dated back to the time when his father opened and headed the branch office there. Pei's design for the typically modernist skyscraper was beset by the particular challenges of the Hong Kong site: it had to be tall, because real estate in the crowded city is prohibitively expensive, and the region was also subject to high winds from typhoons. "I therefore thought about the triangle, which is the strongest structural form," Pei said in a 1999 interview with *Technology Review.* "If the building could essentially consist of shafts with triangular cross sections, it would automatically be very, very rigid. So I made some three-sided sticks and played with them at home, combining them in various arrangements."

The Controversial Glass Pyramid

Despite all of these prestigious projects, it was Pei's plan for an extension of Paris's Musée du Louvre that made him internationally famous. Again, his design proved controversial from the start: Pei was personally selected in 1983 by French President Francois Mitterand, who eschewed the idea of a competition among architects to create improved entrance facilities. The Louvre was already a massive museum, housed in a building constructed in 1546 and added onto in successive centuries. While attendance was rising annually, a poorly situated admission lobby could not handle the traffic or direct it efficiently through the long, unwieldy building. The first phase of Pei's renovation involved constructing a spectacular new entrance. Ground was broken at the center of the Louvre's courtyard for a glass pyramid. It would lead to a below-street level entrance lobby, then take visitors to each wing by a series of corridors. Other user-friendly attractions, such as a pedestrian mall, were also part of the grand plan.

At first, Pei's pyramid design seemed space age and bizarre, and the French media made the entire project the focus of intense debate. However, in Pei's mind the triangle shape was integral to the larger site. "I wanted a pyramid because it has facets, which begin to mirror the level of detail found along the rooftops of the old Louvre–in the form of statues, chimneys, and the like," he told *Technology Review*. Moreover, Pei felt it vital to preserve the visual beauty of the older building, which can be seen through the glass of the pyramid. The main pyramid was constructed with six hundred and ninety-eight panes of glass; three satellite pyramids sit nearby. The revitalized building opened in 1988 to some surprisingly positive accolades. "A vast glass-and-steel structure, it seemed, despite its uncompromising modernism, somehow appropriate to the elegant geometry of the Second Empire courtyard that it dominated," wrote Thomas Hoving and Judith Devereux Fayard in *Town and Country*. Pei completed the second phase of the Louvre renovation in 1993, which involved an 1857 building on the north side of the Louvre courtyard. This building, which became known as the Richelieu wing, had served as headquarters for France's ministry of Finance since 1871. Thus Pei's work was held up by a long battle within the French government over the space, but eventually new offices were built for the Ministry.

Pei's Richelieu wing renovation doubled the Louvre's gallery space, and its skylighted courtyards for sculpture and vast glass windows that looked out on the rest of museum complex earned high marks as a wonderful update for a priceless structure. "The overall effect is to introduce exhilarating illumination and openness to display spaces," opined *Progressive Architecture* writer Thomas Vonier. "For the first time in memory, visitors see, from inside, the palace's layout and its staggering expanse." The expanded Louvre even became the subject of some contention over whether it had become the world's largest art museum; attendance figures deemed it certainly the most visited, at five million in 1993 and rising. But Pei dismissed such absolutes as irrelevant. "It is a mistake to see success of a museum in terms of how many people visit it, or how large it is. More important is how long people stay, and the quality of their experience," Pei was quoted as saying in *Progressive Architecture*.

Rockin' and Rollin'

Pei's next big commission involved a popular museum of far different sort: the Rock and Roll Hall of Fame, which opened in 1995, was a cornerstone of the downtown revitalization of Cleveland, Ohio. The aging China–born architect was an unlikely choice to design the building, but he was selected by the Rock and Roll Hall of Fame Foundation to add some credibility to the entire project. A jazz fan all his life, Pei realized that he needed to familiarize himself with the art form whose spirit was necessary to capture in his design. "I had to start with a good sense of what the music was about," Pei told *Technology Review*. "The problem was that I didn't like the music. My children loved it, but I never did. And yet, since I was selected to do the project, I had to learn about the music. So I went to Graceland to see Elvis Presley's home. I went to Louisiana to listen to jazz and rhythm and blues. And then I began to understand the rich roots of rock and roll."

Pei created a six–story central tower adjacent to a 117–foot–high triangular glass wall. "The building had to express music," he told Michael J. Crosbie in an interview with *Progressive Architecture*. "What is this music? It has a sense of rebellion, of breaking away from tradition. It has a dimension of energy. The generation that made Rock music was much more transparent about their ideas than my generation." Pei attempted to symbolize that transparency though the massive wall of glass. The museum also featured state–of–the–art lighting and multimedia displays that charted the history of rock and roll. "Projecting from the west side of the tower, a cylindrical wing resting on a single concrete column has been likened to a stack of 45s revolving on a turntable spindle," observed William Weathersby Jr., writing in *TCI*. "On the east side, a trapezoidal box housing a theatre thrusts out precariously over the water like a tone arm or blast of sound."

A Far Quieter Project

Pei retired from Pei, Cobb, Freed & Partners at the end of 1990, and became a sole practitioner, under the name I. M. Pei, architect. In his new role, Pei completed his first museum in Japan, the private Miho Museum, which opened in late 1997. Located in the Shigaraki Mountains near Kyoto, on the side of a mountain that is also a nature preserve, the museum was named after Mihoko Koyama, the spiritual leader of the Shinji Shumeikai religious group. Pei had designed a Carillon Bell Tower for a Shinji Shumeikai sanctuary in 1990, which led to his commission for the Miho. The project took seven years in planning and construction, for it involved the excavation of part of a mountain, the construction of the museum, and then the restoration of the mountaintop and the foliage. It was designed to house Koyama's collection of tea–ceremony artifacts, some dating back centuries, and a new collec-

Designed by Pei, the John F. Kennedy Library in Boston contains papers and possessions of the late president.

tion of Silk Road objects. Visitors entered via a six hundred–foot long tunnel. Pei designed this entrance to create a sense of distance from the outside world, and based his idea on a classic fourth century poem by Tang Dynasty scholar Tao Yuan Ming, which recounts a magical lost paradise that is entered through a tunnel. A bridge then led visitors into museum proper, a building constructed from French limestone.

"The Miho physically and visually adapts to its site: elements rise and fall with the contour of the ridge," wrote Janet Koplos in *Art in America*. "It nestles into the earth, inseparable from it even as an image, which is consistent with the traditional Japanese belief that nature is not a thing separate from humanity, but a continuum of the whole." Koplos called the structure characteristic of Pei's style, but with a freer sense of geometry. "For the worlds of art and architecture, it provides a surprising instance of circumspection, a major building with a striking character that does not read as an imposition of style," the *Art in America* writer stated.

If you enjoy the works of I. M. Pei, you might want to check out the following:

The works of Marcel Breuer and Walter Gropius, founders of the Bauhaus school of design and two of Pei's most important mentors.

The works of Ludwig Miës van der Rohe, a key figure in the modernist movement.

The innovative and influential designs of architect Frank Lloyd Wright, whose work Pei greatly admires.

Pei has four children, two of whom became architects, and now have their own firm. As a partner at Pei, Cobb, Freed & Partners he was known for being deeply involved in all aspects of a project, not simply delegating minor details to staff architects. Despite his successes, some architecture critics consider his work too flashy, asserting that his designs attract controversy for its own sake. "I welcome critics because they are bound to have good reasons for their concerns," he told *Technology Review*. "But rather than generalizing about my work, they should look at each project by itself. The basic challenges in building design differ from project to project, and critics have to understand those—where a project is built, and why." He remained focused

on the real purpose his buildings served: "At one level my goal is simply to give people pleasure in being in a space and walking around it," Pei said in the same *Technology Review* interview. "But I also think architecture can reach a level where it influences people to want to do something more with their lives. That is the challenge that I find most interesting."

■ Biographical and Critical Sources

BOOKS

Artists: From Michelangelo to Maya Lin, UXL, 1995, pp. 336–341.
Cannell, Michael T., *I. M. Pei: Mandarin of Modernism*, Carol Southern Books, 1995.
Contemporary Architects, third edition, St. James Press, 1987, pp. 734–736.
Suner, Bruno, *Pei*, Hazan, 1988.
von Boehm, Gero, *Conversations with I. M. Pei: Light is the Key*, Prestel, 2000.
Wiseman, Carter, *I. M. Pei: A Profile in American Architecture*, Abrams, 1990.

PERIODICALS

Architecture, January, 1998, Deborah K. Dietsch, "Hidden Paradise," p. 82; Eric Adams, "Letting in the Light," p. 116.
Art in America, November, 1998, Janet Koplos, "The Hidden Museum," p. 50.
Economist, November 25, 1995, "Ply in the Sky," p. 91.
Interior Design, January, 1991, Stanley Abercrombie, review of *I. M. Pei*, p. 23; December, 1998, So-Chung Shinn, "Postcard from Japan," p. 60.
New York Magazine, May 21, 1990, Carter Wiseman, "Mr. Pei Goes to Hollywood," pp. 73–74.
Progressive Architecture, February, 1994, Thomas Vonier, "The Louvre Grandly Opens Another Wing," p. 17; February, 1995, Michael J. Crosbie, "Raising Rock's Reliquary," p. 62.
Saturday Evening Post, May–June, 1996, Charles P. Miller and Patrick A. Lakamp, "A House Built on Rock," p. 82.
School Arts, April, 1999, Heidi Hinnish, "I. M. Pei's East Building," p. 43.
TCI, February, 1996, William Weathersby, Jr., "Rock & Roll Hall of Fame," p. 38.
Technology Review, April, 1995, "I. M. Pei: A Feeling for Technology and Art" (interview), p. 59.
Town and Country, April, 1994, Thomas Hoving and Judith Devereux Fayard, "Wing Victory," p. 76.

—Sketch by Carol Brennan

Mary Pipher

■ Personal

Full name, Mary Bray Pipher; born October 21, 1947, in Springfield, MO; daughter of Frank Houston and Avis Ester (Page) Bray; married Jim Pipher (a psychologist), October 18, 1974; children: Zeke, Sara. *Education:* University of Nebraska—Lincoln, Ph.D. *Religion:* Unitarian–Universalist.

■ Addresses

Office—3201 South 33rd, Suite B, Lincoln, NE 68506. *Agent*—Susan Lee Cohen, 2840 Broadway, No. 210, New York, NY 10025.

■ Career

Private practice in psychology in Lincoln, NE, 1979—. Faculty member, University of Nebraska—Lincoln and Nebraska Wesleyan University.

■ Writings

Hunger Pains, privately printed, 1987, published as *Hunger Pains: The Modern Woman's Tragic Quest for Thinness*, Ballantine, 1997.

Reviving Ophelia: Saving the Selves of Adolescent Girls, Putnam, 1994.

Diets to Eating Disorders: What Every Woman Needs to Know about Food, Dieting, and Self–Concept, Adams Publishing, 1995.

The Shelter of Each Other: Rebuilding Our Families, Putnam, 1996.

Another Country: Navigating the Emotional Terrain of Our Elders, Putnam, 1999.

■ Sidelights

Laura Shapiro once wrote in *Newsweek* that although Dr. Mary Pipher has "been on *Today* and *Oprah*, and numbers [senator and former first lady] Hillary Clinton among her fans, [she] is probably the least glamorous candidate for guruhood who's ever been hooked to a mike." But that's exactly what this middle–aged clinical psychologist–turned–author became as a result of her "self–help" book *Reviving Ophelia: Saving the Selves of Adolescent Girls*. The themes Pipher deals with clearly struck a responsive chord with readers; the 1994 book was on the *New York Times* bestseller list for almost three years, holding a top spot in the nonfiction category for twenty–eight weeks.

Sara Martin, the editor of the *American Psychological Association Monitor*, explained the astounding popularity of *Reviving Ophelia* by pointing out that "[Pipher] opened America's eyes to the psychological toll that adolescent girls face growing up in a country rife with sexual abuse, school violence and an overwhelming pressure to be thin." Marge Scherer, writing in the teaching journal *Educational Leadership*, echoed those thoughts when she noted: "Although ominous, [Pipher's] words resonate with parents, teachers, and young people alike, perhaps because her solutions are sane and simple and within our reach."

Reviving Ophelia is actually Pipher's second book; the first was the self–published *Hunger Pains* (reprinted commercially in 1997 in the wake of the runaway success of *Reviving Ophelia*), a critical examination of the modern woman's obsession with body image, thinness, and weight loss. This book deals with many of the same issues that Pipher has considered in her subsequent writings. However, as with most self–published efforts, *Hunger Pains* failed to attract national media attention, and so its readership was mostly regional. Not so with *Reviving Ophelia*. Boosted by the marketing savvy and promotional muscle of a major New York–based publisher, the book was available in stores across North America, and it was widely reviewed in the popular press and professional journals.

Offering Solutions

Pipher's theme in *Reviving Ophelia* is as topical as it is straightforward. As *Time* reviewer Elizabeth Gleick explained it, Pipher makes the point that "adolescence is an especially precarious time for girls." A *Publishers Weekly* reviewer noted how the author laments "that, despite the advances of feminism, young women continue to be victims of abuse"— including the kind of self–abuse that is typified by eating disorders and self–mutilation. Pipher argues that our mass–market, consumer–oriented culture— through slick advertising, pervasive media images of sex and violence, fragmented families, the availability of alcohol and drugs, and a population that's under ever–increasing levels of social stress—is ultimately responsible for this problem. While the situation is troubling, unlike most commentators Pipher does more than just sound alarm bells. She offers insight and workable, common sense solutions to the kinds of problems that ordinary people have to confront every day. Scherer observed that Pipher "describes how to rescue young women drowning in a culture that isolates and degrades them."

Reviving Ophelia consists of a series of composite case studies from Dr. Pipher's own practice as a psychologist in Lincoln, Nebraska, where she also teaches at the University of Nebraska—Lincoln and at Nebraska Wesleyan University. "Dozens of troubled teenage girls troop across [the book's] pages," commented Gleick. "[T]here's a girl here for everyone." Gleick attributed the mass popularity of *Reviving Ophelia* to one key factor: the fact that many readers—including parents—can identify with and buy into the message that emerges from at least one of the book's wide–ranging case studies. "For the most part, the culture, not the parents, are to blame [for their daughters' problems]," wrote Gleick. What is more, she noted, as Pipher describes the varieties of therapy that come into play in her own practice, "[she] does offer commonsensical, unthreatening solutions" to problems. Scherer stated that Pipher also provides teachers and parents with advice that is "sane and simple and within our reach."

Pipher revisited the subject of female body image in her 1995 book, *Diets to Eating Disorders: What Every Woman Needs to Know about Food, Dieting, and Self–*

Pipher's 1994 book helped open people's eyes to the disturbing mental and emotional problems facing girls growing up in America.

Concept. The following year, in the book *The Shelter of Each Other: Rebuilding Our Families*, she turned her attentions to the challenges that the typical American family faces in our fast–paced, highly–mobile, and increasingly urban society. In a May 1998 interview with Scherer, Pipher mused about how much the dynamics of the typical family have changed since her own Nebraska childhood in the 1950s. "There's been a total upending of what was considered a virtuous child," said Pipher. For example, she noted how today's society focuses on independence as a virtue for children, rather than traditional obedience. As a result, parents, teachers—and ultimately children—are no longer certain about the relationship between responsibility and accountability.

A "Guru" from Nebraska

Pipher went on to talk about the corrosive effects on family life of shifting social values, our "culture of narcissism," the mass media glorification of sex, violence, and rampant consumerism. All have been factors in the loss of our sense of what Pipher calls "community"—the bonds between parents and children, schools and families, and old people and children. "Community is people with whom you share your stories," Pipher explained. "When we stop having real people to share our stories with, we lose some of our mental health."

Writing in *Educational Leadership*, reviewer Rose Reissman praised *The Shelter of Each Other* as a "lucid, touching book." Ray Olson wrote in *Booklist* that Pipher "movingly advocate[s] an up–to–the–minute cause—reviving American families." A *Publishers Weekly* reviewer stated that Pipher "offers plain and practical talk" for parents struggling to take care of their families. *Newsweek* critic Laura Shapiro echoed all these assessments. "Despite an undercurrent of sharp social criticism, *Shelter* is no diatribe," Shapiro wrote, "neither is it depressing. [Pipher's] uncanny mix of optimism and practicality gives [her] fans a way to resist the worst of the culture around them and substitute the best of themselves. Why not try bikes instead of Prozac? It's about time we had a guru from Nebraska."

Of course, not all reviewers have been as enthusiastic or receptive to Pipher's message or her approach, no matter how well–intentioned they might be. A somewhat more skeptical Lisa Schwarzbaum, reviewing of *The Shelter of Each Other* for *Entertainment Weekly*, wrote that Pipher's empathetic "there–there" approach "fit[s] fashionably into the current, politically co–opted interest in virtues, values, and other comforting words that gussy up the obvious."

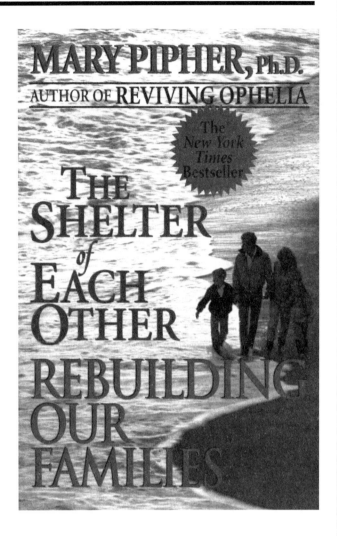

In 1996, Pipher published this critique of the modern American family.

A Different Generation

Pipher's more recent book, following the 1997 reissue of *Hunger Pains*, is *Another Country: Navigating the Emotional Terrain of Our Elders*, which explores the aging process and the nature of the relationship between baby boomers and their elderly parents. Pipher related the meaning of the book's title in a May 1999 interview with *Cincinnati Enquirer* reporter Cindy Kranz (reprinted in *USA Today*). "It's a very old metaphor," Pipher explained. "St. Patrick referred to old age as 'another country.' It also refers to another country to which old people are segregated into assisted living and retirement villages, where they're kept far from the rest of us."

In writing *Another Country*, Pipher uses the same formula that she perfected in *Reviving Ophelia*. She weaves a compelling narrative out of composite profiles of dozens of her own elderly patients and her own advice for communicating and interacting with older parents and loved ones. Pipher recalled in her interview with Cindy Kranz that *Another Country* grew out of her own experiences. While caring for her own aging mother, Pipher came to realize that like the rest of the generation that grew up in the early decades of the twentieth century—during the Great Depression and the Second World War—her mother had a fundamentally different way of looking at the world. The key difference is that she and other members of that older generation were family and socially oriented. Not so their baby boom children, who came of age during the 1950s, the Vietnam War, and the Watergate era, when consumerism and cynicism were rampant. "We behave very differently with people than our parents behaved," said Pipher. "Our parents see us as complaining, selfish, pushy. On the other hand, we see them as being in denial, not assertive. Passive. Neither generation has a monopoly on good mental health."

Once again, Pipher's message rang true with many readers. Ray Olsen wrote in *Booklist*, "[*Another Country*] follows [Pipher's] pro–family *Shelter of Each Other* . . . naturally and is even more appealing, chock–full as it is of engaging and moving stories about the lives of the old people she came to know in her therapeutic sessions and in preparing this book." Other reviewers offered similar praise. A *Publishers Weekly* contributor praised *Another Country* as a "well–written and sensitive investigation of aging."

If you enjoy the works of Mary Pipher, you might want to check out the following books:

Naomi Wolf, *The Beauty Myth: How Images of Beauty Are Used Against Women*, 1992.

Sara Shandler, *Ophelia Speaks: Adolescent Girls Write About Their Search for Self*, 1999.

Daniel J. Kindlon, Michael Thompson, *Raising Cain: Protecting the Emotional Life of Boys*, 1999.

Pipher summarized her optimistic approach to life in a 1999 interview with Susan Ericsson that was posted on the Media Education Foundation's Web site: "One of the things I notice is that when I bring up the phrase cultural change, people's eyes glaze over. They think, 'What can I do to change the culture?' They don't feel powerful enough to change the culture. But what I really believe is cultural change is a million individual acts of kindness and courage." Then, quoting from *Reviving Ophelia*, she added, "Let's work toward a culture in which there is a place for every human gift. In which children are safe and protected, women are respected, and men and women can love each other as whole human beings."

■ Biographical and Critical Sources

PERIODICALS

American Psychological Association Monitor, June, 1998, Sara Martin, "Fortifying Families Is Mary Pipher's Mission."

Booklist, February 1, 1996, p. 898; February 1, 1999, Ray Olson, review of *Another Country*, p. 939; September 15, 1999.

California Lawyer, April, 1999, pp. 68–69.

Contemporary Long Term Care, August, 1999, p. 68.

Current Biography, August, 1999, p. 165.

Educational Leadership, December, 1996, Rose Reissman, review of *The Shelter of Each Other*, pp. 85–86; May, 1998, Marge Scherer, "The Shelter of Each Other: A Conversation with Mary Pipher," pp. 6–12.

English Journal, October, 1995, pp. 128–129.

Entertainment Weekly, April 26, 1996, Lisa Schwarzbaum, review of *The Shelter of Each Other*, pp. 48–49.

Library Journal, April 1, 1994, p. 119; March 15, 1996, p. 88; May 15, 1996, p. 101; August, 1999, p. 165.

Nation, November 3, 1997, pp. 54–57.

National Catholic Reporter, November 21, 1997, p. 14.

New Republic, January 11, 1996, p. 42.

Newsweek, April 8, 1996, Laura Shapiro, "Parents, Take Heart," pp. 56–57.

People, June 24, 1996, pp. 121–124.

Publishers Weekly, February 28, 1994, p. 66; January 29, 1996, pp. 90–92; February 5, 1996, review of *Reviving Ophelia*, p. 37; April 15, 1996, p. 24; January 25, 1999, review of *Another Country*, p. 80; April 12, 1999, p. 32.

Time, February 19, 1996, Elizabeth Gleick, review of *Reviving Ophelia*, p. 73.

USA Today, May 27, 1999, Cindy Kranz, "Talking about Aging with Mary Pipher."

ONLINE

Media Education Foundation, http://www.mediaed.org/guides/pipher/piphrtoc.html (February 2001).*

Marsha Qualey

■ Personal

Surname is pronounced "*kwawl*–ee"; born May 27, 1953, in Austin, MN; daughter of Philip (an attorney) and Gwenyth (a homemaker) Richardson; married David Qualey, 1976; children: Laura, Ellen, Jane, Ben. *Education:* Attended Macalester College, 1971–72; University of Minnesota, B.A., 1976. *Religion:* Baha'i. *Hobbies and other interests:* Reading, maps, Minnesota.

■ Addresses

Home—11525 40th Ave. N., Plymouth, MN 55441. *E–mail*—mqualey@mediaone.net.

■ Career

Homemaker and volunteer, 1978–89; writer, 1990—.

■ Member

Society of Children's Book Writers and Illustrators, Maud Hart Lovelace Society, Author's Guild.

■ Awards, Honors

Revolutions of the Heart won a Minnesota Book Award, was an ALA Best Books for Young Adults, and one of *School Library Journal*'s Best Books of 1993; *Come in from the Cold* was named an ALA Best Books for Young Adults and one of New York Public Library's Books for the Teen Age; *Hometown* won a Minnesota Book Award, and was named one of New York Public Library's Books for the Teen Age; *Thin Ice* was also one of the New York Public Library's Books for the Teen Age, an ALA Quick Pick, and an Edgar nominee; *Close to a Killer* was named an ALA Best Books for Young Adults and was selected as one of the New York Public Library's Books for the Teen Age.

■ Writings

Everybody's Daughter, Houghton, 1991.
Revolutions of the Heart, Houghton, 1993.
Come in from the Cold, Houghton, 1994.
Hometown, Houghton, 1995.
Thin Ice, Delacorte, 1997.
Close to a Killer, Delacorte, 1999.
One Night, Dial, 2002.

■ Sidelights

Marsha Qualey's young adult (YA) novels present average teenagers struggling with unusually challenging situations. Nearly all of her works are set in her home state of Minnesota, and their plots are often driven by intergenerational conflicts between teens and their parents or community. In some cases, a Qualey protagonist must come to terms with the past actions of his or her parents during his or her own young adult years. The American Library Association has praised *Revolutions of the Heart, Come in from the Cold,* and *Close to a Killer* as outstanding novels for teen readers, and Qualey's other books have also earned her critical accolades as well as a devoted readership.

Qualey was born Marsha Richardson in 1953, in Austin, Minnesota, a town whose chief claim to fame is being the home of "Spam," the well–known canned meat product. She was the daughter of an attorney, Philip, and his homemaker wife, Gwenyth; Qualey's grandparents on her mother's side were involved in writing and journalism. Her grandfather had been the editor of a magazine, while her grandmother helped support the family by writing "confession" stories for pulp magazines during the Great Depression. "Perhaps that's one reason early on people expected I'd be a writer," Qualey explained in a biography that is posted on her Web site. "I was never so sure." An avid reader all her life, she has said that her childhood was a pleasant one. "I had a secure home, entertaining brothers, a bookstore and public library a few blocks away, and good friends," she recalled.

Early Memories

Qualey remembers her father making a skating rink in their backyard every winter with a garden hose. "Images like the one I have of my father flooding the yard stick in the mind," she wrote in the biography. "But what's the story behind the lingering picture or the haunting memory? Finding that out—well, that's why I love to write." In junior high, Qualey wrote skits and plays for her friends to perform, but she still harbored no real literary ambitions. As a teenager, she spent much of her summer outdoors. She went to camp, spent summers at her family's cabin, took long canoe trips, and loved to fish. Qualey once recalled: "Three memories. First, from 1969: I was on a canoe trip in Canada and sweating through the final portage of the day. It was a killer, 150 rods, and seemed to be straight uphill. I was carrying the food pack, maybe eighty pounds on my back, and it was a slow climb, especially as the rocky terrain seemed deliberately to keep me back. Roots slithered out and coiled around my legs, brush snickered and snagged my pack, rocks sprang out of the ground whenever I set a foot down, and branches snapped when I reached for a handhold.

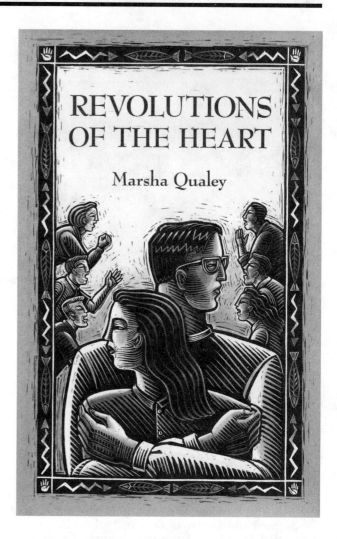

Qualey's second book, published in 1993, centers on the struggle between Native Americans and a group of local townspeople.

"Second memory: The next summer I was seventeen and working as a counselor–in–training at a YMCA camp in northern Minnesota. Three friends and I were up late, walking by the lakefront, when we noticed the display of northern lights. Anyone who spends time in the north sees the aurora borealis fairly often, but never before or since have I seen such a vivid sky show. For almost an hour the four of us lay on the ground, still as could be, while the colored sky danced.

"Final memory: That same summer our group was returning from an easy three–day canoe trip. The four canoes emerged one by one from a placid, narrow, winding river onto the home lake, where we were met by a gale that had transformed the water into a monster. We were all experienced trippers, but only one canoe paddled safely back to camp. The others, mine included, were toyed with, then thrown back to the far shore, by a lake that threatened with every huge wave to rise up and swallow us whole."

"Those two summers I learned how *alive* the sky and the water and the land can be. Most of my writing is set in the lake country of the upper Midwest, and when I now write about the natural world I treat it as another character. That character's influence can be obvious: how would a blizzard affect the plot? Or elusive: how lonely would it be to live in the middle of a great big forest?"

Qualey stayed close to her roots, choosing Macalester College in St. Paul for her first year of college, then transferring to the University of Minnesota, where she studied American history and literature. After earning her degree in 1976, she married David Qualey and they began a family that now includes four children. She began writing short stories for magazines in the mid–1980s, when she had two young children at home. While taking care of her toddlers and her home, Qualey let her mind wander and came up with various interesting scenarios, which she wrote down when she had a spare moment. Her submissions were all returned with rejection slips, but one story sent to *Seventeen* magazine came back with a letter that was encouraging. Qualey decided to expand the story, with its teen protagonist, into a young–adult novel.

Literary Debut

After sending *Everybody's Daughter* to a number of publishing houses, Qualey's manuscript was plucked out of a pile of unsolicited submissions by an editor, and was published by Houghton in 1991. Its protagonist is Merry Moonbeam Flynn, called "Beamer," who is seventeen years old and the daughter of two hippie parents. Beamer's mother and father had been the founding members of a northern Minnesota commune called Woodlands, but gave up the rustic lifestyle when Beamer was ten. They sold the land and used the money to buy a bait shop in the area. Others from the commune also stayed near, and the Flynns' bait shop has become a daily meeting place for the "Woodie" circle. Because Beamer was the first child born at Woodlands, she is considered "everybody's daughter," and her parents' friends take a more active role in her life than usual. As she grows older, she is increasingly irked by this interference, especially when she struggles through a romantic triangle that involves Beamer's high–school boyfriend, Andy,

who demands more time from her, and a college student who is fulfilling an internship opportunity at her town's radio station. "Part of Beamer's indecision about both Andy and Martin is her desire for a long–term relationship rather than just a boyfriend," wrote Ronald Barron in the *ALAN Review.*

The action in *Everybody's Daughter* intensifies when one of the Woodies accidentally kills a security guard by detonating an explosive as part of a protest at a local nuclear power plant. Beamer's parents and their friends draw even closer to pull through this crisis. Her mother provides a valuable piece of advice that helps Beamer come to terms with her dilemmas: "Beamer, as you muddle through life you'll discover the things you can't change and the things you can't escape. Sometimes the best you can do is to have a little fun."

Qualey's debut as a novelist earned positive reviews. *School Library Journal*'s Gail Richmond called the book "an exceptional first novel," commending the main plot as well as Beamer's romantic intrigues and the first–time novelist's ability to characterize life in a northern Minnesota world. "Qualey's smooth writing style and language create poetic, descriptive images," Richmond asserted. Gail Ashe, writing in *Voice of Youth Advocates*, called it "a moving and oftentimes romantic" work that depicts a teen's "struggle to come to terms with her unusual life." A *Bulletin of the Center for Children's Books* review also praised the way in which Qualey depicted Beamer's hippie parents, a characterization admirable for "a depth and respect unusual in the YA genre, which usually boils down the movement to flaky moms who neglect their children."

In her 1993 novel *Revolutions of the Heart,* Qualey creates another interesting protagonist who struggles with the conflicts presented when her own beliefs clash with those of her larger community. When the work begins, Cory Knutson is a popular, happy teen in her small Wisconsin town. That idyll is shattered when Cory, a new driver, loses control of her stepfather's truck on an icy street and crashes into a plate glass window. Her parents take away her driver's license, and she takes a job to help her pay the $500 in damages for which she is liable. Cory's situation worsens when her mother falls ill and doctors put her on a waiting list for a heart transplant. Many of the family's neighbors prove helpful and sympathetic during this difficult time, but many of them also voice their disapproval when Cory begins dating a new student at her high school; Harvey "Mac" MacNamara is a native who lives on the local Chippewa (Ojibway) reservation. Inevitably, small–town prejudices begin to manifest themselves in their harassment of Cory for associat-

"Riveting."
—Publishers Weekly

THIN
ICE

MARSHA QUALEY
author of *Close to a Killer*

In this 1997 work, seventeen–year–old Arden Munro tries to solve the mystery of her brother's disappearance after a snowmobile accident.

ing with a native person. "She becomes the target of crude notes taped to her locker and insensitive comments made in her presence, culminating in the ultimate example when someone stuffs a huge quantity of contraceptives into her school locker," wrote Barron.

As *Revolutions of the Heart* progresses, Cory even loses her job over the fracas, and the situation is further complicated by the Chippewa's' recent battle with local authorities over fishing rights. The natives have returned to spear–fishing, and Cory's older brother, Rob, becomes one of the most vocal

opponents of the practice. The death of Cory's mother plunges the family into grief, a situation made worse by the battles with Rob. When he is arrested at a demonstration, Cory's stepfather throws him out of the house. Though Cory and Mac attempt to stay out of the fishing–rights fray, Mac is inadvertently injured during a demonstration, and the pair flee. After taking a motel room where she can bandage his cuts, the two fall asleep and are discovered. An ensuing ugly argument with her brother ends with Cory breaking her arm. They reconcile at the end, and Rob invites Cory and Mac to a party that serves to symbolize what may be a new, harmonious direction for the embattled town. Cory remembers the words her mother imparted before her death: "Change a heart, you change the world. But doing it one heart at a time is the best you can hope for."

A *Publishers Weekly* review found *Revolutions of the Heart* a bit too issue–focused, but the magazine nevertheless hailed it as "an engaging as well as an enlightening read," and commended Qualey's "believable dialogue . . . and ability to sustain narrative tension." Roger Sutton, writing in *Bulletin of the Center for Children's Books,* liked the fact that the book's Native American characters "never succumb to *nouveau* stereotyping as ecological nature–children," and he commended Qualey's challenged teenage heroine. "It's good to see such confidence matched by such confident writing," wrote Sutton.

Qualey also noted that *Revolutions of the Heart* had several false starts. "It began life as a mystery about four teenagers in northern Minnesota who uncover a marijuana smuggling operation," Qualey wrote in the biographical notes that appear on her web site. "That idea was a dead end. The novel's next incarnation was as a collection of short stories about pregnant girls/young women living in a maternity home in northern Minnesota. . . . Of course, there are no drug smugglers or pregnant teenagers in *Revolutions.* Those elements were lost, but some things that *were* part of the early drafts remained (interracial dating, Indian treaty rights) and are at the heart of the story."

Revisiting Characters

Qualey revived the characters of two of the *Everybody's Daughter* commune dwellers for her 1994 young–adult novel, *Come in from the Cold.* As she wrote on her web site, "I wanted to write about those people, explain why and how some of them made the decision to live that way. I wanted to write about a period in my own life that was so dramatic.

This book is as close to autobiography as I ever want to get." The story, which is set in the late 1960s in Red Cedar, a conservative Minnesota town, follows the lives of two teenagers and the tragedies that bring them together. Jeff is a high–school student in Red Cedar whose older brother is a sergeant in the U.S. Marines. America's military involvement to quash a Communist takeover of the southeast Asian nation of Vietnam is escalating, and Jeff opposes the war. He even convinces the student council of his high school to pass an anti–war resolution. This earns him the scorn of many Red Cedar residents and of his brother. Tom also dislikes Jeff's friends, one of whom is a drug user named Gumbo. To help Jeff meet more wholesome peers, Tom takes his brother with him to a party. There Jeff manages to hook up with the sole anti–war activist present—a church youth minister who introduces Jeff to the organized protest movement. At a University of Minnesota demonstration, however, Jeff is dismayed by the free use of illegal substances that he sees. After Tom's unit is sent to Vietnam, tragedy strikes, and Jeff's brother dies in action. Qualey noted that this was the one incident in her body of work that drew clearly upon her own life.

The other half of *Come in from the Cold* tracks the events in the life of Maud, whose sister has become a radical anti–war activist. Lucy even goes underground, but dies in an attempt to blow up the physics building at the University of Minnesota. However, the bombing incident also appears to have been a cover for Lucy's suicide, and Maud and her family struggle to come to terms with the loss.

While these two tragedies are fresh in their minds, Maud and Jeff meet at a rock show in 1970. Maud emerges from a period of despair as she joins Jeff in anti–war protest activities. They travel to Minneapolis for a large demonstration, and find a ride back north with members of a commune called Woodlands. Jeff enrolls in college nearby, but begins to spend more time at Woodlands, and eventually drops out. When Maud joins him, they begin a new life there together. "Told with a quiet forcefulness, the story of" these two memorable characters conveys the passionate urgency that marked a turbulent era," wrote a *Publishers Weekly* reviewer Others offered equally positive assessments. "The greatest strength" here, wrote *Voice of Youth Advocates* reviewer Jacqueline Rose, "is the skillful way Qualey captures the 1960s ambiance." Reviewing *Come In From the Cold* for *School Library Journal*, Judy R. Johnston called it "fast–paced, well written, and appealing, and [the book] concludes with a strong sense of love and hope."

Hometown, Qualey's 1995 novel, is a sequel of sorts to *Come in from the Cold*. Though it is set in the early

Barrie Dupre has to adjust to her mother's ambiguous past and the crimes that seem to follow her in this 1999 mystery.

1990s, the novel tracks the story of the rebellious Gumbo, who left Red Cedar when his draft number came up and an army stint in Vietnam loomed. As Border, his teenaged son, relates, Gumbo fled to Canada, eventually married, and became a nurse. Divorced, he and Border settled in New Mexico, but Gumbo decides to pull up roots once again when he inherits his family's home in Red Cedar. "Border is unhappy about leaving Albuquerque, where he has become the leader, almost a father, to a collection of teenage misfits and outcasts," wrote Barron in the *ALAN Review*. Their move north coincides with the onset of the Gulf War, which creates groundswell of patriotism in many American communities. Everyone in Red Cedar knows his father was a draft–dodger, but any venom is directed primarily at Border, who is even beat up by his new classmates. He finds solace in a friendship with a classmate, Jacob McQuillan, and even a budding romance with Jacob's sympathetic sister, Liz. With the McQuillans, Border takes part in a local church's drive to send care packages for American soldiers overseas. When some citizens in Red Cedar launch an initiative to erect a veterans' memorial, Border plays his recorder and raises a large sum of money. However, someone at the dedication ceremony makes disparaging comments about Gumbo, and Border courageously steps forward to defend his father's decision. "Border is an admirable but improbable, elusive hero whose self–sufficiency exceeds that of the characters around him," wrote Gerry Larson in *School Library Journal.*

Hometown was the first of Qualey's works to earn criticism as somewhat unsatisfying. The story is told in short, almost vignette–like chapters, and *Voice of Youth Advocates* reviewer Mary Ann Capan found that this shifting perspective works against its impact. Capan also remarked that "the ending is not quite satisfying and the events leading to it are disjointed." A *Kirkus Reviews* assessment, was more positive, terming *Hometown* a "gritty, incisive novel" that "exudes plenty of cool." *Publishers Weekly* also appraised the work more favorably. "Giving this novel uncommon dimension are the author's cunning use of irony," noted the magazine's reviewer, as well as its third–person narrative voice that still asserts Border's inner turmoil and its subplots, which the *Publishers Weekly* reviewer described as "dexterously crafted."

Mysterious Ways

Qualey's 1997 novel *Thin Ice* again takes readers into the frosty woods. It was the author's first mystery story, and Qualey based it on newspaper reports about drunken snowmobilers disappearing when the ice of the frozen lakes cracked and swallowed them. The seventeen–year–old heroine of *Thin Ice,* Arden Munro, has already suffered much heartache in her life when her beloved brother becomes the victim of just such an accident. She was orphaned at the age of six, and Scott left college and found work as a mechanic in order to support her. After the snowmobile tragedy, Arden becomes convinced that it was no accident. Scott's vehicle, wallet, and clothes were recovered, but no body was ever found. Her suspicions intensify when she learns that Scott's girlfriend had recently told him

she was pregnant. Arden believes her brother wanted a more adventurous life, and faked his own death. Others disagree, telling Arden that she must come to terms with the loss.

"Despite the objections of those around her and how it disrupts her life, Arden continues to search for Scott and to try to learn why he disappeared," wrote Ronald Barron in the *ALAN Review.* "Arden's character is full of spunk and self–assurance," noted Helen Rosenberg in *Booklist,* though she asserted *Thin Ice*'s "plot fizzles at the end." Julie Hudson, writing in *Voice of Youth Advocates,* termed Qualey's first attempt at writing a suspenseful novel a first–rate page–turner, and "as a mystery and a novel of self–discovery, *Thin Ice* blends perfectly to equal a most satisfying read."

Qualey's next book, *Close to a Killer,* was another mystery novel for young adults. Sixteen–year–old Barrie Dupre is not entirely happy about her father's decision to send her to live with her mother, an ex–convict, when he and her stepmother go to Europe for a year. Her mother lives in a rough neighborhood, where she is co–owner of a hair salon called Killer Looks; the other business partners have also spent time in prison. Qualey based the mother on a character from one of her earlier novels—in this case the nuclear–power protester who accidentally killed a security guard in *Everybody's Daughter.* Barrie is ambivalent about her mother's past, but settles into her new life with a certain resignation. An avid reader, she makes friends with the owners of a neighborhood bookstore, and befriends the community's homeless.

The plot of *Close to a Killer* is driven by Barrie's worries about two murders that have been linked to clients of Killer Looks. When her mother's home is ransacked and what appears to be arson causes the salon to go up in flames, Barrie becomes even more intensely involved. "Qualey handles the mystery mechanics with exceptional flair," declared *Booklist*'s Stephanie Zvirin, and the author provides "a satisfying assortment of red herrings." However, a *Publishers Weekly* review found the number of subplots and possible suspects confusing, "dividing the novel's focus and diffusing its suspense." A *Bulletin of the Center for Children's Books* review stated that Qualey's attempt to write a novel with dual purposes—a coming–of–age story inside a whodunit—resulted in "shorting both genres," but it did assert that "details of the salon milieu and the shades of the prison past are imaginative and compelling."

Qualey dismisses the classification as an author of young–adult novels in the "problem" genre. "I don't really like the tag 'problem novel' because I think

If you enjoy the works of Marsha Qualey, you might want to check out the following books:

Mary Casanova, *Riot,* 1996.
Eileen Charbonneau, *Rachel LeMoyne: A Women of the West Novel,* 1998.
Linda Crew, *Long Time Passing,* 1997.

it's too often reserved for [young adult] fiction and used disparagingly," she said in her web site interview. "Every novel is a problem novel. Why pin it just on books that happen to be for teenagers?"

■ Biographical and Critical Sources

PERIODICALS

ALAN Review, fall, 1997, Ronald Barron, "Marsha Qualey: 'One Writes What One Would Read,'" pp. 27–30.
Booklist, April 1, 1993, Mary Romano Marks, review of *Revolutions of the Heart,* p. 1994; September 15, 1994, Jeanne Triner, review of *Come in from the Cold,* p. 125; October 1, 1995, Susan Dove Lempke, review of *Hometown,* p. 305l; November 1, 1997,

Helen Rosenberg, review of *Thin Ice,* p. 462; February 1, 1999, Stephanie Zvirin, review of *Close to a Killer,* p. 970.
Bulletin of the Center for Children's Books, March, 1991, review of *Everybody's Daughter,* pp. 174–175; May, 1993, Roger Sutton, review of *Revolutions of the Heart,* pp. 292–293; February, 1999, review of *Close to a Killer,* pp. 213–214.
Horn Book Magazine, September/October, 1993, Elizabeth S. Watson, review of *Revolutions of the Heart,* p. 604.
Kirkus Reviews, September 15, 1995, review of *Hometown,* p. 1356.
Publishers Weekly, May 3, 1993, review of *Revolutions of the Heart,* p. 311; October 17, 1994, review of *Come in from the Cold,* pp. 82–83; November 6, 1995, review of *Hometown,* p. 95; October 27, 1997, review of *Thin Ice,* p. 77; January 4, 1999, review of *Close to a Killer,* p. 91.
School Library Journal, April, 1991, Gail Richmond, review of *Everybody's Daughter,* p. 142; December, 1994, Judy R. Johnston, review of *Come in from the Cold,* p. 130; December, 1995, Gerry Larson, review of *Hometown,* p. 131.
Voice of Youth Advocates, June, 1991, Gail Ashe, review of *Everybody's Daughter,* p. 100; October, 1994, Jacqueline Rose, review of *Come in from the Cold,* p. 215; December, 1995, Mary Ann Capan, review of *Hometown,* p. 308; October, 1997, Julie Hudson, review of *Thin Ice,* p. 247.

ONLINE

Marsha Qualey's Web site, located at http://www.marshaqualey.com (January, 2001).

Charles M. Schulz

■ Personal

Born November 26, 1922, in Minneapolis, MN; died following a heart attack, February 13, 2000, in Santa Rosa, CA; son of Carl (a barber) and Dena (Halverson) Schulz; married Joyce Halverson, April 18, 1949 (divorced, 1972); married Jean Clyde, 1973; children: (first marriage) Meredith, Charles Monroe, Craig, Amy, Jill. *Education:* Studied cartooning in an art school after graduation in 1940 from public high school in St. Paul, MN.

■ Career

Cartoonist and illustrator. Art instructor at Art Instruction Schools, Inc. (correspondence school), Minneapolis, MN; cartoonist, *St. Paul Pioneer Press* and *Saturday Evening Post,* 1948–49; creator of syndicated comic strip, "Peanuts," 1950–2000. *Military Service:* U.S. Army, 1943–45, served with Twentieth Armored Division in Europe; became staff sergeant.

■ Awards, Honors

Reuben Award as outstanding cartoonist of the year, National Cartoonists' Society, 1955 and 1964; Yale Humor Award as outstanding humorist of the year, 1956; School Bell Award, National Education Association, 1960; L.H.D., Anderson College, 1963; Peabody Award and Emmy Award, both 1966, both for CBS–TV cartoon special, *A Charlie Brown Christmas;* D.H.L., St. Mary's College of California, 1969; Charles M. Schulz Award, United Feature Syndicate, 1980, for his contribution in the field of cartooning; Ordre des arts et des lettres (France), 1990; named one of the top twenty–five newspaper people of the 20th Century, *Editor & Publisher,* 1999; Lifetime Achievement Award, National Cartoonists' Society, 2000.

■ Writings

CARTOON BOOKS, MANY COLLECTED FROM NEWSPAPER WORK

Peanuts, Rinehart, 1952.

More Peanuts (also see below), Rinehart, 1954.

Good Grief, More Peanuts! (also see below), Rinehart, 1956.

Good Ol' Charlie Brown (also see below), Rinehart, 1957.

Snoopy (also see below), Rinehart, 1958.

Young Pillars, Warner Press, 1958.

But We Love You, Charlie Brown (also see below), Rinehart, 1959.

Peanuts Revisited: Favorites Old and New, Rinehart, 1959.

You're Out of Your Mind, Charlie Brown (also see below), Rinehart, 1959.

"Teenager" Is Not a Disease, Warner, 1961.

Happiness Is a Warm Puppy, Determined Productions, 1962, enlarged edition, 1979.

Security Is a Thumb and a Blanket, Determined Productions, 1963, reprinted, 1983.

Christmas Is Together–Time, Determined Productions, 1964.

I Need All the Friends I Can Get, Determined Productions, 1964, reprinted, 1981.

What Was Bugging Ol' Pharaoh?, Warner, 1964.

A Charlie Brown Christmas (adapted from the television production; also see below), World Publishing, 1965.

Love Is Walking Hand in Hand, Determined Productions, 1965.

Charlie Brown's All–Stars (adapted from the television production; also see below), World Publishing, 1966.

Home Is on Top of a Doghouse, Determined Productions, 1966, reprinted, 1982.

Charlie Brown's Reflections, Hallmark, 1967.

Happiness Is a Sad Song, Determined Productions, 1967.

It's the Great Pumpkin, Charlie Brown (adapted from the television production; also see below), World Publishing, 1967.

Teenagers, Unite!, Bantam, 1967.

"He's Your Dog, Charlie Brown!" (adapted from the television production; also see below), World Publishing, 1968.

Suppertime!, Determined Productions, 1968.

You're in Love, Charlie Brown (adapted from the television production; also see below), World Publishing, 1968.

Charlie Brown's Yearbook (includes *"He's Your Dog, Charlie Brown!, "It's the Great Pumpkin, Charlie Brown, You're in Love, Charlie Brown,* and *Charlie Brown's All–Stars*), World Publishing, 1969.

Peanuts School Year Date Book, 1969–1970, Determined Productions, 1969.

For Five Cents, Determined Productions, 1970.

It Was a Short Summer, Charlie Brown (adapted from the television production; also see below), World Publishing, 1970.

It Really Doesn't Take Much to Make a Dad Happy, Determined Productions, 1970.

Peanuts Date Book 1972, Determined Productions, 1970.

It's Fun to Lie Here and Listen to the Sounds of the Night, Determined Productions, 1970.

The World According to Lucy, Hallmark, 1970.

Winning May Not Be Everything, But Losing Isn't Anything!, Determined Productions, 1970.

Play It Again, Charlie Brown (adapted from the television production; also see below), World Publishing, 1971.

You're Elected, Charlie Brown (also see below), World Publishing, 1972.

Snoopy's Secret Life, Hallmark, 1972.

The Peanuts Philosophers, Hallmark, 1972.

Love a la Peanuts, Hallmark, 1972.

It's Good to Have a Friend, Hallmark, 1972.

A Charlie Brown Thanksgiving, Random House, 1974.

There's No Time for Love, Charlie Brown (adapted from the television production; also see below), Random House, 1974.

It's a Mystery, Charlie Brown, Random House, 1975.

Be My Valentine, Charlie Brown, Random House, 1976.

It's the Easter Beagle, Charlie Brown (adapted from the television production; also see below), Random House, 1976.

You're a Good Sport, Charlie Brown, Random House, 1976.

Hooray for You, Charlie Brown, Random House, 1977.

It's Another Holiday, Charlie Brown, Random House, 1977.

Summers Fly, Winters Walk (also see below), Volume III, Holt, 1977, Volume III, Fawcett, 1980.

It's Arbor Day, Charlie Brown (adapted from the television production; also see below), Random House, 1977.

The Loves of Snoopy, Hodder and Stoughton, 1978.

Lucy Rules OK?, Hodder and Stoughton, 1978.

The Misfortunes of Charlie Brown, Hodder and Stoughton, 1978.

Snoopy and His Friends, Hodder and Stoughton, 1978.

What a Nightmare, Charlie Brown, Random House, 1978.

It's Your First Kiss, Charlie Brown (adapted from the television production; also see below), Random House, 1978.

Bon Voyage, Charlie Brown, and Don't Come Back! (adapted from the film production; also see below), Random House, 1980.

You're Not Elected, Charlie Brown, Scholastic, 1980.

Life Is a Circus, Charlie Brown (adapted from the television production; also see below), Random House, 1981.

She's a Good Skate, Charlie Brown (adapted from the television production; also see below), Random House, 1981.

Someday You'll Find Her, Charlie Brown, Random House, 1982.

It's Magic, Charlie Brown, Random House, 1982.

Is This Good–Bye, Charlie Brown?, Random House, 1984.

Snoopy's Getting Married, Charlie Brown, Random House, 1986.

Happy New Year, Charlie Brown, Random House, 1986.

Dogs Don't Eat Dessert, Topper, 1987.

You're on the Wrong Foot Again, Charlie Brown, Topper, 1987.

By Supper Possessed, Topper, 1988.

Sally, School Is My World, Sparkler, 1988.

Talk Is Cheep, Charlie Brown, Topper, 1988.

Snoopy, My Greatest Adventures, Sparkler, 1988.

Schroeder, Music Is My Life, Sparkler, 1988.

It Doesn't Take Much to Attract a Crowd, Topper, 1989.

Brothers and Sisters, It's All Relative: A Peanuts Book, Topper, 1989.

An Educated Slice: Starring Snoopy As the World Famous Golfer, Topper, 1990.

Don't Be Sad, Flying Ace, Topper, 1990.

Could You Be More Pacific?, Topper, 1991.

Around the World in 45 years: Charlie Brown's Anniversary Celebration, Andrews and McMeel, 1994.

Being A Dog Is a Full–time Job: A Peanuts Collection, Andrews and McMeel, 1994.

Make Way for the King of the Jungle: A Peanuts Collection, Andrews and McMeel, 1995.

Pop! Goes the Beagle, HarperFestival, 1996.

Life's Answers (and Much, Much More), Collins, 1996.

Bah, Humbug!, Collins, 1996.

Snoopy's Christmas Tree, HarperFestival, 1996.

Your Dog Plays Hockey?, HarperFestival, 1996.

Friends for Life, Collins, 1996.

Way Beyond Therapy, Collins, 1996.

Trick or Treat, Great Pumpkin, HarperFestival, 1996.

Kick the Ball, Marcie!, HarperFestival, 1996.

Love Isn't Easy, Collins, 1996.

Dogs Are from Jupiter, Cats Are from the Moon, Collins, 1996.

Happy Birthday! (And One to Glow On), Collins, 1996.

It's Christmas!, Collins, 1996.

Somebody Loves You, Collins, 1996.

Me, Stressed Out?, Collins, 1996.

I Love You!, Collins, 1996.

Season's Greetings!, Collins, 1996.

See You Later, Litigator!, Collins, 1996.

Birthdays Are No Piece of Cake, Collins, 1996.

Snoopy, Not Your Average Dog, Collins, 1996.

You Can Count on Me, Collins, 1996.

'Tis the Season to Be Crabby, Collins, 1996.

Have Another Cookie (It'll Make You Feel Better), Collins, 1996.

Sally's Christmas Miracle, HarperFestival, 1996.

Insights from the Outfield, Collins, 1997.

Life Is Like a Ten–speed Bicycle, Collins, 1997.

Love Is in the Air, Collins, 1997.

You're Divine, Valentine!, Collins, 1997.

Born Crabby, HarperCollins, 1997.

Charlie Brown: Not Your Average Blockhead, HarperCollins, 1997.

Happy Valentine's Day, Sweet Babboo!, HarperFestival, 1997.

Aaugh! A Dog Ate My Book Report!, HarperCollins, 1998.

Lucy, Not Just Another Pretty Face, HarperHorizon, 1998.

My Best Friend, My Blanket, HarperHorizon, 1998.

You're Our New Mascot, Chuck!, HarperCollins, 1998.

You Have a Brother Named Spike?, HarperCollins, 1998.

Lighten Up, It's Christmas, HarperHorizon, 1998.

Punt, Pass, and Peanuts, HarperHorizon, 1998.

The Round–headed Kid and Me, HarperHorizon, 1998.

Sally's Christmas Play, HarperHorizon, 1998.

Beware of the Snoring Ghost!, HarperCollins, 1998.

Bon Voyage!, HarperCollins, 1998.

Everyone Gets Gold Stars But Me!, HarperCollins, 1998.

A Flying Ace Needs Lots of Root Beer, HarperHorizon, 1998.

The Doctor Is In(sane), HarperHorizon, 1998.

Happy New Year!, HarperHorizon, 1998.

You're the Tops, Pops!, HarperCollins, 1998.

Have Fun at Beanbag Camp!, HarperHorizon, 1998.

I've Been Traded for a Pizza?, HarperHorizon, 1998.

Leaf It to Sally Brown, HarperHorizon, 1998.

Travels with My Cactus, HarperHorizon, 1998.

Our Lines Must Be Crossed, HarperHorizon, 1998.

Shall We Dance, Charlie Brown?, HarperHorizon, 1999.

Now That's Profound, Charlie Brown, HarperPerennial, 1999.

I Told You So, You Blockhead!, HarperPerennial, 1999.

The World Is Filled with Mondays, HarperPerennial, 1999.

Dogs Are Worth It, HarperPerennial, 1999.

Good Grief! Gardening Is Hard Work!, HarperHorizon, 1999.

Calling All Cookies!, HarperHorizon, 1999.

It's Baseball Season, Again!, HarperHorizon, 1999.

Also author of *Snoopy on Wheels*, 1983; *Snoopy and the Twelve Days of Christmas*, 1984; *Peanuts at School*, 1986; and *If Beagles Could Fly*, 1990.

PUBLISHED BY HOLT

Go Fly a Kite, Charlie Brown (also see below), 1960.

Peanuts Every Sunday (also see below), 1961.

It's a Dog's Life, Charlie Brown (also see below), 1962.

Snoopy Come Home (also see below), 1962.

You Can't Win, Charlie Brown (also see below), 1962.

Charlie Brown confronts an unrepentant Lucy in this early "Peanuts" strip from the 1950s.

You Can Do It, Charlie Brown (also see below), 1963.

As You Like It, Charlie Brown (also see below), 1964.

We're Right Behind You, Charlie Brown (also see below), 1964.

There's a Vulture Outside, 1965.

Sunday's Fun Day, Charlie Brown (also see below), 1965.

You Need Help, Charlie Brown (also see below), 1965.

Snoopy and the Red Baron, 1966.

The Unsinkable Charlie Brown (also see below), 1966.

What's Wrong with Being Crabby?, 1966, reprinted, 1992.

Who's the Funny–looking Kid with the Big Nose?, 1966.

You're Something Else, Charlie Brown: A New Peanuts Book (also see below), 1967.

It's a Long Way to Tipperary, 1967.

You'll Flip, Charlie Brown (also see below), 1967.

Peanuts Treasury, foreword by Johnny Hart, 1968.

You're You, Charlie Brown: A New Peanuts Book (also see below), 1968.

A Boy Named Charlie Brown (adapted from the film production; also see below), 1969.

You've Had It, Charlie Brown: A New Peanuts Book (also see below), 1969.

Snoopy and His Sopwith Camel, 1969.

Peanuts Classics, 1970.

Snoopy and "It Was a Dark and Stormy Night," 1970.

You're Out of Sight, Charlie Brown: A New Peanuts Book (also see below), 1970.

You've Come a Long Way, Charlie Brown: A New Peanuts Book (also see below), 1971.

"Ha Ha, Herman," Charlie Brown: A New Peanuts Book (also see below), 1972.

Snoopy's Grand Slam, 1972.

The "Snoopy, Come Home" Movie Book (adapted from the film production; also see below), 1972.

Thompson Is in Trouble, Charlie Brown: A New Peanuts Book (also see below), 1973.

You're the Guest of Honor, Charlie Brown: A New Peanuts Book (also see below), 1973.

The Snoopy Festival, 1974.

Win a Few, Lose a Few, Charlie Brown: A New Peanuts Book (also see below), 1974.

Speak Softly, and Carry a Beagle: A New Peanuts Book (also see below), 1975.

Peanuts Jubilee: My Life and Art with Charlie Brown and Others, 1975.

Don't Hassle Me with Your Sighs, Chuck, 1976.

"I Never Promised You an Apple Orchard": The Collected Writings of Snoopy, Being a Compendium of His Puns, Correspondence, Cautionary Tales, Witticisms, Titles Original and Borrowed, with Critical Commentary by His Friends, and, Published for the First Time in Its Entirety, the Novel "Toodleoo, Caribou!," a Tale of the Frozen North, 1976.

Always Stick Up for the Underbird: Cartoons from "Good Grief, More Peanuts!," and "Good Ol' Charlie Brown," 1977.

It's Great to Be a Superstar: Cartoons from "You're Out of Sight, Charlie Brown," and "You've Come a Long Way, Charlie Brown," 1977.

How Long, Great Pumpkin, How Long?: Cartoons from "You're the Guest of Honor, Charlie Brown," and "Win a Few, Lose a Few, Charlie Brown," 1977.

It's Hard Work Being Bitter: Cartoons from "Thompson Is in Trouble, Charlie Brown," and "You're the Guest of Honor, Charlie Brown," 1977.

There Goes the Shutout: Cartoons from "More Peanuts" and "Good Grief, More Peanuts!," 1977.

My Anxieties Have Anxieties: Cartoons from "You're You, Charlie Brown," and "You've Had It, Charlie Brown," 1977.

Sandlot Peanuts, introduction by Joe Garagiola, 1977.

A Smile Makes a Lousy Umbrella: Cartoons from "You're Something Else, Charlie Brown," and "You're You, Charlie Brown," 1977.

Stop Snowing on My Secretary: Cartoons from "You've Come a Long Way, Charlie Brown," and "Ha Ha, Herman, Charlie Brown," 1977.

The Beagle Has Landed (also see below), 1978.

Race for Your Life, Charlie Brown (adapted from the television production; also see below), 1978.

Snoopy's Tennis Book: Featuring Snoopy at Wimbledon and Snoopy's Tournament Tips, introduction by Billie Jean King, 1979.

And a Woodstock in a Birch Tree (also see below), 1979.

Here Comes the April Fool! (also see below), 1980.

Things I Learned After It Was Too Late (and Other Minor Truths), 1981.

Dr. Beagle and Mr. Hyde (also see below), 1981.

You're Weird, Sir! (also see below), 1982.

Classroom Peanuts, 1982.

Kiss Her, You Blockhead! (also see below), 1983.

And the Beagles and the Bunnies Shall Lie Down Together: The Theology in Peanuts, 1984.

Things I've Had to Learn Over and Over and Over: (Plus a Few Minor Discoveries), 1984.

I'm Not Your Sweet Babboo! (also see below), 1984.

Big League Peanuts, 1985.

You Don't Look 35, Charlie Brown!, 1985.

The Way of the Fussbudget Is Not Easy, 1986.

Duck, Here Comes Another Day!, 1994.

Snoopy's Love Book, 1994.

The Cheshire Beagle, 1994.

Nothing Echoes Like an Empty Mailbox (contains selections from *And a Woodstock in a Birch Tree* and *Here Comes the April Fool*), 1995.

Sarcasm Does Not Become You, Ma'am (contains selections from *Kiss Her, You Blockhead!* and *I'm Not Your Sweet Babboo!*), 1995.

I Heard a D Minus Call Me (contains selections from *Dr. Beagle and Mr. Hyde* and *You're Weird, Sir!*), 1995.

Also author of *Fly, You Stupid Kite, Fly, A Kiss on the Nose Turns Anger Aside, The Mad Punter Strikes Again, Thank Goodness for People, What Makes Musicians So Sarcastic?,* and *What Makes You Think You're So Happy?*.

PUBLISHED BY FAWCETT

Good Ol' Snoopy (contains selections from *Snoopy*), 1958.

Wonderful World of Peanuts (contains selections from *More Peanuts*), 1963.

Hey, Peanuts! (contains selections from *More Peanuts*), 1963.

Good Grief, Charlie Brown! (contains selections from *Good Grief, More Peanuts!*), 1963.

For the Love of Peanuts (contains selections from *Good Grief, More Peanuts!*), 1963.

Fun with Peanuts (contains selections from *Good Ol' Charlie Brown*), 1964.

Here Comes Charlie Brown (contains selections from *Good Ol' Charlie Brown*), 1964.

Very Funny, Charlie Brown! (contains selections from *You're Out of Your Mind, Charlie Brown!*), 1965.

What Next, Charlie Brown? (contains selections from *You're Out of Your Mind, Charlie Brown!*), 1965.

Here Comes Snoopy (contains selections from *Snoopy*), 1966.

We're On Your Side, Charlie Brown (contains selections from *But We Love You, Charlie Brown*), 1966.

You Are Too Much, Charlie Brown (contains selections from *But We Love You, Charlie Brown*), 1966.

You're a Winner, Charlie Brown (contains selections from *Go Fly a Kite, Charlie Brown*), 1967.

Let's Face It, Charlie Brown (contains selections from *Go Fly a Kite, Charlie Brown*), 1967.

Who Do You Think You Are, Charlie Brown? (contains selections from *Peanuts Every Sunday*), 1968.

You're My Hero, Charlie Brown (contains selections from *Peanuts Every Sunday*), 1968.

This Is Your Life, Charlie Brown (contains selections from *It's a Dog's Life, Charlie Brown*), 1968.

Slide, Charlie Brown, Slide (contains selections from *It's a Dog's Life, Charlie Brown*), 1968.

Snoopy, perhaps the most popular of the "Peanuts" characters, faces an existential crisis in his own inimitable fashion.

All This and Snoopy, Too (contains selections from *You Can't Win, Charlie Brown*), 1969.

Here's to You, Charlie Brown (contains selections from *You Can't Win, Charlie Brown*), 1969.

Nobody's Perfect, Charlie Brown (contains selections from *You Can Do It, Charlie Brown*), 1969.

You're a Brave Man, Charlie Brown (contains selections from *You Can Do It, Charlie Brown*), 1969.

Peanuts for Everybody (contains selections from *We're Right Behind You, Charlie Brown*), 1970.

You've Done It Again, Charlie Brown (contains selections from *We're Right Behind You, Charlie Brown*), 1970.

We Love You, Snoopy (contains selections from *Snoopy, Come Home*), 1970.

It's for You, Snoopy (contains selections from *Sunday's Fun Day, Charlie Brown*), 1971.

Have It Your Way, Charlie Brown (contains selections from *Sunday's Fun Day, Charlie Brown*), 1971.

You're Not for Real, Snoopy (contains selections from *You Need Help, Charlie Brown*), 1971.

You're a Pal, Snoopy (contains selections from *You Need Help, Charlie Brown*), 1972.

What Now, Charlie Brown? (contains selections from *The Unsinkable Charlie Brown*), 1972.

You're Something Special, Snoopy! (contains selections from *The Unsinkable Charlie Brown*), 1972.

You've Got a Friend, Charlie Brown (contains selections from *You'll Flip, Charlie Brown*), 1972.

Who Was That Dog I Saw You with, Charlie Brown? (contains selections from *You're You, Charlie Brown*), 1973.

There's No One Like You, Snoopy (contains selections from *You're You, Charlie Brown*), 1973.

It's All Yours, Snoopy (contains selections from *You've Come a Long Way, Charlie Brown*), 1975.

Peanuts Double, Volume I, 1976, Volume II, 1978.

Watch Out, Charlie Brown (contains selections from *You're Out of Sight, Charlie Brown*), 1977.

You've Got to Be You, Snoopy (contains selections from *You've Come a Long Way, Charlie Brown*), 1978.

You're on Your Own, Snoopy (contains selections from *"Ha Ha, Herman," Charlie Brown*), 1978.

You Can't Win Them All, Charlie Brown (contains selections from *"Ha Ha, Herman," Charlie Brown*), 1978.

It's Your Turn, Snoopy (contains selections from *You're the Guest of Honor, Charlie Brown*), 1978.

You Asked for It, Charlie Brown (contains selections from *You're the Guest of Honor, Charlie Brown*), 1978.

It's Show Time, Snoopy (contains selections from *Speak Softly, and Carry a Beagle*), 1978.

You've Got to Be Kidding, Snoopy, 1978.

They're Playing Your Song, Charlie Brown, 1978.

You're So Smart, Snoopy (contains selections from *You're Out of Sight, Charlie Brown*), 1978.

Charlie Brown and Snoopy (contains selections from *As You Like It, Charlie Brown*), 1978.

You're the Greatest, Charlie Brown (contains selections from *As You Like It, Charlie Brown*), 1978.

Try It Again, Charlie Brown (contains selections from *You're Something Else, Charlie Brown*), 1978.

Your Choice, Snoopy (contains selections from *You're Something Else, Charlie Brown*), 1978.

Take It Easy, Charlie Brown (contains selections from *You'll Flip, Charlie Brown*), 1978.

You've Got It Made, Snoopy (contains selections from *You've Had It, Charlie Brown*), 1978.

Don't Give Up, Charlie Brown (contains selections from *You've Had It, Charlie Brown*), 1978.

That's Life, Snoopy (contains selections from *Thompson Is in Trouble, Charlie Brown*), 1978.

You've Come a Long Way, Snoopy (contains selections from *Thompson Is in Trouble, Charlie Brown*), 1979.

Play Ball, Snoopy (contains selections from *Win a Few, Lose a Few, Charlie Brown*), 1979.

Let's Hear It for Dinner, Snoopy, 1979.

Keep Up the Good Work, Charlie Brown, 1979.

Think Thinner, Snoopy, 1979.

Stay with It, Snoopy (contains selections from *Summers Fly, Winters Walk*, Volume III), 1980.

Sing for Your Supper, Snoopy, 1981.

Snoopy, Top Dog (contains selections from *The Beagle Has Landed*), 1981.

You're Our Kind of Dog, Snoopy (contains selections from *And a Woodstock in a Birch Tree*), 1981.

Also author of *Love and Kisses, Snoopy.*

"SNOOPY'S FACTS AND FUN BOOK" SERIES

Snoopy's Facts and Fun Book about Boats, Random House, 1979.

Snoopy's Facts and Fun Book about Houses, Random House, 1979.

Snoopy's Facts and Fun Book about Planes, Random House, 1979.

Snoopy's Facts and Fun Book about Seasons, Random House, 1979.

Snoopy's Facts and Fun Book about Farms, Random House, 1980.

Snoopy's Facts and Fun Book about Nature, Random House, 1980.

Snoopy's Facts and Fun Book about Seashores, Random House, 1980.

Snoopy's Facts and Fun Book about Trucks, Random House, 1980.

OTHER

Peanuts Project Book, Determined Productions, 1963.

(With Kenneth F. Hall) *Two by Fours: A Sort of Serious Book about Small Children,* Warner Press, 1965.

(Contributor) Jeffrey H. Loria and others, *What's It All About, Charlie Brown?: Peanuts Kids Look at America Today,* Holt, 1968.

(Contributor) Robert L. Short, *The Parables of Peanuts,* Harper, 1968.

(With Lee Mendelson) *Charlie Brown and Charlie Schulz: In Celebration of the Twentieth Anniversary of Peanuts,* World Publishing, 1970.

(Author of foreword) Morrie Turner, *Nipper,* Westminster, 1970.

(With Kathryn Wentzel Lumley) *Snoopy's Secret Code Book* (spelling and pronunciation guide), Holt, 1971.

The Charlie Brown Dictionary, Random House, 1973.

Peanuts Jubilee: My Life and Art with Charlie Brown and Others, Holt, 1975.

Charlie Brown's Super Book of Things to Do and Collect: Based on the Charles M. Schulz Characters, Random House, 1975.

Charlie Brown's Super Book of Questions and Answers about All Kinds of Animals from Snails to People!, Random House, 1976.

Charlie Brown's Second Super Book of Questions and Answers: About the Earth and Space from Plants to Planets!, Random House, 1977.

Charlie Brown's Third Super Book of Questions and Answers: About All Kinds of Boats and Planes, Cars and Trains, and Other Things That Move!, Random House, 1978.

Charlie Brown's Fourth Super Book of Questions and Answers: About All Kinds of People and How They Live!, Random House, 1979.

(With Mendelson) *Happy Birthday, Charlie Brown,* Random House, 1979.

(With R. Smith Kiliper) *Charlie Brown, Snoopy and Me: And All the Other Peanuts Characters,* Doubleday, 1980.

Charlie Brown's 'Cyclopedia: Super Questions and Answers and Amazing Facts, Volumes 1–15, Random House, 1980–81.

Charlie Brown's Fifth Super Book of Questions and Answers: About All Kinds of Things and How They Work!, Random House, 1981.

I Take My Religion Seriously, Warner (Anderson, IN), 1989.

Snoopy Around the World, photographs by Alberto Rizzo, Abrams (New York City), 1990.

Why, Charlie Brown, Why?: A Story About What Happens When a Friend Is Very Ill, Topper, 1990.

Peanuts: A Golden Celebration, the Art and the Story of the World's Best Loved Comic Strip, HarperCollins, 1999.

TELEPLAYS; TWENTY–SIX MINUTE ANIMATED CARTOONS

A Charlie Brown Christmas, CBS–TV, 1965.
Charlie Brown's All Stars, CBS–TV, 1966.
It's the Great Pumpkin, Charlie Brown, CBS–TV, 1966.
You're in Love, Charlie Brown, CBS–TV, 1967.
He's Your Dog, Charlie Brown!, CBS–TV, 1968.
It Was a Short Summer, Charlie Brown, CBS–TV, 1969.
Play It Again, Charlie Brown, CBS–TV, 1971.
It's the Easter Beagle, Charlie Brown, CBS–TV, 1972.
You're Elected, Charlie Brown, CBS–TV, 1972.
There's No Time for Love, Charlie Brown, CBS–TV, 1973.
Race for Your Life, Charlie Brown, CBS–TV, 1976.
It's Arbor Day, Charlie Brown, CBS–TV, 1976.
It's Your First Kiss, Charlie Brown, CBS–TV, 1978.
Life Is a Circus, Charlie Brown, CBS–TV, 1981.
She's a Good Skate, Charlie Brown, CBS–TV, 1981.
Why, Charlie Brown, Why?, CBS–TV, 1990.

Also writer of screenplays for feature length animated films, *A Boy Named Charlie Brown,* National General Pictures, 1969, *Snoopy, Come Home,* National General Pictures, 1972, and *Bon Voyage, Charlie Brown, and Don't Come Back!,* 1980.

ILLUSTRATOR

Art Linkletter, *Kids Say the Darndest Things,* Prentice–Hall, 1957.

Linkletter, *Kids Still Say the Darndest Things,* Geis, 1961.

Bill Adler, compiler, *Dear President Johnson,* Morrow, 1964.

Fritz Ridenour, editor, *I'm a Good Man, But . . .,* Regal, 1969.

June Dutton, *Peanuts Cookbook,* Determined Productions, 1969.

Dutton, *Peanuts Lunch Bag Cookbook,* Determined Productions, 1970.

All I Want for Christmas Is . . .: Open Letters to Santa, Hallmark, 1972.

Evelyn Shaw, *The Snoopy Doghouse Cookbook,* Determined Productions, 1979.

Tubby Book Featuring Snoopy, Simon and Schuster, 1980.

Monica Bayley, *The Snoopy Omnibus of Fun Facts from the Snoopy Fun Fact Calendars,* Determined Productions, 1982.

J. C. Suarez, editor and designer, *The Snoopy Collection,* introduction by Nancy Smart, photographs by Don Hamerman, Stewart, Tabori and Chang, 1982.

Dutton, *Snoopy and the Gang Out West,* Determined Productions, 1982.

Charlie Brown's Encyclopedia of Energy: Based on the Charles M. Schulz Characters: Where We've Been, Where We're Going, and How We're Getting There, Random House, 1982.

Terry Flanagan, designer, *Through the Seasons with Snoopy: Based on the Charles M. Schulz Characters,* Random House, 1983.

Flanagan, *Snoopy on Wheels,* Random House, 1983.

Nancy Hall, *Snoopy's ABC's,* background illustrations by Art and Kim Ellis, Golden, 1987.

Hall, *Snoopy's Book of Shapes,* background illustrations by Art and Kim Ellis, Golden, 1987.

Hall, *Snoopy's 1, 2, 3,* background illustrations by Art and Kim Ellis, Golden, 1987.

Harry Coe Verr, *Let's Fly a Kite, Charlie Brown!: A Book About the Seasons,* background illustrations by Art and Kim Ellis, Golden, 1987.

Justine Korman, *Snoopy's A Little Help from My Friend,* background illustrations by Art and Kim Ellis, Golden, 1987.

Hall, *Snoopy's Book of Colors,* background illustrations by Art and Kim Ellis, Golden, 1987.

Hall, *Snoopy's Book of Opposites,* background illustrations by Art and Kim Ellis, Golden, 1987.

Norman Simone, *Come Back, Snoopy,* background illustrations by Art and Kim Ellis, Golden, 1987.

Abraham J. Twerski, *When Do the Good Things Start?,* Topper, 1988.

Margo Lundell, *Where's Woodstock?,* background illustrations by Art and Kim Ellis, Golden, 1988.

Korman, *It's How You Play the Game,* background illustrations by Art and Kim Ellis, Golden, 1988.

Marci McGill, *Snoopy, the World's Greatest Author,* background illustrations by Art and Kim Ellis, Golden, 1988.

Korman, *Snoopy's Two–Minute Stories,* background illustrations by Art and Kim Ellis, Western (Racine, WI), 1988.

Lundell, *Charlie Brown's Two–Minute Stories,* background illustrations by Art and Kim Ellis, Western, 1988.

Diane Damm, *A Charlie Brown Christmas,* background illustrations by Art and Kim Ellis, Golden, 1988.

Linda Williams Aber, *Get in Shape, Snoopy!,* background illustrations by Art and Kim Ellis, Western, 1989.

Aber, *You're a Star, Snoopy!,* background illustrations by Art and Kim Ellis, Western, 1990.

Robert L. Short, *Short Meditations on the Bible and Peanuts,* Westminster/John Knox Press (Louisville, KY), 1990.

Twerski, *Waking Up Just in Time: A Therapist Shows How to Use the Twelve–Steps Approach to Life's Ups and Downs,* Topper, 1990.

Mischief on Daisy Hill: Featuring the Daisy Hill Puppies, Determined Productions, 1993.

Dr. Snoopy's Advice to Pet Owners, Andrews and McMeel (Kansas City, MO), 1993.

Earth, Water, and Air: Based on the Characters of Charles M. Schulz, Derrydale, 1994.

Creatures, Large and Small: Based on the Characters of Charles M. Schulz, Derrydale, 1994.

How Things Work: Based on the Characters of Charles M. Schulz, Derrydale, 1994.

Land and Space: Based on the Characters of Charles M. Schulz, Derrydale, 1994.

People and Customs of the World, Derrydale, 1994.

Twerski, *I Didn't Ask to Be in This Family: Sibling Relationships and How They Shape Adult Behavior and Relationships,* Holt, 1996.

■ Sidelights

In his retirement letter to the public printed in part in *Variety,* Charles M. Schulz maintains that the only thing he "really ever wanted to be was a cartoonist and I feel very blessed to be able to do what I love for almost fifty years." A great admirer of Roy Crane, George Herriman, Al Capp, and Milt Caniff in his youth, he had a hard time selling his own comic strip at first; United Feature Syndicate finally bought it in 1950 and named it "Peanuts." Preferring to name the strip "Li'l Folks," Schulz always disliked his comic being called "Peanuts," a title that endured for nearly five decades. "Peanuts" started in eight newspapers and brought a ninety dollar a month income; by the time of Schulz's retirement, he had written over eighteen thousand strips and had an estimated income of over "one million a week from comic–strip syndication money plus royalties from his books, toys, movies, and commercial endorsements," as noted in an *Entertainment Weekly* article. Schulz is the only cartoonist ever to have won the Reuben Award (the cartoonist's equivalent of the Oscar, designed by and named after Rube Goldberg) twice, in 1955 and again in 1964. Additionally, the National Cartoonists' Society also bestowed a posthumous Lifetime Achievement Award to the "Peanuts" creator in 2000. At the time of Schulz's death, Charlie Brown and his friends reached over 335 million readers daily.

In the last twenty years of "Peanuts," Schulz sometimes drew single-panel strips instead of three or four individual panels.

"Peanuts" has in fact become one of the most popular comic strips of all time. As Lee Mendelson points out in his biography of Schulz, "Charlie Brown has become the symbol of mid century America . . . because [he is] a basic reflection of his time," the "Mr. Anxious" of the age. Commenting on the universality of the appeal of Charlie Brown, the perpetual loser, Schulz says in *Peanuts Jubilee:* "Readers are generally sympathetic toward a lead character who is rather gentle, sometimes put upon, and not always the brightest person. Perhaps this is the kind of person who is easiest to love. Charlie Brown has to be the one who suffers because he is a caricature of the average person. Most of us are much more acquainted with losing than we are with winning. Winning is great, but it isn't funny."

Nonetheless, Schulz contended that there really is no specific "philosophy" behind the strip. An interviewer once noted to Schulz, "There have been various attempts to interpret the strip from a theological or psychological point of view. How do you feel about this?" The cartoonist responded, "The only books that were written about the theological implications were written by Robert Short, and he was not really talking about what my strip was saying. What he was talking about was the ability to gather thoughts from all forms of literature that can lead to some sort of spiritual implications. Robert Short is quite a student of different forms of literature. He's very high on Kafka and Kierkegaard and Bonhoeffer. He realized that I had some things in there that other comic strips didn't have, so he wrote a thesis on the "Peanuts" strip. But he's the only one that's ever been given permission to do this. Since then we've had all sorts of people who have wanted to write a book about math or psychology or languages or anything you can think of, using the strip

as the basis, but I always thought that we were very lucky to get away with it on the Robert Short books, and I didn't want to risk it on anything else. Besides, again, it could become very boring for people to see the strip being used for everything else by other people. I don't want other people using my strip that much, so we put a stop to that a long time ago."

A One–Man Show

Unlike many cartoonists, Schulz did all the work for the strip himself because, as John Tebbel says in a *Saturday Review* article, "'Peanuts' is so much a projection of the Schulz personality that it is inconceivable that anyone else could do it. . . . In the hierarchy of immortal comic strips such as 'Blondie,' 'Little Orphan Annie,' 'Andy Gump,' 'L'il Abner,' and 'Krazy Kat,' Schulz has created something unique, more successful than all the others, but paradoxically more fragile. Perhaps it is because the strip is so personal that it elicits an unprecedented identification and affection from its vast readership." Schulz draws material for the strip from his own childhood memories and from his experiences in raising five children. The popularity of the strip "cuts across every kind of classification," writes Tebbel, "for all kinds of special reasons. Schroeder, the Beethoven–loving character who is usually seen playing the piano when he isn't playing baseball, appeals to people who had never heard of Beethoven before. The little tyrant Lucy is seen by the small fry as a deliciously contrary girl. . . . Linus, with his security blanket, seems to speak to everyone who would like to have a blanket of his own in troubled times. And Snoopy, the beagle who has

Schulz occasionally used his strip to confront social issues, such as book banning.

Van Goghs hanging in his doghouse and a World War I aviator's helmet on his head, is the kind of fantasy dog everyone would like to own."

Some of the most endearing traits of the "Peanuts" characters have come about almost by accident, according to Schulz. He once stated that "frequently something will work out very well and then you wish that you had been more careful with it from the beginning. One example would be Schroeder's playing the piano and another would be the Linus blanket thing. I think actually Charlie Brown was the first one to have a blanket. Then one thing led to another and I got some more ideas and I ended up giving the blanket to Linus. I think even the business with Schroeder playing the piano actually started with Charlie Brown singing a very light passage from Beethoven's Ninth Symphony, and that gave me the idea to use some more musical notes in the script, which I then gave to Schroeder. You don't always know how these things are going to work out; you might say you wish you had planned it a little more carefully, but you never know.

"One of the good things, of course, about a comic strip is that it goes from day to day and you don't have to plan it like you would a novel—everything doesn't have to come out easily at the end. Yesterday's strip doesn't mean anything; the only thing that matters is the piece in the paper today."

Schulz has said that he doesn't expect to please everybody every day. In fact, he declares, "It would be fatal to try. It's wrong to worry about using something that may be directed too much to tennis players or baseball fans or musicians. I think people who are avid tennis players will appreciate it if you treat their sport with respect and authenticity. If a psychiatrist sees something in your comic strip which maybe only he understands, then he'll appreciate it all the more. But if you try to worry about whether everybody is going to understand it, you'll

have a strip that is so bland that no one is going to care anything about it."

"Peanuts" Makes History

Schulz added an extra dimension to Charlie Brown with his introduction to television in 1965. "Peanuts" subsidiaries, licensed by Schulz's Creative Associates, Inc., manufacture everything from clothing, toys, stationery, and cosmetics to furniture, lunch boxes, and Charlie Brown baseballs. Tebbel notes that Charlie Brown and his friends have even "emerged as modern evangelists" in Robert L. Short's two books, *The Gospel According to Peanuts and The Parables of Peanuts.* Snoopy has also been adopted by NASA as a promotional device, and, notes Tebbel, "Snoopy emblems are now worn by more than 800 members of the manned space flight team as rewards for outstanding work." The ubiquitous beagle even made international history as the official name of the LEM (Lunar Excursion Module) of the Apollo 10 manned flight to the moon in 1969. Great Pumpkin sightings are reported almost as often as UFOs, and Schroeder and his toy piano have been immortalized in the stained glass window of the Westminster Presbyterian Church in Buffalo, New York, along with Bach, Martin Luther, Duke Ellington, and Dr. Albert Schweitzer. And all because, as Tebbel concludes, "everyone sees something different, and something of himself, in Charlie Brown and his friends. He's everybody's boy."

Schulz continued to write, draw, and letter "Peanuts" entirely on his own into the 1990s, taking his only official vacation break for five weeks in 1997. Beyond the familiar themes he explored in his strip, he also ventured into broader issues, particularly with his 1990 animated special and book *Why, Charlie Brown, Why?* Dealing with childhood leukemia, *Why, Charlie Brown, Why?* won praise for its truthful depiction of the treatment and aftermath of the disease. "This hopeful, but honest, book could well help children to a greater understanding of a difficult subject," writes a reviewer in *Books for Keeps.* Schulz continued to receive honors, including recognition by France's Ordre des arts et des lettres in 1990 and a star on the Hollywood Walk of Fame in 1996.

When asked which award has meant the most to him, Schulz responded, "I suppose the very first Reuben Award, which I won from the National Cartoonists' Society back in 1955, would have been the most exciting of all because I had only been drawing the strip for four or five years; I wanted so much to be accepted, I wanted it to be a good strip, it was my life's ambition, and then to be chosen totally out of the blue by these cartoonists themselves as the outstanding cartoonist of the year really was a tremendous thrill. I suppose that was the highlight. Winning that first Emmy, too, in 1966 for "A Charlie Brown Christmas" was very exciting. . . ."

"Peanuts" At Rest

A landmark in popular culture was reached in December 1999, when Schulz announced his retirement from "Peanuts" after being diagnosed with colon cancer. He included a farewell message in his final daily strip, which appeared January 3, 2000, expressing gratitude "for the loyalty of our editors and the wonderful support and love expressed to me by fans of the comic strip," and concluding with, "Charlie Brown, Snoopy, Linus, Lucy . . . how can I ever forget them. . . ." Schulz's decision to end his strip as it approached its fiftieth anniversary brought forth regrets and tributes from many

sources. Longtime friend Cathy Guisewhite, creator of the comic "Cathy," tells *Newsweek* that "a comic strip like mine would never have existed if Charles Schulz hadn't paved the way. He broke new ground, doing a comic strip that dealt with real emotions, and characters people identified with."

Schulz died in his sleep at home in Santa Rosa on February 12, 2000, only hours before the publication of his final original Sunday strip. The timing underscored how much his life and his work were intertwined and elicited another wave of fond remembrances. "For 50 years, 'Peanuts' has shown us the way," says "Doonesbury" creator Garry Trudeau. "There is not a cartoonist alive who is not indebted to him, and all of us will miss his gentle and wholly original talent." Sergio Aragones, veteran cartoonist with *Mad* magazine, remarks that "in a couple of centuries, when people talk about American artists, he'll be one of the very few remembered. And when they talk about comic strips, his will be the only one ever mentioned."

Schulz's legacy showed no signs of fading away at the start of the new century. At the time of his retirement, "Peanuts" appeared in twenty–six hundred newspapers in seventy–five countries and twenty–one languages. According to *Editor & Publisher,* some ninety percent of them decided to continue on with reruns of the strip. Plans proceeded for the establishment of the Charles M. Schulz Museum, a twenty–two–thousand–square–foot facility to be attached to Santa Rosa's Redwood Empire Ice Arena, a "Peanuts"–themed property opened in 1968. When completed, the museum will display "Peanuts" original artwork and memorabilia in a permanent gallery, as well as offer a ninety–nine–seat theater and a research center.

Snoopy demonstrates his grasp of social niceties in this 1996 strip.

If you enjoy the works of Charles M. Schulz, you might want to check out the following:

The cartoon work of Jim Davis, creator of the "Garfield" strip.

The works of "Cathy" cartoon strip creator Cathy Guiswite, who credits Schulz as an influence.

The works of cartoonist Bill Watterson, whose retired "Calvin and Hobbes" strip focused on the fantastic adventures of a boy and his stuffed tiger.

Looking back, critics found considerable significance and enduring social relevance in Schulz's body of work. Summing up the broad appeal of "Peanuts," James Poniewozik writes in *Time* that "Most of us will lose more often than we win. That's the joke of Peanuts. Schulz made it funny with characters who faced a Sisyphean suburban world of kite–eating trees and yanked–away footballs with resilience and curiosity. Sincere as a pumpkin patch, his lifework is a reminder that self–awareness and a refined sense of irony do not mean affectlessness, that being a loser does not mean being defeated."

■ Biographical and Critical Sources

BOOKS

Johnson, Rheta Grimsley, *Good Grief: The Story of Charles M. Schulz*, Pharos, 1989.

Mascola, Marilyn, *Charles Schulz, Great Cartoonist*, Rourke Enterprises, 1989.

Mendelson, Lee, and Charles M. Schulz, *Charlie Brown and Charles Schulz: In Celebration of the Twentieth Anniversary of Peanuts*, World Publishing, 1970.

Schulz, Charles M., *Peanuts Jubilee: My Life and Art with Charlie Brown and Others*, Holt, 1985.

Schulz, Monte, and Jody Millward, *The Peanuts Trivia and Reference Book*, Holt, 1986.

Trimboli, Giovanni, editor, *Charles M. Schulz: 40 Years Life and Art*, preface by Umberto Eco, Pharos, 1990.

PERIODICALS

Art in America, March–April, 1976.

Booklist, November 1, 1974; December 15, 1999, p. 750.

Books for Keeps, September, 1991, review of *Why, Charlie Brown, Why?*, p. 11.

Christian Science Monitor, November 29, 1968; November 11, 1970.

Detroit Free Press, February 14, 2000, p. A1.

Editor & Publisher, January 10, 2000, "For United Media, Happiness Is a Warm Response to Reruns," p. 33.

Entertainment Weekly, February 25, 2000, "Good Grief: Why Did We Love Charles Schulz and His Unforgettable Peanuts Gang? Got a Nickel?," p. 28.

Life, March 17, 1967.

New Republic, December 7, 1974.

Newsweek, January 1, 2000, "So Long, Snoopy & Co.," p. 18.

New Yorker, March 18, 1967.

New York Times, May 26, 1969; June 2, 1971.

New York Times Book Review, March 12, 1967; December 7, 1975; December 11, 1977; October 26, 1980.

People Weekly, February 28, 2000, p. 52; March 6, 2000, p. 72.

Saturday Evening Post, January 12, 1957; April 25, 1964.

Saturday Review, John Tebbel, April 12, 1969.

Time, March 3, 1957; April 9, 1965; January 5, 1970; December 27, 1999, Poniewozik, James, "The Good and the Grief: Charles Schulz's 'Peanuts,'" p. 146.

Washington Post, April 4, 1970.

Washington Post Book World, September 16, 1979.

■ Obituaries

PERIODICALS

People, February 28, 2000, p. 72.

TV Guide, March 11, 2000, p. 42.

USA Today, February 14, 2000, p. D1.

Variety, February 21, 2000, p. 56.*

William Sleator

■ Personal

Surname is pronounced "*slay*–tir"; born February 13, 1945, in Havre de Grace, MD; son of William Warner, Jr. (a physiologist and professor) and Esther (a physician; maiden name, Kaplan) Sleator. *Education:* Harvard University, B.A., 1967; studied musical composition in London, England, 1967–68. *Politics:* Independent.

■ Addresses

Home—77 Worcester St., Boston, MA 02118. *Agent*—Sheldon Fogelman, 10 East 40th St., New York, NY 10016. *E-mail*—WSleator@aol.com.

■ Career

Author, composer, and musician. Royal Ballet School, London, England, accompanist, 1967–68; Rambert School, London, accompanist, 1967–68; Boston Ballet Company, Boston, MA, rehearsal pianist, 1974–83; freelance writer, 1983—.

■ Awards, Honors

Fellowship, Bread Loaf Writers' Conference, 1969; American Library Association (ALA), and Honor List citation, *Horn Book,* both 1971, and American Book Award for Best Paperback Picture Book, 1981, all for *The Angry Moon;* Children's Book of the Year Award, Child Study Association of America, 1972, and Notable Book citation, ALA, both for *Blackbriar;* Best Books for Young Adults citation, ALA, 1974, for *House of Stairs,* 1984, for *Interstellar Pig,* 1985, for *Singularity,* and 1987, for *The Boy Who Reversed Himself;* Children's Choice Award, International Reading Association and Children's Book Council, 1979, and CRABbery (Children Raving about Books) Award honor book, Maryland Library System, 1980, both for *Into the Dream;* Notable Book citation, ALA, and Honor List citation, *Horn Book,* both 1984, both for *Interstellar Pig;* Best Book of the Year Award, *School Library Journal,* 1981, for *The Green Futures of Tycho,* 1983, for *Fingers,* and 1984, for *Interstellar Pig;* Golden Pen Award, Spokane Washington Public Library, 1984 and 1985, both for "the author who gives the most reading pleasure"; Junior Literary Guild selection, 1985, for *Singularity;* Notable Book selection, ALA, and Best Book for Young Adults designation, ALA, both 1993, both for *Oddballs.*

Also contributor of short stories to the collections *Am I Blue? Coming Out from the Silence,* edited by Marion Dane Bauer, and *Things That Go Bump in the Night,* edited by Jane Yolen and Martin H. Greenberg. Composer, with Blair Lent, of musical score for animated film *Why the Sun and Moon Live in the Sky*, 1972. Composer of scores for professional ballets and amateur films and plays.

■ Adaptations

The Angry Moon was released on audiocassette by Read–Along–House; *Interstellar Pig* was released on audiocassette by Listening Library, 1987.

■ Work in Progress

Collaboration with composer Wes York on the opera *The Escape Artist*.

■ Sidelights

A popular and prolific writer of fiction for children and young adults, William Sleator is regarded as a particularly original and imaginative author whose works use the genres of fantasy, mystery, and science fiction to explore personal relationships and growth. Sleator incorporates current scientific theories, suspense, and the supernatural in his books, which challenge readers to take active roles in the stories while allowing them to resonate with the feelings and experiences of his characters. Depicting boys and girls who are often reluctant heroes, Sleator takes his characters from their everyday lives into confrontations with unusual, even unnerving situations. His protagonists encounter alien beings, doppelgangers, ESP, telepathy, telekinesis, black holes, evil spirits, malevolent dolls, weird scientific experiments, time travel into the past and the future, and other strange phenomena. In addition, the characters must learn to deal with their brothers and sisters—sibling rivalry is a consistent theme—as well as with their parents and peers. Through their physical and emotional journeys, the young people in Sleator's stories discover strength and confidence within themselves while developing a greater understanding of life in general. Characteristically, Sleator appears to end his books with the situations resolved and his characters secure; however, he is fond of including surprising twists, hinting that perhaps things are not quite so rosy as readers may think.

As a writer, Sleator is often credited for setting a tone which is often referred to as darkly humorous. Although many of his books are scary, he often laces the suspense with tongue–in–cheek humor. The author is praised as a skilled creator of plot and character as well as for his ability to blend the real and the surreal. In addition, Sleator is lauded for his insight into human nature, especially in the area of family relationships, and for creating fully realized worlds in haunting, thought–provoking page–turners. Although his works are often considered demanding and disturbing and his use of ambiguous endings is sometimes questioned, Sleator is generally considered a talented author of rich, fascinating books that appeal to young readers on several levels. Writing in *Children's Books and Their Creators*, Peter D. Sieruta noted, "Sleator has continued to show growth as a writer, and his skillful translation of scientific theories into entertaining fiction has resulted in an important body of work." *School Library Journal* contributor David Gale commented on the author's "singular talent for writing astonishing science fiction novels," while in *Horn Book*, Roger Sutton dubbed him "the master of the juvenile creepy–crawly." Writing in *English Journal*, Margaret L. Daggett stated, "Sleator succeeds with adolescents because he blends enough scientific realities with supernatural possibilities to tantalize the mind and the imagination. Readers feel refreshed after the intellectual and emotional challenges in Sleator's novels. . . . He sets us in a reality and helps us stretch our imaginations."

> *"My goal is to entertain my audience and to get them to read. I want kids to find out that reading is the best entertainment there is."*
>
> —William Sleator

Childhood Encouragement

Born in Havre de Grace, Maryland, Sleator is the eldest son of William Warner Sleator, Jr., a physiologist and professor, and Esther Kaplan Sleator, a physician. Sleator and his siblings—two brothers, Daniel and Tycho, and a sister, Vicky—grew up in University City, Missouri, a predominantly Jewish suburb of St. Louis where the family moved after the author's father was hired by the University of St. Louis. "My parents," Sleator told *Authors & Artists for Young Adults* (*AAYA*), "always encouraged us to be whoever we were." Sleator began studying the piano at the age of six. At around the same time, he wrote his first story. "From that point on," he wrote in his biographical sketch for *The Scoop*, "I was always writing or composing something. And almost from the very beginning, I was fascinated by the grotesque and the macabre." For example, one of his first musical compositions was called "Guillotines in the Springtime." Sleator once said: "I suppose it came from the kind of stories, mostly science fiction, I read as a kid." As a small boy, he wrote a story, "The Haunted Easter Egg," for a school assignment about Easter. Sleator recalled that his parents "thought it was great. Of course, that was before they realized that I was going into this bizarre career without any security, but they encouraged me at the time."

In addition to science fiction and comic books, Sleator began reading works about the physical sciences. He said: "Everybody in my family is a scientist except me. I always liked science but was never good enough to be a real scientist; I was the dumbest person in the advanced class. Still, I learned a lot. I prefer science fiction that has some basis in reality; psychological stories, time–travel stories, but especially stories about people." In high school, Sleator continued writing poems and stories and composing music; he also learned to play the cello. He wrote in *The Scoop*, "When the school orchestra played one of my compositions at an assembly, everybody thought I was a genius. I did nothing to correct this impression." However, as Sleator remembered: "I wasn't a complete nerd. I rebelled with drugs, sex—all the things every kid goes through. My parents weren't happy about it, but they were looser about it than most."

Music Leads to Writing

After high school, Sleator attended Harvard University, where he intended to study musical composition. However, he felt that the nature of the music program was too restrictive, so he become an English major. Sleator continued to write music for student plays and films while at Harvard. After receiving his bachelor's degree in 1967, he moved to London, England, where he studied musical composition for a year while working as a pianist at the Royal Ballet School and the Rambert School. During this period, Sleator lived in the middle of a forest in an ancient cottage that had once been a pest house for people with smallpox. He shared the cottage with his landlady, a sixty–ish woman who tried to treat Sleator as a son. This experience became the subject of his first book for young people, *Blackbriar*. Before its publication, Sleator collaborated with his

friend, illustrator Blair Lent, on the picture book *The Angry Moon*. A retelling of a Tlingit Indian legend, the story describes how a girl, Lapwinsa, is taken away by the moon after she laughs at it. Her friend, the boy Lupan, rescues her by making a ladder out of arrows and climbing into the sky. A reviewer in *Publishers Weekly* noted that "books like *The Angry Moon* appear only once in a blue moon." The critic stated that Blair Lent "has topped himself with this one, perhaps because William Sleator gave him such a strong story to illustrate." Writing in *School Library Journal*, Ann D. Schweibish added that *The Angry Moon* is a "highly successful adaptation and visualization" of the traditional tale.

In *Blackbriar*, which, like *The Angry Moon*, is also illustrated by Blair Lent, Sleator describes how Danny, a teenage boy, struggles for independence from his middle–aged guardian, Philippa, with whom he shares a haunted, isolated cottage in the English countryside. Danny and Philippa are shunned by the locals because of the perception that they are linked to Satanism. After Philippa and her cat are kidnapped, Danny and his friend Lark search for her. In the process, Danny discovers himself and learns the secret of the cottage, which served as a pesthouse during a seventeenth–century plague. A critic in *Kirkus Reviews* advised, "Bolt the cellar door, watch your cat closely for personality changes, and follow him—vicariously." Ashley Darlington Grayson, writing in *Fantasy Review*, stated that Danny "fails to earn any reader respect because he is thick as a post." However, Paul Heins of *Horn Book* noted that "the effectiveness of the story lies in its characterization and in its narrative skill."

In 1974, Sleator began working as the rehearsal pianist for the Boston Ballet while continuing to write fiction. With the dancers, he toured the United States and Europe and wrote three ballets performed by the company. *House of Stairs*, a book published the same year that Sleator joined the Boston Ballet, is considered among his best. A young adult novel set in a huge room that contains a labyrinthine maze of stairways leading nowhere, the story outlines how five orphaned sixteen–year–olds learn to survive in a world without walls, ceilings, or floors. The young people, who eat only if they perform dance–like rituals in front of a machine, eventually realize that they are part of a stimulus/ response experiment in which food is dispensed when the subjects display hostile behavior to each other. When two of the protagonists refuse to perform the cruel acts that are required to obtain food, the scientists end the experiment. Compared by critics to such works as *Brave New World* and *Lord of the Flies*, *House of Stairs* is generally regarded as an exceptional study of human behavior as well as an exciting story. Called "brilliant, bone–chilling," by a reviewer in *Publishers Weekly,* the novel is dubbed "[f]orceful sci fi based on Skinnerian precepts that will have readers hanging by the skin of their teeth" by *School Library Journal* reviewer Pamela D. Pollack. Writing in her *Thursday's Child: Trends and Patterns in Contemporary Children's Literature,* Sheila A. Egoff concluded that the story is "one of the most brutal in science fiction, all the more sickeningly compelling because of its finely controlled, stark writing." Sleator told *AAYA,* "In *House of Stairs,* the kids who refused to become conditioned by hate were being human in the end, as opposed to trained animals. I always stress that. I'm not saying to be nice to other people because it's good; I'm saying, think about how other people feel because it's practical. I'm not making any moralistic, goody–goody kind of point. You will get along better with people if you are able to understand them." Sleator has also written other stories for young people that explore behavior; in addition, he is the author of *Take Charge: A Personal Guide to Behavior Modification,* an informational book for adults on which he collaborated with William H. Redd.

"The more books I write, the more they represent who I really am...."

—William Sleator

Sleator considers *The Green Futures of Tycho,* a story for middle graders, to be a watershed book in his career. He named the title character, the youngest of four children who is tormented by his siblings, after his youngest brother. While working in his family's garden, eleven–year–old Tycho finds a strange silver egg that was planted by aliens thousands of years before. The egg, a time–travel device, allows Tycho to go into both the past and the future. At first, Tycho uses his abilities to tease his brothers and sister. He then meets his adult self in the future and finds that the figure is becoming more and more evil and manipulative. For example, the adult Tycho uses his knowledge of the future dishonestly and also wreaks destruction on his siblings. At the end of the story, Tycho's love for his family leads him to reject his powerful but vile grownup persona; he risks death to bury the egg back in the past. In a *School Library Journal* review Pollack noted, "Sleator's expert blend of future and horror fiction is unusually stark, dark, and intriguing." Writing in *Horn Book,* Paul Heins added that though "the com-

bination of logic and horror gives the telling a Poe– like quality . . . the moral significance" of the happenings becomes clear. Sleator once said: "I really got in touch with my weirdness in [*The Green Futures of Tycho*]. That was the first book into which I was able to inject humor, and I feel humor is important. Even in a basically serious, or even a scary piece, there must be comic relief to reduce the tension. Humor is also very attractive to kids."

Full–time Writing

In 1983, Sleator left his job as an accompanist for the Boston Ballet to become a full–time author. *Interstellar Pig,* a young adult novel published the following year, is regarded by critics as one of his most popular books. In this work, sixteen–year–old Barney faces a boring summer at the beach with his doltish parents. He is intrigued when an interesting trio of strangers—Joe, Manny, and Zena—moves in next door and invites him to join them in playing a role–playing board game called Interstellar Pig. The object of the game is to possess The Piggy, a card named for a pink symbol that is an integral part of the game. However, Barney's neighbors turn out to be hostile aliens masquerading as humans, and the game turns real—and deadly. It places Barney in a life–and–death struggle for survival; at the end of the story, Barney saves both himself and planet Earth by using his head. Writing in *School Library Journal,* Trev Jones stated, "Sleator's science fiction story is compelling on first reading—but stellar on the second." *New York Times Book Review* critic Rosalie Byard called *Interstellar Pig* "a riveting adventure that should satisfy readers in the 12– to 14–year–old range, especially any who happen to be hooked on strategy games." Writing in *Junior Bookshelf,* Marcus Crouch called the novel a "remarkable story" that is "surprisingly readable," adding that "the curious details of the game get right into the reader's system." Sleator told *AAYA,* "*Interstellar Pig* is my funniest book. There were a lot of opportunities for humor in it."

Sleator currently spends half the year in Boston, Massachusetts, and the other half in Bangkok, Thailand. He once told *SATA,* "I feel more at home in Thailand than in practically any other place I can think of. Partly this is because Thailand is so exotic that it feels almost like being on another planet. (Don't ask me why THAT should make me feel at home.) I also like Thai people because they turn almost any situation into an occasion to have fun, and because they are so pleasant and polite that you never know what is *really* going on in their minds, so they are a mysterious puzzle to try to figure out."

The Spirit House, a young adult novel that incorporates Thai beliefs, is considered a stylistic departure from Sleator's other works. In this story, fifteen–year–old Julie meets Bia, an exchange student from Thailand, when he comes to stay with her family. Julie's younger brother Dominic builds Bia a "spirit house," or a traditional household shrine, in the backyard to make him feel at home. However, Bia is convinced that the house is inhabited by a vengeful spirit. Julie leaves offerings for the spirit, who appears to grant her wishes. However, Julie's health begins to decline, and things begin to go badly for her, her family, and Bia. At the end of the story, Julie goes to Thailand with a jade carving containing the spirit in order to restore it to its rightful place. All appears to be well until Julie loses the carving. Calling *The Spirit House* "both scary and convincing," *Bulletin of the Center for Children's Books* reviewer Roger Sutton commented that "all of the events of the story are entirely possible, if unremittingly frightening." In a *Washington Post Book World* review, S. P. Somtow added that *The Spirit House* is a book "that provides no easy answers . . . and the ending packs a satisfying punch." Writing in *Kirkus Reviews,* a contributor commented, "Best . . . is the logical explanation of seemingly supernatural events: the reader suspends belief only to have it systematically restored. That's a feast—and a treat."

Dangerous Wishes, the sequel to *The Spirit House,* features Julie's younger brother, fourteen–year–old Dominic. After three years of bad luck have passed for Dom and his family, he and his parents travel to Bangkok for an extended stay. When everything goes awry, Dom suspects that the cause may be the jade carving that his sister tried, but failed, to deliver three years earlier. Dom and Kik, a Thai boy, try to find the charm and take it to its temple. In the process, the boys are pursued by a malevolent creature from the spirit world. They barely escape, but are able to restore the recovered charm to its rightful place. However, the question remains: will the bad luck end? Writing in *Bulletin of the Center for Children's Books,* Roger Sutton stated that "narrative coincidences that would be trite in realistic fiction here have an otherworldly eeriness that makes them convincing." *Booklist* critic Merri Monks concluded by calling the story "fast–moving." A reviewer in *Horn Book* concluded by calling *Dangerous Wishes* "Vintage Sleator." Sleator told *SATA,* "I recently built a Thai–style farmhouse in the northeast of Thailand, twelve kilometers from the Cambodian border, very close to the Khmer Rouge headquarters. I am the only westerner around for seventy kilometers, so everyone knows me and I rather enjoy it—though of course none of them speak English so they can't read my books. But it is a wonderful place to write and I have a writing room with a beautiful view of checkerboard rice fields, brilliantly green in

the rainy season.... We also have a wonderful lush tropical garden. If I could, I would live there all year!"

Autobiographical *Oddballs*

With *Oddballs,* Sleator created a collection of ten short autobiographical and semi–autobiographical vignettes about his childhood and adolescence. The stories show four creative, talented children growing up in a household run by free–thinking parents who provide minimal supervision. The book is credited for depicting how, through all of their sibling rivalry and joke–playing, the Sleator children developed individuality, confidence, and independence. Writing in *Kirkus Reviews,* a critic favorably commented on Sleator's "splendid sense of comic timing" and "vivid characterizations." Betsy Hearne, writing in *Bulletin of the Center for Children's Books,* added that "Sleator evidently thrived without pause on his permissive parents' steady encouragement to violate social taboos." Writing in *School Library Journal,* contributor Michael Cart predicted, that while "serious" readers will take the book as "a kind of 'Portrait of the Artist as a Young Oddball,'" the majority will "simply relax and enjoy the wacky humor." Sleator, who dedicated *Oddballs* "To my family: Please forgive me!," noted on the flap copy, "I changed the names of everyone outside the immediate family, of course. But as far as I'm concerned, it's all in all a pretty accurate picture of what life was like. My mother, of course, might not entirely agree."

If you enjoy the works of William Sleator, you might want to check out the following books:

Ellen Conford, *The Frog Princess of Pelham,* 1997.
Kimberly Fuller, *Home,* 1997.
Ann Turner, *Finding Walter,* 1997.
Connie Willis, *Bellwether,* 1996.

Regarding his writing, Sleator told *AAYA,* "At the beginning, I was copying other things, but with each book, I've learned to tap deeper into my subconscious. The more books I write, the more they represent who I really am. . . . Also, my style has improved; I'm a better writer, but that goes up and down." He added, "I try to make my books exciting. I also provide incentives in the sense of giving kids a more active role in the story. . . . My goal is to entertain my audience and to get them to read. I want kids to find out that reading is the best entertainment there is. If, at the same time, I'm also imparting some scientific knowledge, then that's good, too. I'd like kids to see that science is not just boring formulas. Some of the facts to be learned about the universe are very weird." Sleator also noted, "In any idea for a book, I want to see how I can explore the personal relations that would manifest from that idea." Writing in *Fifth Book of Junior Authors and Illustrators*, Sleator concluded, "I still consider myself one of the luckiest people in the world to be able to write for young people."

■ Biographical and Critical Sources

BOOKS

Davis, James E., and Hazel K. Davis, *Presenting William Sleator*, Twayne, 1992.

Drew, Bernard A., *The 100 Most Popular Young Adult Authors: Biographical Sketches and Bibliographies*, Libraries Unlimited, 1996, pp. 448–50.

Holtze, Sally Holmes Holtze, *Fifth Book of Junior Authors and Illustrators*, Wilson, 1983, pp. 295–96.

Lerner, Fred, *A Teacher's Guide to the Bantam Starfire Novels of William Sleator*, Bantam, 1990.

Meet the Authors and Illustrators: 60 Creators of Favorite Children's Books Talk about Their Work, edited by Deborah Kovacs, Scholastic, 1993.

Roginski, Jim, *Behind the Covers: Interviews with Authors and Illustrators of Books for Children and Young Adults*, Libraries Unlimited, 1985.

Silvey, Anita, editor, *Children's Books and Their Creators*, Houghton Mifflin, 1995, pp. 605–6.

Sleator, William, *Oddballs*, Dutton, 1993.

St. James Guide to Young Adult Writers, edited by Tom Pendergast and Sara Pendergast, 2nd edition, St. James, 1999, pp. 763–65.

Thursday's Child: Trends and Patterns in Contemporary Children's Literature, American Library Association, 1981, p. 142.

PERIODICALS

Booklist, August, 1995, Merri Monks, review of *Dangerous Wishes*, p. 1942; October 1, 1997, p. 333; June 1 and 15, 1998, p. 769.

Bulletin of the Center for Children's Books, October, 1991, Roger Sutton, review of *The Spirit House*, p. 30; May, 1993, Betsy Hearne, review of *Oddballs*, pp. 295–96; October, 1995, Roger Sutton, review of *Dangerous Wishes*, p. 70.

English Journal, March, 1987, Margaret L. Daggett, "Recommended: William Sleator," pp. 93–94.

Fantasy Review, December, 1986, Ashley Darlington Grayson, "Two by Sleator," pp. 41–42.

Horn Book, August, 1972, Paul Heins, review of *Blackbriar*, p. 378; August, 1981, Paul Heins, review of *The Green Futures of Tycho*, p. 426; January–February, 1994, p. 75; March, 1996, review of *Dangerous Wishes*, p. 200; May–June, 1998, Roger Sutton, review of *The Boxes*, p. 349.

Junior Bookshelf, June, 1987, Marcus Crouch, review of *Interstellar Pig*, p. 137.

Kirkus Reviews, April 15, 1972, review of *Blackbriar*, p. 486; October 15, 1991, review of *The Spirit House*, p. 1350; February 1, 1993, review of *Oddballs*, p. 154.

New York Times Book Review, September 23, 1984, Rosalie Byard, review of *Interstellar Pig*, p. 47; April 24, 1994.

Publishers Weekly, November 23, 1970, review of *The Angry Moon*, p. 39; May 6, 1974, review of *House of Stairs*, p. 68; July 12, 1999, p. 93.

School Library Journal, February, 1971, Ann D. Schweibish, review of *The Angry Moon*, p. 50; March, 1974, Pamela D. Pollack, review of *House of Stairs*, p. 120; April, 1981, Pamela D. Pollack, review of *The Green Futures of Tycho*, p. 133; September, 1984, Trev Jones, review of *Interstellar Pig*, p. 134; August, 1985, David Gale, review of *Singularity*, p. 82; August, 1993, Michael Cart, review of *Oddballs*, p. 189.

Voice of Youth Advocates, February, 1994, p. 386.

Washington Post Book World, December 1, 1991, S. P. Somtow, "Something Weird in the Neighborhood," p. 25.

ONLINE

The Scoop: Biographies, http://www.friend.ly.net/scoop/biographies/ (February 2001).

OTHER

Sleator, William, interview with Dieter Miller, *Authors and Artists for Young Adults*, Volume 5, Gale, 1991.*

Carol Lynch Williams

■ Personal

Born September 28, 1959, in Lincoln, NE; daughter of Richard T. (affiliated with the U.S. Air Force) and Anne Y. (a college teacher) Lynch; married Andrew (Drew) G. Williams (an Internet security–writer), August 13, 1985; children: Sarah Elise, Laura Anne, Kyra Leigh, Caitlynne Victoria, Carolina Grace. *Religion:* Church of Jesus Christ of Latter–Day Saints.

■ Addresses

Home—Houston, TX. *Agent*—Marcia Wernick, Sheldon Fogelman Agency, 10 East 40th St., New York, NY 10016.

■ Career

Author of children's books, 1993—.

■ Member

Society of Children's Book Writers and Illustrators.

■ Awards, Honors

Best Book for Young Adults, American Library Association, and Nebraska Golden Sower Award, both for *The True Colors of Caitlynne Jackson;* Teacher's Choice, International Reading Association and Children's Book Council, 1999, for *If I Forget, You Remember.*

■ Writings

Kelly and Me, Delacorte (New York City), 1993.
Adeline Street, Delacorte, 1995.
The True Colors of Caitlynne Jackson, Delacorte, 1997.
If I Forget, You Remember, Delacorte, 1998.
My Angelica, Delacorte, 1999.
Carolina Autumn, Delacorte, 2000.
Christmas in Heaven, Putnam (New York City), 2000.

"THE LATTER–DAY DAUGHTERS" SERIES

Anna's Gift, Aspen Books (Salt Lake City, UT), 1995.
Laurel's Flight, Aspen Books, 1995.
Sarah's Quest, Aspen Books, 1995.
Esther's Celebration, illustrated by Paul Mann, Aspen Books, 1996.
Marciea's Melody, illustrated by Paul Mann, Aspen Books, 1996.
Catherine's Remembrance, Aspen Books, 1996.

Caroline's Secret, Deseret Book Co. (Salt Lake City, UT), 1997.

Victoria's Courage, Deseret Book Co., 1998.

Laura's Box of Treasures, Bookcraft (West Valley, UT), 1999.

■ **Sidelights**

Carol Lynch Williams is the author of more than a dozen books for young adult (YA) readers. She has written several for the "Latter–Day Daughters" series, which features likable young protagonists whose Mormon faith helps them overcome a crisis in their lives or community. However, Williams's other books, more lighthearted in tone, impart a moral lesson, too. Her heroines grieve a death in the family or resent the arrival of an aging grandparent in their home, but manage to maintain a sense of humor when encountering the usual comic troubles of adolescence. Williams's talent for creating sympathetic heroines and their quandaries has earned her several awards and a devoted readership. "I think stories come about because of an emotion that stirs me," Williams told *Authors and Artists for Young Adults* (*AAYA*) in a 2000 interview. "If I feel something powerfully, doesn't matter the emotion, then I am usually compelled to explore that feeling with a character."

Williams was born Carol Lynch in Lincoln, Nebraska, in 1959, but her father's post with the U.S. Air Force forced the family to relocate twice, first to England and then to Florida. "My father and mother divorced when I was about nine, but Dad left much earlier than that," Williams told *AAYA*. "There were mostly women in my family—my mom and sister and myself, my grandmother and two aunts, and the cousin that I played with. Florida was a wonderful place to grow up. Lots of places to swim, lots of places to play. I explored with my cousins and sister, swam in our lake, went fishing and pretty much enjoyed the outdoors. Once I even went to Brownies (Girl Scouts) but I never went back since there was no food and I thought by the name of the group there would be. Very disappointing."

In Florida, the Lynch family lived in the Orlando area, where their mother enrolled in college. In such a household, the emphasis on learning and history was strong. "I think stories were always in my life. There was lots of reading, lots of oral family history, lots of lyrics written (along with music). At family reunions, somebody was always telling a 'There ain't no way you gonna believe this one' tale when we got together. Lots of laughter when my

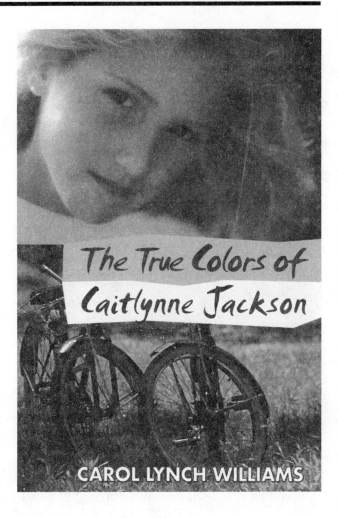

Two sisters learn to confront their abusive and mentally ill mother in this 1997 novel.

grandmother was near." Yet growing up in a one–parent household was sometimes stressful. "I was a very shy child," Williams told *AAYA*. "Life was hard and now, looking back, I see myself kind of wide–eyed and almost surprised at what it offered my sister and me.

"Books were very important to me," Williams continued. "I don't remember how old I was when I began to read (though my sister taught herself at age four), but I know that I loved libraries. When my mother would drive close to one, I would say to her, 'Mom, I smell books,' hoping she would stop. In fact, when I was about nine or so, I was lying in the back of our station wagon reading a *Wizard of Oz* book (I think). A newspaper reporter took a picture of me reading and wrote a little blurb about me. I think that picture exists in an old file somewhere in Sanford, Florida. [*Wonderful Wizard of Oz* writer L. Frank] Baum was a favorite author. I remember when I discovered there was more than just *The Wizard of Oz*. How excited I was! Early on I read *A Tree Grows in Brooklyn* and other books by Betty Smith. Quickly I went to Mark Twain, William Faulkner, Flannery O'Connor, etc. I quit reading kids' books. I've made up for that since. Now I almost always read books for children and teenagers."

Williams added, "I read all the time and at a young age I began to write plays. I loved writing. I tried all different kinds of things and finally, when I was sixteen, I began writing the stories that would end up in my first book, *Kelly and Me*. . . . I didn't like school that much, but I tried to be a good student. As a teenager I read my head off, laughed my head off with my friends, studied my head off in high school and dreamed of getting rich when I published my first book (tee hee). I still correspond with my old high school best friend and she winds up in my books every now and then, too. As a teenager, I became interested in religion and that took up a lot of my life."

Entered Publishing Contest

As a young woman, Williams enrolled in college, but she did not graduate. The creative–writing courses which she took gave her a greater understanding about herself, "and [I] realized I loved making people laugh with my words," Williams told *AAYA*. "I just had this kind of blind faith that I would succeed as a writer. My first book publication is a kind of funny story. I was taking an Independent Study class (work at home thing) when Louise Plummer became my teacher . . . She liked my stuff and encouraged me to send my attempt at a novel to the Delacorte First Young Adult Writing Contest. I had a middle grade novel (though I didn't know that title at the time). The kids were aged ten and eleven, I think. I got the contest rules, saw that I needed the kids to be older. I changed their ages to thirteen and fourteen. The rules also called for the book to be at least one hundred pages. Mine was not, so I enlarged the font size to fourteen point. I sent the novel in. Four or so months later I got a call from Mary Cash at Bantam, Doubleday, Dell. She said, 'We liked your novel. It didn't win though. We'd like to publish the novel if you'd be willing to make a few changes.' 'Of course,' I said. 'Yes, I will!' 'The characters seem too old,' Mary said. 'Would you mind making them younger?' 'I wouldn't mind at all,' I said. And I didn't, either."

That book became *Kelly and Me*, which was published by Delacorte in 1993. Those characters reverted to ten–year–old Leah Orton and her sister Kelly, who is eleven. Their household is disrupted in a not entirely unpleasant way when their energetic grandfather, whom they call "Papa," moves in with them. The two youngsters and their young–at–heart grandparent get involved in a series of adventures that lead them into trouble; the beleaguered Orton parents are forced to play disciplinarian to both generations. Sadly, the mischief turns to grief when Kelly suddenly collapses at breakfast from a fatal brain aneurysm. The family collapses as well, for a brief time. Leah blames her beloved grandfather for the tragedy, but comes to realize her anger is misplaced.

In a *School Library Journal* review, Carolyn Noah praised Williams's ability to chronicle difficult family crises. "Within the space of twelve pages, the family nearly tears apart, then begins to knit together as they share their memories and grief," she observed. Deborah Stevenson, writing in the *Bulletin of the Center for Children's Books*, declared that *Kelly and Me*'s "dialogue and family dynamics are authentic, humorous, and restrained," while *Kirkus Reviews* pronounced it to be "a capable first novel that views both boisterous comedy and wrenching loss with a perceptive eye."

Sequel That Came Full Circle

Kelly and Me was such a hit with critics and readers alike that Williams decided to write a sequel. In *Adeline Street*, Leah, now twelve, recounts events in her life and family since the loss of her beloved sister. Papa is still with them, but time has mellowed him a bit. Leah struggles with the minor crises that arrive along with her status as a pre–teen. Toward the end, she realizes that her parents are expecting a baby. Stevenson, reviewing *Adeline Street* for the *Bulletin of the Center for Children's Books*, wrote that "Williams again displays an easy gift for evocation of place and voice."

Around this time, Williams began to write her Latter–Day Daughters novels, which feature young women and their families who belong to the Church of Jesus Christ of Latter–day Saints. The tenets of this faith, also known as Mormonism, are crucial to the plot or character development in these books. Williams's first in the series was *Anna's Gift*, in which its title character, living in a Mormon community in Illinois in the mid–nineteenth century, befriends the founder of the Mormon faith, Joseph Smith, and realizes that her "gift" is a definite talent for drawing. In *Laurel's Flight*, danger befalls one Mormon community, and Laurel's family is forced to flee westward. *Sarah's Quest* recounts a young girl's search to find a wife for her widowed father,

IF I FORGET, YOU REMEMBER

CAROL LYNCH WILLIAMS

Elyse Donaldson's plans for the summer are changed when she has to deal with her grandmother's Alzheimer's Disease in this Children's Book Council Award winner.

which leads both to the Mormon church. *Esther's Celebration* is set in 1896, when the predominantly Mormon territory of Utah becomes a state. Esther tries desperately to win the lead role in a commemorative play, staged by her father and planned for the statehood celebrations, but the part goes to another girl. Resentful at first, Esther learns to accept the decision and even makes a new friend. *Marciea's Melody* follows a young girl whose mother is instrumental in battling racism in their Mormon community, while *Catherine's Remembrance* returns to early church history and the flight from Illinois to Utah in the 1840s. *Caroline's Secret* is a Mormon spy drama set in 1878, and in *Victoria's Courage*, the title heroine is separated from her family, perhaps forever, when an earthquake destroys San Francisco in 1906.

Tackles Difficult Subjects

William's next novel for Delacorte was *The True Colors of Caitlynne Jackson*, which deals with the tough emotional territory of child neglect and mental illness. As this 1997 novel opens, half–sisters Caitlynne and Cara struggle to survive in a remote rural household headed by their abusive mother. One day, their erratic parent announces that she needs to write a novel and must be alone. She departs with a suitcase, and with her goes her chronic emotion and physical abuse of the girls. Caitlynne and Cara are even relieved to be on their own, but soon realize the difficulty of fending for themselves financially when they run out of food. Caitlynne, a gifted artist, has a supportive boyfriend, but finally they must go to their grandmother for help. Despite their worries, authorities intervene and their mentally ill mother finally begins to receive the help she needs. *Bulletin of the Center for Children's Books* reviewer Stevenson gave the book a strong recommendation. "The story is gripping and believable," Stevenson wrote. "The desperation and up–close parental menace are originally and powerfully depicted."

In her 1998 novel, *If I Forget, You Remember*, Williams returns once again to the adjustments required when a grandparent comes to live in a household formerly dominated by teens. However, Elyse and Jordyn Donaldson's grandmother is no young–at–heart mischief–maker; she is suffering from Alzheimer's disease, and the somewhat self–centered Elyse finds the new situation particularly difficult. She also finds it hard to accept the fact that her single mother is beginning to date. Elyse, a budding writer, finds a new friend in her Granny and a possible boyfriend in her childhood playmate. In doing so, Elyse comes to realize that she and her grandmother share some of the same personality traits, especially when challenged. "Elyse gradually begins to look beyond herself and see the stress life puts on others," wrote Susan Dove Lempke in *Booklist*. *If I Forget, You Remember* won Williams several citations, including a Children's Book Council award.

Williams's next book also features a would–be writer, but Sage Oliver's literary efforts take center stage in the plot of *My Angelica*. Sage is fifteen and plans to earn her living writing historical romance novels, like her mother. Sage has written several chapters of "Angelica and the Seminole Indians," a manuscript in which her stock–character heroine is overwhelmed by relentless stylistic errors. Sage's beloved Angelica has "blacker–than–the–night hair" and "brighter–than–a–blue–sky eyes," and her Native American boyfriend, who is named "247 Bears," predictably is the strong silent type. But Sage has based 247 Bears—whose name changes from page to page—on her best friend. "Sage reads every chapter to George," wrote Patricia S. Brown in *Book*

Faced with the stress of her first year at high school, Carolina McKinney has to confront her feelings about the loss of her father and older sister.

Report. "He is appalled because he knows that the writing is awful." George is silent when it comes to letting Sage know that he has feelings for her, and struggles whether or not to tell her the truth about her melodramatic prose: "Angelica put on her dead husband's favorite white gloves, and wiped a lone tear from her carefully made–up face. Not a bit of make–up smeared."

When their school announces a literary contest, George encourages Sage to write something for it; she is determined to submit "Angelica." To spare her the certain embarrassment, George hides the manuscript, but in a series of comic mishaps it finds its way into the hands of the judges, who declare it hilarious. It wins first prize in the judges' mistaken belief that Sage has written a parody of a romance novel. George's own poems, anonymously submit-

ted paeans to Sage, take second place. Debby Adams, reviewing *My Angelica* for the *Voice of Youth Advocates,* predicted that "[r]eaders will identify with Sage's aspirations to lead a romantic writer's life," but Adams felt that some of the other characters—particularly Sage's unconventional mother—could have been more fully developed. *Booklist* reviewer Shelle Rosenfeld declared that "Williams's skillful, engaging prose and keen observations offer a delightful perspective on matters of the heart, in fiction and life."

Coming to Terms with Loss

Carolina Autumn was Williams's sixth YA novel. Its heroine is Carolina McKinney, who is fourteen and about to begin high school. Garret, her boyfriend, is a year older and lives next door. She worries about their relationship, especially as the first day of school looms. But Carolina is also plagued by a deeper problem: her father and sister are gone. She writes letters to her sister, and is despondent that her older sibling is not here to share the trials and tribulations of freshman year with her. In an effort to connect with her father, Carolina starts using his camera. Gradually, readers learn what happened in the family, and why Carolina's mother is so withdrawn and unavailable to her. A crisis with her double–crossing best friend, who tries to win Garret's affection, finally incites her mother to rally herself for her daughter. "Carolina remains an honestly wrought heroine, whom readers will understand and respect," assessed a *Publishers Weekly* review of *Carolina Autumn.*

Williams wrote another book for publication in 2000, *Christmas in Heaven.* It features a likable twelve–year–old heroine, Honey DeLoach, who lives in a rural Florida town called Heaven. The town's population is primarily the DeLoach family and her grandfather, a famous revivalist preacher whose prayer gatherings attract massive crowds. Much to the disappointment of her grandfather, Honey resists becoming "born again" at one of his revivals. Still, she leads a restricted life in such a household, and yearns for more excitement and worldliness in her life. It arrives in the form of a film star, Miriam Season, who relocates to Heaven and builds a palatial home. One of her two comically named daughters becomes a much–desired best friend for Honey. But Christmas's sister Easter proves to be a troublemaker, and Honey comes to realize that her own brother is not as innocent as he seems. The author, declared a *Publishers Weekly* review, "uses broad, bright strokes to paint the external traits of her motley cast of teenage characters."

A Hectic Household

Williams and her husband live in the Houston area, where she schools her five daughters and a nephew at home. The busy household has presented certain challenges to her as a writer, as she told *AAYA*. "I just recently got an office out of my home. I'm not sure how this is going to work, though I have my fingers crossed it goes well. I have eight children in my home right now and the office thing here at the house had to be changed so kids could have a bedroom. . . . I like to be comfortable when I write (not too cold), and I like it quiet, too. . . As far as writing and work, my family is my work and it comes first. After those needs are met, I find time for myself to write. And since I mostly enjoy writing, it's something I work to find time for. I didn't really decide to write for children. I just wrote and it was for children. I guess I lucked out. Those are the words in my head. . .

If you enjoy works by Carol Lynch Williams, you might want to check out the following books:

Richard Graber, *Doc*, 1986.
Heather Quarles, *A Door Near Here*, 1998.
Sally Pfoutz, *Missing Persons*, 1993.

"My goal as a writer is to write the best story I can, using the best language I can. I don't usually set out to write a specific story. If I feel that emotion I talked about earlier, then I kind of follow that. Sometimes I have an idea in my head, but mostly I watch the story unfold, glad I get to write. Especially if the writing is going well and I'm not having to wrestle the words out of my head. I guess I hope, after a story is done, that people in the situations as my characters, see that things don't always have to be the way the are (like in *The True Colors of Caitlynne Jackson*). Or that there is hope (like in *Carolina Autumn*, *Christmas in Heaven*, or *If I Forget, You Remember*). Life isn't easy. Especially for kids. Maybe as writers we can give readers different ways of looking at things. I think I'd describe my work as—most of the time—revolving around a tough subject. . . . I love life. I love my family. I love that I get to be a writer."

■ Biographical and Critical Sources

PERIODICALS

ALAN Review, fall, 2000, Edna Earl Edwards, review of *Christmas in Heaven*, p. 35.

Book Report, September–October, 1999, Patricia S. Brown, review of *My Angelica*, p. 63.

Booklist, April 1, 1995, Kay Weisman, review of *Adeline Street*, p. 1393; March 1, 1997, Susan Dove Lempke, review of *The True Colors of Caitlynne Jackson*, p. 1155; April 15, 1998, Susan Dove Lempke, review of *If I Forget, You Remember*, p. 1444; December 15, 1998, Shelle Rosenfeld, review of *My Angelica*, p. 744.

Bulletin of the Center for Children's Books, March, 1994, Deborah Stevenson, review of *Kelly and Me*, p. 238; April, 1995, Deborah Stevenson, review of *Adeline Street*, p. 289; February, 1997, Deborah Stevenson, review of *The True Colors of Caitlynne Jackson*, p. 226.

Horn Book, January–February, 1999, Roger Sutton, review of *My Angelica*, p. 72.

Kirkus Reviews, review of *Kelly and Me*, November 1, 1993, p. 1400; February 15, 1995, p. 235; review of *If I Forget, You Remember*, December 15, 1997, p. 1844.

Publishers Weekly, January 5, 1998, review of *If I Forget, You Remember*, p. 68; December 14, 1998, review of *My Angelica*, p. 76; July 10, 2000, review of *Christmas in Heaven*, p. 64; August 21, 2000, review of *Carolina Autumn*, p, 74.

School Library Journal, September, 1993, Carolyn Noah, review of *Kelly and Me*, p. 236; February, 1997, Carolyn Noah, *The True Colors of Caitlynne Jackson*, p. 106; March, 1998, Cyrisse Jaffee, review of *If I Forget, You Remember*, p. 226; January, 1999, Janet Hilbun, review of *My Angelica*, p. 134.

Voice of Youth Advocates, October, 1993, p. 220; August, 1999, Debby Adams, review of *My Angelica*, p. 187; October, 2000, Betsy Fraser, review of *Carolina Autumn*, pp. 271–272.*

—Sketch by Carol Brennan

June Rae Wood

■ Personal

Born September 4, 1946, in Sedalia, MO; daughter of Kenneth Sattler (a cutter and grinder), and Evelyn (a homemaker; maiden name, Evans) and stepfather Olen (a railroad worker) Haggerman; married William A. Wood (a heavy equipment mechanic), December 2, 1966; children: Samantha. *Education:* Attended Central Missouri State College (now University), 1964–66. *Politics:* Republican. *Religion:* Protestant. *Hobbies and other interests:* "Quilting, reading, and granddaughter Rachel, born in 1998."

■ Addresses

Home—P.O. Box 337, Windsor, MO 65360.

■ Career

Whiteman Air Force Base, Whiteman, MO, Civil Service clerk typist, 1967–70; *Sedalia Democrat*, Sedalia, MO, staff writer for "Living Today," 1988–97.

■ Member

Society of Children's Book Writers and Illustrators, Sedalia Writers' Group.

■ Awards, Honors

Mark Twain Award and William Allen White Award, both 1995, both for *The Man Who Loved Clowns;* Friends of American Writers Award for Juvenile Fiction, for *A Share of Freedom;* Edgar Wolfe Literary Award, Friends of the Library (Kansas City, KS).

■ Writings

The Man Who Loved Clowns, Putnam (New York City), 1992.
A Share of Freedom, Putnam, 1994.
When Pigs Fly, Putnam, 1995.
Turtle on a Fence Post, Putnam, 1997.
About Face, Putnam, 1999.

Contributor of articles and short stories to *Family Circle, Reader's Digest, Home Life, The Lookout, New Ways,* and *School & Community.*

■ Work in Progress

Another novel for young adults.

■ Sidelights

"My brother Richard was born [in 1948] with Down's syndrome and a heart defect," author June Rae Wood wrote in the *Sedalia Democrat* in 1995. "The doctor said he wouldn't live, and even if he did, he would never walk or talk. He advised my parents to send Richard to die in an institution, rather than take him home and let the family get attached to him." Wood, the second of what would eventually be eight children, was only two years old when her parents brought Richard, their third child, home from the hospital. Although her parents gave all their children special attention, Richard, whom Wood's mother called her little "Dickey–bird," was doted on and protected by all the family members. This was not just because he was handicapped, but also because Richard was very special to them all. He would eventually become the subject of Wood's award–winning first book, *The Man Who Loved Clowns*. "Richard was a comical little guy," Wood told *Authors and Artists for Young Adults* (*AAYA*) in an interview, "friendly with everybody, even total strangers. He was, in fact, exactly like 'Punky' in the book. He really did pour out the shampoo, tell people they were fat, and fling horn bones behind the TV. He learned to walk at age four, and then he would run away from home—not to be naughty, just to explore. Sometimes he'd be gone when we woke up, and we'd find him throwing dirt clods at the neighbor's chickens, just to hear them squawk. These running–away incidents, which he eventually outgrew, were the only times he was ever alone because our family was very protective of him. If we took him somewhere and people made fun, we would leave as soon as possible."

Richard died in 1985, at the age of thirty–six, when his defective heart gave out. The loss was a painful one for the entire family, but it was his sister who would end up writing about it. At the time, Wood had been writing for three years, but she had had no success publishing her works. Before that, she had not been very interested in writing, although she had always loved to read. "As a child, I enjoyed reading the life stories of Marie Curie, Thomas Edison, George Washington Carver, and many others who made great accomplishments," she told *AAYA*. "I also loved Trixie Belden mysteries and the Laura Ingalls Wilder stories. . . . I remember crying my eyes out at about age twelve when I read Dale Evans' *Angel Unaware*. It was a true story about the life—and death—of a handicapped child, and unlike anything I'd ever read before. I think it touched me greatly because my own little brother had Down's syndrome."

> *"I enjoy writing for kids, but at the same time, it's an awesome responsibility. The words I write will be absorbed by young, impressionable minds, and that's why I work by a certain standard: I never write anything I'd be ashamed for my mom or my daughter to read."*
>
> —June Rae Wood

Growing Up in Missouri

With so many children to take care of, Wood's mother and stepfather struggled to make ends meet. (Her biological father and mother divorced when Wood was still an infant, and she was raised by her mother and stepfather, Evelyn and Olen Haggerman.) Wood described her parents: "Mom wore her straight, brown hair in a ponytail, and her usual attire was a simple housedress. She never wore makeup, and she never spent time on herself. Her 'recreation' was riding in the pickup with Dad and all of us kids to the ice cream store. Chores for her included cooking and cleaning, doing laundry with a wringer washer, caring for a huge garden, and canning hundreds of quarts of food. She was handy with a hammer, and she wasn't afraid to install a window or knock out a wall on her own. She was very creative, and could make prize–winning Halloween costumes out of old curtains, old sheets, old clothes, and a package or two of fabric dye. I used to think she never slept.

"Dad was a small man in size (about five feet, six inches) but big in my eyes. Since he worked for the railroad, his skin was brown and leathery from constant exposure to the weather, and he had a permanent squint. His summer attire was a white T–shirt and overalls, plus a railroad cap or a baseball cap to protect his balding head. In the wintertime, he couldn't wear enough clothes to keep warm. After patrolling track all day in an open motor car, he'd come home nearly frozen, his eyebrows frosted with ice. (Thus the scene in *Turtle on a Fence Post*, when Tree tells Delrita why his family doesn't have enough chairs.) Our family was close–knit and loving and was, in fact, my pattern for the Shackleford family in *The Man Who Loved Clowns*."

While Wood and her brothers and sisters went to school, Richard stayed at home. In the 1950s there were no schools that could accommodate his special needs (although by the time he was seventeen, a school for the handicapped had opened that he attended for four years). At home, there was not much for him to do except watch television, play in the yard, and help watch over the baby of the family—sister Janie, who was born when he was nine. "Years later, Richard also kept an eye on his little nieces and nephews, just as he had with Janie. Thus the scene on page fourteen of *The Man Who Loved Clowns*," Wood explained.

Wood recalled being a good student who graduated second out of a high school class of seventy–four in 1964. "I loved school from first grade on up, and I was very competitive. My first–quarter grade in typing class was an S–minus (same as a B–minus), and I was horrified. I bought myself a portable, manual typewriter so I could practice at home and build up speed. Since I worked evenings after school as a waitress, I started my homework about 8:30 p.m. and did my typing after that. I would type in the kitchen until Dad came thundering down the stairs because my peck–peck–pecking was keeping him awake. The payoff was that I finished the year as the fastest typist in the class." Because of her love of reading, English class was one of her strong subjects. "English came easy for me, but I didn't particularly like writing. I wrote only what was required of me to make a good grade. In high school, I excelled in business subjects: typing, shorthand, accounting, office practice. I thought I would become a business education teacher. It never crossed my mind that I would someday be a writer. I was married and had a twelve–year–old daughter before the writing bug bit me."

Becoming a Writer

While she was still attending business education classes at Central Missouri State College, the future author had a blind date with William A. Wood, an airman stationed at Whiteman Air Force Base. They quickly fell in love and married in 1966. The new Mrs. Wood left school and found work as a clerk–typist at the air force base. Four years later their daughter, Samantha, was born. Wood left her job to raise Samantha, and the family eventually moved to a rural home near Windsor, Missouri. Although Wood was happy to be a mother, she sometimes felt lonely spending all her time at home, so she decided to try her hand at writing. She read how–to books on writing and worked on short stories—for which she has three years' worth of rejection letters—and an unpublished novel called "A Summer's Worth of Trouble." This first book, the author told *AAYA*, "is a story about a girl growing up in a large family in a small town in the 1950s. Although it's

fiction, a lot of it is based on my life. One little brother, for instance, is slow about learning to walk. His nickname is 'Scooter' because he gets around by scooting on his rump, just like Richard did in real life. That book was my 'practice set.' With all those rewrites, I was learning more and more about character, dialogue, and plot—and each new version was better than the last. However, I put that manuscript aside to write *The Man Who Loved Clowns*, and it's been in the drawer ever since. I do plan to work on it again someday."

But before *The Man Who Loved Clowns*, Wood wrote an article for the magazine *Family Circle* that was her first step toward success. Published in the December 3, 1985, issue, a few months after Richard's death, the article was titled "The Boy Who Taught Love" and was about her experiences with her brother. Wood wrote how having Richard in the family was not a burden but a blessing. "God sent him not to be a *learner*, but a *teacher*," she asserted in the article. "And without knowing it, he was the best teacher our family could have had. He taught us understanding and acceptance and compassion." The reading audience was deeply moved. "People all over the U.S. sent letters," Wood told *AAYA*, "telling me how touched they'd been by Richard's life. However, the letters were always from grown-ups, and one day it occurred to me that I should try writing a story about Richard that would appeal to kids. After all, it was kids who'd been afraid of him or cruel to him, and they needed to know what he was really like. That's when I began working on *The Man Who Loved Clowns*."

By the time she started writing the book, Wood was working part time as a staff writer for the *Sedalia Democrat* in Sedalia, Missouri. After many hard months of writing, she submitted the manuscript to Putnam in New York City; the publisher quickly accepted the book for publication with only minor changes. One of these was to make the story's main character, Delrita, thirteen instead of twelve years old. "My editor, Refna Wilkin, said Delrita sounded thirteen and asked me to change her age in the story," Wood recalled. "Refna also said I had a 'natural thirteen–year–old voice.' Don't ask me how that came to be. I just write the way I write." *The Man Who Loved Clowns* is a fictionalization of the author's personal experiences. Instead of giving Delrita a younger brother with Down's syndrome, Wood gives her an uncle with Down's—thirty–five–year–old "Punky." Delrita Jensen adores Uncle Punky, who is fascinated by clowns and crayons and always wears a cowboy hat—but at the same time she is embarrassed by him. She feels uncomfortable when visitors come to their house or when the family goes to church. But the novel is a coming-of-age tale, too, and not just about the difficulties of having a family member with Down's. This is Delrita's story; it deals with such issues as boyfriends, peer pressure, self–esteem, and, finally, death, as Delrita has to face her parents' tragic demise in a car accident. Punky's love and support help Delrita work through her grief, and then in a tragic twist, Punky dies, too, when his ailing heart gives out.

Finding Success

Critics roundly praised *The Man Who Loved Clowns* for its strong characterization and the way Wood realistically portrays difficult problems. Judith E. Landrum, writing in the *Journal of Adolescent and Adult Literacy,* noted how Wood's story challenges preconceptions of what handicapped people are really like, as well as telling the tough truth that "doing 'the right thing' does not always protect people from causing or receiving pain." A *Publishers Weekly* reviewer concluded that in this debut novel, "Wood displays a prodigious writing and storytelling talent."

"Writing *The Man Who Loved Clowns* was therapy for me," Wood told *AAYA.* "It helped me work through my grief after the death of my brother, and the story came from my heart. Society deals with 'differences' much better today than it did when I was growing up, but we still have work to do. For instance, a lot of kids think they can 'catch' Down's syndrome and are afraid to get close to someone who has it. Since *Clowns* was published, I've made a lot of school visits, and I've heard about many methods teachers use to help promote understanding. Here are a few suggestions I'd like to pass along: 1) Invite disabled people into the classroom to talk about their specific challenges— blindness, deafness, Down's syndrome, etc. 2) Provide props such as wheelchairs, crutches, and blindfolds for the students to use while performing simple tasks. Then have them write about the difficulties they experienced. 3) For smaller groups, plan a trip to a sheltered workshop."

After *The Man Who Loved Clowns,* Wood continued to write novels for young adults about characters who face serious challenges in their families. *A Share of Freedom* is about another thirteen year old, Freedom, whose mother is an alcoholic. Because of her mother's problem, Freedom has to take care of her half–brother, Jackie. Freedom and Jackie run away after their mother is sent away for rehabilitation, but they quickly learn that they can't make it on their own and are put in a foster home. Freedom doesn't like her foster father, Martin Quincy, who is always criticizing people. The startling truth that

Freedom discovers is that Martin is actually her biological father. Critics noted that *A Share of Freedom* offers many insights into family relationships. One of the main points in the novel, Wood told *AAYA,* was that people can love each other despite their failings: "I wanted Freedom to realize that her mother did love her, in spite of the drinking." Although some reviewers thought that Martin's being Freedom's father was a bit too coincidental, many praised the novel as another strong work by the author. *Voice of Youth Advocates* contributor Bunni Union called it a "poignant story," adding that the "language reads easily and, at times, almost poetically." A *Booklist* critic said that "teens will sympathize with Freedom, cheer her determination and strength, and enjoy the promising, neatly resolved ending."

> *"Society deals with 'differences' much better today than it did when I was growing up, but we still have work to do."*
>
> —June Rae Wood

In 1995, Wood wrote another novel that included a character with Down's syndrome, *When Pigs Fly.* In this story, thirteen–year–old Buddy Richter has many problems in her life. Her father has lost his job, which has forced them to move into a run–down house in the country, only four miles away from her best friend, Jiniwin; and Buddy worries about watching over her younger sister, Reenie, who has Down's. Buddy's friends also have serious troubles. Jiniwin's parents have divorced and she has started drinking. Another friend, Dallas, has been abandoned by his father. Thus, Buddy's sister's disability is only one of many issues she must face. Although Judy Sasges wrote in *Voice of Youth Advocates* that *When Pigs Fly* is at times too "didactic" about themes such as how money doesn't buy happiness, a *Publishers Weekly* reviewer felt that the "novel treats family conflicts and social concerns with the same sensitivity of Wood's previous titles." Debbie Carton, writing in *Booklist,* also praised the "well developed and believable" characters.

Readers are reacquainted with Delrita Jensen from *The Man Who Loved Clowns* in Wood's 1997 novel, *Turtle on a Fence Post.* After her parents' deaths, Delrita and Punky had moved in with her Aunt

Queenie and Uncle Bert. After Punky's death, Delrita becomes an emotional wreck, who is not ready to love other people, and she feels uncomfortable and unwanted in her new home. Her aunt, she expects, sees her as a burden on the family. Then Queenie's crabby father, Orvis, moves in. Delrita finds Orvis, who is a World War II veteran, very intimidating, and his presence makes the family situation worse. The one bright point in her life is the boy she has a crush on, Tree Shackleford, but even that seems like it will be ruined when another girl starts flirting with Tree. Delrita's life begins to turn around from two unexpected sources: a "teen buddy" program in which she helps Joey Marcum, who suffers from multiple birth defects because his mother had German measles while she was pregnant, and Orvis, who agrees to let her interview him for a school project. By the end of the book, Delrita has learned that she can love again and come out of her shell.

"Before I even thought about writing *Turtle on a Fence Post*," Wood told *AAYA*, "I was assigned to write a story for the newspaper to commemorate the fiftieth anniversary of D–Day. I interviewed five veterans, and the stories these men told, their quiet heroism, their tears fifty years after the fact, had a profound impact on me. Their first–person accounts of the war stoked the fire of patriotism in me. In *Turtle* I wanted to pay tribute to all the veterans of World War II, and that's why I created Orvis Roebuck, Aunt Queenie's father. I needed someone who could talk first–hand about the war." A *Kirkus Reviews* critic observed how this aspect of the book comes out: "An appreciation for those who sacrifice time, effort, money, and even their lives for others infuses this memorable tale of healing." That Wood balances issues such as these, along with the subject of disabilities and other themes, was particularly notable to *School Library Journal* contributor Carol A. Edwards. She remarked appreciatively that "this engaging story is one of a very few that shows average kids interacting enjoyably with special–needs adults without that being the focus of the story."

The Purpose of Writing

When asked by *AAYA* about Edwards' comment, Wood replied, "Actually, I didn't realize I had done that until I read the *School Library Journal* review. I suppose it was a subconscious thing. When I was growing up, it was normal for us to hide the shampoo and to find chicken bones behind the TV. Why? Because we were used to Richard and his little quirks. It was no big deal. Evidently, this was in the back of my mind when I was writing about Joey. I wanted the readers to see his quirks, yes, but not as

any big deal." Wood sees her characters with disabilities simply as one more aspect of her main characters' lives. "The subplots are necessary to make a believable story," she said. "Delrita would be a flat, unlikable character if she did nothing but go to school and go home again. Who cares about that? 'Cares' is the key word. I do my best to make my readers care about my protagonists. I want them to feel Delrita's love for 'Punky,' her insecurity, her grief, her anger. If they don't feel, then I have failed."

If Wood could have her books get across one message to her readers, it would be: "Happiness is not having what you want, but wanting what you have," as she told *AAYA*. This is a direct quote from her 1999 novel, *About Face,* which features thirteen–year–old Glory Bea Goode. Glory is very shy, due to a large, red birthmark on her face. But then she meets Marvalene Zulig, whose parents work at a carnival that is in town. Marvalene is a tough girl who is bitter because she feels that her family's hard life led to her mother having a stroke and giving birth to a stillborn baby. Wood alternates viewpoints between Glory and Marvalene, showing how their friendship and emotional support help Glory gain some self–confidence and Marvalene to appreciate her life more. "Readers may not want to trade lives with either heroine," commented a *Publishers Weekly* critic, "but they will enjoy vicariously experiencing the warmth of their growing camaraderie." A reviewer for *Booklist* called *About Face* an "engaging ramble, well stocked with laughs, tears, spats, and reconciliations."

Wood is working on a sixth novel for young adults, but she's reluctant to reveal more than that. "If I talk about works in progress," she said, "I lose my steam." When getting an idea for a new book, Wood draws her stories "from real life—my own and other people's," as she told *AAYA*. "If I hear a good story, I make a note of it. If I see an interesting 'character' on the street, I make a note of that, too. I clip newspaper articles that catch my attention. Also, the articles I wrote for the *Democrat* have proved to be a valuable resource. A case in point: I once wrote a story for the paper about a lady who cooked on a riverboat. In my most recent book, *About Face,* the character 'Pansy' used to cook on a riverboat—and because I had the newspaper story to fall back on, her dialogue is authentic." After Wood has a story in mind, she creates a short outline. "For each of my books, I've written about a three–page outline. Each outline is basically like a letter to myself. It tells me, who the characters are, what problems they will have, and how they will resolve them. The details come later with the actual writing, but I have to know how a story will end before I start."

If you enjoy the works of June Rae Wood, you might want to check out the following books:

Sara Harrell Banks, *Under the Shadow of Wings,* 1997.
Sharon Creech, *Chasing Redbird,* 1997.
Jean Little, *His Banner over Me,* 1995.
Jerrie Oughton, *The War in Georgia,* 1997.

Wood has no immediate plans to write novels for audiences other than young adult readers. "I enjoy writing for kids," she said, "but at the same time, it's an awesome responsibility. The words I write will be absorbed by young, impressionable minds, and that's why I work by a certain standard: I never write anything I'd be ashamed for my mom or my daughter to read. No foul language, no sex, and no violence just for the sake of entertainment." Not only do Wood's novels deliver their messages of the importance of appreciating what you have—love, friends, self–respect—but they serve as examples of the type of entertainment she strongly believes children and young adults need more of these days. As she pointed out in an article she wrote for the *Democrat,* "Children are great imitators. We adults must provide them with appropriate role models and wholesome books to read and movies to watch." Evidence of Wood's effect on her young readers can be seen in the letters she has received. One student wrote, "My favorite novels were *Jurassic Park* and *Mortal Kombat* until [we] read *The Man Who Loved Clowns*"; and another fan of Wood's first novel said, "I like this book because it inspired me. I had this feeling it was like burning in my fingers. I just wanted to read."

■ Biographical and Critical Sources

PERIODICALS

Booklist, September 1, 1994, Chris Sherman, review of *A Share of Freedom,* p. 36; December 1, 1995, Debbie Carton, review of *When Pigs Fly,* p. 638;

November 15, 1997, Debbie Carton, review of *Turtle on a Fence Post,* p. 564; October 15, 1999, John Peters, review of *About Face,* p. 447.

Family Circle, December 3, 1985, June Rae Wood, "The Boy Who Taught Love," p. 24.

Journal of Adolescent and Adult Literacy, December, 1998, Judith E. Landrum, review of *The Man Who Loved Clowns,* p. 289.

Kirkus Reviews, September 1, 1997, review of *Turtle on a Fence Post,* p. 1396.

Publishers Weekly, November 9, 1992, review of *The Man Who Loved Clowns,* p. 86; September 26, 1994, review of *A Share of Freedom,* p. 71; July 24, 1995, review of *When Pigs Fly,* p. 65; October 11, 1999, review of *About Face,* p. 77.

School Library Journal, September, 1997, Carol A. Edwards, review of *Turtle on a Fence Post,* pp. 227–228.

Sedalia Democrat (Sedalia, MO), October 19, 1993, June Rae Wood, "Happiness Is 'Still a Good Book' for This Local Author," p. 4; August 4, 1994, June Rae Wood, "Some Things Are Better Left to the Imagination"; January 5, 1995, June Rae Wood, "Special Child Had Special Purpose"; May 4, 1995, June Rae Wood, "Brother Lives in Writer's Words, Kids' Thoughts."

Versailles Leader–Statesman (Versailles, MO), April 23, 1987, June Rae Wood, "To a Different Drummer," p. 5B.

Voice of Youth Advocates, April, 1995, Bunni Union, review of *A Share of Freedom,* p. 30; December, 1995, Judy Sasges, review of *When Pigs Fly,* pp. 311–312.

ONLINE

June Rae Wood's Web site, located at http://www. redrival.com/ (August 5, 2000).

OTHER

Wood, June Rae, in an interview with *Authors and Artists for Young Adults,* conducted September 11, 2000.

—*Sketch by Kevin Hile*

Author/Artist Index

The following index gives the number of the volume in which an author/artist's biographical sketch appears: